University of Cambridge Department of Applied Economics

OCCASIONAL PAPER 48

DOMESTIC MONETARY MANAGEMENT IN BRITAIN, 1919–38

Domestic Monetary Management in Britain

1919–38

SUSAN HOWSON
Junior Research Fellow
Wolfson College, Cambridge

CAMBRIDGE UNIVERSITY PRESS

CAMBRIDGE

LONDON : NEW YORK : MELBOURNE

Published by the Syndics of the Cambridge University Press
The Pitt Building, Trumpington Street, Cambridge CB2 1RP
Bentley House, 200 Euston Road, London NW1 2DB
32 East 57th Street, New York, NY 10022, USA
296 Beaconsfield Parade, Middle Park, Melbourne 3206, Australia

© Department of Applied Economics, University of Cambridge 1975

First published 1975

Set by E.W.C. Wilkins Ltd, London and Northampton,
and printed in Great Britain at the University Printing House, Cambridge
(Euan Phillips, University Printer)

Library of Congress Cataloguing in Publication Data

Howson, Susan, 1945–
    Domestic monetary management in Britain, 1919 –38.

    (Occasional papers – University of Cambridge, Department
of Applied Economics ; 48)

    Bibliography: p. 206

    1. Monetary policy – Great Britain. I. Title.
II. Series: Cambridge. University. Dept of Applied
Economics. Occasional papers ; 48.

HG939.5.H65   332.4'941   75-21032

ISBN 0 521 21059 3 hard covers
ISBN 0 521 29026 0 paperback

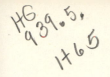
HG
939.5.
1765

Contents

List of Charts and Tables   vii
Acknowledgments   ix

1 INTRODUCTION   1

2 THE POSTWAR BOOM AND SLUMP   9
Monetary Policy 1919–20   11
Causes of the Boom and Collapse   23
Monetary Policy during the Slump   25

3 THE DOLDRUMS   30
Bank Policy 1924–9   33
Treasury Policy 1924–9   36
Monetary Statistics   43
Interest Rates and the Capital Market   47
Investment and Income   54

4 THE GREAT DEPRESSION   64
Bank Policy 1929–31   66
Treasury Policy 1929–31   68
The Financial Crisis   75
Reactions to the Suspension   79
The Development of the Treasury's Views   82
The Introduction of Cheap Money   86

5 CHEAP MONEY AND RECOVERY   90
Treasury Policy 1932–5   90
Debt Management 1932–6   95
Monetary Statistics   99
Interest Rates and the Capital Market   104
Recovery   108
The Authorities' Reaction to Recovery   118

6 REARMAMENT AND RECESSION   120
Rearmament Finance   120
Monetary Policy 1936–8   126
Monetary Statistics and Interest Rates   133
The 1937–8 Recession   135

7 CONCLUSIONS   140

APPENDIX 1 Statistics   146

APPENDIX 2 Official holdings of the National Debt   160
APPENDIX 3 The Term Structure of Interest Rates   167
APPENDIX 4 Treasury discussions on sterling policy,   173
        September 1931 to March 1932
ABBREVIATIONS   180
NOTES   181
BIBLIOGRAPHY   207

Charts and Tables

CHARTS

1	Monetary series, monthly, 1919–23	17
2	Monetary series, monthly, 1923–31	44
3	The yield on 2½% Consols over three twenty-year periods	47
4	The yields on government securities, by class of maturity, 1919–38	48
5	Monetary series, monthly, 1929–36	100
6	Monetary series, monthly, 1935–8	133
7	Monetary series, monthly, 1919–38	158
8	Treasury bills, total and market holdings	162
9	Yield curves for British government securities, 1925–39	171

TEXT TABLES

1	Government debt issues, 1919–30	38
2	Estimated private sector holdings of national debt, by maturity class, as % of total private sector holdings, 1920, 1924, 1929	41
3	Interest rates, annual, 1920–9	50
4	Yields on new issues, annual, 1920–9	51
5	New capital issues, 1920–9	52
6	Gross and undistributed profits, 1920–38	55
7	Decadal and intercyclical rates of growth of G.D.P., 1866–1939	57
8	Rates of growth of G.D.P., 1920–38	58
9	Investment in the 1920s and 1930s	59
10	Investment, Income, Prices, 1920–9	60
11	Government debt issues, 1932–8	96
12	Interest rates, annual, 1930–8	104
13	Yields on new issues, annual, 1930–8	104
14	New capital issues, 1930–8	105
15	Building society rates and advances, 1930–8	107
16	Values and volumes of imports and exports, quarterly, 1930–2	110
17	Bowley's estimates of cost of house purchase, 1925–37	113
18	MacIntosh's estimates of cost of house purchase, 1930–7	114
19	Private unsubsidized housebuilding, 1930–8	115
20	Investment, Income, Prices, 1930–8	117
21	Rearmament: the Problem for the Treasury	122
22	Rearmament: the Outcome for the Economy	122
23	Estimated private sector holdings of national debt, by maturity class, as % of total private sector holdings, 1932, 1933, 1937	136
24	G.D.P. by category of expenditure, at constant prices, 1936–8	137

APPENDIX TABLES

Appendix 1:

1	Monetary series, quarterly averages of monthly figures, 1919–38	148
2	Interest rates, quarterly, 1919–38	150
3A & 3B	L.C.E.S. Indices of security prices and yields, quarterly, 1919–38	152
4A	Central government accounts, calendar years, 1920–38	155
4B	Budget and Sinking Fund payments, financial years, 1919–38	156
5	Components of real G.N.P., 1919–38	157

Appendix 2:

1	Private sector holdings of national debt, by maturity class, 1919–38	161
2	Private sector holdings of national debt, by maturity class, as % of total private sector holdings of national debt, 1920, 1925, 1929, 1932, 1933, 1937	162
3	Distribution of outstanding Treasury bills, quarterly, 1922–36	163
4	Currency Note Redemption Account holdings of government securities, 1919–28	165
5	Issue Department holdings of government securities, 1929–38	165

Acknowledgments

Over the four years that I have been working on interwar British monetary policy I have incurred many debts. I should first of all like to thank those people who commented on and encouraged me in my work from an early stage, Professor R.S. Sayers, the late Sir Ralph Hawtrey, and particularly Donald Moggridge, who supervised the preparation of this study as a dissertation for the Ph.D. degree in the University of Cambridge.

I should also like to thank Professor Sayers and Donald Moggridge again, and M.V. Posner, Professor Donald Winch, Lord Kahn, and Jonathan Reizenstein, who read all or part of the completed dissertation; I am very grateful to them for their help and constructive criticism. None of them should be blamed for the defects in the final product.

I have also to thank the Controller of Her Majesty's Stationery Office for permission to cite Public Record Office documents, Lord Kahn for allowing me to use the Keynes Papers, the Bank of England for providing me with a consistent monthly series for currency in circulation and for allowing me to cite cables from the Bank to the Federal Reserve Bank of New York in 1925, 1930 and 1931, Mr Collinson of H.M. Treasury for giving me access to the Treasury's Currency Note Redemption Account and Issue Department ledgers, the late Sir Ralph Hawtrey for permission to use part of his unpublished chronicle of Second World War financial policy, Lady Ursula Hicks for permission to reproduce some of the charts from her book *The Finance of British Government 1920–1936*, and Messrs. Pember and Boyle for permission to reproduce a chart from *British Government Securities in the Twentieth Century*. I am very grateful to the Social Science Research Council, the Houblon-Norman Fund and particularly the President and Fellows of Wolfson College, Cambridge, for financial assistance, and to Coral George for her help with the typing.

1

Introduction

In the years 1919–38 the British monetary authorities tended to rely in varying degrees on monetary policy in their intermittent attempts at controlling the trade cycle. During this period cyclical fluctuations were pronounced, and the authorities have been accused of either increasing the amplitude of the fluctuations or at least failing to reduce them. The recent availability of the government records of the time makes it possible to discover both the authorities' objectives and the role they attributed to their monetary policy. In this study I have used the Treasury and Cabinet papers in the Public Record Office to describe why the Bank of England and the Treasury adopted particular domestic monetary policies, and what effects they expected them to have. I have then tried to assess the actual effects of policy on the money supply, on interest rates, and hence on other economic variables.

The government records provide a wealth of information on the process of policy-making within the departments and at Cabinet level. The Treasury papers, particularly the personal papers of "Treasury knights" Bradbury, Niemeyer, Hopkins, Phillips and Leith-Ross, throw a good deal of light on these men's views on economic policy and the economic theories which underlay their views. One of the most interesting developments in economic policy-making in the interwar years is the change in the theories on which policy was based. Although I have not ignored the role of economists, and have in particular made considerable use of the Keynes Papers, my major concern has been with the consequences of the theoretical views held by the Treasury men, rather than with the influences that caused them to hold those views. Another limitation of this study is that the description of the views of the Bank of England is based on the Treasury records supplemented by Sir Henry Clay's biography of Montagu Norman, who was Governor from 1920 to 1944. This means that there are some conjectures about the Bank's attitude to various policies which may be disproved (or, hopefully, confirmed) by Professor R.S. Sayers' forthcoming history of the Bank of England.[1]

A chapter has been devoted to each of the major cyclical episodes: the violent postwar boom and slump; the period of slow growth under the gold standard; the great slump of 1929–32; recovery 1932–7; and the recession of 1937–8. In monetary policy there were two main phases: a "dear money" policy lasting from late 1919 until Britain gave up the attempt to retain the gold standard at prewar parity, and the "cheap money" policy established by the conversion of 5% War Loan in mid-1932 and maintained up to (and after) the Second World War. Each phase more or less covers two complete cycles. Chapters 2 and 3 therefore cover the origins of dear money in 1919–20 and the maintenance of the gold standard policy up to 1929.

Chapter 4 describes the authorities' reactions to the great depression and the introduction of cheap money, Chapters 5 and 6 the maintenance of that policy through the periods of recovery and recession. In the remainder of this introduction I discuss certain theoretical issues and empirical evidence relevant to the assessment of the role of monetary policy in business cycles.

In tracing the effects of the authorities' policies I have used data on interest rates and the working of the capital market as well as data on the money supply and on investment and incomes. This is for two reasons: (1) monetary policy always works through interest rate changes and the adjustment of asset stocks to such changes,[2] and (2) Keynesian theory suggests that the magnitude of fluctuations in output and employment partly depends on the behaviour of the financial system in response to any disturbance in the economy.[3]

The monetary authorities may increase the money supply by open-market purchases of securities or by a budget deficit. Budget deficits were not common in Britain in the interwar years, so that fiscal policy was not usually a source of expansion in the money supply. In open-market operations one should include the Treasury's debt management operations, because as with monetary policy proper (i.e. open-market operations in short-term securities) they induce readjustment in people's portfolios of financial and other assets. The difference observed will be in the interest rates first affected. In order to increase the money supply by open-market operations the central bank has to offer holders of a certain class of securities, say Treasury bills, a price higher than the current market price of bills in order to induce them to sell (some of) their holdings to the central bank. The resulting change in the interest rate on Treasury bills induces some holders of bills to switch to other securities which are otherwise a close substitute for Treasury bills but now offer a relatively higher rate of return. The increased demand for these other securities raises their price and lowers their interest rate, inducing further substitutions by individuals between financial assets.

The rearrangement by individuals of their asset portfolios in response to changes in the stock of money brought about by open-market operations in short-term securities such as Treasury bills affects the yields and prices of alternative liquid financial assets, and these effects are then transmitted to less liquid assets. The effects of operations in longer-term government bonds may be transmitted sooner to the less liquid assets as they affect longer-term interest rates more directly.[4] In either case the individuals' substitutions between assets in their portfolios may at some stage include switches from financial assets into real assets, either consumption goods or investment goods. The general fall in interest rates on financial assets means a higher rate of return, in the form of consumption services or future profits, on real assets relative to the return, in the form of interest, on financial assets.

At this point there enters a difference of opinion between the "monetarist" and "Keynesian" schools of thought. Keynesians have tended to see the effect of monetary policy as "a ripple passing along the range of financial assets, diminishing in amplitude and predictability as it proceeds farther away from the initial disturbance. This 'ripple' eventually reaches to the long end of the financial market, causing a change in yields, which will bring about a divergence between the cost of capital and the return on capital."[5] There may be effects on consumption expenditure if that is sensitive to changes in interest rates on (some) financial assets. Monetarists have tended to regard these effects on consumption as being of the same order of magnitude as those on investment; they believe, therefore, that monetary policy will cause a small but pervasive change in all planned expenditures, whether on goods or financial assets. The Keynesian analysis suggests that monetary policy could be undertaken with greater certainty by acting directly to influence and control interest rates than by seeking to control the money stock, and that to assess the impact of monetary measures one should look at interest rates rather than the money stock; the monetarists believe that the money stock is the better indicator.[6]

On both these issues, which are usually referred to in the literature as the question of the "channels of monetary policy" and the "targets and indicators" problem, there are theoretical considerations and relevant empirical evidence to be taken into account. With respect to the channels of monetary policy, one would expect that expenditure on the more durable real assets will be more responsive to a fall in interest rates than will expenditure on less durable goods. The demand price for a long-lived good will depend on the purchaser's estimate of the stream of yields (services or profits) and the rate of interest at which these future yields are capitalized; the longer the life of the good, *ceteris paribus*, the more will a change in the rate of interest affect the demand price. Investment in housing, public utilities, etc. can therefore be expected to be more interest-elastic than investment in working capital, and expenditure on consumer durables to be more interest-elastic than other consumption expenditure. Empirical tests seem to confirm this. They tend to attribute to housebuilding the most marked sensitivity to monetary conditions; the reaction of other investment to changes in monetary policy is also significant, though subject to a substantial lag. There is also evidence of a "wealth effect" of monetary policy on consumer durable expenditure, i.e. a switch by consumers from financial assets to real assets in response to a fall in interest rates which raises the value of their wealth in the form of financial assets.

The latest survey of the econometric evidence for the effects of monetary policy on the United States economy concludes:

> "Changes in monetary policy in the United States have had an important impact on the course of total demand and this impact has been transmitted through three main channels, viz. by changing (1) the cost of capital, (2) the availability of funds in financial markets and (3) the market valuation of financial assets held by the private sector. The first, which tends to operate with a longer time lag than the others, primarily affects private investment expenditures, while the impact of availability is felt particularly in the housing market; changes in private sector wealth affect private consumption. Thus the effects of major changes of monetary policy have been felt more quickly in the markets for consumer goods and housing than in investment demand."[7]

The rapid and sizeable impact of monetary policy on housebuilding results from both the durability of the product and certain related institutional factors. A lowering of interest rates generally tends to increase the flow of funds to the mortgage-lending institutions who finance most house purchase. These institutions tend to react to changes in the inflow of funds by increasing the availability of loans rather than the rate of interest which they charge on their loans. The famous Oxford surveys of the late 1930s[8] convinced many economists that investment was relatively interest-inelastic. Most of the more recent econometric tests on the determinants of investment, however, suggest that changes in monetary policy can exert an important though not rapid influence on investment decisions.[9] There is some difference of opinion over the reasons for the findings. The "neoclassical" theory of the determinants of a firm's optimal capital stock tested by Jorgenson implies that it is the cost of capital in the sense of the cost of external funds that causes investment to be interest-elastic; while other studies, such as that of Meyer and Kuh, indicate that it is the availability of liquidity in the form of internal funds that is more important in determining investment. Jorgenson has argued that the liquidity theory is empirically inferior to his neoclassical theory;[10] on the other hand the Jorgenson tests can be attacked on the grounds that the underlying theory fails to take account of uncertainty. Fortunately for my purposes both sets of studies indicate a sensitivity of business investment to financial conditions. The strongest evidence for the wealth effect on consumption comes from the Federal Reserve-MIT-University of Pennsylvania econometric model of the U.S. economy, which is the most comprehensive study of the channels of monetary policy at present available.[11] There is some doubt about the reality of the effect even within the model; the high correlation between the value of equity shares traded on the stock exchange and consumer durables expenditure may reflect a common dependence on expectational variables, rather than a direct wealth effect.[12] Nonetheless the finding suggests that one should at least look to see if there is any sign of a change in consumer durables expenditure following a change in monetary policy. This evidence on the channels of monetary policy relates to the U.S. economy; similar results for housebuilding at least have been found for Britain and Canada in the postwar period.[13]

With respect to the measurement of monetary policy, policy instruments such as Bank rate do not define policy satisfactorily because, as Tobin puts it, "it doesn't seem very useful to say that a 3½% discount rate is 'easier' policy than a 4% one if the 3½% rate happens to be in the midst of a depression and the 4% in an inflationary boom." As for the variables which represent the goals of policy,

> "If there were a single numerical target of monetary policy—a value for G.N.P. or for unemployment or for the rate of change of prices . . . then we could define and evaluate monetary policy by its markmanship . . .
>
> "This approach attributes to the monetary authorities complete control of economic performance, so that they can be presumed to have caused, or at least to have acquiesced in, whatever happens—obviously a great exaggeration as the authorities themselves would be the first to explain . . .
>
> "Evidently, therefore, we must turn to the vast category of indicators intermediate between instruments and goals"

particularly those which are easier to control than target variables and are links in the chain of causation from instruments to goals. Tobin argues that variables which indicate the cost of acquiring capital goods provide the most information, on the grounds that the fundamental criterion of ease or tightness of monetary policy is whether it makes capital investment more or less attractive.[14] This line of argument suggests using as an indicator of monetary policy either, as Tobin favours, an index of equity values, which represents the cost of financing investment by new capital issues, or long-term rates of interest, which represent the opportunity cost to firms of acquiring real investment goods. Even if one recognizes that monetary policy may have a "wealth effect" on consumption, one can justify the use of long-term interest rates as indicators of monetary policy on the grounds of the larger effect of monetary policy on investment and on a Keynesian view of business cycles.

Keynesian theory implies that there cannot be a purely monetary explanation of the business cycle. Such an explanation would have to rest on the neoclassical theories of interest and of growth. According to the former the "natural" or long-run equilibrium real rate of interest is determined by the real forces of productivity and thrift. In the short run a change in the money supply affects interest rates and other economic variables, but these are merely impact effects which will be reversed by the time the economy regains equilibrium. The role of the temporary interest rate changes is to create forces (increased spending on consumption and investment) tending to move the economy back to equilibrium, in which real interest rates will be at their original levels. Similarly, the neoclassical model of economic growth assumes that the economy is naturally tending (in the long run) toward an equilibrium state (a balanced growth path). Although the economy may be subject to disturbances emanating from the monetary sphere, the disturbances and the adjustment processes to which they give rise constituting the "monetary" business cycle, these do not affect the equilibrium values of real variables (including real interest rates).[15] In the long-run equilibrium there is full employment of the available labour force but the assumptions required to guarantee the attainment of such an equilibrium are rather restrictive, namely malleable capital and/or perfect foresight. Recognition of the existence of uncertainty and the dependence of people's behaviour upon their expectations suggests that there may be no guarantee that the economy is tending towards an equilibrium growth path.[16]

On a Keynesian view of growth and cycles in a closed economy, the trade cycle, which is characterized by large fluctuations in fixed investment, is caused essentially by fluctuations in the marginal efficiency of capital (the expected rate of profit) on which investment depends. Other features of the cycle (fluctuations in income, employment, consumption and prices) are to a large extent consequences of the variation in the rate of investment. Since the rate of investment governs the rate of growth, cycles and growth are determined by the same factors, namely all those which influence investment—including monetary factors. Fluctuations in the marginal efficiency of capital are likely to occur because of the nature of organized investment markets which is such that when disillusion at over-optimistic estimates of yields sets in the marginal efficiency of capital is likely to collapse, and because of the length of life of durable goods and the carrying-costs of surplus stocks which tend to delay the recovery of the marginal efficiency of capital in a slump.[17] While monetary policy can offset such fluctuations to some extent there is no presumption that monetary policy is a necessary or sufficient remedy for the trade cycle.

This theoretical issue over the role of money in business cycles is also relevant to this study because of the interwar Treasury's views on monetary policy. For instance, at the bottom of Hawtrey's monetary theory of business cycles lay neoclassical assumptions about the working of the capital market. For Hawtrey the trade cycle was a consequence of the instability of credit, of the interdependence of the demand and supply of bank credit. Not only did an increase in the demand for credit tend to call forth an increased supply but the effects of the trade financed by the initial expansion of credit, by raising prices and hence profits, increased the demand for credit further. Since Hawtrey assumed monetary policy works through *short-term* interest rates and their effects on traders' stocks, he believed that the remedy for the trade cycle was an appropriate central bank discount policy.[18] Although other Treasury officials did not necessarily hold Hawtrey's views, they were inclined, on occasion, to use his analysis as justification for their policy.

In this study I have tried to assess whether monetary factors contributed to the timing or development of particular cycles rather than to provide a monetary explanation for each cycle. I have not at this stage carried out any econometric testing; my intention has partly been to discriminate between the many hypotheses available about the causes of the cycles observed in Britain in the interwar years as a preliminary to statistical testing. Although the lack of econometric analysis means that one cannot properly estimate in quantitative terms how much monetary policy contributed to the determination of the level of economic activity, one can indicate the role of policy-induced changes in monetary conditions at cyclical turning-points and also, given the fundamental reorientation of monetary policy in 1931–2, compare the experience of the economy in similar phases of the cycle under two different monetary policies.

Some econometric work has already been carried out on British interwar monetary data, on Sheppard's annual monetary series, and on the monthly data which I have used in this study. Walters and his associates have used Sheppard's annual data to estimate the demand for money, as a function of interest rates and income, and monetary multipliers. They found, as others have also found, that the demand for money is interest-elastic and the function is stable over a long period of U.K. monetary history.[19] The difficulties of interpreting "monetary multipliers" are legion. The two major problems are the unspecified transmission mechanism and the exogeneity of the money supply. When it is not known how far changes in the money supply can be regarded as determined by the authorities' policies rather than by changes in economic activity, a high correlation between monetary variables and income or expenditure says nothing about the direction of causal influence, nor, therefore, about the magnitude of the contribution of monetary policy to observed behaviour. Walters' work has, however, provided some information about the length of the lag entailed in the effect of monetary policy, namely that the lag between a change in the money supply (or its rate of growth) and the subsequent change in money income is of the order of six months. This lag may be variable, but it is not likely to be outside the range of 3–12 months.[20]

Sheppard has used his data for the years 1880–1962 to:
(1) regress several different monetary magnitudes against various measures of income and expenditure;
(2) estimate the income velocity of money;
(3) estimate the stability of the public's preferences for different financial assets; and
(4) test various hypotheses about bank behaviour.[21]

The last is particularly useful in the present context, since it bears on the exogeneity or otherwise of the money supply. The statistics show considerable variation in the composition of bank portfolios. Even in 1920–9, a relatively stable period, the oscillations were sizeable and "must have exerted a considerable impact on financial market conditions given that up to 1930 total bank assets accounted for a full 50%

of . . . total financial institutions' assets".[22] The ratio of bank cash to deposits showed less variation than other bank asset-deposit ratios,[23] but its variation was sufficient to invalidate any simple multiplier theory of deposit creation and hence casts doubt on the exogeneity of the money supply. Sheppard used the money supply model, which has also been used by Goodwin for the U.K. and by Friedman and Schwartz for the U.S.A., whereby

$$M = H \cdot \frac{\dfrac{D}{R}\left(1 + \dfrac{D}{C}\right)}{\dfrac{D}{R} + \dfrac{D}{C}}$$

where M = money supply $(C + D)$
       D = bank deposits
       R = bank reserves
       C = currency in the hands of the public
       H = high-powered money $(C + R)$.

He found that while there was a fairly close correlation between movements in the money supply and in high-powered money, the deposit-reserve and deposit-currency ratios varied considerably, and the deposit-reserve ratio in particular, tended to offset changes in high-powered money.[24]

This is consistent with a "portfolio approach" to bank behaviour, that is the assumption that banks choose between the assets available to them, namely reserves (cash and balances at the Bank of England), investments (in government securities), and advances (to customers), on the basis of the risks and returns they estimate to be attached to each of these assets. This implies that while high-powered money may be exogenously determined by the monetary authorities, as seems to have been the case in Britain in most of the interwar period, the total money supply is to some extent endogenous because it depends partly on the banks' asset choices. Changes in the interest rates on the different assets and in the banks' estimates of risks will cause variations in the deposit-reserve ratio, evidence for which has also been found for the London Clearing Banks in the interwar period by A.J. Brown.[25]

Goodwin has also examined the question of the exogeneity of the U.K. money supply in the interwar period, using the monthly data for the London Clearing Banks; he came to a similar conclusion as Sheppard. He also anticipated later economists in finding a stable money demand function, non-constancy in the income velocity of money, fairly high correlations between monetary and real variables, and the importance of interest rates in explaining the observed behaviour of these variables.

In his study Goodwin first looked at the factors determining the proportion of cash held by the non-bank public and found currency in circulation did not in fact bear much relation to movements in bank deposits.[26] Turning to the banks' reserves he found evidence of deflationary pressure by the Bank of England in the 1920s in the form of concurrent declines in the Bank's security holdings and in the banks' reserves; he also found evidence of expansion after 1932, when bank reserves varied with movements in public deposits caused by the operations of the Exchange Equalization Account. He concluded:

"Central bank control plainly depends very much for its effectiveness in certain situations on the governmental financial policy, and they should not be separated . . . The shorter the period the more tenuous appears to be the Bank of England's control over the level of deposits . . . The amount of expansion or contraction necessary to achieve a given end will depend on the state of trade and may depend on government borrowing."[27]

This conclusion was based on his examination of the London Clearing Banks' habit of "window-dressing" their balance sheets, the behaviour of the deposit-reserve ratio, and the relation between current and deposit accounts.[28] His third chapter concentrated on the behaviour of velocity and the possibility of explaining it in terms of interest rates. He found that neither the behaviour of velocity nor that of prices in the 1920s could be explained on a purely monetary theory of the cycle.[29] The recovery of the 1930s also "provide[d] a striking example of the short-run inadequacy of the . . . quantity theory",[30] and suggested that an explanation of velocity in terms of interest rates was much more promising.[31]

In this study I have found Goodwin's work invaluable. Relying on his thorough analysis of the limitations and usefulness of the data, I have followed him in using monthly monetary data. This means that my "money supply" is a proxy, being the sum of currency in circulation and the total deposits of the London Clearing Banks. The sources are discussed in Appendix 1. I have relied on Goodwin's analysis of "window-dressing" and of the determinants of banks' lending behaviour, particularly in Chapter 3. His findings have also encouraged me in my decision not to try at this stage to explain the behaviour of prices, a decision based partly on the current state of the theory[32] and partly on the intrinsic difficulties of explaining the determination of prices in an open economy. Goodwin's work further encouraged me not to undertake econometric study before looking at the authorities' behaviour. To this latter task I now proceed.

2

The Postwar Boom and Slump

After the Great War the U.K. economy experienced one of the most violent fluctu-ations in its history—a short-lived but extravagant boom followed by severe and prolonged slump. The unfortunate consequences coloured U.K. economic history for the rest of the nineteen-twenties, and are attributable to both the government's initial failure to control the boom and the restrictive nature of the policy eventually adopted in an attempt to gain control, namely dear money imposed in several steps from the autumn of 1919, culminating in the raising of Bank rate in April 1920 to 7% (where it remained for a year). This first time that the Bank rate technique had been used primarily to control the domestic economy rather than just the exchanges has repeatedly been criticized for being both too late and too severe.[1] This chapter discusses the origins of that policy and its effects on the economy in the years 1919–23.

For about a year after the War, conditions were tailor-made for a boom. There was a large budget deficit; money was cheap and plentiful; and there were large quan-tities of short-term government debt in the hands of the public, especially the banks, as a result of wartime government finance. There was a strong effective demand for both consumption goods and capital goods (stocks as well as equipment), the absorp-tion of resources by the war effort having meant neglect of replacement investment and a cutback in consumption goods production. A strong overseas demand could also be expected.

After the Armistice there was an initial six-month "Breathing space"[2] before businessmen realized prospects were so bright. During that time prices remained stable (at double their prewar levels) and employment increased as demobilization proceeded.

The boom is generally believed to have begun in April 1919 and lasted a year,[3] during which prices and, after a lag, wages, rose rapidly. By March 1920 wholesale prices were treble their prewar levels. By the end of 1919 boom conditions had brought with them something like full employment.[4] Industrial production rose about 10% above the 1918 figure, almost reaching its 1913 level in 1920, a level not attained again until 1924; real gross domestic product was also up to its 1913 level, which was well above the levels of the next five years (even after making a rough correction for the inclusion of Southern Ireland in the 1913 and 1919 figures).[5] Pigou estimated money income increased by 25–35% between April 1919 and April 1920.[6]

This was obtained, however, at the cost of the rapid inflation and widespread speculation which have been seen as the outstanding features of the boom. There was much speculative buying of commodities, securities, and real estate, and the "flotation of new companies, the sale of old ones, and the issue of new shares became almost a daily event in 1919".[7] The volume of new issues began to increase as soon as the ban on domestic capital issues was removed in March 1919 and continued to increase until late 1920.[8] Speculative excesses were worst in the older industries such as cotton and shipbuilding, at the time enjoying abnormally high demand and abnormally high profits: as a result all too many firms found themselves in no fit condition to face the lean years ahead, because of overcapitalization and a heavy burden of debt which increased with falling prices.

The banks played a large part in financing these transactions—Pigou estimated £500–550m of bank credit was made available between April 1919 and April 1920 for industrial and other purposes.[9] In 1930, Mr R.H. Brand, a director of Lloyds Bank in 1919, recollected:

> "My impression of Board meetings . . . at that time was that we ladled out money; we did it because everybody said they were making and were going to make large profits, and while you had an uneasy feeling yet you thought that while they were making large profits there could be nothing said about ladling out the money."[10]

The boom broke in about April 1920. There were signs of a falling-off in demand before then in consumer goods industries, which had led the upswing,[11] and these signs were noted at the time. The Board of Trade reported to the Cabinet in January 1920 that in some industries there was reason to fear a slump in the near future;[12] in February *The Economist* noted that for home trade "the outlook was very obscure".[13] However, observers expected overseas demand (which had revived after home demand)[14] to keep the boom going. Exports did in fact hold up longer than domestic demand, until the end of 1920; then their collapse aggravated the slump.[15]

The slump was very severe—the 1919 gains in production and income over their wartime levels were lost within a year and unemployment reached a *non-strike* peak of 18% (Ministry of Labour figure) in December 1921. The accompanying fall in prices was considerable and prolonged: wholesale prices fell by March 1922 to half their March 1920 levels, but the cost of living and wages did not fall so far or so fast. Recovery was slow: it did not come until early 1923 according to Pigou (although other writers date the trough earlier).[16]

The strength of a monetary explanation of these developments is that monetary conditions were initially favourable to a boom, they were exploited by bankers and businessmen during the boom, and they changed between December 1919 and April 1920.

During the period of cheap money *the* important rate of interest in the money market was the Treasury bill tap rate. During the war and until April 1921 Treasury bills were on sale only on tap. Bank rate was ineffective, because if the Bank tried to raise market rates above the Treasury bill rate by open-market sales of securities, the banks could run off their large Treasury bill holdings, forcing the government to borrow on Ways and Means from the Bank. Control of the market therefore rested with the Treasury via its control of the tap rate, kept at 3½% (for three months bills) from February 1918 till October 1919, raised to 4½% in October, to 5% in November, when Bank rate was raised from 5% to 6%, and to 6½% in April 1920 when Bank rate went to 7%.

10

Another feature of the wartime monetary arrangements was the unlimited note issue: as one of the measures introduced to deal with the financial crisis in August 1914, the Treasury had begun to issue Currency Notes, available to bankers on demand from the Bank of England.[17] The dear money policy imposed at the end of 1919 included limitation on this note issue.

Monetary Policy 1919–20[18]

The authorities' first steps in 1919 were to unpeg the sterling–dollar exchange (pegged at about \$4.76½ to the £ since 13 January 1916) on 20 March and officially to leave the gold standard on 31 March.[19] The latter, which was interpreted at the time as the defeat of the "dear money party",[20] occurred despite the Cunliffe Committee's recommendation that dear money should be imposed in order to restore the gold standard at prewar parity as soon as possible.[21]

I said above that in 1919 control of monetary policy rested with the Treasury rather than the Bank of England. In fact in the first half of 1919 the Treasury was not in control either, monetary policy being, as everything else, a matter for the Prime Minister, Lloyd George, and his ministers. The Treasury had to work hard to get its policies adopted, but by the end of the year it prevailed.

The minutes of the ministerial conferences on Unemployment and the State of Trade in February, March and April 1919 show that the government unpegged the exchanges and abandoned the gold standard because of the cost of support and fear of unemployment if the Bank took restrictive measures in order to avoid a heavy drain of gold once the exchange fell. They do not support the claim that the British government decided to abandon the gold standard only with the firm intention of returning to it as soon as possible.[22] Fear of unemployment dominated the Cabinet's thoughts on economic matters if only because of the labour unrest it would surely bring (a possibility brought home vividly to it by "Fortnightly Reports on Revolutionary Organizations in the U.K." by the head of what was later "Special Branch" of Scotland Yard).[23] The conferences were a manifestation of this preoccupation and began on 17 February when Lloyd George confronted his ministers with the fact that "trade in the country was more or less at a standstill". Something had to be done and he wanted to know what was being done.[24] The outcome of this meeting was eleven more conferences and a report in April on the subject by Auckland Geddes, the Minister of Reconstruction.[25]

Although the unpegging of the exchanges followed a recommendation by some ministers at one of these conferences, there was virtually no discussion of the merits and demerits of the gold standard. At the sixth conference on 25 February Geddes urged his colleagues to have such a discussion there and then, because there was a serious conflict between the policy recommended by the Cunliffe Committee and supported by the Treasury and the policy of social reform Geddes thought the government was pledged to carry out.

His colleagues could not, or would not, respond. Lloyd George "did not see where the clash came in". To Austen Chamberlain (Chancellor of the Exchequer) and Bonar Law (Lord Privy Seal and a former Chancellor), who tried to impress on him that capital was not unlimited and large scale government borrowing might become impossible, he replied:

"All I know is this. I always used to hear from Mr. McKenna, when he was Chancellor of the Exchequer, that we could not borrow beyond the 31st March, and that then there would be an end. Then he brought it up to September."

Geddes tried again: "Are we, or are we not, going to try and get back rapidly to the gold standard . . . ? . . . If we are going to get rid of the inflation I see enormous social . . . and political difficulty." Bonar Law agreed. Chamberlain asked, "What happens then? . . . Does Mr. Bonar Law contemplate . . . [letting] the exchanges go? If we do, then of course gold will be shipped." Bonar Law replied that the government's policy ruled out deflation, but Chamberlain had the last word: "I do not think we . . . shall be able to keep the exchange going." The reasons were the cost of support and the U.S. Government's reluctance to help. Ministers then turned away from and did not return to the question of the gold standard; the meeting broke up without having faced the conflicts between alternative policies.[26]

At the tenth conference on 17 March the ministers present, at the suggestion of Chapman of the Board of Trade, recommended to Chamberlain in his absence that pegging should cease because it hindered the revival of the re-export trade.[27] Chamberlain, who had already made up his mind on the subject,[28] then let the exchanges go.

Pegging ceased on 20 March and the pound began to fall against the dollar. On 27 March Chamberlain met the Committee of Clearing House Bankers, and the Governor and Deputy Governor of the Bank of England (Cokayne and Norman), to "discuss whether in view of the removal of the control of the American exchange any steps ought to be taken to safeguard our gold reserves". The bankers unanimously favoured prohibiting gold exports. Cokayne and Norman, however, said they preferred to try to safeguard their reserves by informal measures, but an export prohibition now would be less damaging to credit than later if the attempt failed, and in view of the bankers' advice they thought Chamberlain had no alternative.[29]

The Treasury's Views

The Treasury's views were set out by Bradbury (Joint Permanent Secretary) in a memorandum to Addison (then Minister of Reconstruction) in February 1918 and in his "evidence" to the Cunliffe Committee, of which he was a very influential member. He was also instrumental in getting the Treasury's policy adopted by the government in 1919.

For both Treasury and Bank the menace was inflation: because of this Bradbury refused Addison an assurance that after the War essential reform measures would not be held up on the grounds of expense. He forecast a strong postwar boom:

> "the demand for capital for the restoration of industry in the period immediately following the conclusion of peace will undoubtedly be far in excess of the supply . . . [The] plethora of purchasing power . . . is, in the absence of things to be purchased, a national peril of a very serious character. . . . Freedom to use it cannot be accorded without forcing up prices to a level which would dislocate all economic relationships."

Bradbury advocated reducing purchasing power by using the proceeds of taxation to repay debt, employing an argument which was frequently to recur in Treasury memoranda, that this, far from "absorbing capital", would enable former debtholders to purchase private securities, putting more capital at the disposal of industrialists, who would invest all the capital available in productive enterprise.

Further government borrowing in large amounts for public expenditure was frowned upon. Because of the risk of inflation,

> "any new government expenditure after the war must not be by way of creation of new credit but by diversion of the power to use existing credit from private hands to the hands of the government."

Such a diversion of capital (and of labour and raw materials) would remove from entrepreneurs the resources which "if economic forces were allowed free play would undoubtedly be employed for purposes of the most pressing economic necessity", namely food and exports. Government borrowing on top of private demand for capital would push up interest rates, making it more difficult for the government to renew its already large short-term obligations. Hence,

> "It is not suggested that even in the period immediately following the conclusion of peace it may not be possible and desirable to raise loans of moderate amounts . . . [but] the amount which can be so raised without grave risk to the whole financial fabric within any given time can only be determined from time to time as events develop."

To give the assurance that Addison sought "would be to follow the historical precedent set up by King Canute in relation to the activity of the tides".[30]

The Cunliffe Committee's discussion of postwar currency policy took for granted eventual return to gold at prewar par and was, therefore, concerned with the transition from wartime arrangements to an effective gold standard (without internal gold circulation), over a period expected to last ten years. Bradbury pointed out that to prevent the pound falling further from par, inflation must be avoided by restricting bank credit, at present being fed by unlimited issue of Currency Notes and government borrowing. He asked the Committee

> "to give early attention to the conditions likely to arise immediately after peace. There was a general demand in commercial and other quarters for easy money conditions after the War. The continued issue of Currency Notes would mean a cumulative rise of prices and an eventual breakdown of the exchanges . . .
>
> "[He] doubted the possibility of total stoppage immediately . . . [Therefore] the first essential was to reduce Government expenditure . . . within revenue and . . . to provide a net sinking fund to pay off debt."[31]

Cessation of government borrowing was in the circumstances practically the only way to reduce inflation.[32] As for the restriction of the Currency Note issue, the Governor's suggestion of a statutory annual reduction in the fiduciary issue, although sound in theory, would be too drastic in practice.[33] Having agreed that the Bank should aim at a gold reserve of £150m, and that this should determine the post-transition size of the fiduciary issue,[34] Bradbury suggested that during the transition the issue of Currency Notes should remain with the government but that

> "any postwar expansion . . . should be covered not by the investment of the proceeds of the new Notes in Government securities, but by taking Bank of England Notes from the Bank and holding them in the Currency Note Reserve, and that as and when opportunity arises for making reductions in the fiduciary issue the same procedure should be followed."

This would reduce the reserve of the Banking Department of the Bank, and render it necessary to raise Bank rate.[35] Bradbury agreed with the other members of the Committee that dearer money was necessary to restore the gold standard at prewar par.[36]

Bradbury later managed to effect this arrangement of earmarking Bank notes against any further increase in the Currency Note circulation. After a while it did bring dearer money. Bradbury's influence also made itself felt in that his recommendations on the size of the fiduciary issue, cessation of government borrowing, and limitation of the note issue were adopted by the Committee and put in its report.[37]

The Bank's Views

The Bank of England had been urging its policy on the government since the last months of the War. Its aim was the restoration of the pre-1914 financial system, including, of course, the gold standard at prewar parity. Its longer-run policy recommendations were the same as those of the Cunliffe Committee; its immediate objectives a swift and drastic reduction of the floating debt, funding of other short-term debt at the earliest possible date, and dearer money.

In September 1918 the Governor (Cokayne) rejected a request by Bonar Law then Chancellor for a lowering of Bank rate on the grounds that money was too cheap already and further cheapening would make dear money even harder to achieve after the War.[38] In October Cokayne urged an immediate funding loan before the War ended, while money was still cheap and investment overseas was prohibited.[39] Law was non-committal and suggested discussion with Bradbury. Cokayne and Norman tried again at a meeting at the Treasury on 17 December, when the Chancellor asked the advice of the Clearing Banks' representatives on immediate funding.[40] "According to Norman's diary . . . when the Governor announced the scheme, 'the Chancellor . . . said at once he was wobbly.' Quite understandably be became more wobbly as he listened to the discordant views of the so-called experts."[41]

When Chamberlain became Chancellor on 10 January 1919, the Governors suggested dearer money (not only a higher Bank rate but also higher rates on bankers' deposits, fixed at 3% since May 1918) and a funding operation to bring the exchanges to par before the signing of the peace treaty.[42] Not surprisingly, Chamberlain did not act upon this suggestion, nor upon Norman's idea for a compulsory funding loan based on income tax assessments.[43] Cokayne also protested in February against government borrowing on Bank Ways and Means Advances; the Chancellor's reply (drafted by Bradbury) suggested the Bank was unduly alarmed.[44]

The Treasury offered 4% Funding Loan 1960/90, and 4% Victory Bonds, in June–July, but the results were disappointing and the floating debt was only temporarily reduced.[45] This was to aggravate the authorities' problems later in the year; in the meantime it prompted another approach by the Bank.

On 10 July Cokayne urged a reduction of Ways and Means to zero by the end of September. He went on:

> "We regard it as urgent in the public interest that power to control the market should at once be restored to the Bank,—it may become absolutely necessary to raise the market rate for money in the near future if we are to avoid such a break in the Exchanges as might produce a dangerous situation.
> "The first step necessary is that the Banks should be released from their

undertaking to limit their Deposit rate to 3%; and the conclusion of the Loan Campaign would seem a very fitting time for their release."[46]

Chamberlain's reply (again drafted by Bradbury) was non-committal, but he raised the matter at the first meeting of the Cabinet Finance Committee on 24 July. He referred to the Bank's request to free deposit rates as well as to a memorandum by Bradbury on the agenda.[47] Bradbury's memorandum advocated lifting the restrictions on the export of capital, giving two reasons:

(1) They were no longer effective. There was no longer cable and postal censorship; and the Capital Issues Committee were finding it difficult to turn down applications for capital for reconstruction of war-stricken areas of Europe.

(2) The slump in the exchange made the present time opportune.
Bradbury continued:

> "Whether the restrictions are removed or not and more particularly if they are removed, I think it is essential that immediate steps should be taken to erect the proper economic barriers against the outflow of capital . . .
> "This means higher money rates in this country . . . This will have to come sooner or later and I am strongly of opinion that we are now at the parting of the ways and that the sooner it comes the better . . .
> ". . . I think public opinion is now ripe for taking the initial step toward restoring sound currency in accordance with the recommendation of the Cunliffe Committee."

The first step suggested was the simultaneous repeal of the restrictions on capital export and earmarking Bank Notes against any further increase in the Currency Note circulation.[48]

Bonar Law "doubted the expediency of doing anything"; Chamberlain could not see any point in waiting. Lloyd George wanted to know the Bank's views. Bradbury said that he had shown a copy of his memorandum to the Governor, who had agreed but suggested removal of restrictions should wait until the three months Treasury bill rate had reached at least 4%. Lloyd George then asked for Bradbury's own view; Bradbury repeated his contention that there was nothing to lose by lifting the restrictions now. Chamberlain pointed out that only new issues could be controlled, and summed up the conclusions of the meeting as:

(1) control should be maintained over new overseas issues;

(2) all other restrictions should be removed, including that on the bankers' deposit rate. These conclusions were accepted.[49]

The other result of the meeting was that from 6 August the Bank adopted Bradbury's suggestion of matching increases in the Currency Note circulation by setting aside Bank notes to the Currency Note Reserve.[50] The parting of the ways had indeed come: this arrangement (continued until 6 October 1920)[51] led directly to the interest rate rises in the autumn and the following spring.

The second half of 1919 witnessed mounting alarm at the state of the government's finances; in consequence the government accepted the Treasury's views on "economy"[52] and on monetary policy. In August and September 1919 the Bank urged Chamberlain to increase the Treasury bill rate to 4½%. According to Norman, the Chancellor was not unwilling but doubted Cabinet agreement owing to opposition from Bonar Law and Milner.[53] Therefore Chamberlain

> "invited the Governor to reply briefly and with formal protest only to the

usual application for Ways and Means Advances over the next quarter and to address a reasoned statement on home and foreign finance, in the nature of a state paper, which after agreement as to contents he would receive and circulate to his colleagues." [54]

The five page letter, sent on 25 September, is among the papers of the Finance Committee: there is no record of its discussion. It began with the state of the exchanges, with the fact that the pound was now 15% below parity, and continued:

"If the Bank had been free to exercise their proper functions they would long ago have taken steps to raise the value of money in the Country in order to protect the Exchanges . . .

"The Court fully understand that a Chancellor . . . should hesitate to raise the rate at which he is borrowing . . . I submit with all deference that, so long as Treasury operations prevent the Bank from performing this duty to the State, the Treasury become responsible for its performance and is justified in incurring expense to enable it to be performed."

The best solution would be a funding operation to reduce the floating debt, but that was impracticable at present. "Meanwhile in the opinion of the Court the raising of money rates is urgent." "Turning now to the internal situation of the Country", the Bank noted the low level of its reserve, and the credit expansion which had led to price inflation and "extravagant living". The inflation had depreciated the dollar exchange and must be corrected: and

"*the general private extravagance* is an obvious evil when the country has overspent its resources, and it would seem fitting that at a time when the Government is wisely bent on retrenchment in its own expenditure the people should also be induced to economise."

For the time being the Bank requested only help in making its 5% Rate effective (in the form of an increase in the three months Treasury bill rate to 4½% and the six months rate to 5%); if this were not done the Reserve would fall further.* Finally,

"the Court regard the restoration of the gold standard . . . at the earliest possible moment as of vital importance to the Country as a whole and consider that it is well worth a temporary sacrifice to that end." [55]

The three months and six months bill rates were raised to 4½% and 5% on 6 October.

The progress of the boom, by increasing the transactions demand for currency and hence, given the earmarking practice, reducing the Bank's reserve,[56] soon brought the Bank to the Chancellor again, this time for help in raising Bank rate. On 7 November the three months Treasury bill rate was raised to 5%, Bank rate having been raised to 6% the day before.

However, the government still did not have the "avowed policy . . . to re-establish our country on a gold basis at the pre-war parity as soon as . . . practicable" that it has sometimes been said to have had since March 1919.[57] As from 15 December it did have such a policy: Chamberlain announced in the House of Commons that the government had accepted the Cunliffe Committee's recommendations on the cessation of government borrowing, particularly on Bank Ways and Means, economy in public expenditure, and note issue limitation. Two Treasury Minutes were issued,

---

* Thanks to the acceptance of Bradbury's trick, which the Bank admitted was "in some degree responsible".

16

Chart 1 *Monetary series, monthly, 1919–23*
    Source: See Appendix 1

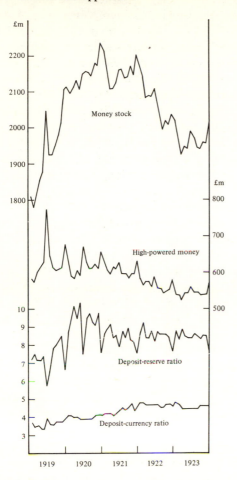

announcing that, as recommended by the Committee, the actual maximum fiduciary issue in any one year was fixed as the legal maximum for the next, and the arrangement in force since 1914 whereby the banks could obtain Currency Notes from the Bank was discontinued. Bradbury's suggestion of earmarking Bank notes for the Currency Note Reserve had, of course, already been put into practice.[58]

Bradbury's trick also played a major role in the next step in April 1920, the raising of Bank rate to 7%. First, however, what effects had the steps already taken had on the money supply? (See Chart 1)

From December 1919, the money supply began to grow at a slower rate than before, though it did not begin to decline until February 1921. Between January 1919 and January 1920 it grew by 17%, between January 1920 and January 1921 by 5%. This was due to an even greater drop in the growth rate of deposits, which grew by 22% in 1919 and 6% in 1920, actually falling in the months of February and April 1920. Currency in circulation which had risen steadily throughout 1919 continued to rise in the first half of 1920.

High-powered money (the sum of currency in circulation and the reserves—cash and balances at the Bank of England—of the clearing banks) fell in the first four months of 1920, but the period of rapid increase in this figure had ended in July 1919; in August it had fallen below its April 1919 level where it remained until the seasonal rise in December. This was due to a fall in reserves which had commenced in the summer of 1919 and continued through the rest of the year and the first three months of 1920. This fall in reserves and high-powered money began when Bank Ways and Means Advances to the government had begun to decline.[59] The banks had offset this decline in reserves by increasing their deposit-reserve ratio substantially (from 7.2 in April 1919 to 8.4 in January 1920), a rise accelerated in the first quarter of 1920 (the ratio was 9.4 in February, 10.4 in March) despite the fall-off in the growth of deposits. Thus the authorities' actions at the end of 1919 had the result of accelerating the trend of declining reserves and rising deposit-reserve ratio which began the previous summer.

After the turn of the year the banks became increasingly less able to offset the decline in high-powered money; by April 1920 the ratio had risen to 30% above its April 1919 level. April 1920 saw a sharp but temporary rise in reserves (the ratio fell to 9.4), and though reserves fell again in May, the next month saw the beginning of a steady rise (the ratio had fallen to 8.7 by January 1921). The money stock and high-powered money also rose suddenly in April and fell again in May. A sharp but temporary fall in deposits occurred a month later. As we shall see, the bankers' attempt to replenish their reserves by letting Treasury bills run off (their holdings had been steadily declining as their holdings of commercial bills rose during the second half of 1919)[60] precipitated the rise in Bank and Treasury bill rates in April 1920, forcing the reluctant hand of Chamberlain.

In February 1920 Chamberlain was under pressure from both the Bank, who wanted to carry the restrictive policy further because of the continued speculation, and from some of his colleagues, especially Lloyd George and Bonar Law, who wanted a return to cheaper money to facilitate the issue of Housing Bonds, to reduce the cost of government borrowing, and, by putting up the price of securities, to allow the banks, now fully "loaned-up", to liquidate their position. This pressure from his colleagues "the Chancellor was resisting, but [he] felt the need of support."[61] Clay records that he asked the Bank for another "reasoned statement", but he also sought other advice, from Blackett (Controller of Finance), Niemeyer (then Principal Assistant Secretary and later Controller of Finance) and Hawtrey (Director of Financial Enquiries) within the Treasury, and from Keynes (who had left the Treasury only eight months previously).

Cokayne sent the Bank's memorandum on 25 February with a covering letter warning Chamberlain that he would soon have again to ask him to raise Treasury bill rates to support a 1% increase in Bank rate.[62] According to the memorandum, the November rise in Bank rate had had the expected beneficial effects on prices, speculation,* and the exchanges, but dearer money would be needed to bring about the fall in prices necessary for a return to gold.

> "The first and most urgent task before the Country is to get back to the gold standard by getting rid of this specific depreciation of the currency.

* These contentions are not supported by the statistical evidence available.

"This end can only be achieved by a reversal of the process by which the specific depreciation was produced, the artificial creation of currency and credit, and for this the appropriate instrument is the rate of interest.

"The process of deflation of prices which may be expected to follow on the check to the expansion of credit must necessarily be a painful one to some classes of the community, but this is unavoidable."[63]

Niemeyer's brief memorandum listed six arguments for high money rates:

1. In accordance with the Cunliffe Committee's recommendations, the U.K. would need higher money rates than in other financial centres in order to bring sterling to a par with gold, sterling being at present depreciated because of undue credit expansion.

2. A high Bank rate would check credit expansion.

3. A high Bank rate would also "encourage merchants to trade quickly (they cannot afford to hold down stocks) . . . [which] tends (a) to bring down prices and (b) to stimulate export, however unpleasant its immediate taste."

4. Though it had been said that the higher Bank rate since November had been in-effectual, it must have stopped *some* new issues.

5. The reason why more were not stopped was that it was still cheaper to borrow here than elsewhere.

6.   "Finally, a reversion to cheap money will undo all the educative effect of even 6%. People will say: scarcity is over: money is cheap: there is no need for economy: and rush down the steep place of inflation until the shilling goes the way of the franc and the mark."[64]

To Hawtrey, a rise in Bank rate was necessary to check credit expansion and hence price inflation, but as soon as expansion had ceased (and he believed that a rise in Bank rate would stop expansion almost immediately, by changing expectations with respect to the future course of prices), it should be lowered again to prevent serious trade depression and unemployment.[65]

Keynes, however, not only wanted a rapid increase in Bank rate but he also wanted to keep it up for a long time. On 28 December 1919 he had written to Chamberlain as follows:

"I was immensely glad to read of your decision about Currency Notes. *The Times* may sneer at it as an illusory step; but in fact it is, if anything, too drastic and will have far reaching consequences. I believe that the Treasury Minute if it is maintained, must logically end in a very high Bank Rate and corresponding rates for Treasury Bills. I was nearly moved to write to *The Times* in defence of the new policy; but decided that it had better work its remedy in silence for the present."

On 2 February Chamberlain wrote to Keynes asking him if he still held this opinion.[66] Keynes called at the Treasury on 4 February and ten days later he sent Chamberlain a written statement of his views. In his letter Chamberlain had asked Keynes what he would reply

"to McKenna and others who argue that in the special circumstances of the time the raising of the Bank rate or Treasury bill rate has no effect upon borrowing or upon the exchanges except raising the price of money against the government itself?"

Keynes agreed a moderate increase might have little effect and might merely make government borrowing more expensive without deterring other borrowers. However credit inflation had to be stopped, and given that the only alternative to dear money, discrimination (rationing of borrowers by banks) could not be effective in the absence of wartime controls, now abandoned, a very stiff dose of dear money had to be contemplated. As Chamberlain put it, "K. would go for a financial crisis (doesn't believe it would lead to unemployment). Would go to whatever rate is necessary— perhaps 10%—and keep it at that for three years."[67] According to Keynes's notes,

> "Dear money will do good by checking bankers' loans, diminishing foreign loans, and, not least, by bringing the mind of the business world to a better realisation of the true position. As a result of rising prices profits in trade are now so high that money may have to be made very dear before the necessary results are achieved. This fact has to be faced and a rate of even 10% . . . contemplated."

Inflation must be stopped because

> "Very grave issues are at stake. A continuance of inflationism and high prices will not only depress the exchanges but by their effect on prices will strike at the whole basis of contract, of security, and of the capitalist system generally."

Therefore he recommended

> "the rate for money should . . . be put to 7% and then again soon after to 8%. The results of this action would have to be watched. But . . . I should not be surprised if 10% would be required . . ."[68]

Blackett, however, did not actually advocate a rise in rates, although he implied it might become necessary in order that sufficient Treasury bills could be sold. According to his memorandum the enormous price rise was the result of an increase in the public's purchasing power (caused by government borrowing, particularly on Bank Ways and Means, coupled with the issue of Currency Notes) in the face of a decrease in the volume of goods produced. Since inflation had been greater here than in America, sterling had depreciated against the dollar. The only effective remedy was to bring prices down to a level approximately equal to their proportionate level as compared with dollar prices before the war, and hence bring sterling back to par. This would require reduction of the public's purchasing power, which could be brought about either by the banks' restricting advances (which Blackett did not think they would do voluntarily) or by the government's securing control over part of the public's purchasing power. The government could not rely solely on a budget surplus to achieve this end; the most effective instrument was to be found in Treasury bills, if enough could be sold to repay Ways and Means as well as to meet maturing bills. Blackett continued:

> "The Banks can let Treasury Bills run off to a considerable extent and so prevent deflation, but their power to do so is not unlimited and has in fact not enabled them to prevent some deflation [i.e. a reduction of Bank Ways and Means] in the period from November 1, 1919 to February 7, 1920 in spite of an excess of Government expenditure over Revenue during that period.
> "It is claimed that this result has been achieved by making Treasury Bill rates attractive enough to compete with private borrowers. It is admitted that rates must not go so high as to check production and it is recognised

that so long as prices continue to rise, trade borrowing will not be easily checked because profits are so high, but it is argued . . . that every rise in Treasury Bill rates successfully checks some borrowers and that once it is realised that deflation is being pursued steadily and being achieved, the hope of huge profits from continuously rising prices will no longer operate, and deflation will succeed by success."

Thus Blackett, like Hawtrey, believed a rise in rates would not have to be prolonged; he also emphasized the disadvantages of dear money.

"Deflation must therefore be very gradual and cautious . . . a policy of dear money can only be pursued to a degree so moderate that the question inevitably arises whether it is worth pursuing at all.

"For the moment a Bank rate of 6% is probably as high as it is safe to go on political and social grounds."[69]

On 21 February Blackett told Chamberlain that he thought the banks were now feeling the pinch due to the government's repayment of Ways and Means, and beginning to demand higher interest rates from their customers. However he warned that once interest rates became high enough that banks began to take advantage of the Bank's offer to rediscount at 6%, the Bank would be compelled to raise its rate.

"The moment will come . . . when the Governor . . . will ask you to raise Treasury bill rates to help him in making his new bank rate effective and it will then be for consideration whether you should let Bank rate go up independently of Treasury bills. I am not satisfied yet that you could not safely do so, but the choice will be difficult."[70]

The moment would come within a week, Blackett told Chamberlain on 4 March.

"The statistical position leaves to my mind no question that Bank rate should go up. In the four weeks to March 3rd, the figure of other securities in the Bank return has gone up by £9,880,384, that is the market has forced the Bank to create that amount of additional credit, thus replacing to that extent the credits which have been wiped out recently by the repayment of Ways and Means Advances out of Revenue."

Meanwhile, the Bank's Reserve had fallen.

"The bankers are responsible for this state of things. . . . Mr. Holland Martin [Chairman of the Bankers' Clearing House] told me privately (1) that since January 1st bankers' loans have considerably increased, (2) that many of the bankers would have liked to have checked the increase but were afraid of the competition of others . . . and (3) that although bankers have retained . . . their official rate for deposits at 4% for seven-day money, they are in fact taking very large amounts on deposit for ten days at 5% or even 5¼%.

"Since February 16 the bankers have probably not increased their loans, as they began to take alarm at the success of the Government's deflationary policy, but they are still too much afraid of each other to reduce the amount lent."

As to whether the Treasury bill rate should be raised,

"I am reluctantly convinced that it is essential. What is said above shews that it is no good hoping to prevent competition with a 5¼% Treasury bill by persuading the bankers to maintain deposit rates at 4%."

According to Blackett money was being attracted away from Treasury bills and Ways and Means Advances were increasing, as were Currency Notes, for the first time since Christmas. At the same time repayment (in gold) of the 1915 Anglo-French loan was imminent. Although the Treasury could lay its hands on some of the £40m required for shipment to New York, £14m would have to come from the Bank's published reserves and by taking the gold out of the reserves on the day Bank rate went up, a good reason for the rise could be presented to the public. Blackett also drew the Chancellor's attention to a letter from Pigou to *The Times* of 1 March recommending an 8% Bank rate, and he urged that a rise in Bank rate to 7% should be accompanied by raising the three months bill rate to 6½%, ending the sale of six months bills, and offering twelve months bills at 6½%. In conclusion he stated: "I do not conceal my fear that even 7% will not be sufficiently effective and that a further rise to 8% . . . may be necessary before long." [71]

Thus Blackett had now joined the chorus urging higher rates. Chamberlain, however, decided to call a meeting with the bankers on 9 March. By this time the Bank, because of the impending Anglo-French loan repayment, had asked the Treasury to consent to higher rates, and Chamberlain had replied that he wanted to consult the bankers and consider alternatives. [72] At the meeting, Chamberlain said that the government's policy of deflation was being frustrated by the banks' letting Treasury bills run off and forcing the government into the Bank. Cooperation was necessary and it was needed immediately because of the Anglo-French loan repayment which would require a decrease in the currency circulation. The only action the Chancellor could take unaided was to raise the Treasury bill rate. The bankers, naturally enough, did not relish the prospect of dearer money. Some said it would not be effective; others said it would harm trade; they all wanted time to consider how they could help the Chancellor. McKenna (Chairman of the Midland) asked that

> "the Bankers might be given an opportunity to considering whether they
> could not help the Chancellor . . . in the only way that was possible by
> agreeing to limit their advances to customers to a certain percentage of
> their resources provided that the Bank . . . also agreed to cease lending."

The Governor (he and Norman were also present) replied that "it would not be possible for the Bank of England to refuse to lend money on approved Government securities".

The bankers met the Chancellor again on 11 March. Blackett told Chamberlain beforehand that the least the bankers should have to undertake in order to avoid an increase in Treasury bill rates was: (1) to reduce their total loans at once by an amount sufficient to restore their proportion to what it was on 1 January, (2) not to increase the total of their advances to customers beyond such total, and (3) to employ any cash set free in taking up additional Treasury bills. Chamberlain asked the bankers if they would do this; they refused. [73]

Blackett concluded "the only safe course and the only fair course all round may be to raise Bank rate on Friday [12 March]". [74] Nevertheless it was not raised till 15 April. The reason for this delay is to be found in a letter from Blackett to Keynes on 30 March.

> "We are really doing rather well for the moment in keeping down inflation
> and though the bankers are kicking I think we shall succeed in making them
> assist in a little deflation. We hold the threat of an increase in money rates
> over their heads and the market's, and for the moment it is nearly as effec-
> tive as an actual rise." [75]

But this threat did not in the end prove effective enough: between Wednesday 17 March and Monday 12 April, Treasury bill sales fell, by £16m; total Ways and Means Advances increased by £88m, the Bank's by £40m; the circulation of Currency Notes increased by £15m; the fiduciary issue approached its legal maximum; the Bank's reserve fell by £11m to £24m and its Proportion from 23.5% to 14.9%. On the latter date Norman (now Governor) wrote to Blackett begging him to bring these facts to Chamberlain's notice.[76] Norman saw the Chancellor the next day, the Treasury bill rate went up the day after, and Bank rate followed on Thursday.

The imposition of the 7% Bank rate has been judged harshly, because of the severity of the slump which followed, but the step was not taken lightly, let alone in haste. The Chancellor was in the end forced to it by the state of Treasury bill sales. However, this was a serious situation for the authorities only because they had committed themselves to a deflationary policy and could not ease the banks' position by expanding the currency, and the step can, therefore, be seen as ultimately dictated by gold standard considerations, via the acceptance of Bradbury's recommendations for limitation of the note issue.

Causes of the Boom and Collapse

There is no shortage of reasons for a postwar boom (above pp. 9–10). The problem to be explained is, therefore, its timing, in particular (since the dispute has centred on this), why it should have ended when it did.

It began when businessmen's uncertainty, particularly with respect to government policy on the continuance of controls and the disposal of stocks, was dispelled.[77] Given the strength of the underlying real forces making for a boom, all that was needed for entrepreneurs to recognize the abundant possibilities for profitable investment. The initial optimism was well-founded and the realization of the expected high profits encouraged even more optimistic expectations, speeding up the pace of activity still further, as did the rise in prices which proceeded faster than that of wages. The pace was not retarded by financial or physical controls, and the banks were prepared to, and could, offset the pressure on their reserves which began in the summer of 1919, because of the high expected rate of profit and their large secondary reserves of Treasury bills.

In the first quarter of 1920, the monetary situation changed. Although budgetary conditions changed at the same time, the first quarter of 1920 showing a surplus rather than a deficit, there is room for doubt whether the 1919/20 budget was actually inflationary;[78] indeed it is arguable that the important change came in the spring of 1919. The published deficit for 1919/20 was only a third the size of those in the preceding four years, and Feinstein's figures for the government's current account for calendar years show a larger drop in expenditure and a more substantial increase in revenue in 1919 over 1918 than in 1920 over 1919.[79] In other words, budgetary measures were operating against the boom throughout its duration. However, it is difficult to argue that the increase of Bank rate to 7% precipitated the collapse of the boom. If the turning-point occurred in April 1920, then the economic system would have to be so sensitive to variations in short-term interest rates as to react with a negligible lag. Hawtrey has argued that traders (wholesalers), whose business depends on the carrying of stocks, are very sensitive to small changes in short rates, and that because of this and because of its effect on their expectations of future short rates, when Bank rate went to 7%, "then at last the corner was turned." There are theoretical and practical difficulties with this hypothesis.

(1) Interest costs are just one of several factors a trader has to take into account; among others are (expected) price fluctuations which can swamp variations in interest charges.[80] Even though the large volume of stocks implies that even weak sensitivity to interest rate changes could produce a large aggregate effect, the major determinant of *actual* (as opposed to desired) levels of stocks is unplanned changes in inventories arising from the lagged response of output to sales.[81] It is also difficult on Hawtrey's theory to account for the variations in fixed capital investment that characterize the business cycle.[82]

(2) Empirical studies of the lag in the effect of monetary policy in the U.K. suggest its length is similar to that found in the U.S.A., i.e. of the order of six months or more.[83]

(3) There were signs before April 1920 that the boom was breaking anyway due to a fall off in consumer demand (above p. 10).

Therefore, if any monetary action had contributed to the breaking of the boom it would seem to have been the actions taken toward the end of 1919, though they were themselves a continuation of a deflationary trend begun in the summer of 1919 as the monetary statistics show. The authorities' persistent pressure on the banks' reserves meant that, given the bankers' limited ability to offset this decline in reserves, a point was bound to come when the banks were forced to limit their lending. On the other hand, this occurred at a time when consumer demand was slackening, so the lag between a change in the growth rate of the money supply and a change in consumer demand would have to have been very short, and, furthermore, it is doubtful whether consumer demand depended much on bank credit.

The importance of the effect of the restrictive policy on the banks would seem to be the way it dictated the final step in the imposition of dear money. The 7% Bank rate came just at the right time to ensure that the (over-) optimistic expectations of businessmen (who had apparently believed the prosperity generated by the restocking boom would last for ever[84]) which were fading fast, and had been for some three to four months,[85] were replaced in the shortest possible time by deep pessimism, which was later reflected in a drastic downturn in investment.[86] This pessimism was all the stronger (and well-founded) given that the authorities had left no room for doubt that dear money once imposed would be consistently maintained, by the announcement in December of their acceptance of the Cunliffe Committee *Reports.*

Finally, could (and should) the boom have prevented? The Treasury has been criticized for its tardiness in raising rates in 1919, but since the banks were so successful in offsetting pressures on their reserves for so long, deflationary measures would have to have been taken in the first quarter of 1919, before the expected rate of profit exceeded the interest rates that the authorities could impose. The desirability of drastic measures so soon after the War was doubted then and is still doubtful now. What could have helped was a continuation of the wartime controls, which, thanks to the government's fear of unemployment, had been all too hurriedly relaxed,[87] and which had given the signal for the boom to commence.[88] This was Keynes's conclusion[89] and his advice was acted upon after the Second World War, when "the policy followed was . . . that of sitting on the postwar boom till it blew itself out" (in 1952).[90]

Monetary Policy during the Slump

Once imposed, the 7% Bank rate was maintained for almost a year. Dear money was thus one of the factors which made the slump so severe. Other factors were:

(1) Budgetary policy: Chamberlain announced a deflationary policy in April 1920, raising taxes and reducing expenditure* in order to achieve a substantial surplus, which turned out to be even larger than he anticipated;

(2) The Treasury's continuation of its policy of reducing expenditure and short-term debt;

(3) The continued rise in money wages after prices began to fall;

(4) The financial difficulties of those who had bought income-yielding instruments at inflated prices during the boom, particularly those who had borrowed money to do so;

(5) The widespread cancellation of orders in 1920;

(6) The collapse in exports after the end of 1920;

(7) The coal strike of 1921.

Why, then, was a restrictive monetary policy pursued so long?

The Treasury was satisfied with the dear money policy adopted between October 1919 and April 1920. In June 1920 Blackett noted it was producing the desired effects, namely credit deflation, a fall in prices, and an improvement in the sterling–dollar exchange. He admitted that "the intense hostility to the Government's financial procedure is only natural" but he was optimistic (as Keynes had been) about both the future prospects of British industry and the wisdom of Treasury policy. "There are potential demands all over the world sufficient to keep employment up to the highest level for a long time to come." There was a danger from the psychological effect of falling prices, but "in truth the community as a whole stands to gain enormously from the improved standing of British credit . . . [Our] policy will surely stand the verdict of history."[91] The Bank shared this complacent view.[92]

During 1920 and early 1921 the authorities' main concern seems to have been their difficulties in controlling the market. The Bank was still dependent on the Treasury's cooperation in raising Bank rate, and the Treasury refused such a request in August 1920.[93] The tender system for Treasury bills was reinstituted in April 1921, but "additional bills" continued to be issued through the tap at rates fixed slightly below the previous tender until 1925 and occasionally thereafter.[94] The volume of tap bills was reduced in the year beginning August 1921 from £540m to about £150m, and Morgan dates the resumption of a "normal" relationship between the Bank and the market as the spring of 1922, when there were no Bank Ways and Means for the first time since the War.[95]

The Treasury was faced with its persistent problem of renewing short-term debt. With respect to Treasury bills, the troubles of the spring of 1920 recurred in the

---

* The pre-Keynesian businessman of 1920 would have been depressed not by the Chancellor's announcement that the budget must and would be balanced—indeed he would have welcomed it as a return to sound finance—but by the increase in taxation (especially on profits). In June 1920 the Board of Trade noted "the realisation that the abandonment of war profits taxation did not mean exemption from the need for finding large sums of money by other taxes such as Excess Profits Tax" had, along with credit restriction, caused "fears of the future" on the part of industrialists (Cab. 24/108, G.T. 1583).

autumn. Bank Ways and Means shot up in October after total Treasury bills outstanding fell off. On 2 October the Bank was discounting below the official rate for
those who wanted to apply for Treasury bills; a month earlier it discounted October
Treasury bills only on condition that the proceeds were invested in December bills.[96]
The Chancellor met the bankers again on 15 September and "warned them that any
increase in the Treasury bill rate was largely dependent on their own action".[97]
These measures must have been successful for not only were rates not raised but also
the total outstanding and the clearing banks' holdings of Treasury bills were up very
considerably in October and November on the earlier months of the year.[98] One
would expect Treasury bill holdings to rise and commercial bill holdings to fall as
depression set in but Treasury bill holdings increased very sharply and remained at
very high levels long after Treasury bill rates had fallen while commercial bill holdings
remained high till the end of 1920.[99]

Measures to deal with other short-term debt were less successful. Issues of 5%
Treasury Bonds to cope with current maturities brought in little cash, and the "nadir
of government borrowing" came with the much-criticized April 1921 offer on
generous terms of 3½% Conversion Loan to holders of National War Bonds, of which
only a quarter were converted.[100] The Treasury justified this operation as follows:

> "What was the position in the spring of 1921? We had not long ceased to
> borrow new money and we had not convinced investors that we would and
> could look after our maturing debt. We had not made any start with funding.
> We had a Floating Debt of £1,300m (Treasury Bill rate 6%). Obviously if
> we were to avoid the gravest risk of this debt becoming unrenewable except
> out of pure credit manufactured by the Bank, we had to decrease this
> floating debt. This we could not do if we also had to meet other large debt
> maturities. Now in 1921 we had £100m Exchequer Bonds maturing and
> about £600m of 5% War Bonds maturing in a year or so, much of which had
> become 'short' money largely in the hands of the money market and Banks.
> We had to make a start to clear this out of the way before we could reduce
> Floating Debt.
> "It follows that we *could not* wait. We had to act at once . . .
> "The proof of the pudding is in the eating.
> "3½% Conversion Loan was our first step in the very long road of converting
> our enormous war debt. We have now [1924] reduced our floating debt to
> manageable proportions and pay a low interest on it . . .
> "I think it is true to say that if we had not in 1921 taken the plunge—expen-
> sive though it was at the moment—we should not now be where we are: and
> we should probably in the interval have paid in higher interest etc. far more
> than the cost of the plunge."[101]

The Treasury's borrowing problems eased with deepening depression. Treasury
Bond issues in 1921 and 1922 were more successful, and by March 1923 a "rather
complicated set of operations . . . had gone a long way towards bringing about the
objects that had been pursued so strenuously and so unsuccessfully for the previous
three years".[102] Thanks to the operations and a budget surplus, some (mostly external) debt had been repaid and the floating debt had been reduced to £821m.

1921 also saw a lowering of interest rates. In February Norman reported to the
Bank's Committee of Treasury that for political reasons Treasury bill rate might have

to be lowered.[103] It was lowered on 10 March, to 6%. Bank rate came down six weeks later, after the restoration of the Treasury bill tender, and, more significantly, after the lowering of some Federal Reserve discount rates.[104] Norman had been inclined to lower Bank rate in December 1920 but not unless the New York rediscount rate fell too, because although he wanted to keep in line with the Treasury he wanted to keep his rate a little higher than New York.[105] Hawtrey blamed the "deplorable conditions" in the U.K. on this waiting on Federal Reserve policy.[106]

The average rate of interest on three months Treasury bills fell quite rapidly after tendering was resumed, but Bank rate was only very gradually reduced, 3% (a high rate for a deep depression) not being reached until July 1922. There is evidence that this, too, was due to waiting on New York.[107]

The Treasury's reason for maintaining its 6% rate till March 1921 was, of course, the problem of renewing Treasury bills. That problem was made more acute by the self-denying ordinance to limit the fiduciary issue; similarly, the low state of the Bank's reserve was partly due to Treasury policy. The decline in the reserve in the last nine months of 1920 was almost exactly matched by the increase in Bank notes in the Currency Note Redemption Account, which transfer was largely governed by the need to keep the fiduciary issue within the legal limit and to a lesser extent by the Treasury's policy of accumulating Bank notes, even when not strictly necessary, in the Account.[108] The Treasury was thus adhering to the Cunliffe Committee recommendations: as Niemeyer remarked, "If we are to get back to an effective gold standard with a free market for gold . . . which has been and still is the policy of His Majesty's Government, it is certain there must be some deflation", a fall in the money supply relative to physical output.[109] Furthermore, Niemeyer's memorandum went on to show that there had been no real deflation so far, only a cessation of inflation. At the same time Blackett argued against attempting an expansionary policy as follows: "An artificial stimulation of home demand will merely mean encouraging people in this country to take in each other's washing and waste their energies in so doing" since "the only form of demand which will really help the situation is demand from abroad." "The vital matter" was to get down costs of production, i.e. wages and prices, at home. Expansion of the currency would hinder the *natural* process of recovery by setting up "a new cycle of rising prices and rising wages . . . just at the moment when with a little patience the most difficult period of the painful process of a return to sound conditons will begin to be succeeded by a revival on a new basis of reduced wages and reduced prices".[110] This also ruled out loan-financed public works, budget deficits, etc.[111] and the Treasury joined the Bank in objecting to the short-lived Trade Facilities Act (passed in November 1921 and revoked in 1927) which empowered the Treasury to guarantee loans towards capital development schemes designed to relieve unemployment up to a maximum of £25m.[112] Thus the Treasury was as firmly committed to a deflationary policy as the Bank and primarily for the same reasons.

However, despite the preoccupation with the exchanges, for a brief period in 1922 the Bank eased its restrictive policy somewhat. The gradually declining Bank rate was not effective, and in the spring the Bank used its newly regained power over the market to carry out open-market purchases of government securities. Morgan suggests the intention was to offset the Treasury's deflationary policy,[113] but Norman presumably preferred such operations to any further lowering of interest rates. The sterling–dollar exchange had improved considerably by March 1922 ($4.43) from its February 1920 low ($3.40), and Norman could not have wished to risk any deterioration; a deterioration in June 1923 was followed by a 1% increase in Bank rate the next month.

The Bank's policy was not expansionary for long: open-market purchases were soon replaced by sales—in July and August 1922—and market rate was raised to 2½% by the middle of August, having been 1¾% at the beginning of July.[114] Although the City apparently did not see it as such,[115] it is hard to believe that the rise in Bank rate to 4% in mid-1923 was not Norman's first step toward the higher interest rates that a return to the gold standard would require. As Morgan points out, "there was nothing in the state of trade at home to call for it; there were no unusual demands upon the Bank; the reserve had remained very stable . . . and . . . was increasing"; on the other hand, there was a fall in the exchange, the New York rediscount rate had been raised in February and market rates there were about 4%.[116] Despite their common aims, the Treasury did not approve of the Bank's action. Shortly before the rise, Niemeyer had written to Norman opposing any upward change in Bank rate, because of its effects on the unemployment situation, the cost of industrial credit, and the cost of government borrowing. Since it would be hard to show any positive results given that the exchange weakened every autumn, these effects would be intensified by fear of a further rise in Bank rate.[117] According to Clay, Norman was well aware of these arguments, but he raised Bank rate all the same.[118]

This concern on the Treasury's part for the effects of monetary policy on unemployment was rather belated, though it was to accompany every upward change in Bank rate till 1929. Recovery was underway by then. It was nevertheless consistent with the Treasury view that the economy was self-righting so that nothing should be done to hinder either the progress of or recovery from a depression. The merit of the gold standard was that it provided on an international level an automatic mechanism of readjustment to disequilibria of prices and costs.

There is no shortage of reasons why the authorities pursued a deflationary policy during the slump of the early 1920s: the Bank's desire to regain control of the market, the recurring problem of Treasury bill sales, the ever-present problem of renewing government short-term debt, acceptance of the Cunliffe Committee recommendations, and a lively horror of inflation. Norman's objective was a return to gold; the fundamental reason for the Treasury officials' deflationary policy probably lies in its consistency with their economic theories. Although "their motives were mixed, they sought to strengthen the pound, at the cost of economic distress, in order to get back to gold, and they were at the same time thinking of the disasters that would befall if they chose a less austere course",[119] there was no conflict between different objectives; fulfilment of all their aims pointed in the direction of a deflationary policy. The conflict between the Bank and Treasury in 1920–3 was about means, not ends. For both Bank and Treasury inflation was the major fear, heightened by observation of the European hyperinflations.

> "[Though] inflation may give a very temporary fillip to trade, . . . this fillip is in all the circumstances only temporary because prices and wages very rapidly catch up with the increased profits of industry. At the present time, when the peoples of the world have been taught the effects of inflationary finance by well known examples, the reaction takes place very quickly.

The ultimate effect is wholly bad . . . [This means that] the object to be kept steadily in view is to arrive at a parity between sterling and gold."[120] Inflation would also be the undoing of the Treasury's other policies: reduction of expenditure, debt repayment by means of a budget surplus, funding of short-term debt, and renewal of Treasury bills at moderate rates of interest. Fear of inflation was a logical consequence of holding the classical economic theory, whereby the volume of output and employment were determined by real factors, inflation being a purely monetary phenomenon. In consequence, the authorities did not intend to moderate, let alone reverse, their deflationary policy. This is reflected in the monetary statistics (see Chart 1).

The money stock grew throughout 1920 (by 5%); after a sharp fall February to April 1921, it recovered to the end of the year (though the December 1921 figure— window-dressed—is less than the December 1920 figure, the difference is small and the October figures are almost the same: the decline from January 1921 to January 1922 was only 1%). Another sharp, and more prolonged decline followed, from December 1921 to March 1923, and then three years of constancy, at about the level of July—August 1919. High-powered money soon recovered from its low March—April 1921 figures and showed a rough constancy in the second half of 1920; thereafter it steadily declined from the end of the year to March 1923, falling below its February 1919 level early in 1922. It continued to decline, more slowly, until 1931.

The deposit-reserve ratio, after declining slowly (with considerable month-to-month fluctuation) from March 1920 to April 1921, remained more or less constant for six years; the deposit-currency ratio rose by 23% from mid-1920 to January 1922, and was then almost constant for five years. The behaviour of the money supply reflects the behaviour of deposits. Both are affected by the fact that "when monthly statements were published again from January 1921, the banks put a good face on their position with the aid of rather more window-dressing".[121] From the same time, the month-to-month fluctuations of reserves and the deposit-reserve ratio were reduced in amplitude. The steady decline in high-powered money was primarily due to a steady decline in currency in circulation. Monetary deflation thus did not cease until after the trough of the slump. Recovery happened "naturally", as the authorities expected.

3

The Doldrums

"The Slump . . . did not so much end as peter out. . . . The ending of the slump was the beginning of the Doldrums. In these we might say the country remained more or less—not of course completely—becalmed until the Wall Street crash in 1929 heralded a second and greater slump."[1] This gloomy judgment of the state of the U.K. economy in the 1920s has often been echoed.[2] It was also the opinion of contemporary commentators—*The Economist* reported that in 1922 "economic life . . . has been at a very low ebb", in 1923 though there was "definite progress in the economic sphere" there was a setback in the middle of the year, that 1924 was a "mixture of achievement and disappointment", and "the economic history of the year [1925] to a large extent centres around depression in [the iron and steel and coal industries] and the crisis in the latter to which this depression gave rise. Worse was yet to come: 1926 was "a year of unqualified disaster", 1927 "a year of convalescence" which was followed by two "years of disappointment", 1928 and 1929.[3] The decade was characterized by the persistence of heavy unemployment, stagnation in the basic industries, falling prices, and slow rates of growth of income and output, at a time when other countries, particularly the U.S.A. where a "new era" had dawned, and Germany after 1924, were enjoying boom conditions.

These economic ills have often been attributed to Britain's returning in April 1925 to the gold standard at the prewar parity, a rate which overvalued sterling by something like 10% and which thus at the very least aggravated the already serious difficulties of the staple export trades which had been created by the changes in the international economy since 1914. The effects on the U.K. economy of the return to gold can in principle be separated into the effects on the balance of payments (together with the repercussions of depression in the export trades on income and employment in the rest of the economy) and the effects of the financial policies pursued by the authorities in the attempt to return to and stay on the gold standard. The so-called "monetary" explanations concentrate on the latter set of consequences of the gold standard policy. Friedman has summarized the monetary interpretation as follows:

> "The prewar parity . . . overvalued the pound by some 10% or so at the price level that prevailed in 1925 at the time of resumption (prices by then having fallen about 50% from the postwar price peak); hence the successful return to gold at the prewar parity required a further 10% deflation of domestic prices; the attempt to achieve such further deflation produced, instead, stagnation and widespread unemployment, from which Britain was unable to recover until it finally devalued the pound in 1931. On this

interpretation, the chain of influence ran from the attempted deflation to the economic stagnation."[4]

Hawtrey believed that:

"The return to the gold standard, with the attendant reimposition of dear money, had interrupted the progress of recovery from the severe depression of 1922. . . . The true efficacy of dear money as a support to the gold position was to be found in the deflationary effect on this country,"[5]

while Keynes wrote in *A Treatise on Money:*

"Whilst it is arguable that there existed at the end of 1924 a slight tendency to a mild profit inflation accompanied by a still milder income inflation, the deflation required for the return to gold amounted to far more than the counteraction of that tendency. But the authorities at the Treasury and Bank of England knew nothing about the difference between an income deflation and a profit deflation, with the result that they greatly over-estimated the efficacy of their weapons of credit restriction and bank rate—which had often shown themselves effective against a profit inflation—when applied with the object of producing out of the blue a cold-blooded income deflation. . . . The loss of national wealth entailed by the attempt to bring about an income deflation by means of the weapons appropriate to a profit deflation was enormous."[6]

On the other hand, Sayers has argued that:

"There is little sign that the Bank consciously used Bank Rate to force a deflation of the home price and income structure. Depression in the export trades and the competition of imports were the powerful deflationary forces at work; it was through these conditions rather than through high interest rates that the gold-standard policy was depressing the Britich economy."[7]

He has also "venture[d] to doubt whether a choice of 4.40 as the 1925 parity . . . would have made much difference in any but the very short run."[8]

While the return to the gold standard was not the *fundamental* cause of Britain's problems, this does not mean a lower rate for sterling would not have been beneficial: Moggridge's discussion of the implications of $4.86 shows that "a lower exchange rate in 1925, though it certainly would not have solved all the problems of the British economy of the 1920s, certainly would have provided a better basis on which to solve those problems which centred round the transition of the industrial structure from the nineteenth to the twentieth century."[9] Given the authorities' goals (which can be summarized as the maintenance as far as possible of the prewar position) sterling was overvalued at $4.86 to the pound.[10]

In what follows, I shall assume the overvaluation of sterling, since this implies that, *ceteris paribus*, domestic deflation would be necessary to enable Britain to stay on the gold standard at the prewar parity. The purpose of this chapter is to test the "monetary" explanation of the doldrums, to assess whether and to what extent the authorities' financial policy actually exerted a deflationary pressure on the British economy in the years 1920–9. I shall not discuss the reasons behind the authorities' decision to return to gold in 1925 nor the effects via the balance of payments of that decision, but am concerning myself with that decision only in so far as it caused the Bank and/or the Treasury to try to offset the effects of overvaluation by deflation of U.K. prices and incomes. The first thing to consider, therefore, is the Bank's and the Treasury's intentions with respect to aggregate financial policy in the years 1924–9 (the earlier years having been covered in the previous chapter); the second is to assess the potential deflationary impact of their policy by looking at figures on the money supply and interest rates; and the third is to look at the behaviour of investment and incomes.

It has become fashionable in recent years to challenge the traditional gloomy picture of these years: on the basis of new statistical data,[11] some historians have stressed the statistical "fact" that Britain's rate of growth was not particularly unfavourable compared with her past and future performance or with that of other countries, and/or the development of the so-called new industries, as reasons for viewing the 1920s as years of progress rather than of stagnation.[12] Such writers usually play down the role of monetary factors in determining the course of economic activity, seeing the growth of particular industries and of the economy as a whole, as determined by long-run trends. Monetary policy is seen as being only a temporary disturbing influence. Thus Aldcroft and Richardson write:

> "Over the 1920s as a whole . . . monetary factors had on balance a destabilising effect. Yet it is difficult to accept that they were a major depressant on the British economy. Interest rates (though higher than the average before 1914, in the 1930s and in the cheap money phase of the post-1945 period) were moderate compared with recent experience, and it is improbable that investment demand was sufficiently interest-elastic for many viable investment decisions justified by market conditions to be postponed."[13]

From the evidence to be presented in this chapter, I come to a conclusion the opposite of Aldcroft's and Richardson's. The role of monetary policy in short-term fluctuations was limited, but the policy pursued by the authorities, particularly the Treasury's debt policy, was deflationary over the decade as a whole, in its effect on the level of interest rates and hence on investment, incomes and employment. The authorities' consistent pursuit of these policies also tended to dampen profit expectations, further aggravating an already difficult situation. It may be true that not many "viable investment decisions justified by market conditions" were postponed; the trouble was that, then as now, market conditions were not independent of government policy.

Before outlining Bank and Treasury policies in the years 1924–9 to see if they were deflationary in intention, it is necessary to point out the ambiguity in the word deflation, whose different meanings correspond to different theories of the relation between monetary and fiscal policy on the one hand and prices and incomes on the other.

Traditional quantity theorists who regard the price level as a purely monetary phenomenon, determined by the quantity of money in circulation, use the word deflation both in the sense of a fall in prices and money incomes and of a reduction in the money supply, since the latter would cause the former. Some quantity theorists, for example Hawtrey, would include in the term "monetary deflation" a reduction in the volume of bank credit; the modern monetarists use the term to describe a reduction in the money supply or its rate of growth. The Treasury knights of the 1920s used "deflation" in the traditional quantity theory senses.[14]

At this time Keynes, in his *Tract on Monetary Reform*, noting the varying senses in which different writers used the words inflation and deflation, distinguished between deflation (and inflation) of cash, of credit, and of real balances.[15] Later, in the *Treatise on Money*, Keynes distinguished between profit and income deflations (and inflations), i.e. between changes in the price level of output as a whole resulting from changes in profits (which would occur if there was a discrepancy between savings and investment) and changes in prices due to changes in wages.[16] The relevance of this distinction to this chapter lies in Keynes's contention that the traditional weapons of monetary policy (variations in Bank rate, open-market operations) "whilst capable of being used efficiently . . . for the avoidance or mitigation of credit fluctuations, [are] singularly ill-adapted for achieving an Income Deflation".[17] In the *General Theory* Keynes spoke of inflation and deflation of *effective demand*, noting that whilst a deflation of effective demand below the full-employment level would diminish employment as well as prices, an inflation of effective demand would merely affect prices.[18] Therefore, he defined "true inflation" to be a rise in prices, without limit, after full employment has been reached.[19] The view (held in the Treasury in the 1920s) that any increase in the money supply would be inflationary was "unless we mean by *inflationary* merely that prices are rising . . . bound up with the underlying assumption of classical theory that we are *always* at full employment".[20]

Post-Keynesian economists who have followed Keynes in recognising (1) that the main impact of monetary policy is on interest rates and incomes, not just on prices (in the long run as well as the short run) and (2) the variety of factors determining prices, have usually defined inflation as a sustained rise in prices.[21] They have also regarded policy, monetary or fiscal, as deflationary if it tends to reduce income and employment (whether or not it also affects prices). Here a deflationary policy is any government economic policy which could be expected to have a depressing effect on demand and incomes; "monetary deflation" is reduction of the money supply or its rate of growth; "price deflation", "profit deflation" and "wage deflation" refer to falls in prices, profits and wages, however caused.

Bank Policy 1924–9[22]

It has been claimed that "there is no evidence that a deliberate policy of deflation was adopted in order to prepare the way for returning to the gold standard, at least prior to 1924".[23] It is clear from the previous chapter that the authorities' policy was almost consistently deflationary from 1920 onwards, the Bank's short-lived easing policy being counteracted by the Treasury's restrictive budgetary and debt policy; furthermore, both the Bank and the Treasury were, at least partly, motivated by a desire to get back to gold at the prewar parity. The Bank took its first post-slump step towards the restoration of the gold standard in the summer of 1923; it took its second the following summer, when it made effective the hitherto ineffective 4% Bank rate. Market rate had been 3–3½% between the summer of 1923 and the spring of 1924 and had then fallen to a little under 3% by June.[24] The Federal Reserve Bank of New York reduced its rediscount rate from 4½% to 3% in three ½% steps in May, June and August, with the deliberate intention of helping the pound back to the gold standard by maintaining lower rates of interest in New York than in London.[25] Norman, being unable to find a reason for raising Bank rate, as he told Strong (the Governor of the F.R.B.N.Y.) in a letter in June,[26] effected his part of the cooperative strategy by getting the joint stock banks to agree to raise their rates on short loans to the discount houses and thus hitching market rates up nearer Bank rate.[27] As well as this understanding with the London Clearing Banks and an informal embargo on foreign issues, the Bank "toughened up its market policy. There was no great reduction in the normal level of either 'securities' or 'government securities', but the Bank curtailed the amount of aid granted in times of scarcity . . . The result was that market rate was kept at about 3¾% from August 1924 to January 1925".[28]

At this stage (i.e. mid-1924), though the discussions leading to the decision had begun in March,[29] the authorities had not yet committed themselves to a return to gold in 1925. Norman himself, though anxious for a clear statement of policy by the government in the near future given that the Gold & Silver (Export Control) Act 1920 would expire on 31 December 1925, was not in any particular hurry to return.[30] However, by taking advantage of the opportunity for strengthening sterling offered by Strong in the summer of 1924, Norman helped to bring about by the end of the year the conditions favourable to a return that were a significant factor in the decision that was taken on 20 March 1925.[31] A further move, "the last stage in the campaign for a return to gold",[32] was taken by Norman on 5 March 1925 when Bank rate was raised by 1% to 5%, following the ½% increase in the New York rate on 27 February, but the rise to 6% that Norman thought would be necessary if free gold payments were resumed in April proved to be unnecessary because of the unexpected strength of sterling.[33]

The first year of the gold standard saw three more changes in Bank rate, beginning with a reduction to 4½% on 6 August. Sayers conjectured that this move, and also the further ½% lowering on 1 October, were in response to political pressure;[34] Clay, on the other hand, recorded that Norman explained the reduction to Schacht (Governor of the Reichsbank) as "simply following traditional lines of pre-war policy" given the inflow of funds to London. There was indeed Treasury pressure: Niemeyer wrote to Norman on 21 July 1925, pointing out "money is becoming so easy here that even I am beginning to wonder whether we ought to keep up Bank rate at its present level".[35] Norman replied that the situation was not really so favourable as it appeared, the gold that had come to London was not likely to stay long, and signs of speculation on the New York stock exchange led him to expect a rise in rates in New York in September.[36] In fact, Norman had been considering the possibility of a reduction in Bank rate in May but the threat of a coal strike had delayed it till August when the dispute was temporarily settled.[37] The arguments for a reduction given by Norman to Strong in May included the statement that it "would make it easier for us to increase our rate at any time after summer"; both communications dwelt upon the dangers of the optimism-inspired flow of short-term funds and the consequent lowering of market rates. On this evidence Clarke describes Norman's tactics thus: "He followed what were then believed to be the traditional rules of the game, and he did so with some vigor, in order, in the end, to return to the tight money policy that was necessary [for staying on the gold standard]".[38] The October reduction in Bank rate was in furtherance of Norman's object of dearer money, which was not attained until December when the Treasury had difficulty in renewing Treasury bills in sufficient volume to avoid recourse to Ways and Means borrowing from the Bank. Bank rate then went back to 5% where it stayed till 21 April 1927.[39] This interpretation would seem to conflict with the Deputy Governor Harvey's Macmillan Committee evidence according to which the Bank was reluctant to go back to 5%;[40] but the conflict is only apparent: Norman, anticipating a return to a 5% Bank rate, was unwilling to raise the rate in the absence of a rise in the New York rate.[41]

Thus in 1925, though Norman's moves were apparently what the rules of the gold standard game would dictate, he was operating within the constraint of Treasury reactions to any move he might make; he therefore sought an easily justifiable excuse before making each move.[42] Treasury reaction to his raising of Bank rate in December 1925 was not at all favourable: the Chancellor, Churchill, telephoned to protest vigorously against the increase.[43] Though the Bank rate decision was unaffected, it prompted a Treasury inquiry into the relations between the Treasury and the Bank; the replies emphasized that Bank rate decisions were in the hands of the Bank alone.[44]

The Bank continued to look at New York rate policy when considering its own moves. "The Committee of Treasury had wished to follow the New York rate down in April 1926 but was deterred by the imminence of a coal strike. In the autumn a revival of speculation in New York was accompanied by a renewed outflow of gold to America. German borrowing involved further losses for London, and any reduction in Bank rate was deferred till the following spring".[45] However, despite these problems and also difficulties with Treasury bill sales which recurred again in November, 1926 was a relatively quiet year for the Bank.[46] Norman managed to enforce "a strict monetary discipline. Reduction in holdings of securities and in discounts and advances more than offset the expansionary effects of the rise in its gold holdings and of a continued reduction in note circulation, with the result that bankers' and other deposits at the Bank of England declined 6.2% in the year ended November 1926".[47]

In 1927 Bank rate was reduced to 4½% on 21 April, following the Bank of France's repayment in March of the 1916 Anglo-French loan and a rise in the dollar exchange. Norman had wished to lower it earlier but he had considered the exchange position made it unwise.[48] May witnessed the attempt of Moreau, the Governor of the Bank of France to check the heavy inflow of funds into France following the *de facto* stabilization of the franc in December 1926, by forcing an increase in Bank rate on the Bank of England by means of converting sterling holdings into gold and dollars. The immediate problem was solved and an increase in rates avoided by cooperation following the 27 May meeting of Moreau and Norman, and by the New York Federal Reserve Bank's easing of monetary policy after the Long Island meeting of Norman, Schacht, Strong and Rist in July.[49]

The next source of strain was speculation in New York, drawing funds from Europe from mid-1928 until the stock market crash in October 1929, a situation aggravated by the inability of the Federal Reserve system to do anything because of internal dissension as to the measures necessary.[50] Being acutely conscious of the "political" constraint,[51] Norman managed to keep Bank rate at 4½% until 7 February 1929.[52] According to Clay, "the Bank was anxious to assist industry, and therefore in addition to keeping rates lower than it would have liked, helped to keep the Clearing Banks liquid. At the same time, current propaganda for 'easy money' was ignored: when gold reserves rose, their effect was offset by reducing Banking Securities, so that the volume of credit varied little over the period." In fact, since the effects of gold outflows were not offset, the Bank's policy tightened markedly after mid-1928.[53]

Bank rate was raised to 5½% while Norman was in New York, because of difficulties with Treasury bill sales and continued reserve losses.[54] This did bring some relief but it was short-lived. Throughout the summer a rise in Bank rate seemed inevitable but political pressure stayed Norman's hand until six days after the Hatry scandal broke on 20 September: Bank rate was then raised to 6½%.[55]

Thus the Bank's intention with respect to the domestic economy from 1926 onwards was to be as far as possible (i.e. as far as was consistent with its primary aim of remaining on the gold standard) neutral.[56] Harvey told the Macmillan Committee in 1930 that "The Bank's policy [since 1925] has been . . . to maintain a credit position which will afford reasonable assurance of the convertibility of the currency into gold in all circumstances, and, within the limits imposed by that objective, to adjust the price and the volume of credit to the requirements of industry and trade".[57] As for the Bank's alleged policy of deflation, "I know of no such policy and I think it is sometimes forgotton that whatever policy the Bank might adopt, they are without the power to enforce it, except to a definitely limited extent, now that we are working again under a gold standard".[58]

It is a matter for conjecture how far concern for the domestic economy was a result of Treasury pressure, but it showed itself in an increasing use of open-market operations and also in the development and use of a number of other devices to maintain the gold standard while avoiding Bank rate changes.[59] These open-market operations were, however, limited in extent as the Bank's security holdings did not permit intervention on a large scale.[60] Furthermore, the Bank tended to more than offset the effects on the cash basis of gold and foreign exchange gains by selling securities in amounts greater than the amount of reserves gained, while less than fully offsetting reserve losses.[61]

The Bank was also more inclined to increase Bank rate when it was losing gold and foreign exchange than to lower it in times of reserve gain.[62] Thus the deflationary tendency of Bank policy increased after mid-1928. The effects of this slight but steady pressure directed at the case base and short-term interest rates, on the money supply and its components, and on the level of interest rates generally, will be considered further below.

Treasury Policy 1924–9

Despite its protest over every Bank rate increase in the years 1923–9, there is no doubt that the Treasury was in favour of returning to the gold standard and of staying on it once the return was accomplished. The disagreement was over the methods of achieving an agreed end. When opposing any Bank rate increase in 1923 on the grounds that it might well increase unemployment, Niemeyer pointed out that the agreed gold standard policy did not at that time necessitate a rise in Bank rate since a rise in American prices, which he suggested might perhaps be assisted by gold shipments from the Bank to the U.S.A., might bring the exchanges to par.[63] One reason the Treasury officials may have been more concerned about the effects of Bank rate on unemployment is that they did not share the view apparently held by Norman that the influence of Bank rate changes was almost entirely confined to the short-term money market;[64] they recognized the discouraging effect of high interest rates on trade and industry and hence on employment. Another reason for the Treasury's concern may have been Churchill's sensitivity to critics such as Keynes and McKenna, who were all too fond of pointing out the consequences in terms of unemployment of the gold standard decision. Churchill asked his officials on several occasions for their replies to the critics;[65] he also asked them to persuade the Bank not to increase its rate in 1925, 1928 and 1929.[66]

The Treasury's concern about the effects of a deflationary policy manifested itself in words rather than actions; this was necessarily so with respect to monetary policy since that was now officially the Bank's responsibility, but its own financial policy with respect to the national debt was hardly expansionary, being a continuation of that initiated in 1920–1, i.e. reduction of debt, particularly floating debt.

Debt Management 1924–9

"The circumstances [in which interest rates were raised in 1920] had repercussions on the monetary history of the entire inter-war period . . . The consequence was a resolution—ruling debt policy for twenty years—to reduce the floating debt whenever reasonable opportunity allowed."[67] Niemeyer told the Colwyn Committee in 1925: "Policy . . . must always be to reduce the Floating Debt steadily".[68] His reasons were:

"1. Uncertain charge.
   In recent years the discount on Treasury Bills has been below 2 percent and above 6 for considerable periods. On £500m these rates represent £10m and £30m per annum respectively . . .
2. Leaves State at mercy of Banks. The Banks when trade is slack have a safe, convenient and liquid investment waiting for them: but they can always withdraw and force the State on to Ways and Means (pure inflation)—a most dangerous one-sided option.
3. The danger in a crisis obvious—war—civil commotion—even so far as foreign holdings remote European squalls (exchange crisis) or flight from sterling owing to foolish inflationary gossip . . .
4. Even apart from crisis if trade bills increased, an excessive floating debt may over-burden the resources of the banks. With given liabilities the banks can only make room for it by restricting other assets. Whether this means any embarrassment to trade depends on circumstances."[69]

Of these reasons, (2) is the legacy of the 1920 experience, and (3) reflects the Treasury's commitment to the gold standard. (1), the greater variability of the interest charge on short-term debt than on long-term debt, is no reason in itself against a large floating debt,[70] but when the ultimate objective is to maximize the amount of debt repaid and, therefore, the largest possible sinking fund is desired, it is a nuisance because it makes it difficult to lay down in advance the amount to be provided in each year's budget to cover interest.[71] (4) was the only "theoretical" reason given for a policy of funding, and rests on a mistaken theory of bank behaviour (see below pp. 40–1).

The Treasury also wanted to reduce the total of the debt. To Niemeyer as to Bradbury debt repayment meant

"returning to trade so much of the money that is raised by taxation. The effect of taxation is to force saving fairly generally over the community . . . When debt is repaid out of money collected by taxation from the citizens at large it is used to pay off loan holders, that is the portion of the community

Table 1 *New government issues, 1919–30*

			£m
1919	National War Bonds	Cash and conversion	27.5
			41.7
			5.4
	4% Victory Bonds	Cash and conversion	359.5
	4% Funding Loan 1960/90	Cash and conversion	409.1
1920	5¾% Exchequer Bonds 1922/25	Cash and conversion	166.7
	5% 5–15 year Treasury Bonds	Cash and conversion	23.6
1921	3½% Conversion Loan	Conversion	266.1
	5½% Treasury Bonds 1929	Cash and conversion	245.2
	5½% Treasury Bonds 1930	Cash	134.7
1922	5% Treasury Bonds 1927	Cash	41.1
			69.0
	3½% Conversion Loan	Conversion	215.9
	4½% Treasury Bonds 1930/32	Cash and conversion	121.3
	3½% Conversion Loan	Conversion	211.5
1923	4% Treasury Bonds 1931/33	Cash	64.6
1924	4½% Conversion Loan 1940/44	Conversion	152.9
			57.7
	4½% Treasury Bonds 1934	Conversion	24.3
1925	3½% Conversion Loan	Cash	59.7
			30.0
			40.0
1926	4% Consols	Cash and conversion	215.1
	4½% Treasury Bonds 1934	Conversion	85.8
1927	4½% Treasury Bonds 1934	Cash	65.0
	3½% Conversion Loan	Conversion	111.7
	5% Treasury Bonds 1933/35	Cash and conversion	217.3
1928	4% Consols	Conversion	156.6
	5% Treasury Bonds 1933/35	Cash	35.0
	4½% Treasury Bonds 1932/34	Cash and conversion	150.1
1929	4% Consols	Conversion	4.4
			10.9
	5% Conversion Loan 1944/64	Cash and conversion	293.0
		Cash	30.0
1930	4½% Conversion Loan 1940/44	Cash and conversion	92.8
	4% Treasury Bonds 1934/36	Cash	105.0

Source: Pember and Boyle, *British Government Securities in the Twentieth Century*, pp. 42–64 (even numbers).

that is more inclined to save than the rest and the tendency will be for the investor who is paid off to reinvest his money in other securities." [72]

Debt operations in 1924–9 were on a smaller scale than in 1919–23 (see Table 1), but 1924 saw the beginning of the Treasury's efforts to deal with £2,000m 5% War Loan 1929/47, which was eventually converted to a lower rate of interest in 1932. Along with the problem of the redeemability of War Loan in 1929 and the desire to fund at all costs, the Treasury had also to cope with a large number of current maturities and a high Bank rate due to the maintenance of the gold standard. All the Treasury Bond issues were made to cope with maturing debt, and so were the first two issues of 3½% Conversion Loan (in January and March 1925), an issue of the same stock in September 1927, and the issues of 4% Consols in 1928 and 1929. [73]

The Treasury began to "nibble" at War Loan in April 1924 by offering £200m of 4½% Conversion Loan 1940/44 to holders of War Loan. Niemeyer explained the problem to the Chancellor:

> "In 1927–8 we have to deal with £350,000,000 Treasury Bonds and National War Bonds and 1928–9 with £508,000,000, so we are limited to 1924–7 when other maturities are relatively light for operations on 5% War Loan. Therefore I believe we must make a start almost at once, certainly this year. . . .
>
> "If we do not start now, when are we to start? Is it so clear that if trade revives . . . we shall do better by waiting? Is even ¼% saving on £200m, i.e. £500,000 a year, to be sneezed at? Finally, the transaction mustn't be judged by itself. It would be the forerunner to further conversions on terms by degrees more favourable to the State in the next two or three years." [74]

£150m of this offer was taken up,* but the next "nibble", the December 1926 issue of 4% Consols, was rather more successful. This was also offered for cash because of the Treasury's "funding complex". According to Niemeyer,

> "To keep our market Treasury Bills at about last year's figure we ought to raise about £50,000,000 from the public in some other form. This is the least we can do to prevent the ordinary laws of supply and demand putting up Treasury Bill rate against us and consequently also putting up commercial bill rate. We really ought to decrease Treasury Bills, not merely maintain them at a stable figure.
>
> "It may be thought that we ought not to take the money out of the commercial market just as trade is starting again. But . . . owing to the size of our public expenditure we have got to take the money out in any case. Having failed to get it by taxation we must take it by borrowing; and . . . taking it by a stock issue . . . is probably the lesser competition with liquid trade requirements.
>
> "We cannot take [it] by . . . Ways and Means (i.e. sheer inflation) firstly because we couldn't get it, secondly because that would mean a very high Bank rate; and thirdly because it would hopelessly compromise our whole financial position for the future.
>
> "A more pertinent criticism might be that money rates being now high, this is not the moment to fund; it is better to pay present or even higher Treasury Bill rates for a while; and leave funding till rates fall. The answer to this is (a) that on "Wait and see" rates will never come down; they only do that when we diminish or at least do not increase the demand [for short-term funds]; (b) that with the liabilities of the next few years before us we can't afford to wait. We want rates down as soon as we can get them. This result can't be achieved if the floating debt is increased." [75]

One result of this operation was that

> ". . . the City, which has made up its mind that we shall not be able to deal in 1929, to any great extent, with 5% War Loan, is now coming to think that there is life in the old dog yet. And I believe that if we manage our

---

*   4½% Conversion Loan was also offered to holders of 5¾% Exchequer Bonds maturing in February 1925, who took up £57.7m.

psychology properly, we may be able to do quite considerable things when the day comes."[76]

Norman and Niemeyer suggested an issue of 3½% Conversion Loan in 1925, in order to prevent the floating debt increasing as a result of a budget deficit, and they recommended making it in September because they thought interest rates might soon become higher due to the unsatisfactory exchange position.[77] Just as the Bank's attempts at maintaining the gold standard became more difficult after mid-1928 so did the Treasury's issues.[78] This caused not only complaints from Churchill[79] but also no new debt operations for a year.[80]

Although the New York stock market crash in October 1929 opened up the prospect of lower interest rates, the issue in November 1929 of 5% Conversion Loan, which had been proposed some time before to meet debt maturing early in 1930, was not delayed. This was because:

> "The Governor . . . holds it is not safe to wait longer when the January maturity is so close at hand. Moreover there is no sign up to the present of a definite end to the drain of gold to France."

Sir Richard Hopkins (who had succeeded Niemeyer as Controller of Finance in August 1927) believed that:

> "much benefit would result from such an issue as would not merely provide for the January maturity but also leave over a large sum for reduction of State floating indebtedness . . . If we are ever going to tackle the conversion of the main body of the 5% War Loan it will be an essential preliminary to reduce our floating debt to the lowest possible dimensions."[81]

For the same purposes the Treasury issued 4½% Conversion Loan 1940/44 in February 1930.[82]

These two issues, particularly that of the 5% stock in November, met with considerable criticism.[83] To the Macmillan Committee, therefore, Hopkins tried to justify the two operations, on the grounds of (1) the Treasury's fear of repetition of its 1920 experience, (2) the maintenance of the gold standard, and (3) the effect on short-term interest rates.

(1) "For some years past we have been occupied with recurrent maturities of National War bonds. It has been difficult to keep pace, and at times we have tended to fall behind and increase the volume of Treasury Bills. . . . "So large a volume of Bills is not merely inconvenient; in times of pressure and high money rates it may at any time become difficult to secure that the market will take all that the Government need to offer. They may themselves become the cause of an increased bank rate."

(2) He expected beneficial results on the exchanges because the government issues would take up money which would otherwise be lent abroad, and the shortage of Treasury bills would encourage lending by the London money market on sterling commercial bills.

(3) ". . . the non-renewal of Treasury Bills which had previously used up a certain proportion of the money in the short money market leaves the money free to compete for other business, and tends, while there is a shortage of Bills, to facilitate low money rates . . . It should augment and strengthen the general tendency towards cheap money engendered by the American slump . . . and thereby oil the wheels of trade."

The criticism that paying off Treasury bills is deflationary "does not apply when the gold standard is in force. If there is no corresponding deflation elsewhere any deflationary effect will be counteracted by drawing gold."[84]

The analysis, and its conclusion that "the issue of the Conversion Loans and the reduction of the floating debt . . . reconciled cheap money with a favourable exchange", were Hawtrey's.[85] The crucial assumption was that it was the behaviour of the *short*-term rate of interest that determined whether policy was deflationary or not. The effect on investment of the increase in the long-term rate that funding caused was not acknowledged. The policy-induced reduction of short rates would stimulate bank lending which would be on commercial bills and/or advances because of the lack of Treasury bills.* Therefore, as long as the Bank did not reduce the banks' cash base which determined the volume of lending, the Treasury could not regard its policy as deflationary. By 1932 the Treasury had acknowledged the important role of long rates of interest, but some confusions remained for years, particularly with respect to funding (see Chapters 5 and 6).

Although the current and impending maturities and the maintenance of the gold standard created difficulties for the Treasury in carrying out its policy of reducing the debt, especially the floating debt,† they did not prevent the Treasury from very significantly lengthening the maturity structure of the debt. In order to assess the effect of this it is necessary to estimate the departmental holdings of the debt and hence the private sector's holdings. The results of this exercise (see Table 2 and Appendix 2, para. 1) show that the liquidity of private holdings decreased markedly in the 1920s. Such a reduction in liquidity would, *ceteris paribus*, have been deflationary and could have contributed to keeping interest rates up; this is discussed further below.

Table 2 *Estimated private sector holdings of national debt, by maturity class, as % of total private sector holdings of national debt 31 March, selected years*

	Floating debt and debt under 5 years	Debt with maximum life of 5–15 years	Debt with maximum life of over 15 years or redeemable only at government option
1920	24.8	12.1	41.5
1924	21.7	4.4	52.4
1929	13.9	2.8	62.3

Source: See Appendix 2, para. 1 and Tables 1 and 2.

* This "Treasury view" of bank behaviour, that there is a fixed volume of money which has, if not spent, to be lent, is of course related to the so-called "Treasury view" of investment behaviour, i.e. the neoclassical notion that there is a fund of savings for whose use the private and the public sectors have to compete, which appeared in the Treasury's reply to the Liberal manifesto "We can Conquer Unemployment" [Cmd. 3331, Memorandum on Certain Proposals relating to Unemployment (1929); see also Macmillan Committee, *Minutes*, QQ. 5561–5689] and which was set out by Hawtrey in "Public Expenditure and the Demand for Labour", *Economica*, March 1925.

† Other problems encountered were increases in the charges on Treasury bills and savings certificates, and a decline in the amount of funds in the hands of government departments that the Treasury could borrow free of interest (T. 175/15, Phillips to Hopkins, 7 November 1927).

The Treasury's aim was balanced budgets, or preferably, slightly surplus ones to permit debt redemption. All the different strands of the Treasury's case against budget deficits are to be found in a 1922 memorandum by Blackett. This began with the statement:

> "The British financial system has for generations been held up to the admiration of the world as a model, and it owes its pre-eminence largely to the stern observance of the rule that expenditure must be covered by revenue and must include a reasonable provision for the amortisation of debt."

In consequence, "it would come as a terrible shock to the world to see Great Britain budgeting for a deficit." Blackett dwelt on the inflationary dangers of a large floating debt, and pointed out that only a large budget surplus in 1920 and 1921 had enabled the Treasury to cut down the floating debt. There were political dangers in borrowing to cover expenditure:

> "Once admit that expenditure can proceed without relative taxation and the floodgates are opened. Why not reduce income tax at once to the prewar level and make good the loss out of the newly found gold mine? Why not double Old Age Pensions? Why waste money on Treasury officials? The ultimate end of the new system is . . . currency depreciation."

Then came the familar argument that "every penny devoted by Government to reducing debt goes straight back to help trade". Moreover,

> "the taxation . . . will certainly have resulted in some enforced saving which would not have been effected if the individual taxpayer had been free to spend his money as he liked. The capital fund of the country is thereby increased to the advantage of the community as a whole." [86]

Blackett did not deny that reducing taxation would in itself be helpful to trade. In fact one of the Treasury's aims was to reduce taxation, but this was subordinate to the aim of a balanced budget, for the reasons given in Blackett's memorandum. Reductions in taxation could only come about if expenditure was reduced; keeping up taxes in order to pay off debt was a necessary preliminary to lowering taxes, because one of the largest items of expenditure was interest and management expenses on the debt—hence the pressing need to do something about 5% War Loan and the need for the maintenance of sinking fund payments.

One reason for maintaining the sinking fund year in and year out was, according to Niemeyer, "political":

> "To get the value out of your sinking fund it seems to me that what you have to bind yourself to do is to produce each year . . . at any rate a minimum amount . . . I do not want to have elasticity. You would be bound to get in practice every year endless arguments as to whether this was a case when you should have the higher figure or the lower figure, and I am afraid those discussions would be conducted on political grounds. It is putting temptation in the way of the Treasury to which they had much better not be subjected."

However, since the heavy maturities of the years 1927 onwards were "in the Treasury view . . . the great governing fact of our immediate debt" the strongest argument in favour of maintaining sinking fund payments was not that it would permit debt redemption but that it might improve the chances of being able to deal on favourable terms with the heavy maturities.[87]

When Balwdin was Chancellor of the Exchequer he provided in the 1923 Finance Bill that the future normal sinking fund should be £50m a year, which would have redeemed the debt in 150 years. In the 1928 Budget Churchill established a "New Sinking Fund", a Fixed Debt Charge of £355m p.a. This sum, which would each year meet the interest on the debt, including Savings Certificates, and a Sinking Fund (initially £50m) which would increase each year as the growing volume of debt redeemed diminished the requisite sum for interest, was estimated by the Government Actuary as necessary to amortise the debt in 50 years, on the assumption that the Treasury Bill rate would be around 4%. The Treasury did not in fact expect the system to last for 50 years; the point of the innovation was that whereas with a fixed sinking fund "the Chancellor of the day must legislate every time he wishes to increase debt redemption", with the new "accumulator" "the Chancellor of the day must legislate specially if he wishes to prevent an increase in debt redemption".[88] (For actual sinking fund payments, see Appendix 1, Table 4B.)

However, Churchill's budgetary bias was in favour of expansion, though he managed to present nominally balanced budgets by ingenious devices.[89] Also, despite Snowden's notorious orthodoxy in financial matters, there was some relaxation in his 1924/25 budget compared to those of his predecessors.[90] The results were, according to Feinstein's figures for calendar years, small deficits on central government current account (and a larger one in 1926 because of the Strike).[91] Nonetheless, the government had an overall deficit only in 1926 (Appendix 1, Table 4A).

Monetary Statistics

The first thing that strikes one about the money series for 1923–9 is their stability compared with the wild fluctuations of the immediate postwar years (see Chart 2).

After the substantial fall of 12% from the end of 1921 to March 1923, the money stock began to rise, a rise of 2% March 1923–November 1924 (i.e. 0.11% per month) which was soon undone by a 2% fall in the first half of 1925, so that by May 1925 the money stock was back at the level of March 1923. By October 1925 the money stock was still below its level the previous autumn, and in the next seven months (excluding window-dressed December), it fell again by another 2% (these months saw the beginning of the coal strike in April and the General Strike in May). Thereafter for almost three years the money supply rose steadily, but slowly, at a rate of 0.24% per month, so that it had risen 8% by November 1928; this growth levelled off in 1929.

The behaviour of high-powered money is very different from that of the money stock: its steep fall from 1920 came to an end in March 1923 but it continued to decline through 1930. From January 1923 to January 1930 it declined by 3.5% (0.56% p.a.) from £540m to £521m. Its lowest value in the interwar years occurred in March 1930, £501m; the lowest in 1924–9 in February 1928, £511m. The deposit-currency ratio was almost constant in the years 1922–6, averaging 4.6. There was a slight fall in February–June 1926, followed by a slight rise 1926–8 and levelling off in 1929. The deposit-reserve ratio was from 1921 to 1926 roughly constant (with fluctuations, of course) about an annual average (excluding June and December figures) of 8.6, though by the end of 1926 it was beginning to rise. Over the next three years it rose by 12% to 9.6 in 1929 (annual average excluding June and December).

Chart 2 *Monetary series, monthly, 1923–31*
       Source: See Appendix 1

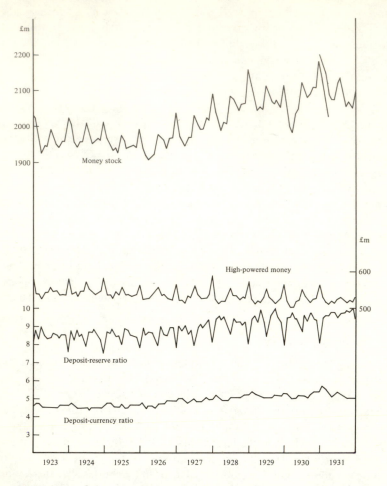

The components of the money supply show a similar pattern. The decline in high-powered money is reflected in a slightly greater (3.8% compared with 3.5%) decline in currency in circulation. Although the steep fall in currency in 1920–3 was followed by a rise in 1924, currency in circulation fell steadily from then until 1930, when the annual average was £339m compared with £429m in 1920. Reserves also declined 1921–3; the next eight years saw a slower but steady (except for a slight rise in 1927) decline. Over the ten years 1921 to 1931 the annual average of the monthly figures declined by 13%. Deposits, on the other hand, were fairly constant 1923–6 and then rose steadily until 1929. The rise in deposits was of course faster than that in the money supply, given that currency was declining. Reserves were also declining, so that the rise in deposits and the money supply after 1926 was made possible by a rise in the deposit-reserve ratio, and to a lesser extent by the slight rise in the deposit-currency ratio. These rises in the two ratios thus offset the effects on the money supply of the Bank's deflationary pressure on high-powered money. The 1923–4 rise in the money supply was apparently due to the slight increase in currency in 1924;

44

the early 1926 drop in the money supply was due to the short-lived fall in the deposit-currency ratio.

Goodwin has examined Keynes's hypothesis that the rise in the deposit-reserve ratio after 1927 was due to the Midland Bank's reduction of its reserves to deposits ratio, which had previously been higher than those of the other banks, a reduction which permitted an increase in the aggregate deposit-reserve ratio without an increase in that of any of the other banks.[92] His results show that a significant part of the increase in this ratio was due to the Midland's behaviour, but by no means all. Noting that Keynes largely established his case for the constancy of the bankers' cash to deposit ratio by attributing the drop in this ratio after 1927 to the changed practices of the Midland, Goodwin also spelt out the implication of his findings for the exogeneity or otherwise of the money supply in these years. "No plainer evidence could be given of the degree to which banks are independent of their cash reserves and are influenced by the state of trade ... It has often been said to have been a period of monetary deflation, but, whatever may have been the intentions and efforts of the Bank of England, this cannot be said to be true as long as the word refers to operation through the quantity of money."[93]

Another aspect of the monetary series upon which it is necessary to comment is the effects on them of the practice of window-dressing. This phenomenon and its effects have been discussed by Sayers, Morgan and Balogh,[94] but I shall rely on Goodwin's thorough analysis which covers the years 1920–38.[95]

Window-dressing* not only serves the purpose of making banks appear more liquid than they are but also permits them to maintain stability in their deposits in the face of fluctuations in their reserves, which are in fact far from stable, while at the same time avoiding the risk of lack of confidence by the public that a freely fluctuating ratio might cause.[96] Goodwin's plotting of annual averages of the true cash and the true ratio against the untrue shows clearly that average yearly window-dressing was by no means constant, having nearly doubled from 1921 to 1927, a variation that was "neither accidental nor negligible but ... related to the whole monetary development".[97] The outcome was much greater stability in the published

---

* The Macmillan Committee described the practice thus: "The monthly figures published by the clearing banks are not true daily averages but are averages of one selected day in each week of the month. It seems that, in order to present a better appearance, most of the banks concerned are at pains to manipulate their balances with the Bank of England on the selected day of the week so that they stand at a higher figure than usual. Moreover, each of the four biggest institutions pursuing these practices selects a different day of the week for the purpose, calling in loans from the money market on its own selected day, but returning them next morning in time for the next big bank to call them for its making up day. Thus a certain part of the published reserves of the clearing banks in the shape of deposits with the Bank of England is like a stage army, the same liquid resources doing duty four times over in the course of each week." (Committee on Finance & Industry, *Report*, Cmd. 3897, para. 368).

There is also the further practice of window-dressing at the half-year and year ends when all the banks have to make up their balance sheets together. Then they swell their cash reserves by forcing the money market into the Bank of England. In using seasonally unadjusted figures I have allowed for this by omitting the months of June and December from calculations. Goodwin uses three-months moving averages of current accounts, deposit accounts and reserves except for the study of monthly variations ("Studies in Money", p. 25).

ratio than in the true one. In fact in the years 1921–7, a change in the true ratio was completely concealed by an opposite one in window-dressing.[98] Thus the observed constancy of the deposit-reserve ratio in these years is only apparent: the banks were in fact managing to offset (by increasing their deposit-reserve ratios) the policy-induced monetary deflation in the years prior to 1925 as well as in the later 1920s. Balogh and Sayers suggest that, for the 1920s at least, the effect of the practice of window-dressing on monetary policy was only to lengthen the time-lag between the Bank of England's taking action and the impact on bank lending, but in the 1920s the consequences were rather more serious from the Bank's point of view: window-dressing enabled the banks to thwart the policy of monetary deflation.

Offsetting was more successful after 1925 than before. For this there are two possible reasons:

1. The Bank was trying harder to bring about deflation before the return to gold than afterwards. This suggestion has also been made by Goodwin[99] and there is some evidence for it both in what is known of the Bank's intentions and in the monetary statistics.

2. The banks' lending policies are related to the state of trade: Goodwin has produced evidence for this. Observing that the ratio of reserves to deposits is positively correlated with banks' cash but that this relation does not always hold up nor is it uniform, he examined the relation of advances to the state of trade (taking the employment figures as an indicator) and concluded: "The result [of the banks' passive policy with respect to advances] is a regular cyclical pattern quite independent of the many vagaries of the level of deposits. If banks behaved in a similar way towards all assets then the quantity of money would be cyclical and largely independent of banks' cash in the short run."[100]

Goodwin's conclusion from his study of the supply of the bank money was:

> "The level of banks' cash does not control the amount of deposits; it is only the most important among several elements. It is not feasible by means of multiple correlation analysis to determine exactly what elements do enter in and their relative influence. There is no numerical measure of the broad factor of the state of trade. The employment series constitutes only the best available rough approximation. The banks' reactions to it depend on many indefinite, changeable and certainly unmeasurable things such as the degree of competition, bankers' feelings about the present and their estimates of the future. There would be no assurance that any of the relations thus determined would remain unchanged in the future. Finally the number of factors which should be included would make it unmanageable and the results unreliable. . . .
> "Broadly speaking the operation of the banking system has been in part in accordance with the line of thought held by the Banking School in nineteenth-century controversies. Such operation has not been accepted as desirable by most economists on the grounds of considerations deriving from the quantity equation. These conclusions are of doubtful validity when applied to short-run, cyclical phenomena, because they rest on the bad assumption that any amount of money will always be spent with roughly the same rapidity as in the past."[101]

Goodwin's thesis contains a seasonally adjusted series for current accounts of the London Clearing Banks which shows some differences in behaviour from the total deposits series. Whereas total deposits did not reach their postwar peak till the beginning of 1922, current accounts fell from January 1920 through to mid-1925. Their subsequent slow rise (slower than that in total deposits, but steadier, there being no fall in 1926) was interrupted at the end of 1928 and was followed by a sharp fall. There is thus more evidence of monetary deflation in the narrowly defined money supply. It is unlikely that this "concealed measure of deflation"[102] had much to do with policy: the ratio of deposit accounts to total deposits had fallen drastically during the Great War from its prewar normal level of around 50% to 34% in 1919[103] and thereafter it steadily climbed back to its prewar level by 1929. However, as Goodwin notes, this secular trend was interrupted, the ratio *falling* between 1921 and 1923, and the upward trend when resumed was less steep than before. An explanation is once again to be found by introducing the state of trade as an explanatory variable: "current accounts show a much closer relation to the state of trade than do total deposits".[104] Goodwin concludes: "There can, I think, be no doubt that this distinction between the two kinds of accounts makes the supply of money even more variable independently of the amount of bankers' cash." The rate of interest paid on deposit accounts turned out to be a major factor in determining the ratio between the two types of accounts.[105]

One other comment on the Bank's "neutral" monetary policy should be made. The Bank apparently viewed a constant money supply as neutral. But a growing economy needs a growing money supply if only to meet the need for larger transactions balances (though there may be secular trends working in favour of lower transactions balances, and high interest rates may encourage the economising of cash balances). Over the period 1923–9 real gross domestic product grew by 15% (2.36% p.a.) and the money supply by 6% (0.98% p.a.). If the money supply is growing more slowly than income and failing to meet transactions requirements, then this should be reflected in a rise in velocity and in interest rates. Velocity in fact was more or less constant over 1923–9.[106]

Interest Rates and the Capital Market

Relative to earlier periods of U.K. history, interest rates were high between the Wars, and while they (especially long rates) showed greater fluctuations after 1914 than before, in the years 1922 to 1930 they were stable, at a high level (see Charts 3 and 4).

Chart 3 *The yield on 2½% Consols over three twenty-year periods*
      Source: U.K. Hicks, *The Finance of British Government*, p. 313

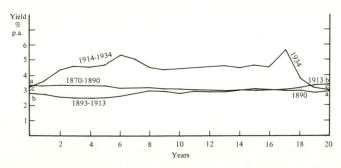

Chart 4 *The yields on government securities, by class of maturity, 31 December 1919–38*
     Source: Pember and Boyle, *British Government Securities in the Twentieth Century*,
     p. 579

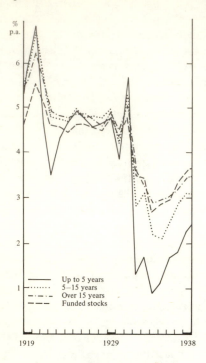

The stability and height of the short rate reflects the stability and height of Bank rate in the 1920s compared with prewar.[107] The most unusual feature of interest rates in the 1920s is the relation between short and long rates. An unprecedented gap between short and long rates made its appearance in the 1920s and persisted for the rest of the interwar years. For at least sixty years before the Great War, discount rates and long-term rates on fixed-interest securities (averaged over a number of years) moved very closely together. This closeness continued with the rise in rates in the War and immediate postwar years, but then the discount rate fell considerably more than the long-term rate. After the introduction of the cheap money policy in 1932 the gap widened further.

Three reasons have been suggested for this phenomenon. One is purely technical, the 1920 reduction by the London bankers of rates offered on deposits from 1½% to 2% below Bank rate.[108] However, the Bank of England did several times during the 1920s persuade the banks to bring their other short rates up nearer Bank rate,[109] thus tending to narrow the gap between short and long rates. Of the other two explanations, one concerns the demand side, the other the supply side, of the market. On the demand side Morgan has suggested that one result of the War and its aftermath was that liquidity preference increased so that investors required higher rates on long-term securities to hold the same proportion as before of such securities in their portfolios..

> "The political and economic uncertainties of the past 25 years [to 1944] have led to the placing of an increased value on both the emergency and risk

48

factors [in the advantages attached to holding short-term securities] and this in itself may go a long way towards explaining the growth of the gap between short and long rates."[110]

With respect to the supply side, Hicks has emphasized the vast increase in the national debt and the increased (and increasing as the decade wore on) proportion of long-term securities in the total debt.

"This vast mass of debt has had to be held somehow; and it could not possibly be held unless investors, on the average, were prepared to hold a larger proportion of their assets in the form of long-term Government stock than they had been used to do. Now it is reasonable to suppose that investors will be prepared to hold a certain proportion of their wealth in the form of Government stock, even if the yield on such stock is very low; its relative security and ready marketability make it an attractive second line of liquid reserves. But if they are required to increase their holding beyond a certain point, they will require a better return; they do not need any more of it as a liquid asset, it has to compete more and more with other property as a source of income."[111]

These two explanations are, of course, complementary rather than competing, but in order to assess the validity of either of them it is necessary to discuss the various theories of the term structure of interest rates and the evidence bearing on them, since one hypothesis, for which there is some evidence, denies the existence of liquidity premia and allows debt management little if any role in determining the term structure.

The discussion in Appendix 3 shows that the present body of knowledge (i.e. the theories that have been tested and the results of those tests) seems to support the Keynes–Hicks theory that the existence of a liquidity premium causes long rates normally to exceed short, except when offset by expectations that rates are going to fall. In other words, both investors' expectation of future interest rates and their liquidity preference determine the term structure. This implies debt management can, by changing the maturity composition of the outstanding debt, influence the pattern of rates on securities of different maturities.

It does not of course necessarily follow that Treasury debt policy in the 1920s did cause the rate structure to be what it was in that period; that expectations of future interest rates are a major determinant of actual interest rates is supported by the evidence (see Appendix 3), and an explanation of the 1920s rate structure in terms of expectations can be devised.* But the rate structure was unusual and not what one would normally expect on the expectations hypothesis, high interest rates being accompanied by a wide spread between short and long rates. At the same time debt management did greatly increase the average maturity of the outstanding debt. Therefore it seems at the very least plausible to conclude that debt management played a significant role in creating the term structure observed. Furthermore, if the expectations hypothesis were the true explanation this would imply that the Bank's policy, if not the Treasury's, had much to do with the height of interest rates in the U.K. in

* The high level of interest rates can be explained by high short-term rates (due to Bank of England policy) creating expectations of high future short rates. In fact, interest rates were expected to fall; revision of expectations in the face of the failure of the long rate to fall would result in a narrowing of the gap between long and short rates which did indeed happen.

49

the 1920s.[112] Also the expectations hypothesis does permit the authorities' operations on long bonds to influence the shape of the yield curve and not just its height in so far as they influence expectations. Expectations were certainly influenced by, for instance, the fact that the huge block of War Loan was due to mature in 1929 and must therefore have been influenced by debt operations that gave the public some indication of how the Treasury was likely to deal with War Loan when the time came to do so.

Table 3 *Some interest rates, annual averages, 1920–9*

	Bank rate	Average short rate	Treasury bill rate	Short-dated gilt edged yield	2½% Consols
1920	6.7	5.42	6.21	6.23	5.32
1921	6.1	4.76	4.58	5.70	5.21
1922	3.7	2.30	2.57	4.78	4.42
1923	3.5	2.30	2.62	4.39	4.31
1924	4.0	2.95	3.39	4.36	4.39
1925	4.55	3.19	4.09	4.51	4.44
1926	5.0	3.25	4.51	4.35	4.55
1927	4.65	3.98	4.25	3.98	4.56
1928	4.5	3.86	4.15	4.73	4.47
1929	5.5	4.94	5.27	5.08	4.60

Sources: Goodwin, "Studies in Money", and L.C.E.S., *Key Statistics*, Table M.

The interest rate figures in Table 3 show that there were two curious features in the movement of the Consol rate. In the first half of the 1920s it failed to fall to its usual prewar level of 3¼%, and towards the end of the second half of the 1920s it rose more than did short rates. The first period, especially the years 1921–3, was the one in which the floating debt was so drastically reduced and long-term debt increased even though it meant offering high rates of interest (e.g. on the 3½% Conversion Loan in 1921). The years 1924–7 were characterized by several debt operations intended to be the first steps on the "long and stony path of straightforward debt redemption and continual conversions" towards dealing with the mass of 5% War Loan 1929/47.[113] From mid-1928 to autumn 1929 the scale of debt operations was reduced and the floating debt increased; at the end of 1929 5% Conversion Loan was issued in an attempt to reduce the floating debt (above pp. 38–40).

The same behaviour of long-term rates can be seen in the L.C.E.S. index of yields on four fixed-interest securities (see Appendix 1, Table 3A). Like the yield on Consols, this index fell 1920–3, with the sharpest fall occurring between 1921 and 1922, rose 1924–9, the rise levelling off 1926–7, fell in 1928 and rose sharply in 1929.

It would appear that Treasury and Bank policy combined to keep long-term gilt-edged rates at a high level throughout the decade. If high interest rates had a dampening effect on investment in the 1920s, the effects of the authorities' policies should also be seen in interest rates on industrial securities and in the volume of capital raised in the industrial capital market. On the other hand, one cannot expect yields on ordinary shares to follow gilt-edged rates closely because of the variety of influences to which share prices are subject, in particular profit expectations. Similarly, investment is affected by profit expectations and the effects of government policy could be offset by changes in expectations in the opposite direction. In fact some writers have thought the capital market "was hampered surprisingly little" and that its shortcomings were not due to government policy.[114]

The yields on ordinary shares and gilt-edged securities moved in the same direction 1921–4 and then diverged, the former continuing to rise 1924–8 (Appendix I, Table 3A). Differences are also observed between the behaviour of the yields on new debentures and that on new preference share issues (Table 4). On both rates were higher in 1921 than 1920, and then dropped sharply in 1922. The yield on preference shares continued to fall 1923–5, rising in 1926, falling again in 1927 and rising sharply in 1928; while the yield on new debenture issues *rose* 1923–4, falling in 1925, rose in 1926 and then fell for the rest of the decade. Thus the series for yields on new preference shares behaves more similarly to the index of ordinary share prices (except for 1926 and 1928, which can be explained by the strikes and the new issue boom respectively) than does the series for yields on new debenture issues. After 1921 the latter behaves fairly similarly to the gilt-edged series.

Table 4 *Yields on new issues, annual, 1920–9, % p.a.*

	Debentures	Preference shares
1920	7.92	8.09
1921	8.09	8.39
1922	6.32	7.17
1923	6.40	6.59
1924	6.61	6.27
1925	6.43	6.10
1926	6.48	6.70
1927	6.21	6.67
1928	6.10	7.37
1929	6.10	6.58

Source: The Economist, selected issues.

The data on new issues in the 1920s lend some support to the idea that the authorities' policy did not have such a dampening effect in the later 1920s as in the earlier years, due to a revival of confidence in future prospects after the return to gold (at least after the strikes of 1926 were over). The volume of new issues tended to move with movements in share prices, rising steadily from 1923–8. Furthermore, the volume was greater after 1925 (until the onset of the world slump) than before (Table 5). On the basis of these figures, Grant contended:

> "stabilization—by making prospects appear more favourable—probably stimulated activity far more than hindering it through rates being kept higher on account of the restored international standard. If the export industries were hit, there was no hindrance on new developments finding finance in the stock market. Stabilization strengthened the capital market, rather than the other way about."[115]

It cannot, however, be concluded from this that high interest rates had no effect on the flow of funds into new investment; there is evidence that this flow was affected adversely in at least three ways. To begin with, the fact that the total volume of new issues increased with the return to the gold standard does not mean the flow into domestic industry was increased to the same extent. Total new issues in the 1920s included a higher proportion of both financial and speculative issues than did

Table 5 *New capital issues, annual, 1920–9, £m (Midland Bank figures)*

	Home	Empire	Foreign	Total
1920	324.6	40.6	19.1	384.2
1921	100.0	90.8	24.9	215.8
1922	100.5	75.5	59.7	235.7
1923	67.6	87.6	48.6	203.8
1924	89.3	73.5	60.7	223.5
1925	132.1	57.4	30.4	219.9
1926	140.9	52.0	60.4	253.3
1927	176.0	87.7	50.9	314.7
1928	219.1	86.1	57.3	362.5
1929	159.4	54.4	39.9	253.7

Source: Grant, *A Study of the Capital Market in Britain 1919–36*, p. 134

the prewar total.[116] This was particularly true at the time when the stock market was most active, i.e. during the "new issue boom" of 1927–8, and it has been blamed (by the writers already mentioned) on the structure of interest rates. Grant suggests:

"A fall in the long-term rates on safe borrowing might have tempted established businesses into the market on a greater scale from 1926 onwards. The characteristic of the 1928 new issue boom is the part played by the speculative appeal . . . a fall in long-term interest rates would have attracted a better class borrower and reduced the appeal of the more speculative element . . . It might have had a considerable effect on investors' judgments by making them more modest in their expectations. Money might have gone into housebuilding and other relatively safe employments rather than into the purchase of the more extravagant kind of security which was appearing so frequently between 1926 and 1929." [117]

While in the 1930s money did flow into housebuilding (below pp. 106–8), the 1928 new issue boom was dominated by speculative securities of the quick-return and high-yield type. "A feature of the year [1927] has been the repeated over-subscription of speculative issues, the attractions of whose deferred shares as gambling counters were more regarded by the public than their merits as an investment".[118] The speculative issues were mostly either purely financial (for the formation of investment trusts, holding companies, etc.) or for such purposes as the production of films, gramophones, radio and photographic equipment, safety glass and artificial silk. Many were entirely new ventures, which soon collapsed.[119] Consequently, the volume of funds raised through these issues that could have gone into physical investment must have been small. The "boom" collapsed in 1929;* this must have had a dampening effect on expectations generally (though by this time the world was about to plunge into depression so that any such effects were soon overwhelmed). Thus the apparently favourable effect of the return to the gold standard in promoting capital issues was hardly an unmixed blessing for the U.K. economy.

* The reasons, according to Grant, were:
  (1) rise in Bank rate to 5½%;
  (2) attraction of funds to New York stock market boom;
  (3) disillusionment of investors whose anticipations the previous year of quick returns had not been realized; and
  (4) (later in the year) the Hatry failure and the collapse of the New York market.
  (*A Study of the Capital Market*, pp. 144–5)

Another way in which the high interest rates may have adversely affected the availability of funds was that just as they prevented the Treasury from carrying out any large-scale funding operations (above pp. 38–40), they also precluded conversions by businesses. Businesses remained highly geared and the resulting high interest charges on past debt must have discouraged further borrowing.[120] This was particularly serious in view of the overcapitalization stemming from the 1919–20 boom: "the 1920s were dominated by a struggle for cash to pay fixed charges. In a falling market, debentures found their way into the banks, which also acquired an interest in industry through frozen overdrafts . . . Overcapitalization [thus] involved the banks deeply in declining industries and may . . . have slowed down transformation by making capital scarce for the new industrial leaders".[121] Certainly Nevin shows that the introduction of cheap money in 1932 resulted in conversion operations by businesses on a large scale.[122]

A third possible factor is the "Macmillan Gap".[123] This may have been a phenomenon dating back to prewar days, but the state of the capital market in the 1920s was not the most conducive to reducing it. For instance, at the same time that small firms were becoming more dependent on the capital market, investors had a strong preference for quoted securities of well-established firms.[124] Furthermore, "Nothing helps the small firm so much as a liberal fiscal policy, good times and general economic growth".[125]

Assuming then, that high interest rates reduced the availability of external funds for new investment for one or all of these three reasons, would this have adversely affected investment? With respect to the objection that the state of entrepreneurial expectations may render high interest rates ineffective, there is evidence that businessmen *thought* high interest rates were depressing investment.[126] Whether or not the belief was rational the fact that businessmen held it implies that they did not hold optimistic expectations with respect to future demand and profits, and it is unlikely their expectations *offset* high interest rates.

A more serious objection is that if internal financing is prevalent, as it was in the 1920s,[127] then the cost of borrowing will relate only to a small proportion of available funds. Both direct enquiries of businessmen and econometric analysis of statistical data have found internal liquidity considerations and a strong preference for internal financing are prime factors in determining the volume of investment.[128] This does not mean, however, that either financial market conditions or the authorities' policies are unimportant.

There is first the point that securities are an asset alternative to physical capital goods for a firm to hold. The funds (accumulated profits) available for internal finance of physical investment may be used to purchase securities if the firm's estimates of the risk and the returns attached to each of the alternatives make securities the more desirable "investment". Security holdings were in fact large in the interwar years. Eleven large firms, for instance, held in 1936 a total of £85m securities, which amounted to 35% of their total nominal paid-up capital and which was mostly government stock.[129] An example of a small firm is the engineering firm of Mather and Platt; at the end of 1922 its total assets of £2½m included £936,916 real assets and £786,924 securities, of which all except £39,500 was in 5% War Loan, 4% War Loan and 3½% Conversion Loan.[130] The high rates of return obtainable on such securities in the 1920s would have increased their relative attractiveness as an asset.

Furthermore, financial conditions will affect the choice between internal and external funds by altering the terms on which the latter are obtainable, though the relation between ease of borrowing and the use of external sources of funds will not necessarily be direct. The terms for a particular firm will depend on its liquidity position and/or its stock market valuation and the (present or anticipated future) need to borrow will lead a firm to use a proportion of its internally-generated funds to build up its liquid assets and/or increase its dividend payments rather than spend them on investment. The easier the terms on which a firm expects to be able to borrow whenever it needs to, the more it can use its internal funds on investment.[131] Thus both current and expected future monetary conditions can be important.

There is empirical evidence that suggests (1) small and new firms have more need for external funds than large and old ones, while the latter find it easier to obtain funds; (2) firms with older real assets favour larger liquid asset stocks, use less external finance, and invest less (i.e. slowly-growing firms follow conservative policies and, therefore, continue to grow slowly); while fast-growing firms finance a greater proportion of their investment from external sources, and also pay higher dividends and hence improve their future borrowing power; (3) the relative importance of internal liquidity considerations in investment decisions increases in the depression phase of the business cycle, and at the same time the relative advantage in obtaining funds (for continued expansion and/or tiding over setbacks) of the large established firm over the smaller or newer firm increases.[132] These are consequences of the fact that the prime source of internal funds is, of course, profits. Internal liquidity becomes an operative constraint on investment when firms cannot expect internal funds to be replenished quickly. In a situation of low current and/or expected future profits, tight financial conditions will increase a firm's cautiousness in the use of funds, even when investment is normally financed internally. In these conditions, which held in the U.K. in the 1920s, monetary policy can affect the pace of investment by its influence over financial markets and its effects on profit expectations.

Gross profits in real terms were in the 1920s both much lower on average than in the 1930s but also grew very little over the years 1923–9, and the same is true of (real) undistributed profits (see Table 6).

Investment and Income

Having argued that monetary conditions could have adversely affected investment and hence income and employment over the decade, I now look at the behaviour of these variables, dealing first with the fluctuations and the relation of these to monetary policy, and then with the growth of the economy in the 1920s.

The period from the trough of the post-war slump to the 1929 downturn is usually regarded as the upswing of a Juglar cycle.[133] The National Bureau reference cycles, however, include some minor fluctuations.

Contraction	November 1918	– April 1919
Expansion	April 1919	– March 1920
Contraction	March 1920	– June 1921
Expansion	June 1921	– November 1924
Contraction	November 1924	– July 1926
Expansion	July 1926	– March 1927

Table 6

	Gross trading profits of British companies and public corporations at constant (1920) prices, 1920–38, £m	Undistributed income of British companies, after tax and before depreciation, at constant (1920) prices, 1920–38, £m
1920	621	252
1921	385	74
1922	583	356
1923	661	290
1924	701	309
1925	688	344
1926	627	273
1927	724	332
1928	729	329
1929	746	345
1930	632	169
1931	571	141
1932	528	126
1933	638	213
1934	798	386
1935	870	340
1936	1,060	433
1937	1,134	502
1938	1,040	387

Source: Calculated from Feinstein, *National Income*, Tables 32 and 61.

Contraction   March 1927   – September 1928

Expansion   September 1928 – July 1929[134]

The troughs of June 1921 and July 1926 are determined by the coal strikes, which lasted for three months from April 1921 and for six months from 1 May 1926. The turning-points needing explanation are the peaks of November 1924 and March 1927.

Although the absolute bottom of the postwar slump came in June 1921, thanks to the coal strike, recovery did not really get under way till the beginning of 1923, and it was not complete when it was interrupted at the end of 1924. To decide whether the mid-1924 tightening of monetary policy was at all responsible, as has been claimed by, for example, Hawtrey,[135] it is necessary briefly to consider the forces making for recovery in 1923. *The Economist* saw the year 1922 as one in which "a trade recovery for which the economic conditions* were favourable was held in check and delayed by the state of international politics".[136] In 1923 "the [French] occupation [of the Ruhr] produced a temporary expectation of higher prices and stimulated certain special trades in this country"; increased American prosperity also improved British trade.[137] These quotations alone indicate the dependence of recovery on conditions abroad. The figures show there were marked temporary increases in the value of U.K. exports to Western Europe, in the value of non-manufactured exports, and in coal production in 1923.[138] The end of the revival which "faded away" after May 1924[139] can also be attributed to export behaviour, attributable in its turn to the appreciation of the pound (from $4.32 to $4.86 in ten

---

*   Specifically mentioned were the liquidation of stocks, adjustment of wages and other costs to the new price level, and the credit situation.

months after June 1924, a rise of 12.5%). Insofar as the appreciation was due to U.K. monetary policy, that policy can be blamed for the setback.

The Bank's policy was, as noted above, part of a cooperative strategy with New York. The New York Federal Reserve Bank's easy money policy of 1924 was intended to "change . . . the interest relation between the New York and London market", to direct foreign borrowing to the New York market, and thus "to render what assistance was possible by our market policy toward the recovery of sterling and the resumption of gold payments by Great Britain"[140] and it succeeded in these objectives. There was a significant shift in long-term foreign borrowing from London to New York and "there can be little doubt that this shift contributed significantly both to the strengthening of sterling and, to a lesser degree, the reversal of the gold flows to the U.S."[141] But other factors were also involved in the appreciation. *The Economist* noted the effect of the revival of confidence (due to the Dawes reparations settlement and the return of a Conservative government to power in Britain) in bringing foreign balances to London. Speculation on the appreciation of sterling (stimulated by the widespread speculation that Britain would soon return to the gold standard) was certainly a major influence, and there was also the fortuitous development of an exceptionally heavy demand during the autumn and winter of 1924–5 from continental European countries for sterling commodities, such as Australian wheat, the result of a bad European harvest in 1924.[142] Clarke has emphasized that it was this complex of forces in which monetary policy did not play a large part that, by its effects on the exchanges and on British and American export prices, enabled Britain to return to gold in the spring of 1925 in a way "that not only achieved technical success, but, in doing so, also avoided jerks and jolts".[143] Clarke has also pointed out that favourable developments abroad prevented any serious threat to Britain's maintenance of the gold standard in the first couple of years after the return to gold.[144] On the home front, however, the return brought in its train the Coal lock-out and the General Strike in 1926. The economic history of that year is, as *The Economist* pointed out, dominated by those events, which show up clearly in the aggregate figures (see Table 10).

The next two and a half years were the most prosperous Britain enjoyed in the 1920s. At last it seemed as though the problems due to the War were being overcome. However, though U.K. exports and income and expenditure were expanding in the years 1927–9, they did not grow anything like as fast as those of other countries; for this the overvaluation of sterling deserves some of the blame. "The later effects of the gold standard have perhaps been overrated, but it certainly ensured that when European reconstruction at last went ahead (in 1926–9) and emerged as a resurgence of competitors rather than customers, British industry should be fully exposed."[145] In general, over the years 1924–9, "the export sector, rather than being an engine of growth . . . merely allowed domestic expansion to proceed relatively unimpeded . . . [and even that] depended on an expanding international economy".[146]

The 1927–8 contraction reflects mainly a fall in housebuilding due to the cutback in government subsidies and also a cessation of the stockbuilding that had followed the end of the strikes of 1926. From 1923–7 public sector investment, which was predominantly in dwellings, had risen steadily.[147] * In 1927 local authority house-building (and hence total public investment) reached its maximum for the 1920s and in 1928 it fell, because of the reduction from the end of 1927 of both the 1924 Wheatley subsidy and the 1923 Chamberlain subsidy.[148] Stockbuilding, much increased in 1927 over 1925 and 1926, became negative in 1928.[149]

This very brief outline of the minor fluctuations in the U.K. 1923–9 does not lend much support to a monetary theory of business cycles. It is now necessary to consider the impact of the deflationary monetary policy on economic growth.

The "new view" historians (above p. 32) rest their claims about Britain's economic growth in the 1920s largely on Feinstein's and Lomax's data on income, industrial production and productivity. The most recent figures confirm the impression that Britain's growth was *respectable* compared to her past performance (see Table 7).

Table 7 *Decadal and inter-cyclical rates of growth of G.D.P., % p.a.*

1870–79	1.7	1866–73	2.4
1880–89	2.1	1873–82	1.9
1890–99	2.4	1882–90	2.0
1900–13	1.5	1890–1900	2.1
1913–19	0	1900–07	1.5
1919–20	−9.0	1907–13	1.6
1920–29	2.0	1924–29	2.6
1930–39	2.0	1929–38	1.9

Source: Feinstein, *National Income*, Tables 6 and 1.8

Growth rate calculations are, however, very sensitive to the initial and terminal dates chosen; when comparing prewar and interwar growth the above figures probably underestimate prewar growth and overestimate interwar growth;[150] the figures are also subject to very wide margins of error.† With the interwar years the major difficulty is choosing the initial date, 1924 usually being chosen for comparison of 1924–9 with 1929 to 1937 or 1938 since the levels of unemployment were similar,[151] but this biases the result toward the 1920s, because the early, depression years are omitted. Omitting the depression years of *both* decades real gross domestic product grew about 2.4% p.a. in the 1920s and 3.7% p.a. in the 1930s (see Table 8). Similar comments can be made about the figures on industrial production, which show industrial output grew 2.8% 1920–9 and 3.3% 1929–37.[152]

These calculations tend to ignore the historically high levels of unemployment between the Wars and the point that:

"[Though] 'success' and 'failure' may be subjective terms . . . we now know that modern economies can grow three times faster than the British economy did at that time; that they can employ even the 'hard core' of 1–1½ million permanently unemployed . . . and that they can show some growth every year instead of concentrating it . . . in the later 1930s."[153]

* The rise in public investment was not only in housing; non-housing public sector investment also grew over the period, providing 35% of total non-housing investment in 1920–4 and 50% in 1930–4 (Feinstein, *Domestic Capital Formation*, p. 48).

† The figures prior to 1907 are merely grade D conjectures with margins of error of more than 25%; those for 1907–29 are rough estimates (margins of error of ± 15–25%). This means margins of error, as percentage of growth rate, of at least 21% for the years up to 1929 (Feinstein, *National Income*, pp. 20–2).

Table 8 *Rates of growth of G.D.P., selected periods, 1920–38, % p.a.*

1922–9	2.39
1923–9	2.36
1924–9	2.29
1932–7	3.71
1932–8	3.65
1932–9	3.70

Source: Calculated from Feinstein, *National Income*, Table 6.

Interwar economic growth does not look so respectable when one remembers the potential output lost as a result of unemployment. If one estimates for each year 1921–38 how much unemployment was in excess of the prewar average and multiplies the figure by output per man employed recorded for that year, to arrive at a conservative estimate of output foregone each year, and then adds these up, the total foregone is approximately equal to the 1938 gross national product. This calculation, made by D.E. Moggridge, produces a conservative estimate because it takes no account of any increases in productivity that would have materialized if output growth and employment had been higher. It also assumes unemployment could not have been reduced below the average prewar percentage. This figure (4.7%) is that for members of certain trade unions, this being the only series available; the interwar figures relate to insured employees.[154]

Matthews has argued that *the* reason for the higher employment in Britain since the Second World War is the high level of investment relative to previous levels.[155] Investment figures for the interwar years (Table 9), show an increase in gross domestic fixed capital formation (at constant prices) in the second half of the 1920s over the first half, but they also show that most of the increase was in local authority investment. Furthermore, investment was consistently lower in the 1920s than in the 1930s (with the exception of 1932 and 1933 in the net investment figures). Even in the relatively prosperous years 1927–9 there was no boom in investment to match the boom on the stock exchange.

Why was investment relatively so low in the 1920s? Comparison of U.K. and U.S. experience shows that the same "autonomous" impulses making for growth were present in both countries. However, the extent to which the resulting potential demand (for houses, new consumption goods, etc.) can be made effective depends on the growth of aggregate demand.

"The outstanding fact about the movement of total capital formation [in the U.S.A.] in this decade is the high level reached by 1923 and the maintenance of this level for as long a period as seven years. . . . We thus have a picture of a prolonged investment boom."[156] The main factors responsible for the high level of investment were:

(1) pent-up demand for plant and equipment created by the War;
(2) the direct and indirect effects of the automobile;
(3) the rapid expansion of other relatively new industries such as electric power, electrical equipment, radio and telephones, air transportation, motion pictures and rayon;
(4) rapid pace of technological change, leading to great increases in labour productivity;
(5) the rise to a peak of a long building cycle.

58

Table 9 (a) *Investment in the 1920s and 1930s*

	G.D.F.C.F. at constant prices, 1920–38, £m	N.D.F.C.F. at constant prices, 1920–38, £m
1920	284	30
1921	326	67
1922	300	37
1923	308	41
1924	359	84
1925	410	127
1926	397	110
1927	442	150
1928	438	142
1929	461	154
1930	463	146
1931	454	128
1932	396	65
1933	409	74
1934	498	163
1935	518	176
1936	565	215
1937	584	218
1938	592	219
1939	530	156

Source: Feinstein, *National Income*, Tables 40 and 48.

(b) *G.D.F.C.F. at current prices, by sector, 1920–9, £m*

	Private	Central government	Local authorities	Total
1920	379	13	90	482
1921	299	18	141	458
1922	261	11	109	381
1923	246	13	75	334
1924	277	15	82	374
1925	298	17	105	420
1926	264	16	121	401
1927	283	16	127	426
1928	295	16	109	420
1929	319	15	106	442

Source: Feinstein, *National Income*, Table 39.

Superimposed on these were a wave of optimism, a fairly high propensity to consume, and an elastic credit supply.[157]

It seems unlikely that in the U.K. (1) should have been satisfied in the postwar boom: the boom lasted longer than in the U.S.A., but the U.K. economy had been affected by the War considerably more than the American economy had.

(2) "On any other ground than comparison with the American industry, the growth of the British [automobile] industry has been great and noteworthy."[158] Recovery from the postwar slump was rapid and the great continuous expansion was only temporarily halted by the 1929–32 depression.[159] It was also one of the largest of the newer trades. However, the industry remained, in the 1920s, only a small employer relative to the old staples. Although there were heavy licence and insurance charges and a high fuel tax,[160] the difference between the size of the industry in the two countries is mainly to be explained by the higher level of American incomes.[161]

(3) *The New Industries:* The electrical industries were among the most important

Table 10 *Investment, income, prices, 1919–29*

Year	Industrial Production Index (1913 = 100)	Investment G.D.F.C.F. at constant prices £m	N.D.F.C.F. at constant prices Dwellings £m	Total £m	Income G.D.P. at constant prices £m	Prices Board of Trade wholesale price index (1913 = 100)	Cost of living index (1914 = 100)	Wages Average weekly wage rates (1913 = 100)	Unemployment among insured workers (annual averages of monthly figures) %
1919	89.8	172	-31	-52	4,580	250	215	215	(6.6)
1920	99.8 / 97.9	295 / 284	3	30	4,273 / 4,096	307.3	249	257	(7.9)
1921	79.7	326	42	67	3,857	197.2	226	256	17.0 / 14.3
1922	92.2	300	33	37	3,992	158.8	183	198	11.7
1923	97.6	308	26	41	4,115	158.9	174	176	10.3
1924	108.4	359	51	84	4,238	166.2	175	178	11.3
1925	112.7	410	73	127	4,449	159.1	176	181	12.5
1926	106.6	397	98	110	4,243	148.1	172	181	9.7
1927	122.8	442	110	150	4,539	141.6	168	179	10.8
1928	119.5	438	77	142	4,617	140.3	166	177	10.4
1929	125.5	461	91	154	4,726	136.5	164	176	

Sources: Feinstein, *National Income*, Tables 51, 40, 48, 5 and 65; Mitchell and Deane, *Abstract of British Historical Statistics*, pp. 447–8; L.C.E.S., *Key Statistics*, Table E; Pigou, *Aspects of British Economic History 1918–1925*, pp. 221, 234.

Notes: The figures above the dotted lines include Southern Ireland. The unemployment % for 1919 and 1920 is for December of that year.

and once the supply industry had been reorganized and the "grid" established in 1926, great progress was made and the industry's investment (particularly the construction of the grid) made a large contribution to total investment. Most of this investment, however, took place (for technical reasons) between 1929 and 1932;[162] before 1926, "expansion of electrical output in Great Britain was long retarded by the same general factors that retarded the modernization of her industrial plant—the real and psychological deadweight of the past".[163] The other new industries also grew rapidly in the decade. The "new view" historians have argued that the shift of resources to the new sector of the economy was the major contributor to Britain's growth in the 1920s.[164] There is no doubt that the new industries' growth was rapid; but their net output only accounted for just over 16% of manufacturing production by 1930[165] and their investment accounted for only one-third of total capital formation in the eleven years 1920–30.[166] Their exports also grew rapidly but they were unable to compensate for the loss of export markets by the old industries,[167] and their rapid growth did not serve to "mop up" the unemployed.

(4) *Technical progress* was in fact "spectacular"[168] and it was taken advantage of by British entrepreneurs, particularly in the new industries. There is also evidence of increased productivity in some older industries as a result of technical progress, increasing mechanization, and improved methods of production.[169] The result was an increase in productivity (output per man-hour) in the aggregate.[170] Within the aggregate, industry productivity growth rates were correlated with output growth rates.[171] Salter's study of twenty eight manufacturing industries over the period 1924–50 suggests this correlation is explicable mainly in terms of (the uneven impact of) technical progress and also partly by economies of scale. Observed structural changes originated in the same factors, being the response to the changing pattern of prices and costs resulting from uneven rates of technical change.[172]

Aldcroft and Richardson contend that such technologically-determined shifts in the allocation of resources caused the "respectable" economic growth of the interwar years, but such shifts, and technical progress itself, are not determined by supply conditions (e.g. the current state of science and technology) alone.[173] There are several reasons in theory for this. Demand-side considerations are a major, if not the major, determinant of variations in the allocation of inventive effort to specific industries, since entrepreneurial perception of an as yet imperfectly satisfied need for some consumption or capital good will induce investment in research and development designed to find a feasible and profitable way of meeting that need.[174] This implies the faster the growth of investment and income, the greater will be the incentive (and the ability) to invest in R & D, and the more technical progress there will be. The same conclusion is one of the "economic implications of learning-by-doing": the production and use of new products will show up deficiencies in the original designs and induce further investment (and technical progress) to improve the product. The continued use of the same new process of production may also result in improved productivity in producing the final product.[175] Scientific research and technical progress in one area also lead to new possibilities in other fields. In other words, inventions and innovations are *both* determined to some extent by economic factors.[176]

This Richardson and Aldcroft deny. For them the rate of invention is given,* and at any time the current supply of innovations made possible by past invention is being embodied in the gross investment that is going on.[177] They admit that the number of innovations embodied will increase with an increase in investment, but they explain the actual rate of investment in terms of the overcommitment of resources to the older declining industries, due to the imperfection of the capital market, the immobility of labour and the conservatism of entrepreneurs,[178] and leave it at that, as though that were not further explicable in economic terms (see pp. 51–4 above and p. 63 below).

The conditions that render technical progress endogenous were in fact present in Britain in the years 1919–39: Sayers found that the course of technical improvement was in large part dictated by market conditions, that the effect of depression in 1921 and 1922 and in 1931 and 1932 was to retard technical progress, and that they were considerable interrelations between innovations.[179] Therefore technical progress and productivity growth would have proceeded faster if aggregate demand and investment had been growing faster.

(5) *Building:* There was, as in the U.S.A., a considerable expansion: "Building activity expanded almost uninterruptedly in the years 1924–29. This long-lived boom was a boom in housing."[180] But this "boom" was mild compared with the 1930s boom (on which see below pp. 108, 111–16). It was also mainly due to government intervention in the form of subsidies. Unsubsidized housebuilding in the 1920s remained small and relatively steady.[181] The stimulus to subsidized housebuilding was provided by the Chamberlain and Wheatley subsidies of 1923 and 1924. The Conservative government reduced both subsidies on all houses completed after 30 September 1927 and abolished the Chamberlain subsidy on houses completed after 30 September 1929,[182] thus inducing peaks in building in 1927 and 1929.[183] Local authorities responded far more than private builders to these subsidies,[184] whereas the 1930s boom was due almost entirely to private unsubsidized building. Given that on theoretical grounds one would expect private building to be sensitive to changes in monetary conditions, and that there was a potentially large demand for housing,[185] it is reasonable to suppose restrictive monetary policy played a dampening role, a supposition strengthened by the experience with cheap money in the 1930s.

The standard explanation of Britain's difficulties in the decade points to the decline in exports, particularly of the old staples. Britain certainly had a major problem of adjustment to changed world conditions; but could a different monetary policy have made the adjustment any easier? The suggestion of the "new view" historians is that a lower exchange rate and an easier monetary policy would not have solved the problems of adjustment and would probably have retarded it, because if the older industries had remained prosperous then resources would have stayed tied up in them rather than shifting to the new industries which provided the basis for recovery in the 1930s. Thus Aldcroft writes:

> "In point of fact, the sharp contraction of some of the older industries was a positive long-term advantage since structural change would no doubt have

---

*   They justify their assumption of autonomous technical progress by pointing to the fact that innovations were often made abroad (Aldcroft and Richardson, *The British Economy 1870–1939*, p. 38), but this implies only that technical progress is *partly* autonomous.

been delayed even longer had these industries maintained the dominant position in the export economy which they had held formerly . . . Had this transition not taken place in the 1920s the British economy would have been without the viable base which assisted its recovery from the Great Depression of the early 1930s."[186]

The flaw in this argument is the assumption of a limited stock of resources, limited in the aggregate by exogenous technical progress and within that aggregate "over-committed" to the production of the old staples by "structural" factors. Technical progress and structural factors are not independent of aggregate demand and with one million unemployed there could have been more expansion in the new industries even if the old were not declining, if aggregate demand had been growing sufficiently to create profit expectations favourable to investment in the new industries (primarily domestic-based). The new industries thrived in the 1930s when they "encountered a rising demand in the context of a more intelligent monetary and credit policy than had prevailed in the twenties".[187]

Against this it has been said that the unemployed were concentrated in particular regions different from those in which the new industries were being built up. This is of course true but there is evidence that mobility in the form of a drift to the South of England increased considerably in the 1930s when employment opportunities there were seen to be expanding rapidly.[188] After all,

"In periods when certain industries obviously need more workers . . . a worker out of a job, who wants to move, has no difficulty in deciding where to go. But, when the only obvious thing is that his present industry needs less workers, such a man has great difficulty. . . . If [he does] move, will [he] not merely find [himself] unemployed in some other job or some other place? The temptation to stay where [he is] in the vague hope that something will turn up is very strong."[189]

To conclude (in Sayers' words):

"The low incomes of the depressed areas meant unpropitious markets for domestic industries . . . [These] low incomes . . . and the monetary conditions arising from the gold standard policy and the Wall Street boom, all conspired to limit markets both at home and abroad, and the splash on the Stock Exchange was not matched by any great employment of real resources in the new lines. There were no obvious openings to which surplus labour from the depressed areas could move, and the world boom came and went leaving that hard core of a million unemployed untouched."[190]

4

The Great Depression

"The economic blizzard of 1929–32 was something that struck Britain from outside".[1] Accordingly, the main question to be considered in this chapter is: How did the U.K. monetary authorities react to this situation?

The first, preliminary, step in answering the question is to settle a matter of timing: just when did the Great Depression hit the U.K.? This cannot be decided without some consideration of the causes of the depression, in particular the question of whether it began in the U.S.A. and was transmitted from there to Britain in the autumn of 1929, or whether the events of later 1929 which apparently ushered in the worldwide slump were the culmination of deflationary forces already operating elsewhere in the world, especially in primary-producing countries, impinging on both the U.K. and the U.S.A. Given the U.K.'s greater dependence on foreign trade, and hence its greater vulnerability to depression overseas, one would on the latter hypothesis expect Britain to be suffering from the external deflationary forces earlier than the U.S.A. which did not feel their full force until its investment boom had spent itself and its prosperity (and the expectations of its businessmen and investors) had become very shaky.

Hodson has remarked: "To open the tale of the world depression with the stock market crash in New York in October 1929 is like starting the story of a flood at the moment when the last sod in the dyke gave way."[2] Among the already present deflationary forces that had been concealed by the boom, Hodson emphasizes the steady fall in commodity prices due to the relative overproduction of primary commodities and their consequences first for the debtor countries and then, given the disruption of trading patterns thus caused, for the whole international economy.[3] Sayers gives two major origins for the world depression: one, this overproduction of primary commodities and two, the collapse of the speculative fever in the U.S.A.;[4] a third factor, the instability of the international monetary system in the 1920s, has been stressed by Brown and Kindleberger.[5]

A complete explanation of the Great Depression has, as Kindleberger has emphasized,[6] to give reasons why it was so wide, so deep, and lasted so long; Kindleberger finds them in the working of the international monetary system as it had developed after its disruption by the First World War rather than in the misguided monetary policy pursued by the Federal Reserve System, as Friedman and Schwartz would have it.[7] Here, however, my concern is with how and where it originated. Both explanations of the course of the depression allow that deflationary forces were at work before the New York stock market crashed in October 1929, as is borne out by the fact that the downturn in activity in both America and Britain occurred earlier in the year. The National Bureau reference dates for the upper turning-point for the U.S.A. and the U.K. are August 1929 and July 1929 respectively. Further light on timing is shed by the calculations of Corner[8] which give the following turning-points in British and American exports and imports.

	U.K.	U.S.A.
Exports	May 1929	November 1928 or March 1929
	Trend: February 1929	Trend: March 1929
Imports	January 1929 with second peak August 1929	April 1929
	Trend: July 1929	Trend: May 1929

Given that the propensity to export (as a percentage of disposable income) of the U.K. is 21% compared with 6.6% for the U.S.A.,[9] the impact of a decline in foreign demand would be much greater on the U.K. economy than on the U.S. Furthermore, the U.S.A. did and the U.K. did not, enjoy a boom in the later 1920s, so that the evidence points to an internally-caused downturn in activity in the U.S.A. and an externally-generated one in the U.K. Given that the turning-point came earlier in U.K. than in the U.S., this does not in itself imply that the contraction in the U.S. caused that in the U.K., *unless* the forces making for the downturn in the U.S.A. made themselves felt in the U.K., owing to its greater vulnerability, earlier than in the U.S. One factor, the effects of the speculation in New York, was felt overseas before in America: after mid-1928 American foreign lending was very sharply curtailed.

U.S. lending overseas had greatly increased after the adoption of the Dawes plan in 1924, and reached a new high plateau of more than $900m a year, rising above $1,250m in 1927 and 1928.[10] The most sensational increase was in the volume of loans to Latin America and Europe, and much of the latter virtually kept the German economy going, until 1928. Kindleberger has estimated that there was a swing of something in the order of $2,000m in U.S. lending between the eighteen months from 1 January 1927 to 30 June 1928 and the fifteen months from 1 July 1928 to 30 September 1929;[11] such an enormous cutback could hardly fail to have serious consequences for the rest of the world, and for the former recipients of American loans in particular. The effects were particularly serious for the primary-producing countries, which had been suffering since the War from overproduction of their main commodities (due partly to the War and partly to technical innovations).[12] Trade with these countries was particularly important to Britain, much more so than to the U.S.A.[13] Corner's evidence suggests the following sequence of events:

> "There was an early decline in demand in certain of the U.K.'s overseas markets, notably those of the low income per head primary producers—South America, British India, the British Colonies and the Far East. This fall in U.K. exports induced deflationary pressure on the U.K. economy. The United States also experienced the pressure of similar forces but not nearly to the same extent as the U.K. Once the slump got under way in the U.S.A. and internal demand started to fall off total U.S. imports declined rapidly consequently inducing a second bout of deflationary pressure on the British economy."[14]

Phelps Brown's and Shackle's series show that export-sensitive employment stopped rising in 1927, the drop into severe depression occurring in March 1929. Downturns in employment in consumer durable industries followed in July 1929, and in producers durable and consumers durable industries in October.[15]

The drain of funds from Europe to New York in the fifteen months preceding the Wall Street crash also increased the pressures on interest rates in European money markets and hence on the Bank of England in its attempt to keep Britain on the gold standard. The result was a tightening of monetary policy in the U.K. from mid-1928 onwards.[16] I described the Bank's operations in those fifteen months in Chapter 3; I now turn to the Bank's, and the Treasury's operations in the period from the New York stock market collapse to the beginning of the international financial crisis in May 1931.

Bank Policy 1929–31

The authorities' first reaction to the crash in New York was relief, because it opened up the prospect of lower interest rates. "The collapse of the New York stock market boom in October 1929 relieved London and the Bank of a strain that had preoccupied the Governor for more than a year. . . . Now he could respond to domestic claims. Beginning on October 31 the Bank reduced its rate, in step with New York, from 6½% to 3% by May [1930]."[17] There Bank rate stayed until 14 May 1931, when it was reduced to 2½%.

Sayers has suggested that "after the collapse of the 1929 boom the Bank of England, to some extent in concert with other central banks, had adopted a cheap money policy partly as the classical reaction to the relaxation of strain upon the supply of money, and partly as a deliberate effort to reverse the world-wide slump. This cheap money policy was interrupted by the international liquidity crisis of 1931".[18] Monetary policy was eased, virtually simultaneously, in all the major financial centres.[19] The central bankers wanted to see a revival of international capital flows (interrupted since mid-1928) which they "sought . . . with rare harmony. They agreed that the revival was necessary for the success of the Young Plan and for the maintenance of exchange stability. In addition, each had special reasons of his own. For Norman, the renewed American outflow was desirable because it supported sterling and facilitated the reopening of the London capital market."[20] In consequence there was a major drop in money market rates in all the major financial centres, and a remarkable revival in American foreign lending in the first half of 1930.[21] However, while money was certainly cheaper in Britain as elsewhere in 1930 than in 1929, it is not so certain that this represented a significant easing of the monetary situation. On the one hand, as Clarke points out, "in the capital markets . . . the cost of long-term borrowing was still about the same level as in the first half of 1929 even for the British Government";[22] on the other, the U.K. monetary statistics (see Chart 2) show that both high-powered money, which had been constant for the previous couple of years, and the money stock, whose growth of 1926–8 had levelled off in 1929, fell in the first half of 1930. Both recovered only slightly in the second half of the year. The decline and subsequent recovery of deposits may have been partly due to the similar change in the banks' Treasury bill holdings.[23] The money supply then fell from the end of 1930 to February 1932; high-powered money remained constant till the spring of 1932. The deposit-reserve ratio rose very slightly 1929–31; the deposit-currency ratio was constant over the same period. The fall in bank deposits was more marked in current accounts than in total deposits.[24]

Although the Bank may have wanted to pursue an easier monetary policy, it was constrained by its determination to stay on the gold standard, a task which became more difficult as 1930 went on and the depression deepened. The exchanges were never strong enough to avoid the need for constant watching;[25] although 1930 was a relatively quiet year for the Bank,[26] first reports of the distrust of sterling arrived before its end.[27] In consequence there were no reductions of Bank rate between May 1930 and May 1931. In June 1930 the Bank did not follow New York down, "having regard to the general weakness of our exchanges".[28] In August Norman told Harrison (Governor of the New York Federal Reserve Bank) that he thought: "Under existing conditions we could perhaps work with a 2½% Bank rate but the general position is such that little or no advantage could be expected. A reduction in the rate now would deprive us of the means of helping if and when the business situation becomes more promising."[29] The Bank on at least two occasions attempted to narrow the gap between market and Bank rates, in March 1930 by means of foreign exchange operations at a time when money was tending to be tight because of tax payments, the final call for the conversion loan and the popularity of late June Treasury bills,[30] and in January 1931.[31] Clarke also says that: "The Bank of England, which previously had at least partly offset the effects of gold movements, reversed its policy. During the eleven months beginning July 1930 open market sales reinforced the cash drain that resulted from the outflow of gold so that bankers' balances at the Bank of England averaged 5% lower than a year earlier".[32] However, throughout the years 1925–31 the Bank tended to offset the effects of inflows of gold and foreign exchange on the cash basis but not to offset reserve losses,[33] so its policy in the eleven months mentioned by Clarke was in fact a continuation, not a reversal, of an established policy: the result was that the deflationary tendency of the Bank's policy that had increased after mid-1928 was not diminished after 1929.[34]

Other central banks' attempts at an easier monetary policy were also halted in mid-1930. This was due to the fact that the initial "hopes that the depression would be mild and that a renewed outflow of U.S. capital would restore the international economic balance were undermined by the further deterioration of the international economy during the eleven months that followed the flotation of the Young Loan [in June 1930]".[35] As a result, "The monetary policies of the major countries combined with the continued decline in production and prices and the rise in defaults, devaluations, and political disturbances, to kill the revival of the long-term capital flow. In the year beginning July 1930, new issues for foreign account fell in both Britain and the U.S.A. to only about one-third the rate in January–June 1930."[36]

How much monetary policy contributed to this second cessation of international lending is debatable; international commodity prices also resumed their downward course in the spring of 1930.[37] Sayers judged that the central bankers did not have a chance because the forces making for depression were too great.[38] Once the capital flow ceased the worldwide deflationary forces gathered momentum. This increased the pressures on London and when a reduction in Bank rate to 2½% was finally made, in May 1931, it was an act of desperation. Norman told Harrison on 5 May: "The general economic outlook appears in every way so discouraging that for my part I should like now to try the effect of reductions of ½% in your and our discount rates",[39] and then reduced Bank rate on 14 May (a week after New York) because "it would be most difficult to maintain 3% effectively" because of falling bill rates.[40]

Treasury Policy 1929–31

The Treasury also wanted cheaper money and saw the events of October 1929 as opening the way to lower interest rates, which it desired not only to facilitate the conversion as soon as possible of 5% War Loan but also because it expected lower rates to have a beneficial effect on trade. According to Hopkins:

> "Though of course these causes take some time to operate . . . cheap money means that enterprise can be financed more easily and . . . prospective profits . . . increased. It stirs the merchant to place orders and it must therefore tend to make enterprise more attractive."[41]

Towards the end of 1930 the Chancellor (Snowden) told his ministerial colleagues that although recent reductions in short-term interest rates would take a long time to show their full effects on long-term rates, "a year ago the short-term rate which was now a little over 2% stood at 6% and he was looking forward in the absence of any catastrophe, to bringing the long-term rate down to 4%".[42] However, although the Treasury had been discussing ways of dealing with War Loan since 1927, preparations for conversion did not begin in earnest till January 1931 (below pp. 71–4). For the Treasury as for the Bank, "1930 was a year of suspense",[43] and the main preoccupation was the budget. The difficulties of balancing the budget became steadily more acute as 1930 progressed. Depression brought declining revenues and increased expenditure, especially on unemployment relief, particularly from the spring onwards when the normal seasonal improvement in employment failed to occur.

Snowden's aims as Chancellor were (1) to balance the budget honestly, i.e. without resorting to the "raids" that Churchill had indulged in, and with a proper provision for debt repayment, and (2) to reduce the intolerable burden of debt. In these he was perfectly in sympathy with the Treasury officials. He was also a convinced freetrader and wished to repeal the few protective duties the U.K. had. This aim and (2) were part of a more general ambition, to shift the distribution of income in favour of the working classes by reducing the returns to the rentier on the one hand and keeping the cost of living low on the other.[44]

In October 1929 Hopkins and his colleagues provided Snowden with a memorandum designed to enable him to paint a gloomy picture to the Cabinet. Grigg, then the Chancellor's Secretary (later at the Inland Revenue), admitted the figures were "a little disingenuous because [they] make allowance for the immediate and complete repeal of the food and protective taxes and the certainty of some reduction in the Navy is mentioned in the text but not allowed for in the Table." But, he added, "it would be natural for you to paint a gloomy picture (with the purpose you have in mind [i.e. impressing upon his colleagues the necessity of limiting expenditure]) and anyhow it isn't a particularly cheerful prospect".[45]

The result of the financial stringency which the worsening economic situation was imposing on the Exchequer was that Snowden did not repeal the McKenna and silk duties, nor the food taxes, though the safeguarding duties were allowed to lapse.[46]

He did not reduce indirect taxation in spite of the fact that Churchill's five budgets had brought about a net increase in indirect taxation of £20,379,000, and a net decrease in direct taxation of £40,588,000.[47].He increased income tax, super-tax, estate duties and the beer duty.[48] He also managed to increase the sinking fund provision by £5m raising the provision for debt charges from £355 to £360m, as Hopkins recommended.[49] This was to make up for Churchill's laxity with respect to the sinking fund, the arrangement being that the borrowing to meet the 1929 deficit of £14½m should be repaid by adding to debt redemption £5m in each of 1930/31 and 1931/32 and £4½m in 1932/33.[50] But Snowden departed from his principles in both this and his next Budget by partially relying on paper transfers from Treasury capital accounts—the Rating Relief Suspensory Fund, and in 1931/32, the Exchange Account—i.e. he adopted the technique of balancing by "raids" and "windfalls" for which he had consistently criticized Churchill.

Snowden's April 1931 Budget

On 14 January 1931 Snowden reported to the Cabinet on the financial situation. He began: "The Budget prospect for 1931 is a grim one . . . As each month passes with no sign of a lifting of the world economic crisis, the financial prospect constantly and steadily deteriorates". His memorandum is worth quoting fairly fully, for two reasons: firstly, the intention as soon as possible to take advantage of lower interest rates to convert War Loan is stated, as part of an argument against raiding the sinking fund; secondly, the need to take drastic measures to balance the budget is stressed.

> "It is sometimes argued that there is no real deficit, on the ground that the Budget provides a sinking fund which should more than offset any deficit and that in times like this we would be justified in curtailing the sinking fund. This plausible argument is entirely fallacious. In the first place, the great bulk of the Budget provision for debt redemption is required to provide specific sinking funds attached to particular loans under the terms of the prospectuses of these loans. Any curtailment of these sinking funds would be a definite breach of the contractual obligations on the faith of which the loans in question were subscribed by the public and the shock to British credit which would be caused by such measures would far outweigh any advantage that we could hope to gain. Secondly, in present conditions it is not true to say that the sinking fund more than offsets the Budget deficit. There is a large expenditure which ought to be charged on the Budget but which we are meeting out of borrowing. In particular, the Unemployment Insurance Fund is borrowing at the rate of £40 millions a year, though there is little or no prospect of any part of this debt ever being repaid. This borrowing, which is unprecedented in peace time, must certainly be brought into the reckoning. Thirdly, the policy proposed would not even pay. Any suspension of the sinking fund would immediately depreciate the whole of the £7,000,000,000 of Government securities. It would increase the cost of the legitimate borrowings which the Government has to undertake each year for Local Loans and similar purposes. It would postpone indefinitely all prospects of the conversion of the war debt to a lower interest basis, which is one of the few hopeful means of securing a reduction of

expenditure in the future. It is possible that the existence of a small 'free' surplus on the sinking fund (i.e. a margin over and above the contractual sinking fund on particular loans), together with some other special factors, might justify some reconsideration of the provision in the last Finance Act requiring the deficit of any year to be redeemed in the succeeding year; but even action of this limited character requires to be considered with the utmost care, or it may well accentuate the evils that it is intended to remedy. "This country cannot afford a Budget with any sort of deficit. From the internal point of view alone there are compelling reasons for maintaining the country's credit. The falling off of revenue coupled with the constant increase of expenditure and the great demands for new capital resources occasioned by borrowing, particularly for the Unemployment Fund, are swiftly bringing back our floating debt to the dangerous high level at which it stood a year ago. The improvement in the short-term position effected by the new issues of the autumn of 1929 and the spring of 1930 will be worse than lost, and . . . if in these conditions the public look upon the Budget as unsound, it will become a question whether they can be induced to subscribe for the short-term accommodation which is vital to finance and equally whether they can be induced to subscribe to any necessary long-term loans, be they required to meet the growing mass of general indebtedness or to be expended on fruitful schemes of national work. Failure to secure the necessary short-term accommodation will prejudice the continuance of cheap money with all that implies. Failure to obtain necessary long-term money at reasonable rates will not merely postpone all prospects of successful conversion of the war debt, but will jeopardise the whole improvement in the long-term rate of interest which has characterized recent months and which, if maintained, is full of promise for business in the future.

"This is not scare-mongering; in present conditions of gloom and anxiety there would follow all the necessary consequences of unsound state finance; nor is the probability of other graver consequences—a breakdown of our financial organization and the removal of great sums abroad—lightly to be dismissed. There are disquieting indications that the national finances, and especially the continuously increasing load of debt upon the Unemployment Insurance Fund, are being watched and criticized abroad . . . It is believed that there is a steady trickle of money being transferred from this country abroad. We cannot afford to let this movement increase . . . Any flight from the pound would be fraught with the most disastrous consequences—not merely to the money market but to the whole economic organisation of the country. It is imperative to take steps to combat this tendency, and to re-assure the world as to our position. It is not merely that we cannot afford the drain of gold which a withdrawal of balances would entail. Beyond this it is the hope of this Government that means will be found to promote a re-examination of monetary policy throughout the world and thus to secure a greater degree of cooperation in regard to the management of credit and the utilisation of the available supply of gold. It will be an ill day when any initiative taken from London on these grave questions is met with the rejoinder that our first business is to put our own house in order. But there are indications that, unless active steps are taken to remedy the admitted defects of our financial position, that is the rejoinder with which we will inevitably be faced."[51]

However, drastic measures were not taken in this budget. With respect to debt policy "financial rigidity was not . . . the distinguishing mark of this Budget" as it had been of the last.[52] The remaining £9½m of the 1929 deficit was not now to be compensated for by increased debt redemption, and as for the current deficit, Snowden

> "suggested that Members [of the House of Commons] neither should nor would expect him to provide for this by increased taxation. He confidently expected that the economy committee [set up under Sir George May as a result of the Economy debate in the House on 11 February 1931] would make recommendations resulting in reduced spending, and it was possible that, during the year, debt interest might be substantially reduced by conversion operations, the savings in either case automatically swelling the amount available for debt reduction, and he expressed the hope that in these ways savings would be effected in the current year wiping off a considerable part of the deficit of £23 million. If this expectation were not realized, he said, 'it would be the duty of Parliament to deal with this matter when better times return'."[53]

Thus this was a stop-gap budget. It was balanced by transferring £33m from the Exchange Account, by increasing the duty on oil and by some jiggling with the income tax, Snowden having emphatically rejected the idea of a revenue tariff.[54]

The idea of departing from strict canons of financial orthodoxy had been recommended to Snowden by Hopkins back in October 1930. Hopkins suggested both the use of money from the Exchange Account and an abandonment of the effort to pay off past deficits; in a later memorandum, intended as a follow-on to Hopkins' memorandum, Fergusson (the Chancellor's Secretary) made it clear that the only reason these devices could be contemplated was the need to avoid an increase in direct taxation. Having pointed out the grave danger, in terms of their effect on foreign opinion about Britain's financial position, of trying any further expedients (beyond those suggested by Hopkins) Fergusson suggested one last alternative, to use the fact that the Royal Commission on Unemployment Insurance and the Economy Committee were now sitting as an excuse to postpone any reduction in expenditure or increase in taxation.[55]

War Loan Conversion Scheme, 1931

The scheme finally adopted in 1932 was worked out in the Treasury in the early months of 1931. Since 1927 the Treasury officials had been looking ahead to a large operation in 1930 or 1931. Not only had they been making an occasional "nibble" at War Loan, they had also been discussing ways of surmounting the problems of dealing with such a large block of stock at one go. The precedent closely studied was, of course, Goschen's operation of 1888, when £600m of 3% Consols was converted into 2¾%, and ultimately 2½%, stock.

Although in April 1927 Niemeyer told Churchill that he had "never believed that a conversion on the scale of £2,000 million in one lump was a conceivable operation",[56] in September 1927 Phillips (then Principal Assistant Secretary) wrote a memorandum on the Goschen operation.* The conclusions were, Leith-Ross (Deputy Controller of Finance) told Hopkins, that "at present Government credit is not sufficiently good to enable us to effect a really favourable conversion: and even if it were, we have no power to redeem and so would have to offer holders some special inducement to convert . . . We are in a better position to make a successful conversion if we wait till after 1929 when we have power to redeem." The difficulty that would then arise of what to do with dissentients could be dealt with by the Goschen procedure of requiring holders who dissented from conversion to apply for repayment, and by converting all holdings for which such notice was not given. Having pointed out that this would probably need Parliamentary authority, Leith-Ross went on to emphasize that the procedure was only "the machinery by which a big conversion scheme must be tackled [and] cannot . . . ensure success"; the offer made must like the Goschen offer be more attractive to holders than cash. Since (1) the authorities could not afford to fail, (2) a high interest rate would be needed now (in 1927) to avoid failure, (3) the object of the exercise was to reduce the interest charge on the debt, and (4) it was hoped that interest rates would fall in the next few years, "We must . . . defer action till Government credit stands on a 4% basis or nearby. We may hope that this position may be reached by 1930 or 1931", and then the Treasury should follow the Goschen precedent. "In the meantime we have plenty to do in meeting existing maturities".[57] How these were dealt with I have already discussed in Chapter 3.

In 1928 another possibility, a proposal to repay holders in instalments over several years, was extensively examined by the Treasury officials, who were in favour of the idea but were stopped by a definite opinion from the Law Officers that it would be a breach of the terms on which War Loan had originally been issued.[58]

* During 1927 Churchill received voluminous memoranda and numerous visits from Mr J. Hanson Lawson, a stockbroker, on the latter's scheme for conversion of 5% War Loan before 1929, which he urged because of the problem that would arise in and after 1929 if holders opted for repayment rather than conversion. The Treasury went "to a great deal of trouble in examining this scheme, and [came] to the clear conclusion that it will not work", because Lawson had assumed institutional holdings of War Loan were larger than they were in fact (T.176/18, Leith-Ross to Stamp, 8 December 1927). An important cause of their trouble was Churchill's prodding. In May he complained to Niemeyer:
"We have assumed since the War, largely under the guidance of the Bank of England, a policy of deflation, debt repayment, high taxation, large sinking funds and the Gold Standard . . . [which] has produced bad trade, hard times, an immense increase in unemployment . . . [and] fierce labour disputes. . . . Now our debt policy has reached a complete *impasse*."
(T. 175/11, Churchill to Niemeyer, 20 May 1927)
When Hopkins replaced Niemeyer as Controller of Finance at the Treasury during the summer of 1927, Churchill urged him to look again at Hanson Lawson's scheme, because:
"Sir O. Niemeyer and the Governor were entirely without any solution or wish to move: and perhaps there is no solution. But we ought not to accept this melancholy conclusion until after we have *hopefully* and *helpfully* explored every well-informed and serious suggestion. No one can regard the Debt policy as a success at present, the cost mounts and the total swells in spite of enormous sinking funds."
(T. 188/11, Churchill to Hopkins, 5 October 1927)

In January 1931 Phillips stated the current alternatives:

"1. *4½ Treasury Bonds 1934*

We can give notice to repay 1 February 1932 . . . Probably inadvisable . . . It is a gamble, as we cannot be sure on what terms we could raise cash in 1932. Plenty of later chances of dealing with these bonds.

2. *4½ Treasury Bonds 1930–2*

If not previously redeemed the Bonds will be redeemed at par 15 April 1932. We mustn't let this drift much longer without a clear understanding with the Governor. . . . the question is simply what is best date for operation between now and then [i.e. April 1932]. If there is serious fear of short interest rates rising there is everything to be said for an early operation before Budget Figures make everyone gloomy.

3. *Nibbles at 5% War Loan*

Conditions are not too brilliant for this." [59]

None of these suggestions was acted upon: in fact no new government issues were made in 1931. At the same time that Phillips wrote the above memorandum, a Cabinet Committee of J.H. Thomas, A.V. Alexander and W. Graham was sitting under Snowden to consider possible ways of balancing the budget. All three were in favour of all-round cuts that included the rentier; Alexander actually suggested conversion.[60] When one remembers Snowden's remarks to his Cabinet colleagues, it is at least plausible to assume that Treasury discussion of a large conversion scheme in the near future began in January 1931, an assumption that the fact that the Phillips memorandum is the first on a file labelled "Papers leading up to the Conversion Operation" renders more plausible.[61]

In May 1931 Phillips stated the alternatives open to the Treasury rather differently:

"(i) to do nothing

(ii) to have another nibble by offering a stock in conversion without giving notice to pay off dissentients

(iii) to give notice to pay off the 5% War Loan in full on 1 December next, coupled with an offer which it would be hoped would induce most holders to convert.

"In favour of doing nothing it might be argued that interest rates have not yet reached bottom and that a further wait which might enable us to convert it at substantially better than 4% in a few years would be the correct course financially.

Against a policy of inaction are fairly weighty arguments:

(a) the present opportunity is at least fairly good and may not recur for a long time

(b) so long as £2,000m of 5% stock remains unconverted, Government credit never will get to a really satisfactory level

(c) a successful conversion, which reduced the income of the rentiers, would greatly ease the passage of the economy measures.

"As regards [(ii)] . . . the Bank advise that this would have to take the form of a 4½% stock redeemable at or after a fixed date and that not more than £500m of such stock would be converted.

"The possible objections . . . are (a) expense and (b) likelihood of failure . . .

[Two previous conversions, in April 1924 and November 1929, offered favourable terms to holders but had disappointing results.] Opinions differ very much as to the prospect of better success on the present occasion, but it is certainly a large order to assume we can convert £500 millions. In any case the fact that we limit our offer to £500 millions may lead holders to abstain on the ground that they are bound to get a second chance since at least £1,500m of the 5% War Loan will remain. Such an amount is hardly less formidable than the present £2,000m and a further offer by the Treasury on reasonable terms is certain later. For that reason people may hold back in the expectation of a reasonable offer later after an interval during which they have continued to earn 5% on their holdings.

"The remaining possibility is to give notice to repay on 1st December coupled with an offer of conversion to a lower rate of interest.

"The important questions are (a) the risk . . . and (b) the terms . . . The risk is essentially an exchange risk . . . dissent by foreign holders (who including the Irish Free State may hold £200m) may be a serious matter leading to withdrawal of gold, and an attempt by English dissentients to invest their redemption money abroad would increase the difficulty . . . [As to the terms, the Bank think 4% is possible.]"[62]

This last suggestion was accepted: the rest of the file consists of memoranda dealing with a bill, to be called the War Loan (Redemption and Continuance) Bill, to give the government the necessary powers to act on the Goschen precedent, and draft prospectuses dated 30 June 1931 offering redemption on 31 December 1931 or conversion to 4%. The file ends on 19 July 1931, by which time the international financial crisis had caused the scheme to be temporarily shelved. As Phillips said later, two conditions were essential for undertaking the operation:

"(a) Interest rates must be low enough to make it worth doing (it would be a murderously expensive mistake to convert at any rate substantially above 4%), and

(b) Calm conditions must be assured for at least four or five months ahead.

"The operation would have been launched this year in June or July when interest rates were favourable, had condition (b) also been satisfied. The Chancellor was stopped however by the signs of disturbance in Austria and Germany."[63]

As it turned out, the operation was postponed for a year; in the meantime the Treasury took advantage of the opportunity of a second budget in September to obtain the necessary legal powers (see pp. 76, 88 below).

Before discussing the financial crisis and post-crisis monetary policy, it should be noted that the expectation of lower interest rates generally and the hope of reduction of the interest burden of the debt by conversion of War Loan were widely shared.[64] As the months went by and Britain's already weak economic position rapidly worsened under the impact of the world slump (see Tables 9, 16 and 20), these hopeful expectations turned to pessimism.[65] Although public expenditure did not fall in 1930, and consumption expenditure fell relatively little, thanks partly to the favourable movement of the terms of trade, unemployment reached two and a half million by the end of the year and nearly three million a year later as a result of the immense loss of exports and the decline in investment.

The Financial Crisis

The crisis began in Austria in May with the failure of the Credit-Anstalt, a banking concern whose assets consisted mainly of industrial and commercial loans in Austria and neighbouring countries, and had spread to Germany almost immediately because the embarrassments of the Credit-Anstalt were realized to be shared by many institutions in Europe given that debtors everywhere were facing ever more serious difficulties as a result of the continued fall in prices.[66] Creeping insolvency due to falling prices had already become a problem in 1930 and early 1931, especially in the great international short-term creditor nations such as America and France, both of which experienced acute internal bank failures.[67] The mad scramble for liquidity in mid-1931 could not be stopped by credits from the Bank for International Settlements, the Bank of England, the Bank of France and the Federal Reserve Bank of New York to the Reichsbank, nor by U.S. President Hoover's offer of a one-year moratorium on all inter-governmental debts on 20 June; on 13 July the Darmstadter Bank failed and thereupon the entire German banking system was closed.

Attention shifted to Britain, which was by now suffering from an adverse balance of trade, serious budgetary difficulties, most obviously due to the ever-growing expenditure on the "dole", and whose banks were reputed to have lent to Germany substantial sums of money which were now immobilized. "The check to confidence was great. A withdrawal of foreign money from London set in immediately on a formidable scale. In a fortnight the Bank of England had lost £32m of gold. Bank rate was raised from 2½ per cent to 3½ on the 23rd July and to 4½ on the 30th."[68] The drain on London occurred not only because of doubts abroad about Britain's solvency but also because of foreign bankers' fears that the German and Austrian difficulties would spread to their own countries: to bolster their own liquidity these bankers drew down their sterling balances.[69]

Confidence was partially restored by the announcement at the beginning of August of credits to the Bank of England from the Bank of France and the Federal Reserve Bank of New York, but the budget remained unbalanced and the drain continued. The potential favourable effects on confidence of the announcement of the credits were considerably diminished by the publication of the May Committee's report the same day. This forecast a budget deficit of £12m for 1932/33 and recommended £97m of cuts in public expenditure. "This confirmed in the minds of foreign observers their worst fears. The credits were interpreted as a sign of weakness and the increase in the fiduciary issue [extended by £15m by the Treasury, at the request of the Bank, on the same day] as evidence of inflation."[70] Already the publication of the report of the Macmillan Committee in mid-July had, by revealing the volume of London's short-term debts, increased doubts abroad about the solvency of the U.K. financial position.

While the crisis had begun for the Bank on 15 July with a sudden drop in sterling, it began for the Labour Government on 11 August when the Prime Minister, MacDonald, arrived back from his home in Lossiemouth in response to a letter from Snowden which enclosed a letter from Harvey. The Cabinet economy committee, appointed on 30 July to examine the report of the May Committee and originally scheduled to meet on 25 August, met the next day (i.e. 12 August) and again on 13, 17 and 18 August. On 13 August the Treasury asked the Bank to sound New York as to the possibility of a credit to the government. Harrison replied that he thought the government could raise loans in New York and Paris as long as the government took steps to balance the budget which would be acceptable to the Opposition and hence to Parliament. From 19 August the Cabinet discussed its economy committee's report, which consisted of a list of economies amounting to £78.6m, and then (from 21 August) a revised version, a list of economies amounting to £56.4m plus a 10% cut in the standard rate of unemployment benefit, every day until 23 August. The Cabinet meetings were punctuated by consultations with representatives of the Bank, the Opposition and the General Council of the Trades Union Congress. The Bank and the Opposition having made it clear that the economies would have to include a reduction in the standard rate of unemployment benefit, the Cabinet finally split over such a reduction. The government then resigned and MacDonald formed a National Government on 24 August.[71]

In the course of the Cabinet's deliberations/wranglings over economies, "consideration was given . . . also to other matters, such as proposals for Debt Conversion and a Revenue Tariff" on 19 August. Debt conversion was not mentioned again—it was definitely not on in present market conditions—but there was discussion of a revenue tariff and of suspension of the sinking fund on 21 August. Snowden rejected the former, but with respect to the latter, though Snowden opposed this too, the Cabinet agreed "that for the purpose of their present calculations the possibility of deducting £47½m in respect of the sinking fund from the gross deficiency should be taken into account." Accordingly, MacDonald said he would submit the latest list of economies (£56m) *and* the sinking fund proposal to the Opposition and Bank representatives. The next day Snowden told the Cabinet that the sinking fund proposal had been rejected on the grounds that, in Snowden's words, "any attempt of this kind to camouflage the true position would be at once detected, and that it was of paramount importance that the Budget should be balanced in an honest fashion and not by recourse to borrowing". At the same time Snowden justified his own determination that Britain should remain on the gold standard by the inflation which would follow suspension and would "reduce the standard of living of the workmen by 50%." The Treasury was also opposed to suspension of the sinking fund, as it "will pro tanto render it more difficult to get back to the possibility of a large conversion operation".[72] Instead they considered the possibility of a tax on the rentier and ways of raising £90m in new taxation.[73]

On 28 August loans to the new government were raised in Paris and New York. On 10 September a second budget for the year and on the following day an Economy Bill, were introduced in the House of Commons. To meet a current deficit of £74½m and a prospective deficit for 1932/33 of £170m, there were economies worth £70m in a full year, increased in income tax, super-tax, and the beer, tobacco, petrol and entertainments taxes, worth in all £57½m in a full year, and the non-contractual part of the sinking fund (£20m) was suspended![74] Another notable feature of the budget was the provisions to facilitate the conversion of 5% War Loan, by enabling the authorities to follow Goschen's procedure for dealing with dissentients, so that the authorities would be "fully armed to seize any opportunity that arises".[75] It seems that Snowden would have liked to announce conversion at this stage.[76]

However, "it was too late to stem the flood of panic. For some days indeed the stream of withdrawals of money abated. But the world was in a state of extreme nervousness . . . A scare about unrest in the Navy in connection with . . . proposed cuts in pay [on 15 September], contributed to revive the panic."[77] This does not mean that, as has often been claimed,[78] that the alarm that the budgetary difficulties aroused abroad caused the gold drain and hence the suspension, as the balance of payments figures suggest Britain would have been forced off the gold standard some time in 1931 or 1932.[79]

Harvey, the Deputy Governor of the Bank, formally asked to be relieved of the obligation to sell gold on demand in a letter to the Prime Minister and the Chancellor of the Exchequer on Saturday, 19 September.[80] The actual decision was taken at a meeting between the Prime Minister and Harvey and Peacock of the Bank of England, at 9.45 p.m. on Friday, 18 September, at which Sir Warren Fisher (Permanent Secretary of the Treasury), Leith-Ross and Phillips, Sir Maurice Hankey (the Cabinet Secretary), and Duff (the Prime Minister's Secretary) were also present. The previous day the Cabinet Committee on the Financial Situation had discussed the gold drain:[81]

> "Mr [Neville] Chamberlain (Minister of Health) summed up the position resulting from the discussion as follows. There were three possible courses:
> (1) For the Government to remain in office and announce whatever measures they thought best adapted to restore the trade balance;
> (2) To obtain extended credits abroad;
> (3) To go off the gold standard.
> The first course was open to great objections and all were agreed that the third should be avoided. Consequently every effort should be made to obtain extended credits."[82]

The Prime Minister reported to the Cabinet that day that "the Bank of England [was] firmly of opinion that the efforts to maintain the pound sterling must be continued."[83] However, discussion within the Treasury on suspending the gold standard began that day, when officials began to draft the Gold Standard (Amendment) Bill;[84] given the nature of the Financial Situation Committee's conclusions, their preparations are hardly surprising.

On Friday evening,

> "the Deputy Governor stated that the losses during the day had amounted to over £17,000,000. This had exhausted the dollar credit. There was still £15,000,000 available from France. He had been in touch with Harrison who felt that a banking credit would not be likely to be available and that for a Government loan the authorisation of Congress would be necessary . . . The Deputy Governor did not himself think that we could raise enough to save the situation, and if the situation could not be saved it was merely a waste of more money. In reply to a question from the Prime Minister the Deputy Governor could give no estimate of how much money would be required to save the situation: but he did not see that it was worth while raising £100,000,000 if people were only going to draw it out. The Prime Minister agreed that if one could not see one's way through it was better to acknowledge it now.
> "In reply to a question from the Prime Minister as to what he proposed to do tomorrow, the Deputy Governor said that the Bank had £15,000,000 French money. Tomorrow being a short day they would hope to carry through it and to go on on Monday till they were forced to stop. The Prime

Minister asked if it were decided to stop tomorrow what is the process? Sir Warren Fisher replied that if an inroad on our gold stocks were involved he, on the Chancellor's behalf, would instruct the Deputy Governor to act as though the Act of Parliament relieving him of the need to pay out gold bars were already in operation.

"The Prime Minister enquired as to the procedure on Monday, to which Sir Warren Fisher replied that a Bill must be put through all its stages, including the Royal Assent, on Monday ... The Deputy Governor stated that it was better to stop on Monday morning as that would give time to warn the press, and the public could be stopped from rushing the banks. ...

"In reply to a question by the Prime Minister as to whether there is any means of pegging the pound and preventing it from going flop altogether, Mr Peacock replied that nobody knew what would happen: he hoped the pound would make a sudden dip and then come up again. He thought that it would not change *internally* for a bit. Pegging was a very complicated operation, and he thought that we should watch the situation for a bit before making any commitment.

"The Prime Minister observed that all the theorists would at once rush into print. Was there any way of using them? We ought to enlist every brain and it would be a case of all hands to the pumps ... A number of names were mentioned, and it was decided the Prime Minister should see [Sir Josiah] Stamp in the morning with a view to collecting a body of persons whose names would carry confidence with the various sections of the community, who should be constituted a Council or Committee to watch and advise on the situation."

Discussion on the arrangements for Monday and the necessary Proclamation was then resumed. At the conclusion of the meeting,

"Mr Peacock said that no-one could accuse this country of not having made every effort before letting the pound go, and it was pointed out that by having balanced the Budget, whatever happened, this country had at least demonstrated her will to play the game at all costs."[85]

The Prime Minister met Harvey and Peacock again the next day. This meeting was also attended by Fisher and Leith-Ross of the Treasury and Sir Robert Vansittart of the Foreign Office (after a quarter of an hour) and by Baldwin and Samuel (towards the end of the meeting). Harvey reported that all the credits were now exhausted. Most of the discussion was on the draft of the Gold Standard (Amendment) Bill that was to go through both Houses of Parliament on Monday; exchange control was also discussed. Leith-Ross stated that "the Treasury felt there were considerable dangers in control".[86] Discussion on exchange control by Fisher, Harvey, Leith-Ross, Stamp and Keynes, continued after the meeting in Sir Warren Fisher's room in the Treasury. Again, and against Stamp and Keynes, Leith-Ross "vigorously opposed the suggestion of exchange control".[87] In fact some restrictions on exchange dealings were imposed on 21 September but only temporarily: they were allowed to expire in March.

The public announcement of the suspension of the gold standard was made on the evening of Sunday 20 September after a special Cabinet meeting;[88] the Gold Standard (Amendment) Act was passed on Monday 21 September; and Bank rate was raised to 6% the same day.

Reactions to the Suspension

In spite of the strenuous efforts that the authorities had made to maintain the gold standard, and the support they had received in their attempts,[89] the City and the authorities received the news calmly.

> "The suspension of the gold standard caused no panic in London. Markets were confused and hesitant, and the Stock Exchange was closed for a couple of days; but there was no suggestion of a run on banks and no signs of any flight of capital . . . By the end of the month, the exchange with New York had settled down to a rate around 3.90. Opinion at home and abroad was reassured by the balancing of the Budget and by the return of a National Government at a general election on October 27 by a large majority."[90]

To Norman, of course, who did not learn of the suspension until 23 September, "Nothing could have been a greater blow. He was profoundly depressed and for a time his temper showed it."[91] Niemeyer (who had been at the Bank since 1927) regarded the suspension as "for this country, for foreign countries and for the general restoration of world confidence, a very great disaster".[92] Siepmann (also at the Bank) thought three things should be said: "if we have anything to be proud about at all, it is the strenuous fight we made, and not our failure to win it"; "since we were defending the national and general interest in attempting to retain our hold on $4.86\frac{2}{3}$, we cannot expect anything but a net loss, in the short and in the long run, to result from what has happened"; "there is no alternative to the gold standard as an international monetary system".[93] Both were concerned that the government should immediately make it plain that inflation would not be allowed to follow the suspension. On the other hand, Siepmann immediately accepted that "$4.86\frac{2}{3}$ was gone for ever" and Niemeyer rejected the idea of pegging sterling at a new rate. Niemeyer thought "the urgent thing is to show signs of having a policy" and suggested forming a sterling block.*

Such a reaction, that going off gold was bowing to the inevitable with a good conscience because of the fight we had put up, and that one should make the best of it by formulating new policies, was apparently shared by the Treasury, if not by Norman.

Before the suspension of the gold standard, the Treasury officials were firm believers in putting up a fight. At the end of July Hopkins told the Chancellor,

> "I feel it is my duty to say that the Governor's words to you yesterday evening put in precise form apprehensions which I and my colleagues . . . have entertained in growing volume for some days past . . . Unless we take such steps as are open to us to rectify the situation, there is a real danger of our being driven off the gold standard . . . Unless action . . . is taken . . . the consequences may be very grave,"

in particular the effect of depreciation on the cost of living, given Britain's need to

---

*   Keynes had earlier suggested converting disaster into success by taking the initiative in forming a sterling block on the basis of a devalued pound; Niemeyer's suggestion can be taken as confirmation of Keynes's belief that "many people in the city, far more than might be expected . . . are now in favour of something of this sort" (Keynes to MacDonald, 5 August 1931, Keynes Papers L/31). However, Keynes was also advocating a deliberate departure from the gold standard, something with which Niemeyer would undoubtedly not have agreed.

import food and raw materials.[94] The Cabinet received an even more thoroughly alarmist memorandum on the same lines by Warren Fisher on 16 September.[95]

On 30 September, however, Fisher calmly noted that the necessary measures to avert the evil consequences had been taken. Such measures were:

"*Fundamentals*

(1) Confidence in settled Government at home and abroad
(2) No inflation; this includes
   (a) continuance of balanced Budget
   (b) close watching of prices, especially of food supplies
   (c) no multiplication of paper pounds
   (d) floating debt to be kept down
(3) [Measures to correct] balance of trade . . .

. . .

"*Arrangements in being*

(1) P.M.'s Committee to advise as to financial problems domestic and international that ought to be considered
(2) E.A.C. Committee under Stamp dealing with Balance of Payments, first report (EAC(SC)1) available
(3) Treasury in close contact with Bank of England is dealing with all matters in its sphere e.g. currency, floating debt, exchanges
(4) Board of Trade in contact with Treasury is watching stocks and prices of commodities and allied questions
(5) Supply and Transport Committee under the directions of the Home Secretary
(6) Regular liaison between Bank of England, Joint Stock Banks and Committee of Stock Exchange; Bank of England and Joint Stock Banks committees on problems connected with exchange and other matters
(7) Joint enquiry by Treasury, Bank of England and Bankers in relation to "mobilisation" of foreign securities
(8) Continuous contact between Treasury and other departments on all matters arising out of the crisis, e.g. India Office, Dominions Office, Post Office."

Some "less immediate" questions had still to be settled:

"(1) ultimate level of pound
(2) War Debts and Reparations
(3) international cooperation in regard to monetary and credit policy."[96]

"Stamp's Committee" was the Economic Advisory Council's Standing Committee on Economic Information, whose first report appeared on 25 September and recommended a 25% depreciation of sterling.[97] The Prime Minister's Committee on Financial Questions was "unanimous in holding that it would be a great mistake if the Bank of England were to make it their aim to return to the gold standard at the old parity as soon as circumstances permit it." In order that the Bank should not be allowed to make this its aim, the Cabinet should make an early decision to tell the Bank not to do so. Some, but not all, members of the Committee were concerned that a tariff should not be imposed, because depreciation made it unnecessary and an additional blow to foreign exporters might provoke retaliation.[98] There was also a difference of opinion over whether "we should aim at ultimately restoring the pound to a gold basis with a new and lower parity, or at securing the adoption of a standard of value of a type designed to keep the purchasing power of money over commodities stable". The second alternative might also have the advantage that other countries which have "suffered like ourselves from the instability of the price level in recent years" might opt to link their currencies with sterling rather than with gold, so that Britain would become the centre of a sterling area. However with respect to immediate policy the Committee was agreed that "for the time being we should pursue a waiting policy and allow sterling to settle at whatever level circumstances suggest is most appropriate." As far as international action was concerned, the Committee suggested an international conference in the early future to explore, on the one hand, the question of cooperation for the purpose of steadying prices, and on the other, the question of war debts and reparations. With respect to immediate problems, there was dispute over whether the exchange restrictions that had been imposed by the Treasury were desirable, and on the question of a tariff; pegging the exchanges, within fairly wide limits, was generally agreed to be "worth considering".[99]

At the meeting on 29 September the Committee, after pointing out that the question of long-term policy was now a matter for the Government rather than the Bank, told the Prime Minister that "the Bank of England should as a provisional policy endeavour to keep sterling within certain limits, by buying sterling at the lower limit and selling foreign currencies at the higher" and that the Bank should be "invited to state their views" on this question and on the limits within which sterling should be held.[100]

In the following months the Prime Minister and other ministers were reassured by the Committee that the course of the exchanges was satisfactory.[101] In line with the suggestion of a waiting policy, the Chancellor told ministers on 10 November that they should not attempt to state when the pound sterling could be stabilized or when an International Conference on the monetary situation could be arranged. They "would be on safe ground if they confined themselves to the immediate need of balancing the Budget and maintaining the internal value of the pound sterling".[102]

In the meantime the Treasury had been discussing the same questions, in particular pegging the exchanges, the standard by which sterling should be managed, and an international conference. The Treasury had sought the views of the Governor of the Bank, who had not been very helpful, and of certain "outsiders". The development, outlined below, of the Treasury's views appears largely in its opinions on the advice received.

The Governor's Views

On 8 December, at Leith-Ross's suggestion, the Chancellor, together with Hopkins, Phillips, Leith-Ross and Waley of the Treasury, met the Governor and Mr Hambro of the Bank, to inquire of them (1) the causes of, and possible remedies for, the recent slump in the exchanges, and (2) their views on immediate and future policy toward sterling.[103] According to Clay,

> "The Governor . . . took a memorandum to the Chancellor . . . which shows the development of his views. The fluctuations in the exchange were more serious for trade than the actual level; the Bank could moderate these fluctuations, but had not the resources to peg the rate or even to withstand a determined speculative attack; attempts to arrange with the holders of large

sterling balances to retain them would only suggest that the United Kingdom was arriving at a standstill, as would any approach to other Central Banks; they had not enough gold and foreign exchange to carry through a long-term policy, and the Government should avoid any statement that seemed to commit it to stabilisation. It was agreed that the Bank should do what it could to iron out fluctuations."[104]

Clay also states that "the fall in sterling in December alarmed the Government and disinclined them to do anything to ease credit";[105] but the minutes of the meeting show that it was the Governor, not the government, who objected to easing credit. The minutes also provide a summary of Norman's views on sterling policy.

He rejected all the possible short-term measures suggested by the Treasury, namely, selling gold, loans, agreements with other central banks, exchange controls, clearing arrangements, with the exception of import restrictions; that he "said was a political question and he would not say anything about it". As for long-term policy,

"We should eventually return to gold, not necessarily at the former parity but we could not decide the rate until we had

(a) An active trade balance,

(b) A settlement of reparations and war debts,

(c) A budget balanced now and in the future, and

(d) A competitive price level.

The Governor was not in agreement with those who thought that we must wait until there was agreement on the part of other countries to 'play the gold standard game according to the rules', whatever this exactly might mean. Foreign lending would begin when confidence was restored . . . It would be dangerous to make any statement as to the time or rate of stabilisation . . . It must be recognised that we have not the means to peg exchange."

As for liaison between the Bank and the Treasury, "the Governor entirely agreed with this proposal and arrangements will be made accordingly."

The Chancellor then asked whether the Governor considered that trade recovery depended on a rise in wholesale prices. Norman agreed but thought that there was nothing the authorities could do to bring this about.[106]

Two days later the Cabinet "had a preliminary discussion on the subject of the policy to be pursued by the Government as to the stabilisation of sterling". It agreed that the Chancellor should prepare a memorandum to be considered by a Cabinet Committee of the Chancellor (Neville Chamberlain), the Lord President of the Council (Baldwin), the Lord Privy Seal (Snowden), the President of the Board of Trade (Runciman), and the Minister of Health (Hilton Young).[107] The Treasury soon set to work, using as a basis a memorandum by Hopkins on Keynes's views; Hopkins, Phillips, Waley and to a lesser extent Leith-Ross, all had a hand in the production though Phillips' views eventually prevailed.

The Development of the Treasury's Views

The chronology and the evidence are in Appendix 4; here I shall concentrate on the principles discussed.

1. *Return to the Gold Standard*

The Treasury officials did not spend much time on this question. Within a week of the fall from gold Phillips wrote:

> "Ignoring all the other charges against the gold standard the fact remains that *in less than two years* viz. since October 1929, the appreciation of gold has:
>
>> Lowered wholesale prices by 25%;
>> Lowered cost of living by about 10%;
>> while wages have been practically unchanged.
>
> Now all these things were out of harmony already in 1929. By the beginning of this month the disharmony was becoming fantastic . . .
>
> "This is what was crushing our farmers and manufacturers for the benefit of the rentier, the distributive trades and the fixed income man, while the working classes were losing as much from unemployment as they were gaining from an increase in real wages.
>
> "Why go on with it? . . .
>
> "[Therefore any] stabilisation must be de facto and not legal, and . . . our subsequent policy should be governed by the course of gold." [108]

From then on, the problem was seen as that of managing the sterling exchange so as to give more benefit to British industry than had been possible under the gold standard. Only Leith-Ross remained wholeheartedly in favour of an early return to the gold standard and he therefore played only a minor role in the discussions. Hopkins thought that ultimately we ought to return to the gold standard but this might well not be for several years. Phillips was prepared to contemplate that we might never return (see Appendix 4).

2. *Pegging the Exchanges*

Because of the Bank's apparent lack of gold and foreign exchange reserves* Leith-Ross and Hopkins doubted the feasibility of pegging. Phillips, who initially thought the rate at which sterling should be pegged would depend on "what practical exchange experts think we can manage", became less sceptical, not presumably because of knowledge superior to that of his colleagues on the Bank's holdings, but because by the end of 1931 he was no longer concerned to *raise* the rate. The apparent practical problem of support was solved by the strengthening of sterling in the first quarter of 1932 (below p. 87).

---

* The Bank held foreign exchange in both the Issue Department and the Banking Department but was required under the Currency & Bank Notes Act 1928 to tell the Treasury only of the former. From the passing of this Act to the fall from gold the Treasury knew only of up to £13.5m foreign exchange held in the Issue Department rather than the Bank's total holdings of between £13m and £28m (Moggridge, *British Monetary Policy*, pp. 160–1, 183–4). At the end of November and December 1931, while the foreign exchange reserves of which the Bank had to inform the Treasury were zero (H.M. Treasury, Issue Department monthly statements), the Bank's total foreign exchange reserves were £14m and £20m (the figures, provided by D.E. Moggridge, are a continuation of the series in *British Monetary Policy*, pp. 178–9). Treasury knowledge of the latter figures would not be entirely consistent with its often-expressed concern (Appendix 4) about the Bank's lack of foreign exchange reserves: one can only suppose that the Bank was still keeping the Treasury in the dark.

3. Alternative standards and methods of currency management

Given that sterling could be controlled, on what principles should it be fixed/varied? There were three views circulating in the Treasury, those of Hawtrey, H.D. Henderson and Keynes.

Hawtrey thought "the predominant consideration" should be "the course of trade activity and the movement of commodity prices".[109] He believed that "the strain that forced the country off the gold standard arose from a disastrous divergence of the world price level from the wage and debt structure of the country . . . The suspension of the gold standard gives us the opportunity of eliminating this divergence", by a depreciation which should be of the order of 30% on the assumption that there was "tolerable" equilibrium between wages and prices in 1925 and world prices had fallen approximately 30% since then. He therefore suggested pegging the pound initially at $3.40 and raising (or lowering) it *pari passu* with the world price level. The pegging should be carried out mainly by purchases and sales of bills and securities supported by suitable movements of Bank rate.[110]

Henderson advocated an interim policy of pegging the pound at $3.90, using Keynes's *Tract on Monetary Reform* proposal of variable buying and selling prices for gold announced from time to time by the Bank, and then altering these prices according as gold was flowing in or out. The advantages would be a fair measure of exchange stability and a free hand as to future policy, since the options of an eventual return to gold and of a currency managed so as to stabilize the price level would be left open.[111] Commenting on this suggestion, Hawtrey did not think gold movements should be the criterion for changing the exchange rate, and Phillips could not see why the Bank should not deal in francs and dollars as well as in gold.[112]

Keynes wanted sterling managed on the lines of his proposals in *A Treatise on Money*, Book VII, i.e. in accordance with an index of the prices of the main raw commodities of international trade, by means of the technique of variable gold prices.[113] Although Hopkins and Phillips agreed with Henderson's objection that the bottom of a world slump was not the best time to put such a scheme into operation, they were in favour, while Henderson was not, of managing sterling with prices as the criterion. They differed from Keynes in that they wanted to see a substantial rise in prices before letting the pound rise rather than to commit themselves to raising it as soon as primary product prices started to rise (see Appendix 4).

4. $3.40 or $3.90?*

In September 1931 Phillips was thinking of $4.0, a month later of $3.65, and from December to March 1932 he was arguing the case for $3.40 against the $3.90 favoured by Henderson and, until a late stage, Hopkins. Hopkins came down from $4.0 to $3.60–3.70; Leith-Ross stuck to $4.0–4.25; Hawtrey and Keynes were $3.40 men. The choices depended on the assumptions made about the response of (the different components of) the balance of payments to depreciation, and also the behaviour of wages and prices. It should be noted at the outset that the Treasury tended to reckon the balance of payments in gold prices in terms of which the unfavourable initial effects of depreciation are greater than in sterling. In September 1931, when the problem was set to him by Hawtrey and Henderson, Phillips thought the rate should

---

* These rates represent 30% and 15% depreciation respectively.

not be above $4 because prices were too low relative to wages. It should not be below $4, because

(1) The initial effects of depreciation on the balance of trade would be less favourable with a lower pound. He cited Henderson on the effect on exports (see below).
(2) Invisible items, being largely in sterling, would fall heavily in gold value.
(3) Below $3.65 wages would rise, and an increase in wages would set off a vicious spiral of inflation.

However, he also thought that at $3.65 prices would return to their October 1929 level while the cost of living would not rise much and wages would rise very little. Therefore a week later he favoured $3.65 on the assumption that equilibrium between wages and prices existed in 1929. The notion of an equilibrium rate at which prices and wages would be stable was Hawtrey's, but Hawtrey thought equilibrium had not existed since 1925 and therefore favoured $3.40.

Henderson was in favour of $3.90 because:

(1) Depreciation would by lowering the price of exports to foreigners increase the volume of exports, and since gold prices would be lower the gold value of exports would be lowered until the volume of exports had risen to compensate for this, which would take some time.
(2) At the same time the value of shipping receipts, short interest and banking commisions, net government receipts, and income from overseas fixed-interest investments, which were mostly denominated in sterling, would fall heavily in gold value. The balance of payments would, therefore, deteriorate markedly in the short run, and the lower the exchange rate the greater the deterioration.
(3) In the longer run, a low pound would cause inflation, by substantially raising, in turn, import prices, the cost of living, and wages. He estimated that a 30% devaluation could raise the cost of living by more than 10%.
(4) If the authorities tried to fix the exchange rate too low, they would adversely affect confidence abroad and induce a withdrawal of funds by foreign holders of sterling.
(5) Any substantial fall of the pound would depress the level of gold (i.e. world) prices and aggravate financial insolvency abroad.

In consequence, he thought depreciation should be limited to 15%, which was "as much in the way of a windfall as it is ever good for anyone [i.e. British exporters] to get, and as much in the way of disturbance as a strained world economic system can be expected to cope with".[114] He also objected strongly to Hawtrey's notion of an equilibrium exchange rate. Phillips accepted this criticism of Hawtrey, but ended up arguing for $3.40 as against $3.90 (see below).

Hopkins in December 1931 was a $4 man, because a low rate would reduce confidence, raise the cost of living unduly, and lower the value of investments abroad.[115] In January he adopted Henderson's arguments (and his words) to argue for $3.60– 3.70: a lower value would affect other countries adversely, would lessen the improvement in the balance of payments because it would reduce revenue from exports (in the short run) and from fixed-interest investments abroad, would raise import prices and hence the cost of living and might lead to foreign withdrawals of sterling balances.[116]

Phillips wrote the final version of the statement to the Cabinet. In it he pointed out the advantages of a high value ($3.90) for the pound, namely import prices would be lower, the price of foreign exchange and gold (which the authorities wanted to buy in order to build up reserves) would be lower, and fixed-interest investments (denominated in sterling) would bring in more income (in gold value). But he went on to the "more theoretical . . . but for all that . . . extremely strong", and "decisive", arguments in favour of a lower value ($3.40). These were:

(1) The Treasury *wanted to raise* wholesale prices.
(2) The burden of the debt would be lower.
(3) The Treasury wanted to help exporters, and though the present state of world trade might prevent much of an increase in exports, depreciation was the best method of assistance available.

In future, if world prices fell further the authorities might have to lower the pound further, and they should not raise the exchange rate unless and until sterling prices had risen at least 25% over the September 1931 level.[117] As Phillips later explained to Leith-Ross:

> "The question of our own price level is the fundamental matter. There may be theoretical considerations which suggest that a country may retain a considerable degree of prosperity with a low price level, but practically such considerations could not apply to England. The size of our national debt and the rigidity of wages and other costs in this country make a falling price level peculiarly dangerous to us.
>
> "It is not merely that falling prices, unaccompanied by falling wages, affect the manufacturer directly—they have also important psychological reactions tending to damp down business activity.
>
> . . .
>
> "It is suggested (i) that our departure from gold has accelerated the fall in world prices, (ii) that a rise in the value of sterling would tend to raise the world price level. I think both statements are very likely true but I doubt very much their practical importance.
>
> . . .
>
> "These considerations suggest that a (relatively) low value of the pound is desirable—not because that is a good thing in itself but because it seems the only way to prevent sterling prices following gold prices down."[118]

Thus a low exchange rate was desired in order to encourage a rise in domestic prices; cheap money was also wanted for the same reason. According to Phillips again:

> "First and foremost the Bank rate should be reduced as rapidly as may be to say 3 per cent . . . we want cheap money and plenty of it to stimulate industry. The great objection to cheap money . . . that it causes a drain of gold and weakens the foreign exchanges"

does not apply in present circumstances.[119]

The Introduction of Cheap Money

Cheap money and a low exchange rate were also recommended to the government by the Prime Minister's Advisory Committee in its report on Sterling Policy, which was circulated to the Cabinet at the same time as the Treasury memorandum. The Cabinet did not discuss either the memorandum or the report, and there is unfortunately no record among the Cabinet papers of any meetings of the Currency Questions Committee.[120] The memorandum was, however, obviously accepted as the settled policy of the Treasury. The Treasury, having provided a statement of its objectives, proceeded during 1932 to put its (or rather, Phillips') ideas into practice. The two major ways in which this was done were the establishment of the Exchange Equalization Account (E.E.A.) and the conversion of 5% War Loan.

The first post-crisis step towards cheaper money was, however, taken by the Bank, which lowered Bank rate to 5% on 18 February 1932, and progressively lowered it further in the spring and early summer. As usual, movements of Bank rate should not be discussed without reference to the movements of the sterling-dollar exchange, which are also relevant to the origins of the E.E.A.

Immediately after the suspension the pound fell sharply to $3.40 on 25 September. It soon recovered to 3.90 but was falling again in November, and reached a low of 3.23 at the beginning of December. This was followed by a period of stability, at about 3.40, and then a recovery due to a revival of confidence. This was helped by the repayment of the Central Bank credits at the end of January and the announcement on 2 March of arrangements for repaying the Treasury credits,[121] and took sterling to 3.80 on 31 March. In line with this recovery of sterling, Bank rate was lowered to 5% on 18 February, to 4% on 10 March, and to 3½% on 17 March.

Nevin has conjectured that the delay in lowering Bank rate from 6% was due to the Bank's desire to take advantage of the growing strength of sterling to acquire foreign exchange in order to repay the credits from the U.S.A. and France.[122] This was undoubtedly the case; the Bank was also supported in this by the Treasury who believed the credits could not be renewed.[123] One can attribute a large measure of responsibility to the Treasury, since the Bank, given its views, particularly its fear of inflation, would not have wanted to lower Bank rate earlier, and the Treasury, given its views and the closer liaison between the Bank and the Treasury, would have pressed it to do so if there had not been the problem of the Treasury credits. Also, the Bank continued after the February reduction to be reluctant to lower Bank rate; it wanted the exchange to rise, a proposal with which the Treasury emphatically did not agree, wanting a rapid reduction of Bank rate to at least 3% for two complementary reasons: to keep the pound down by repelling foreign money and to stimulate industry.[124] The Treasury regarded the inflow of foreign money as a nuisance because it threatened to undo the reflationary policy before it had even begun.[125] Therefore, in order to overcome the Bank's lack of resources with which to buy foreign exchange to keep down the pound, Phillips thought up the device of the Exchange Equalization Account. The principles of E.E.A. operations had of course been evolved by the Bank in its foreign exchange dealings in 1925–31,[126] but the machinery was, apparently, devised in the Treasury.[127] The Bank would buy foreign exchange for the Treasury's Exchange Equalization Account which was authorized to borrow the sterling needed to purchase foreign exchange by issuing Treasury bills. The Treasury would cover any future loss on the Account's purchases due to appreciation of the exchange. Although the actual exchange operations were left to the Bank, the Treasury retained control over the rate of exchange to be supported.[128] In the 1930s the management of the Account "fell chiefly to Phillips and Waley—a big responsibility for two officials".[129]

The E.E.A. was announced in the budget on 19 April, and officially came into

into existence on 1 July, though it was conducting operations unofficially for a month or so before that.[130] The Governor told the Bank's Committee of Treasury on 13 April that the E.E.A. would be established by means of clauses in the Finance Bill;[131] a week later Bank rate was reduced to 3%, and it was further reduced to 2½% on 12 May, and on 30 June to 2% where it remained until August 1939.

The next step was the conversion of War Loan, which was announced in Parliament on 30 June, the day Bank rate was reduced to 2%. Preparation for the conversion had not ceased when the international financial crisis intervened to change the original timetable in May 1931. The War Loan (Redemption and Continuance) Bill originally intended was replaced by clauses in the September 1931 Finance Bill (above, p. 76). On 26 November W.R. Fraser of the Treasury wrote to G.W. Wise of the Bank of England suggesting the second preliminary step: "We ought to be preparing draft War Loan Regulations under . . . Finance Act 1931, though we shan't be able to settle them finally for some time to come"; a discussion on the subject took place at the Bank on 18 January.[132] At the same time the Governor was seeking the advice of brokers, bankers and investors on ways of ensuring the cooperation of the market.[133]

Having taken advantage of the postponement caused by the financial crisis to get the necessary legislative and administrative preliminaries out of the way, the Treasury was from January 1932 onwards only biding its time until the Bank should tell it that market conditions were favourable. On 7 June the Bank told the Chancellor that conversion was now possible on a 3½% basis.[134] On 29 June Chamberlain returned from the reparations conference at Lausanne to tell his ministerial colleagues (hitherto kept in the dark), which he did the next day before making the announcement to the House at 9.30 p.m.[135]

The operation was a great success: £1,920,804,243 (92%) of £2,084,994,086 5% War Loan 1929/47 outstanding on 31 March 1932 was converted to 3½% War Loan 1952. The many factors that made for success can be divided into two over-lapping sets: (1) the measures taken by the authorities to ensure success, and (2) the causes of the post-crisis recovery of gilt-edged security prices in early 1932 which made conversion possible in mid-1932.

(1) (i) The Chancellor in making his announcement appealed to the patriotism of the holders of War Loan.[136]

(ii) The Treasury and the Bank directly appealed to the chief classes of holder; the Bank interviewed brokers and jobbers; the Treasury held a conference with the bankers.[137]

(iii) An informal but effective embargo on all new issues was imposed.[138]

(iv) Other government issues had been dealt with or postponed.[139]

(v) An increase in high-powered money and hence the money supply in 1932.[140]

(vi) The establishment of the E.E.A., which "raised liquidity-assessment both by indicating the new power of the authorities to regulate the internal credit structure independently of the state of the foreign exchanges and by the promise it embodied of greater stability in the foreign exchange markets" and "by enabling the Bank of England to acquire additional gold . . . permitted the authorities to proceed with credit expansion without endangering the state of confidence through an unwitting calling-up of the latent devil of inflation fears."[141]

(vii) Measures taken to restore confidence, which were thus a cause of recovery of gilt-edged prices: a balanced budget and the maintenance of a high Bank rate assured the public that inflation would not be allowed to follow departure from the gold standard.[142]

(2) This last assurance and the return of a National government at the October general election increased the confidence of investors at home and abroad in British government credit, and together with other factors caused a very substantial rise in security prices and a fall in interest rates. The movement in interest rates meant that acceptance of the conversion offer by holders of War Loan was not merely a patriotic step but an obviously profitable one.[143] The general expectation which emerged early in 1932 that the government would soon make a large conversion offer, if only to provide relief to the Budget, also helped interest rates to fall.[144] The recovery in gilt-edged prices accompanied the revival of confidence in sterling; here too the authorities' policy of balancing the budget and keeping up Bank rate played a role in creating that confidence. Nevin has shown that these factors changed the liquidity preference of the investing public.[145] One other expectation on the part of the public was necessary to ensure success, a belief that low interest rates once established would remain in being. When Bank rate came down, there was no problem in creating this expectation, as the public had been expecting a period of lower interest rates ever since the New York stock market crash in 1929.

Nevin has claimed that "the cheap money policy of the 1930s was . . . originally an offshoot of foreign exchange policy [which] survived the exchange problems of 1932 and [then] flourished in its own right", that "the original impetus for the credit expansion sprang from the desire to prevent the appreciation of sterling in the face of an influx of foreign capital",[146] and that "between [the] two stages—cheap money as an aid to foreign exchange policy and cheap money as a means of assisting recovery—there occurred . . . cheap money as a means of achieving budgetary relief".[147] The story of the origins of cheap money as I have told it here implies a different conclusion. Cheap money, in the sense of lower long-term interst rates, was desired by the Treasury from at least the onset of the slump (in fact the Treasury had wanted lower interest rates from the mid-1920s, though the effects of its debt management policy actually worked in the opposite direction),[148] and it was desired as an aid to recovery. In 1931 with the growing budgetary difficulties a large conversion operation on 5% War Loan was also desired as a means of reducing expenditure; foreign exchange policy became a major preoccupation of the Treasury after the suspension of the gold standard in September 1931 and ceased to be one after the establishment of the E.E.A. in the late spring of 1932. In those months cheap money was still wanted primarily as an aid to industry and even in so far as a cheap money policy can be regarded as a corollary of exchange policy, it has to be remembered that exchange policy was nothing less than an attempt to manage the currency in order to promote U.K. prosperity by helping exports on the one hand and reducing its vulnerability to external pressures on the other.

Cheap Money and Recovery

"Cheap money was maintained until the eve of the Second World War. . . .
[It] accompanied and helped a steady expansion of trade and industry.
The Chancellor, so Norman complained in 1934, was quite satisfied that
Cheap Money and the Ottawa policy had solved the country's economic
problem."[1]

This chapter will discuss the questions of how and why the authorities pursued a
cheap money policy in 1932–5, how the economy recovered from the depression in
that period, and whether the Chancellor's claim was justified. The next chapter will
deal with the maintenance of cheap money after 1935 and the 1937–8 recession.

Treasury Policy 1932–5

The Treasury had two major, and conflicting, aims with respect to financial policy
in the 1930s:

(1) maintenance of cheap money in order to bring about recovery from the slump;

(2) funding of the short-term and floating debt, especially Treasury bills.

After 1935 the pursuit of these objectives was complicated by the necessity of financing rearmament and the appearance of inflationary tendencies.

In 1932—and in 1933 and 1934—the Treasury's "main object . . . [was] to get
trade going with as much vigour as adverse world conditions permit. It [was] highly
desirable that the present low rates of interest should gradually permeate the economic structure and quicken industrial enterprise", especially in housebuilding.[2] In
the spring of 1932 the Treasury had wished to keep the pound down in order to prevent sterling prices falling with gold prices. Now that interest rates had been lowered,
it wished to keep money cheap in order to bring about a rise in U.K. prices. This was
desired because "the greatest obstacle to prosperous British trade [was] the discrepancy between costs and wholesale prices".[3] "The malady [to be remedied was] a
marked divergence between prices (not above pre-war) and costs (of which the leading
item, wages, [was] 66% above pre-war)" and "the remedy being pursued [was] cheap
money, fairly abundant credit and avoidance of exchange complications, [because] it
[was] . . . undesirable and . . . in any case impossible to close the gap by lowering
wages".[4] The Chancellor publicly announced the objective of raising prices at the
Ottawa Imperial Conference shortly after the announcement of the War Loan Conversion, and reiterated it many times in the next few years. Although "a rise in sterling
prices would suffice for our purpose even if world gold prices did not change", a
worldwide rise in wholesale prices would be better. To the Treasury "the importance

of the World Economic Conference [held in London in 1933 was] that it enable[d] a plea to be made for international action with a view to raising wholesale commodity prices".[5]

With the exception of the tariff, which was introduced on Chamberlain's initiative (below p. 93), and funding (below pp. 95–9), the other elements of the government's economic policy were designed to support the cheap money policy. Phillips later described the recovery policy as intended

> "to restore the conditions under which industry and commerce could expand . . . [for] if we can hold out to industry a prospect of stable or rising prices, a reasonable stability in the exchanges, cheap capital and easy money, a check to the rise in taxation and possibly some reduction, and a guarantee against revolutionary and dislocating new departures in public enterprise, confidence will revive, enterprise will quicken and employment will expand."[6]

Whereas in the 1920–1 slump the authorities believed that policy should be designed to let recovery come about naturally, the Treasury now wanted to promote recovery by a positive policy. However, as the underlying economic theory was the classical theory, there was still a belief that government measures would accelerate a *natural* process of recovery by strengthening the tendency of interest rates to fall in a depression. In October 1932 Phillips said that he was more in sympathy with the view of Gregory, Hayek, Plant and Robbins that "if there is a shortage of new issues, the flow of money into existing securities lowers the long term rate of interest and so stimulates capital outlay and new issues until equilibrium is reached", than with "MacGregor, Pigou, Keynes, Layton, Salter [and] Stamp [who believed] investment in securities is sterile because want of confidence blocks the flow of new industrial securities into the market". Accordingly, he believed that "the trouble is much more due to the greatly curtailed volume of savings themselves than to any reluctance to bring out new issues at least equivalent to the savings, such as they are".[7]

Hopkins however, did not "know that [he] altogether agree[d] with Mr Phillips' attitude towards private saving", and when sending Phillips' memorandum to the Chancellor, he pointed out:

> "It seems useless to endeavour to follow professional economic teaching, for there is no criterion for determining the proper economists to follow, and whoever one chooses, one is apt to find oneself led into actions which are either repugnant to commonsense or incapable of practical achievement.
> . . .
> "At the root of everything lies the question whether we are going to secure an increase of the wholesale price level. If we are well and good: if not the future is gloomy in the extreme. Towards a higher price level cheap and plentiful money may prove to be able to contribute a good deal: for the rest we must look to international economic re-adjustments which seem almost unattainable and to the natural return of that spirit of confidence which makes people anxious to trade: the return of that confidence may be helped by the adoption of policies which are generally accepted on common sense, whether they pass the test of the higher economics or not."[8]

Despite his "theory" of savings and investment, Phillips (inconsistently) recognized, as did the other Treasury officials, that mere ease and cheapness of borrowing would not do much good if entrepreneurs were so pessimistic about future prospects that they did not wish to borrow funds to expand their business.

> "Monetary remedies . . . are effective only to the extent to which trade and industry in fact make use of the facilities provided. A cure is not therefore to be expected from monetary remedies alone. [However] it does not follow that monetary conditions are unimportant or can be neglected. On the contrary it is essential that monetary conditions should to the maximum extent which conditions permit be such as to encourage a rise in prices and increased commercial activity." [9]

From this followed the emphasis on creating confidence:

> "A general expectation that trade will be bad and prices will fall further is a powerful factor in causing bad trade and low prices. When people think trade will improve and prices rise . . . conditions tend to improve." [10]

Another reason for attaching importance to confidence was:

> "To create any impression [abroad] that this country was committed to inflation would be dangerous as the stability of sterling and its use as a great medium of international exchange depend very largely on the general conviction that this country does not intend to resort to inflationary measures." [11]

The aim of creating confidence was an important determinant of budgetary policy in the 1930s. The National government regarded this as its first priority on taking office, and Neville Chamberlain's 1932 and 1933 budgets were a continuation of Snowden's policy in his September 1931 budget and Economy Bill. In April 1932 Chamberlain announced that in order to maintain and consolidate the small surplus that Snowden had achieved by his last budget, there could be no reductions in taxation or increases in expenditure despite the increase in revenue due to the introduction of the tariff in February 1932.[12] A year later, though he did reduce the beer duty by a penny a pint, he made no other significant tax concessions, nor did he revoke the economy cuts of September 1931, because of his determination, which he emphasized in his speech, to keep the budget balanced.[13]

The maintenance of confidence was the Treasury's main justification for avoiding budget deficits at this time. Given that a rise in prices was now desired, the avoidance of unbalanced budgets could no longer be justified by pointing to the menace of inflation. The standard argument against unbalancing the budget now ran:

(1) it would undermine confidence which was necessary for the cheap money policy;

(2) it was unnecessary because deficits would bring about inflation only insofar as they were financed by creating credit, something which could be done better (i.e. without the deleterious effects on confidence and without increasing the National Debt) by a cheap money policy.[14]

Similar considerations ruled out public works as a method of promoting recovery. In 1932 the Treasury summed up its objections as:

> "If they do *not* involve reflation, they simply divert money from normal trade to abnormal relief works. If they do involve reflation, it is far better that the additional credit should be used for normal trade and not for hothouse schemes. Relief works have always been found to be exceedingly expensive; they take a very long time to organise; and when they come to an end, they create fresh unemployment." [15]

The more practical of these arguments were regarded as decisive against almost all public works schemes.[16] This did not mean there were *no* public works. As Phillips put it,

> "because public works are not very effective in curing unemployment or in accelerating economic recovery it does not follow that there should not be any. Where schemes well thought out and justified on their merits are presented . . . not only would no obstacle be put in their way, but if help were required the Government will consider giving Government assistance in one form or another."[17]

Help was given to such schemes as the construction of the Cunard liner Queen Mary, new telephone exchanges and the extension of London's Underground railways. The government tended to draw a fairly sharp distinction between recovery policy and unemployment policy. The former consisted almost entirely of the cheap money policy; the latter was a matter of providing relief in the form of maintenance, morale-boosting, and rehabilitation.[18] Public works fell into neither category.

The only way budgetary policy could play a role in promoting recovery was by the reduction of taxes. Since budgets had to be balanced, this could only come about if expenditure was kept down. Therefore the economy cuts and tax increases made in September 1931 were not reversed until April 1934 and then only partially. In his 1934 budget Chamberlain divided the fruits of his and Snowden's attempts to achieve a substantial surplus between those affected by the cuts and the income-tax payers (by increasing unemployment benefit by the full extent of the cut and the pay of civil servants by 50% of the cut, on the one hand, and reducing the standard rate of income tax by 6d, on the other), since the reduction of taxes was

> "the relief that would confer the most direct benefits upon the country, which would have the greatest psychological effect and which would impart the most immediate and vigorous stimulus to the expansion of trade and employment."[19]

Chamberlain made further tax reductions and restoration of salary cuts in 1935 when increased economic activity had brought increased government revenue.[20]

Chamberlain did not, however, reverse the suspension of the sinking fund. In 1933 Hopkins noted of the good intentions of Churchill in 1928 and Snowden in 1930 (above pp. 43 and 69) that: "All this edifice has now tumbled down, and we alter the unalterable debt charge every year."[21] The September 1931 budget reduced the Fixed Debt Charge for 1931 and 1932 to £322m; Chamberlain's first budget reduced the latter to £308½m, and his second budget the charge for 1933 to £224m at which level it remained[22] (see Appendix 1, Table 4B). Although with low interest rates this sum proved sufficient to cover interest payments, the Treasury was not entirely happy with the arrangement. In 1935, for instance, Phillips thought that "it is by no means certain that the smooth weather of the last two years will continue and any political uncertainties towards the end of this year [e.g. a general election] might have a marked effect on interest rates".[23]

Chamberlain's primary object on taking office, was, however, to "direct . . . the government towards a fiscal revolution without breaking it up", that is to introduce a tariff despite the presence of freetraders (Snowden and the Liberals Samuel and Sinclair) in the Cabinet. In this he succeeded, after persuading the Cabinet to set up a Committee under his Chairmanship on the Balance of Trade and then, after much discussion on what to do about the dissenting Ministers, to accept the Committee's recommendations.[24]

Chamberlain's budgets of the years 1932 and 1935 were also determined by his aims on taking office. At the end of 1933 he told his Cabinet colleagues:

> "When he took office he had made it his definite aim, in dealing with national finance, to build up the resources of the nation until they were in an unassailable condition. He had also wanted to demonstrate the strengthening of the national resources by progressive remissions in successive Budgets. So far he had been successful in carrying out that policy. It had been almost an essential of that policy that his first Budget should be an unpopular one. His second Budget had been a little better, and he hoped that his third would be better still. To complete the policy it was important to avoid an anticlimax in the case of his fourth Budget by making all the concessions and remissions in the third Budget."[25]

In line with this policy he had early in 1932 told Hopkins that he would like to estimate how much scope he would have over a period of three or four years for reducing taxes or increasing expenditure. In reply Hopkins and his colleagues produced, at Hopkins' suggestion, an "Old Moore's Almanack" for 1935 giving assumed economic data for that year, which they then used to calculate the budget outturn for 1935 assuming existing rates of taxation and the continuance of the economy policy.[26] The assumptions afford an insight into what the Treasury thought a policy of cheap money could achieve. It assumed that prices would have risen to approximately the level of 1929 (a little higher because of the tariff), while wage rates would remain, as they had done since 1924, substantially unaltered, that "the home trade [would] have regained activity and vigour" though exports would not have recovered to their 1929 level, unemployment would be at about the 1927 percentage and around 1,200,000, the gilt-edged rate of interest would be about 4¼%,* and that progress would have been rapid in 1932 and 1933, so that by 1934 the general level of industry would not be much below that of 1935.[27]

Before turning to consider the other element of Treasury policy, the funding complex, the Bank's attitude towards the cheap money policy should be mentioned. By this time Norman had accepted that the consequences of abandoning the gold standard had not so far been disastrous: according to Tom Jones, he told Lady Grigg in February 1932 that "we have fallen over the precipice, missis, but we are alive at the bottom".[28] He approved the Chancellor's statement at the Ottawa Conference on the question of returning to the gold standard,[29] although he continued to believe that the international gold standard was the best of all possible monetary systems. To him a sterling standard could never be more than a "temporary substitute" for the gold standard and "our objective . . . to return ultimately to gold . . . cannot be changed even if its realisation has to be postponed."[30]

With respect to domestic monetary policy,

> "The Governor did not regard the suspension of the gold standard as a reason for relaxing the control which the Bank and the Treasury together

---

*   This probably reflects the fact that at this time War Loan had not been converted and the Treasury still thought, on the advice of the Bank in 1931, that 4% was the lowest rate to which it could hope to convert the block of War Loan.

94

exercised over domestic credit. Rather the reverse: he was alarmed by the increased scope given to political exigencies by the increased influence in the money market of the Treasury. He felt the loss of the compulsion exercised by the adverse movement of the exchanges on the gold standard, and missed the traditional warning signals which then operated."[31]

The Governor was apparently a reluctant supporter of the cheap money policy. Phillips told the Chancellor in October 1932 that the Governor thought money rates were "exceedingly low" and that "he gave the impression that he holds the view that he is not committed to cheap rates except for the period of the Conversion operation and the Lausanne Conference".[32] But the Bank had no option but to keep its rate at 2% until August 1939, because one of the most important consequences of the abandonment of the gold standard had been a shift of power from the Bank to the Treasury[33] and, in Clay's words, "the Chancellor was wedded to cheap money".[34]

There is something of a problem about the Bank's attitude to public works. Norman is reported as having said on one occasion that "this was almost the only point on which he seriously disagreed with the Chancellor. He also tried to get a more active policy adopted."[35] On the other hand, after seeing Sprague, one of Norman's advisers, early in 1933, Henderson told Keynes: "I'm afraid there's no more in the Bank's advocacy of public works than I'd expected. Don't believe in a miraculous conversion of the Bank of England".[36] Sprague himself told Keynes:

> "Henderson . . . seems very hopeless about anything being taken in hand by the present Government but suggests that I see Sir Horace Wilson [Chief Industrial Adviser to the government]. I sigh for someone in authority with that sort of momentum and imagination which Lloyd George and Winston Churchill alone among public men in this country seem to possess. Were I a British subject I think I might be tempted to resign from the Bank and associate myself with you, should you be willing, in a public campaign."[37]

It is clear from the Treasury documents that Norman's advisers, notably Clay and Sprague, were in favour of public works schemes to back up the cheap money policy, and that in consequence the Bank was prepared to include internationally-coordinated public works in the British government's programme for the World Economic Conference.[38] Unfortunately there is no direct evidence of Norman's own views in the papers available.

One consequence of Norman's attitude to the cheap money policy was that he did all that he could to keep down the volume of Treasury bills held by the market, by persistently advocating funding to the Chancellor, and by increasing the volume of Treasury bills held by the Issue Department of the Bank and by government departments.[39] The consequences of this and of Norman's other actions on the money supply are described below (pp. 99–103).

Debt Management 1932–6

The Treasury did not dispute the desirability of reducing the volume of market Treasury bills and throughout the 1930s it continued its 1920s policy of funding the floating debt. I have discussed the origins and development of this policy in the years 1920–31 in Chapters 2 and 3; here I shall describe the forms this funding complex took in the years 1932–6 and the motives behind each operation (see Table 11).

Table 11 *New Government Issues, 1932–8*

			£m
1932	4½% Conversion Loan 1940/44	Conversion	41.7
	4% Consols	Conversion	73.0
	3% Treasury Bonds 1933/42	Cash	110.0
	3½% War Loan	Conversion	1,920.8
	2% Treasury Bonds 1935/38	Cash and conversion	150.0
	3% Conversion Loan 1948/53	Cash	301.8
1933	2½% Conversion Loan 1944/49	Cash (tender)	55.0
	2½% Treasury Bonds 1937	Conversion	30.2
	2½% Conversion Loan 1944/49	Cash and conversion	151.5
1934	3% Funding Loan 1959/69	Cash	152.4
1935	2½% Funding Loan 1959/61	Cash	200.3
	1% Treasury Bonds 1939/41	Cash	100.0
1936	2¾% Funding Loan 1952/57	Cash	100.6
1937	2½% National Defence Bonds 1944/48	Cash	100.2
1938	3% National Defence Loan 1954/58	Cash	81.2

Source: Pember and Boyle, *British Government Securities in the Twentieth Century*, pp. 68–80 (even numbers).

The three issues of the first half of 1932 can be regarded as preliminaries for the War Loan conversion, as they were intended simply to deal with current maturities of Treasury Bonds.[40] Since there were several more maturities of Treasury Bonds in the next couple of years, and a certain amount of cash had to be found to pay off 5% War Loan holders opting for repayment, the Treasury officials drew up, and the Chancellor agreed to, in August 1932 a programme for the next few months, whereby immediately after the close of the Conversion offer on 30 September, a new issue or issues would be offered, to raise the estimated £400m required, and then, in mid-October, the embargo on all new issues would be lifted. When the time came a month later to discuss the form the issue should take, the Treasury ruled out the idea of a single long-dated issue on the ground that "to try and replace £400 millions of bonds and stock, most of which is held as a short, by a long, is asking for trouble. Moreover the market is so starved at present with Bills at under 10s per cent and Bonds scarce and dear, that it seems almost essential to provide them with some kind of a short". On the other hand, the Treasury did not favour issuing £400m of short maturities, because

> "(i) We ought to take every reasonable opportunity to replace short borrowings by long; and we cannot be sure of a better chance than this.
> (ii) It is highly desirable to get our long-term rate as low as possible . . .
> Our slogan ought to be:
> 2% for shorts
> 3% for longs.
> This is our chance to get it taken up."

The author of this memorandum, A.P. Waterfield, suggested a 3%, 1947/52.[41] The suggestion was discussed by Fisher and Leith-Ross with the Governor and the Deputy Governor of the Bank the next day; as a result of that meeting and further discussions a month later, an offer of £150m of a 2% Treasury Bond 1935/38 at the beginning of October and an offer of £300m 3% Conversion Loan 1948/53 in the first week of November were recommended to the Chancellor.[42] Significantly, the total amount to be raised by the two offers was increased from £400m to £450m at the 27 September meeting with the Governor and Deputy Governor of the Bank. The reason was that

> "it [would] be desirable to take the opportunity to mop up some Treasury Bills, the quantity of which now outstanding is abnormally and unpleasantly large, owing to the need of financing purchases of devisen for the E.E.A."[43]

The next Government issue, of £55m 2½% Conversion Loan 1944/49, was offered along with Treasury bills each week from mid-March till the end of May. This (unsuccessful) innovation was carried out at the Governor's instigation and was intended solely for the purpose of reducing the volume of market Treasury bills.[44]

After a small issue of 2½% Treasury Bonds 1937, a large cash and conversion offer of 2½% Conversion Loan 1944/49 was made in September, in order to provide £50m for repaying 4½% Treasury Bonds 1932/34 due on 1 February 1934 and £100m for reducing Treasury bills.[45] According to Phillips, the market's Treasury bills were "high though not . . . very excessive" because the Issue Department held an abnormal amount of them and the E.E.A.'s requirement was not high.

> "Even if we had no long-term policy of reducing the floating debt, special operations would still be necessary from time to time to prevent it increasing. The growth of the floating debt is a silent and insidious disease constantly undermining our financial health."

On the criticism that a reduction in the floating debt was deflationary, he wrote:

> "All that can be said is that the occasion of debt repayment would be a convenient opportunity for effecting a reduction of the credit basis if anyone desired to do it, but there is no reason why that result should follow automatically and it is perfectly easy for the Bank not to let that result follow."[46]

The next three years saw the issue of three fairly substantial funding loans. In January 1934 Waterfield wrote a note to Hopkins about the redemption on 15 April of 4% Treasury Bonds 1934/36, in which he said that though market Treasury bills had not increased recently they might well do so later in the year, that "it would seem desirable to make a further attack on [the] unwieldy mass of floating debt while conditions are favourable for funding", and that a further (cash and conversion) offer of 2½% Conversion Loan in April would be a possible way of reducing Treasury bills by some £75m, except that the Issue Department was already overloaded with 2½% stock.[47] In March Hopkins told Chamberlain that the Treasury was discussing with the Bank the possibility of issuing a new long-term 3% loan for £150 or £200m, for

> "in view of the very favourable terms on which a long-term stock can now be sold, we agree with the Governor that even if the issue of a long stock in replacement of bonds did cause some slight inconvenience to the market, that consideration is clearly overruled by the national interest."[48]

However, the Governor on the one hand, and the Deputy Governor, Phillips and Leith-Ross on the other, disagreed over the amount to be raised. Norman wanted £200m, the others only £150m, Harvey because of the difficulties the larger issue would create for the Bank with respect to the Issue Department's holdings, and the Treasury because "we favour a gradual rather than too abrupt a reduction in the floating debt". Phillips thought that "it might be well should the Chancellor accept the present proposal for him to stipulate that he does so on the understanding that the Bank will take any measures that might prove necessary to check any deflationary effects following on a reduction in the holdings of Treasury Bills by the Joint Stock Banks".[49] Three days later Hopkins told Fisher and the Chancellor:

> "After very considerable general discussion on two successive evenings, the Governor remains wedded to his opinion, while Sir Frederick and I still prefer our own view.
>
> "On merits, while not associating ourselves with the small school which claims that reduction of the floating debt must intrinsically be deflationary, we think the process should be reasonably gradual and especially so when the total effective issue of Treasury Bills in smaller than of late years . . .
>
> "In addition to this we cannot dismiss from our minds the probable public reception of a new issue to redeem floating debt."[50]

Fisher added: "With Harvey, Hopkins and Phillips in agreement—and Mr Norman and Mr McKenna representing the opposite extremes—I should favour the £150m operation". Chamberlain replied: "I had better see the Governor and settle this matter on Monday."[51]

Clay mentions the Chancellor's interview with the Governor, but not the dispute that led to it. However, he has pieced together from Norman's notes what Norman would probably have said to the Chancellor by way of justifying a determined policy of funding:

> "He would stress the danger of a large amount of outstanding Treasury Bills; there were nearly £400m of maturing bonds to be met in the next five years and any emergency might require sudden borrowing on Treasury Bills. It might be difficult to increase these, it might even be difficult to maintain the present volume, as the demands of trade for credit expanded, without forcing up the rate. Funding, it is true, involved some increase in interest on the debt as a whole; but Funding would be at a lower rate now than the Government could count on in the future, so that, if Funding was desirable, it would be most economical to effect it now. On a long view Funding was a safeguard of Cheap Money."[52]

The Chancellor was not convinced: £150m 3% Funding Loan 1959/69 was offered for cash on 3 April 1934. Neither was Norman convinced of the necessity of offsetting the deflationary effects on the cash base of reducing Treasury bills (see below, p. 102).

In November 1935 Phillips asked the Chancellor for authority for a conversion operation by which the Treasury would issue £100m 5-year 1% bonds which would be "cheap to us and convenient to the market" and £200m of either 2½% Funding Loan 1951/56 issued below par or 3% Funding Loan 1970/80 issued at par (of which Phillips preferred the latter), in order to meet various bond maturities and to fund some of the floating debt.[53] The Chancellor favoured the longer 3% bond,[54] but the Governor wanted the 2½% medium-term bond because Harvey had warned him of the difficulty of placing a long loan with the banks who already had very large holdings of long-term government stock. Phillips recommended the Chancellor take Harvey's advice,[55] but issues of 1% Treasury Bonds and 3% Funding Loan were announced on 3 December 1935.

Eleven months later, Phillips thought "the time ha[d] come [again] when we should take steps to reduce the volume of Treasury Bills outstanding", because market Treasury bills had been increased due to gold purchases by the E.E.A. and were likely to rise further in the next year because of a possible budget deficit, repayment of bonds and rearmament borrowing.

> "The market is not acquainted with the figures of market bills outstanding or the figures of our gold holdings . . . it will therefore be inclined to attribute the whole operation to our need for money for armaments. From that point of view a loan of £100 million might be thought more expedient than one for £150m. On the other hand it is common sense to borrow a fair amount before people get alarmed at budget deficits. I think £150m is the right figure."

It should be a medium- or long-term issue:

> "On general grounds a long term issue, when you are perfectly sure you can make a success of it, is to be preferred to a medium term issue. The long term market is not in the most brilliant condition since fears of a coming rise in interest rates are fairly frequently expressed. If the Governor is satisfied that he can sell long term stock in sufficient amounts then no doubt we should take his advice." [56]

The Governor was dubious of the feasibility of a long-term issue and recommended a 2¾% Funding Loan 1953/58,[57] and a prospectus for 2¾% Funding Loan 1952/57 was issued on 17 November.

The documents cited show not only that the authorities still had their "funding complex" acquired in 1920 and that the Treasury was therefore taking advantage of low interest rates to fund cheaply, but also that Norman wanted to fund floating debt in order to offset some of the effects of cheap money. The results show up clearly in the monetary statistics and interest rate figures. The memoranda also refer to the role of the Issue Department in debt management: on this see Appendix 2.

Monetary Statistics

As Nevin has remarked, "Movements in the money supply during the period 1933–39 are not *a priori* consistent with the statements of official spokesman that the authorities were pursuing a policy of cheap money".[58] The monetary statistics used here show this clearly. However, they also show that the authorities' policy did result in a behaviour of the money supply in the years 1932–6 very different from that of the 1920s (see Chart 5).

The turning-point came in February 1932 when the money supply and high-powered money began to rise rapidly. By the end of 1936 the money supply had grown 34% (a rate of 6% p.a. compared with 2% p.a. in 1926–8; the rise for 1932 was as rapid as 1919). In the same period high-powered money grew by 30% (5% p.a.) after its long decline in 1921–30. Another striking feature is the marked reduction in the size of the increases of the money supply and high-powered money, and of the decreases in the deposit-reserve ratio, at the half-year ends, from mid-1931 onwards. The other sort of window-dressing also decreased, and was less variable, in 1932–8 compared with the 1920s.[59] Also the rise in current accounts was faster than that in total deposits, rather than slower as in the 1920s.[60]

However, the rises in the money supply were not continuous over 1932–6. The seasonal fall was sharp early in 1933 and the money supply recovered only to its

Chart 5 *Monetary series, monthly, 1929—36*
   Source: See Appendix 1

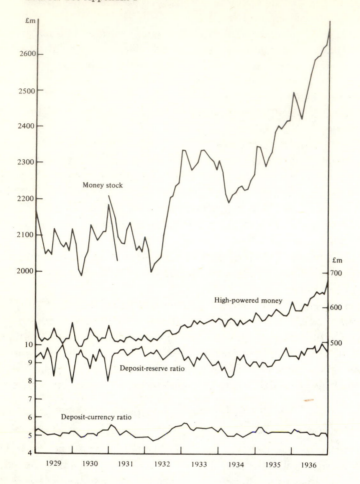

end-1932 level in mid-1933, after which it fell rapidly until March 1934 (at a rate of 0.65% per month). Its rapid growth was then resumed and continued until the end of 1936. High-powered money continued to grow during June 1933—March 1934 but at a much slower rate than previously (0.1% per month compared with 0.7% per month). Its growth ceased in the middle of 1937. The deposit-currency ratio rose substantially from February 1932 until February 1933; it was then fairly constant, though falling temporarily in 1934 and after 1936. The most curious behaviour was that of the deposit-reserve ratio which remained constant in 1932 after rising slightly 1929–31, and then fell sharply from November 1932 until March 1934. It rose in May, June, July and August, fell again in September, and did not rise again until June 1935. The rise of the next twelve months took it to its 1929 level but it declined again during the next two and a half years. Bank deposits behaved in the same way as the money supply. Currency, on the other hand, had already risen sharply before March 1932, from mid-1931 onwards. It levelled off in the remainder of 1932 and recommenced its growth at the end of 1932, accelerating gradually until the second half of 1936. Reserves rose considerably in 1932, but hardly at all in 1933 and 1934; thereafter they grew again but at a slower rate than in 1932.

Thus the rapid growth of the money supply and deposits in 1932 was due to a growth in reserves, which was, of course, one of the measures taken by the authorities to ensure the success of the War Loan conversion operation. What has to be explained are:

(1) the fall in the deposit-reserve ratio which caused the fall in deposits and the money supply between June 1933 and March 1934;

(2) the behaviour of high-powered money in the same period.

(1) As earlier writers have pointed out,[61] the explanation lies in the authorities' policy with respect to the floating debt. The figures in Appendix 2 show the changes in the public's holdings of government debt of various maturities and in the market's holdings of Treasury bills; the Treasury bill figures show that the various debt operations effected significant reductions in market bills in this period. The total supply of Treasury bills was (given that the E.E.A. issued bills to finance its purchases of gold and foreign exchange) the outcome of both the E.E.A.'s operations and the Treasury's funding operations, but in determining the supply of Treasury bills *to the market* it was the latter (helped by the Bank's management of its Issue Department holdings) that was more important. The sharp drop in total private sector holdings of Treasury bills caused by the authorities' policy was faithfully reflected in the London Clearing Banks' bill holdings which having slowly, since 1925, with two considerable setbacks in 1929 and 1931, climbed back in January 1933 to their December 1922 peak, fell very sharply in the next year to their 1931 level (not much higher than those of the mid-1920s) where they stayed for the rest of the year.[62] Not only was there a decline in market Treasury bills but there was also a shortage of commercial bills available for the banks to purchase because of the continued decline of commercial bills and increased competition from foreigners investing funds in London after 1932.[63]

Nevin has shown that although the liquid assets ratio of the clearing banks was not rigid and inflexible, market Treasury bill decreases caused a fall in clearing bank deposits July 1933–March 1934.[64] With respect to the liquid assets ratio he concluded:

> "There is . . . no question of any rigid secondary *ratio* during this period. The reaction of the banks to a decline in liquid assets varied according to the circumstances of the time—the importance attached to the secondary reserve . . . depended on the prevailing trade conditions and general economic outlook and—what is virtually the same thing—the opportunities for the suitable employment of the resources set free as a result of the decline in liquid assets.[65]

The circumstances of 1933–4 were that general economic recovery was still only gradual and had not checked the decline in bank advances (which had begun in 1929). The banks could avoid a reduction in deposits only through purchase of securities, and they were not anxious to do this because cheap money and the reduction in advances had greatly increased the size of banks' holdings of government debt relative to their total investments.[66] This meant that for the banks such securities were no longer safe/highly liquid, because

> "The liquidity of security holdings was seriously reduced . . . when the interest of the banking system in the gilt-edged market became so substantial as to make sales . . . difficult without a serious fall in price, and when such a

101

decline in price would affect the capital value of a large segment of the total assets of the banking system."[67]

As recovery continued into 1935, the banks expanded their advances and their low secondary ratios ceased to be a constraint on deposits.[68]

(2) The answer to the question of the behaviour of high-powered money in 1933–4 lies in the Bank's actions with respect to the credit base, so I shall here discuss the Bank's policy over the period 1932–6.

The Bank followed an expansionary policy in 1932,[69] but as I have already mentioned the Governor seems to have been a reluctant supporter of cheap money after 1932. As Clay says,

> "It followed that . . . [the Governor] avoided increasing the fiduciary issue and took every opportunity to increase the Bank's holding of gold . . . while the Banking Department increased its holding of securities until bankers' balances were brought up [by February 1933] to £100 million, about which level they were kept until the eve of the Second World War."[70]

Clay has described briefly, and Brown in more detail, the measures the Bank took in 1932 and early 1933 to further these ends. In 1932 these were open-market purchases of government securities in March, gold purchases from the E.E.A. in May and June, and more open-market purchases in December to offset the American war debt repayment in gold. However, because of these operations "the balance sheet of the Banking Department . . . had . . . assumed an abnormal aspect." Government securities were exceptionally high while the reserve and the proportion were lower. Therefore,

> "In 1933 . . . the Bank broke completely with . . . tradition and embarked purposefully upon a policy of gold accumulation. In three months, from February to April 1933, it purchased sufficient gold not only to make good the amount used for the war debt payment and to offset the effect of a continued rise in circulation, but also to lift the reserve of the Banking Department to the general level of from £70 to £80m."

It thus restored its reserve and proportion while keeping bankers' balances at £100m. Then, at the end of April 1933, the rising trend of bankers' balances ceased, and thus ended the Bank's positive contribution to cheap money.[71]

Despite the constancy of bankers' balances high-powered money continued to grow, due to a steady rise in currency, but this was partly due to the growth of continental hoarding.[72] The inflow of funds into London which began in the first quarter of 1933 continued until the first quarter of 1938. It was, according to Clay, "an embarrassment" to Norman, because

> "it tended to inflate Clearing Bank deposits, the Bank could not refuse to increase its note issue if more currency was required, and the Treasury Bills, which the Exchange Equalisation Account sold to pay for its purchases of the incoming gold and foreign exchange, threatened to weaken the Bank's control of the market."[73]

Norman's persistent advocacy of a policy of funding Treasury bills was an attempt to prevent the inflow of foreign funds from thwarting his policy with respect to the cash base. Reducing the available volume of Treasury bills would mean that, in Clay's words, "the market would be prevented from securing such a holding that they could at any time force the hands of the Treasury and Bank, and, by refusing to renew

102

Treasury Bills, compel them to create more cash".[74] The memory of 1920 was still vivid to Norman! The Bank not only attempted to persuade the Treasury to keep on funding but also (with the Treasury's acquiescence) reduced the volume of Treasury bills by more direct methods, for example, acquiring them for Government Departments and other central banks, holding them in the Issue Department, and selling gold acquired by the E.E.A. to the Issue Department.[75] The operation of these expedients can be seen by comparing the departmental holdings of Treasury bills with the market's holdings (Appendix 2).

This policy of "non-intervention" by the Bank with respect to the cash base on the one hand, and intervention with respect to the supply of bills on the other was continued till the end of 1936.[76] It was not just the consequence of the fact that the E.E.A. protected the banks' cash reserves from the impact of inflows and outflows of foreign funds only by transferring the impact to the supply of Treasury bills to the banks (and others),[77] but also of the fact that though the Bank was prepared to keep short-term rates of interest low (because changes in these were no longer necessary to protect the exchanges), it did not want abundant credit.[78] Aiding and abetting the Treasury in reducing the supply of Treasury bills to the market enabled the Bank to keep down short-term interest rates without increasing the cash base. As Goodwin has pointed out, operations in Treasury bills were just as effective in controlling the credit base as ordinary open-market operations.[79] It did oblige the Bank to step in in 1934 to save the discount market from the effects of the bill famine, by establishing a floor to the Treasury bill rate of just over ½%, but once this was done, the rate could be kept at this level without substantial open-market operations.[80]

Whereas Norman was indifferent to long-term interest rates,[81] the Treasury officials wanted low long-term rates, which in the years 1932—6 they got, so that there was no need for them to ask the Bank to do anything expansionary. What they were concerned about in these years was that the low rates on long-term government debt should be passed on to industry (above p. 90). Consequently when in the autumn of 1932 they noticed that though the Bank of England had greatly expanded the credit base, bankers' advances were still declining and their investments in government securities still increasing, they considered trying to persuade (at a meeting of the Chancellor, and the Governor if he was willing, with the Joint Stock Banks) the banks to lower their overdraft rates and/or stop increasing their liquidity at the expense of advances.[82] However, they then decided the desired events would come about fairly soon anyway,[83] and indeed by April overdraft rates had come down, further than the Treasury had expected.[84] The Treasury also wanted to see bankers' deposit rates come down, and early in 1933 contemplated reducing the Savings Banks rates on deposits in order to force the banks to lower their rates,[85] but this scheme was also dropped as being unnecessary.[86]

Although this account of monetary policy should dispose of the contention[87] that the authorities' policy 1933—5 was a consequence of their not knowing what they were doing, it does raise the problem of the relative weights the Treasury officials attached to their two objectives (cheap money and funding), and whether they actually realized there was a conflict between them. I shall return to this problem in the next chapter (pp. 130—1).

Interest Rates and the Capital Market

Despite the various and conflicting policy influences on the money supply after 1932, money was cheap, at least until 1936. Short-term interest rates were very low, as a consequence of the shortage of Treasury bills. Although the drop in short-term rates compared with the 1920s had been greater than that in long-term rates, so that the spread between them had widened, long-term rates remained at or below their immediate post-conversion levels until 1939. Although long rates showed a tendency to rise in and after 1936, that was after they had been below 3% for two years, and it was not until 1939 that they regained the level of 1933. The Consol rate 1933–8 averaged 3.15% with 4.62% 1920–9. The Treasury bill rate averaged 0.60% 1933–8 compared with 4.16% 1920–9. Furthermore, low interest rates on government securities gradually spread to other securities (see Tables 12 and 13, and Appendix 1, Tables 2 and 3B).

Table 12 *Interest rates, annual averages, 1930–8, % p.a.*

	Bank rate	Average short rate	Treasury bill rate	Short-dated gilt-edged yield	2½% Consols
1930	3.41	2.49	2.48	4.31	4.48
1931	3.97	3.18	3.59	4.54	4.39
1932	3.01	1.59	1.49	3.64	3.74
1933	2.0	0.69	0.59	2.09	3.39
1934	2.0	0.82	0.73	1.78	3.10
1935	2.0	0.65	0.55	2.46	2.89
1936	2.0	0.69	0.58	2.45	2.94
1937	2.0	0.67	0.56	2.90	3.28
1938	2.0	0.68	0.61	2.72	3.28

Sources: Goodwin, "Studies in Money", and L.C.E.S., *Key Statistics*, Table M.

Table 13 *Yields on new issues, annual, 1930–8, % p.a.*

	Debentures	Preference shares
1930	6.0	6.0
1931	6.3	6.5
1932	5.4	6.3
1933	4.6	5.3
1934	4.5	5.0
1935	3.8	5.0
1936	4.2	5.0
1937	4.1	4.9
1938	4.2	5.1

Source: The Economist, selected issues

The interest rate figures show that yields on existing and new industrial issues followed those on government stock down and, after 1936, up again. Nevin has dealt with the difficulties involved in using the figures and the way they can be overcome[88] and he concluded:

> "When full allowance has been made for the main factors entering into the cost of industrial borrowing, then, it is clear that the prices paid by British industry for new funds in the capital market declined noticeably after the inception of cheap money in 1932. Between that year and 1936 . . . the

statistics suggest that the rise of 29 per cent in the price of Consols was associated with a fall of 25 per cent in the cost of debenture borrowing and a fall of 24 per cent in the cost of borrowing on preference shares . . . The rise of 66 per cent in the price-level of ordinary shares . . . is evidence . . . of the increased facility with which entrepreneurs could approach the market. These movements cannot be wholly attributed to the monetary policy of the period; but cheap money was probably the largest single factor in the change in the cost of debenture borrowing, and was of not inconsiderable significance in the cheapening of preference-share borrowing. It was certainly least important in the realm of ordinary shares, where profit expectations are dominant. But the rise of some 13 per cent in the *Investors Chronicle* general business securities index in July of 1932 immediately after the War Loan conversion announcement is evidence that even here changes in the rate of interest, by adjusting the capitalised value of a given expected yield, is of some importance."[89]

Nevin has remarked:

"While new investment may be financed by many means other than new capital issues, an increased flow of such issues can be taken as *prima facie* evidence of a rise in investment, . . . a reviving capital market is a characteristic of an economy shaking off the inertia of trade depression."[90]

Table 14 *New capital issues (Midland Bank figures), annual, £m*

	Home	Empire	Foreign	Total
1930	127.4	70.0	38.8	236.2
1931	42.6	36.8	9.2	88.7
1932	83.8	28.9	0.3	113.0
1933	95.1	29.8	8.0	132.9
1934	106.7	40.4	3.1	150.2
1935	161.9	18.0	2.9	182.8
1936	190.8	23.4	3.1	217.2
1937	138.8	24.9	7.2	170.9
1938	92.7	20.8	4.1	118.1

Home issues:

	Public Bodies	Production	Trade	Transport	Finance
1927	29.8	53.5	20.4	28.8	43.5
1928	17.6	86.5	43.1	8.2	63.8
1929	3.6	80.1	27.1	3.7	45.0
1930	46.0	34.9	10.3	20.2	15.9
1931	10.3	16.3	4.7	4.3	7.1
1932	32.6	25.3	11.4	8.9	5.5
1933	34.5	34.5	16.6	3.7	5.9
1934	34.3	41.7	18.6	2.7	9.5
1935	24.6	62.2	26.3	32.6	16.2
1936	48.1	73.1	16.8	33.1	19.7
1937	34.7	57.8	18.0	11.1	17.1
1938	27.6	48.3	11.0	0.5	5.4

Source: Grant, *A Study of the Capital Market*, p. 134.

The new issue figures (Table 14) do indeed show such an increased flow, and what is more unlike the 1920s an increase in the total was not due to an increase in new overseas issues. This was of course partly, but not wholly due to the embargo.[91] Also a lower proportion of the total was going to financial ventures than had been the case in the late 1920s. Furthermore, when adjusted for changes in the cost of capital goods, these figures indicate, as Nevin has shown, that:

> "Private capital issues during 1932–4 were nearly twice as great in real terms as in the two preceding years, and . . . the volume of funds raised during 1935–6 was in fact greater in money terms than that raised in 1929–30, and considerably greater in real terms."[92]

By an analysis of prospectuses (of every prospectus issued by British public companies in the 1930s) Nevin has indicated two other important respects in which the behaviour of the U.K. capital market in the 1930s differed from that in the previous decade:

(1) the higher proportion of issues made by smaller firms;[93]

(2) the high proportion of conversion issues.[94]

The conversion operations appear to have reduced the annual interest burden on British industry by just over £2m, not "an immense figure, but in the atmosphere of the early 1930s [this] addition to disposable profits . . . cannot have been other than welcome".[95] Some of the funds thus released were used to retire bank debt and the indebtedness of firms on bank overdrafts and mortgages appears to have declined as recovery proceeded.[96] At the same time, firms raised money from banks by selling securities to them rather than by arranging new overdrafts.[97] There is also some evidence (in the balance sheets of fifty companies) of a decline in internal financing in the early 1930s and increased financing by debenture rather than share issues.[98]

Since these things are what one would expect on theoretical grounds to happen in a period of cheap money and economic revival, one can say that changes in financial conditions, attributable to the 1931–2 change in monetary policy, were such as to facilitate business expansion and investment. These changes were, however, small in comparison with the vast increase in savings going to the building societies.

The growth of U.K. non-bank financial intermediaries in the 1930s was of course part of a longer-term trend,[99] but in the interwar years the building societies' growth was the fastest of all financial institutions,[100] and while their growth was tremendous over the whole period, they were significantly affected by the changes in monetary conditions in the early 1930s. Before 1930 the growth in the deposits of the building societies (and of the Post Office and Trustee Savings Banks) was due mainly to the growth of "small" or working-class savings.[101] After 1930 these savings were joined by funds which would not normally be deposited there, because, first, "as the crisis of 1931 deepened there was a rush—almost a frantic rush—among investors for security above all considerations",[102] and, second, after the War Loan conversion the fall in interest rates on gilt-edged stocks (and other securities) rendered the safer deposits of non-bank financial intermediaries more attractive than they had previously been.[103]

This inflow of funds posed a difficult problem for the building societies, particularly in regard to the rate they paid on their deposits, as Sir Harold Bellman, who was managing director of the Abbey Road Building Society, has explained:

> "The societies, as a settled aim of policy, have never sought to reproduce the more extreme movements of the interest curve, whether high or low . . . primarily in the interests of the borrower, for his is a long-term contract and

frequent fluctuations in his interest rate would make any attempt at budgeting extremely difficult if not impossible ... The decision whether adjustment was required was never easy ... [Though] it was recognized ... that interest rates generally prior to 1932 had, owing to the existence of the great mass of 5% War Loan, been unduly high, ... after the initial adjustment due to the Conversion of War Loan ... the strength and character of the forces operating on interest rates were extremely difficult to assess. Certainly the pressure of funds seeking admission to the societies' coffers was a very misleading guide, for obviously much of this was 'bad' money, which was seeking merely temporary refuge until confidence revived. In fact, so far from being a guide to the state of the market ... this was a problem in itself. For if the societies had made such extreme interest adjustments that all those funds could have been just accommodated, their position would have been very precarious when enterprise was once more astir and other investment outlets regained their attractions. In these circumstances the societies' policy was to make, step by step, such interest adjustments as seemed at the time fully justified and also to impose quantitative restrictions on the amount which an individual investor, and especially a new investor, could place with a society. The restrictions were first imposed on a considerable scale in July, 1932."[104]

These restrictions, only gradually relaxed over the next three years, slowed down the growth of building societies' shares and deposits, and rates on deposits and on mortgages came down slowly over the next few years.[105] The reductions in interest rates were, however, substantial and they were also accompanied by a lengthening in the repayment period and an increase in the percentage of the total value of a house that the societies would loan to the purchaser.[106] The amount advanced on mortgage grew dramatically (Table 15), and financed the purchase of the vast majority of houses built in the housing boom which began towards the end of 1932.[107]

Table 15 *Building society rates and advances, 1930–8*

	Yields on building society shares %	Average rate of interest charged on mortgages, %	New mortgage advances, £m
1930	4.65	5.82	88.8
1931	4.62	5.87	90.3
1932	4.52	5.87	82.1
1933	3.95	5.57	103.2
1934	3.80	5.44	124.6
1935	3.64	5.21	130.9
1936	3.45	4.97	140.3
1937	3.38	4.87	136.9
1938	3.37	4.83	137.0

Source: BESS

So I move on (though not quite immediately) to the question of the effects of cheap money on housebuilding in the 1930s, noting here by way of conclusion to the section that "the main effect of cheap money in this context [the flow of funds] ... was to divert into the outer capital market considerable sums of money which would otherwise have remained in the relatively narrow confines of the trustee and high-class debenture market".[108]

Recovery

"Looking back it is possible to perceive continuous recovery from about September 1932, gathering pace until 1934, then slower recovery through 1934 and much of 1935, and a final brisk improvement until some time in 1937."[109] The National Bureau reference date is August 1932; *The Economist* index of business activity reaches a trough in September–October 1932. Other indicators show a wider range of turning points but, as H.W. Richardson has pointed out at length, given the usual leads and lags, they support the assumption of the trough occurring in the late summer of 1932.[110]

The most noticeable (to both contemporaries and historians) feature of the revival, which was domestically based, was the enormous increase in private investment in housebuilding which began in the autumn of 1932. Cheap money has often been given credit for the great upsurge in housebuilding and hence for recovery. I wish here to discuss that hypothesis. Two main questions are involved:

  (1) Was the increase in housing investment the cause of the revival of investment generally, and hence income and employment?
  (2) Was the increase in housing investment caused by cheap money?

Both these questions can be subdivided into two, because of the ambiguity of the word "cause" which in this context can mean either "initiate" or "sustain". There is in fact little doubt that cheap money helped to sustain housing investment, and housing investment to sustain the recovery;[111] therefore, the question that needs examining is whether the emergence of cheap money in 1932 set the ball rolling.

Given the literature on the subject it is probably best to start with the alternative explanations of the recovery, namely

  (1) depreciation of the pound after September 1931;
  (2) the tariff;
  (3) the rise in real incomes caused by the fall in the cost of living during the slump.

(1) and (2) *Depreciation and the Tariff*

How much the floating of the pound contributed to the course of economic recovery in the years after 1932 cannot be indicated, because it is impossible to allow for all the factors that invalidate any *ceteris paribus* assumption. However, with respect to the impulses which initiated the upswing within a year of Britain's leaving the gold standard, it is the effects of the depreciation of sterling in that first year which matter. In that time the full effects of the "devaluation" cannot be presumed to have worked through and there could have been a deterioration in the balance of payments due to the value of U.K. imports being increased sooner than the value of exports, i.e. the phenomenon which is now known as the J-curve, and which the Treasury officials, under Henderson's influence, took into account in their discussions of the winter of 1931 (above pp. 84–5).

Initially, in the brief "currency-contract period" before pre-devaluation contracts fall due, whether there is a change in the trade balance will depend on whether contracts are denominated in sterling or in foreign currencies. If one assumes U.K. export and import contracts are in sterling then the trade balance in sterling would not change, and in foreign currencies would increase, in this period.[112]

In the next phase, the "pass-through period" in which it can be assumed that quantities of exports and imports have not had time to adjust, the trade balance will depend on the price behaviour of U.K. and other exporters.[113] If the quantity exported and sterling export prices are constant, then the sterling value of exports will also be constant (and prices and hence the value will fall in terms of foreign currency). A rise in sterling import prices would cause an increase in the sterling value of goods imported. The trade balance will, therefore, deteriorate in this pre-quantity adjustment period. Experience of devaluations since 1931 suggests that even when elasticities are such that devaluation should eventually exert a sizeable beneficial effect on the balance of payments, the trade balance may deteriorate, or at least remain unfavourable, in the first year after devaluation, because increases in import prices come through quite rapidly while the decrease in import volume (caused by the sterling price rise) and the increase in export prices (caused by the rise in import prices and hence in exporters' costs) and in export volumes come through more slowly. The last could take up to three years, the other two between one and two years.[114]

In the case of the 1931 "devaluation", U.K. food and materials wholesale prices rose in the last quarter of 1931 and then declined through the rest of the first post-"devaluation" year, so that by the fourth quarter of 1932 they were back to their pre-depreciation levels.[115] The initial rise in the price of imported manufactures was also to a certain extent undone by the continuing depression in the exporting countries. The behaviour of exports and of invisible items in the current account of the balance of payments was also determined by the decline in the volume of world trade. The effects were further complicated by the National government's other expenditure-switching remedy for the balance of payments deficit, the tariff.*

What actually happened in the year from September 1931 to September 1932 is shown in Table 16.

The quantities of food, of materials, and of manufactures imported all rose in the last quarter of 1931, the first two for largely seasonal reasons and the last in order to beat the tariff.[116] In the next three months, the quantity of imported manufactures fell substantially (except for another pre-tariff rise in February)[117] and thereafter stayed down well below the levels of 1930 and 1931. The fall in value terms was more pronounced because of the fall in prices. Imports of food in both value and volume terms fell in 1931 I (because of the seasonal and price factors), but imports of materials rose. For the rest of the year for both these categories of imports the fall was only in value.

On the export side, the rapid decline of 1930 and 1931 in export volumes was arrested in 1931 IV, but the slight rise in quantities of 1932 I and II did not last, and

---

* On 17 November 1931 the government introduced a bill empowering it to impose high temporary duties on any manufactured goods of which imports were abnormally great, and on 4 February 1932 Chamberlain introduced a bill for the imposition of a general tariff, which was passed on 29 February. The Import Duties Act imposed a general 10% duty on all foreign goods except basic foodstuffs and raw materials and goods already subject to duty and provided for an independent Import Duties Advisory Committee to recommend higher duties on particular products (e.g. iron and steel).

Table 16 *Values of unadjusted retained imports and exports of British goods at current and constant (average 1930) prices, quarterly, 1930–32, £m*

At current prices

	Retained imports				Exports			
Quarter	Food	Materials	Manu-factures	Total	Food	Materials	Manu-factures	Total
1930 I	114	67	75	256	12	19	128	159
II	108	52	72	232	11	16	110	137
III	107	47	69	223	13	15	105	133
IV	123	47	68	238	13	15	97	125
1931 I	93	39	58	190	10	12	78	100
II	94	36	58	188	8	12	72	92
III	96	33	60	189	8	11	71	90
IV	113	40	70	123	10	12	70	92
1932 I	91	42	43	176	8	11	70	89
II	85	34	32	151	8	11	73	90
III	86	30	34	150	7	10	64	81
IV	98	36	37	171	9	12	69	90

At constant prices

	Retained imports				Exports			
Quarter	Food	Materials	Manu-factures	Total	Food	Materials	Manu-factures	Total
1930 I	105	60	73	238	12	18	125	155
II	107	50	71	228	11	16	110	137
III	108	48	69	225	13	15	105	133
IV	132	54	72	258	13	16	100	129
1931 I	110	51	65	226	11	13	84	108
II	113	47	69	229	9	14	79	102
III	122	44	73	239	8	12	82	102
IV	143	57	82	282	11	14	82	107
1932 I	116	58	50	224	10	12	85	107
II	111	49	42	202	9	12	88	109
III	115	45	45	205	9	12	79	100
IV	130	51	47	228	11	14	85	110

Source: Board of Trade Journal, selected issues.

the decline in values continued (more slowly than pre-"devaluation", of course). The increase in exports in 1932 I and II was not uniform among commodities, an increase in exports of cotton offsetting decreases in other goods.[118] The increase in imports of materials in the same period was also largely due to cotton.[119]

The outcome for the balance of trade was therefore a large deterioration in 1931 IV and a marked reduction in the deficit in 1932 I–III. This was, as expected, accompanied by a decline in the values of all invisible items which aggravated the 1931 IV situation but was not large enough to prevent the deficit on the balance of payments current account for 1932 being half of 1931, because, principally, of the large fall in the value of imports.[120]

Now, could these developments of January–September 1932 have contributed to the economy's upturn in September?

1. Exports did not rise in any sustained fashion so though a depressing influence was removed, this could not have set the economy on its way up. Further, in 1932 III they actually fell quite sharply.

2. A similar argument applies to the continuation of the current account deficit.

3. Imports did fall substantially in 1932, by more than the fall in real income in 1932 over 1931 can account for.[121] This was a stabilizing influence since it improved the position of the economy compared to the situation in which it would otherwise have found itself. The substitution of domestically-produced goods for imported goods that subsequently occurred seems to have been due more to depreciation than to the tariff,[122] but the big post-"devaluation" fall in imports (in real terms) did not occur until late in 1932, almost half the total fall in imports in 1932 over 1931 occurring in the fourth quarter (Table 16).

4. Although the terms of trade were not, as the Treasury officials feared, worsened by depreciation, they improved negligibly (by less than 1%) in 1932 as compared with 1931, whereas in the previous three years they had risen by at least 21%. The next year's rise was only 3% and did not continue in subsequent years.[123]

5. The tariff may have improved expectations of entrepreneurs in certain trades, but if so then the London and Cambridge Economic Service quarterly index numbers of production for the protected trades should have shown some increase in 1932 II and III for this phenomenon to be an explanation of the September 1932 upturn. In fact they do not.[124] As contemporaries noted, a small immediate post-"devaluation" burst of activity in the textile and iron and steel trades soon petered out.[125] This burst of activity showed itself first in employment and, to a lesser extent, production, in 1931 IV and in imports (of materials) and exports (of manufactures) in 1932 I and II (above p. 110). Investment in iron and steel was encouraged by the tariff and showed an increase in 1932 over 1931, but the big post-tariff increases came in 1934 when the tariff was made permanent.[126]

6. Probably the most important way in which the depreciation of the pound and tariff can be seen to have encouraged recovery *in the first year* after Britain left the gold standard is the freedom it gave to the monetary authorities to introduce the long-desired policy of cheap money.

(3) *Rise in real incomes*

This has been used as an explanation both of the housing boom and of recovery.[127]

Between 1929 and 1932 average annual money wage and salary earnings fell by 3% and the official cost of living index by 12½%, so that for those in employment there was a rise of over 10% in estimated average annual real earnings. This was associated with the favourable movement in the terms of trade and like that it did not persist throughout the 1930s. There was a further slight rise between 1932 and 1935 but from then on real earnings declined. Although "there must . . . have been a useful additional increase in the ability of potential owner-occupiers to give effective expression to their long-standing desire for better housing",[128] it is nonetheless difficult to account for the actual timing and development of the housing boom on this hypothesis alone.

Nevin has suggested that the rise in real incomes cannot explain the continuation of the housing boom after 1933:[129] over the two years 1933 and 1934 when the number of houses completed increased by 100% the rise in real incomes was 8%.[130] Richardson has criticized this argument as "neglect[ing] the role of lags, that the sharp rise in average annual real earnings between 1929 and 1931 may have affected the demand for houses not in those years but in 1932 and 1933".[131] However, if one allows the relevant lags to be long enough that the 1933–4 rise in housebuilding can be explained by the preceding rise in real incomes, one still faces the problem that a rise in real incomes of around 10% caused an increase in housebuilding of 100%. Even if one ignores the possibility that not all of the gain in real income would have been devoted to housing and the fact that the gain went only to those in employment,[132] one is still assuming a very high income-elasticity of demand for housing. Empirical studies for the U.S. suggest a permanent income-elasticity of demand for housing in the range of 0.8−1.5 for rented housing and moderately above 1.0 for owner-occupiers.[133] For the U.K. in the period 1955−70 Christine Whitehead has found even lower income-elasticities, well below 1.0, and on the same data far higher elasticities with respect to interest rates. Further, simulations of her model predicted substantial and fairly rapid effects of interest rate changes on housebuilding, which tends to suggest that one might have to add another factor, namely the change in monetary conditions, to the rise in real incomes to explain the origins of the 1930s housing boom.[134] In other words, although one should not underestimate the importance of the preceding rise in real incomes, which may have been a necessary condition for the boom to occur, it is doubtful whether it could have been a *sufficient* condition.

Richardson has argued that increased expenditure on all consumer durables, rather than on housing, caused by the rise in real incomes during the depression was the cause of the revival. He believes "consumption was undoubtedly the most crucial cyclical determinant in the 1930s"[135] and has summarized his major argument as follows:

> "The relative stability of aggregate consumption was a moderating factor in Britain's economic depression in the early 1930s . . . [Further] consumers were reallocating their expenditure between non-durables and durables . . . The increased sales of certain groups of consumption goods helped recovery to get under way by inducing new investment in plant and equipment; high capital-output ratios in some of the industries concerned meant that this new investment was of more than marginal significance."[136]

Now it is true that expenditure in real terms on motor cars and motor cycles, furniture, floor coverings, electrical goods, etc., unlike most other categories of consumers' expenditure except housing and "other services", showed a significant increase in 1932 over 1931,[137] but the series showed a very strong upward trend throughout the interwar years. Purchases of furniture and furnishings rose uninterruptedly from 1921 until 1936 at an average rate of 5% p.a. and this growth slowed down very little in the depression.[138] For cars, too, there was a marked upward movement of demand over the two decades (accompanied by a comparable fall in price). Here there was a fall in 1929−31 and a small increase in 1932;[139] the large post-slump increases came in 1933 and 1934.[140] If the floor to expenditure provided by these steadily expanding industries initiated an upswing in activity generally, then its effect should be observable in investment in these industries.[141] There are indeed substantial increases in investment in the "newer" manufacturing industries but not until 1933 and 1934, particularly the latter year,[142] i.e. after the beginning of the housing boom. Although the new industries could, on a buffer theory of the cycle, have initiated revival, it appears that they did not in fact do so in this instance.

So I come back to the importance of the upswing in housing investment and the question of the role of cheap money in its initiation. A major reason why other writers have sought alternative explanations of recovery is that they have located the turning points in building and in monetary conditions so as not to allow a sufficient lag. At this point one should mention another explanation of the rise in housebuilding, the fall in building costs.[143] Richardson and Aldcroft have used this as an argument against Nevin's analysis.[144] They claim that "the house purchase market was turning upwards before the conversion to cheap money" because

(1) annual figures for houses built by unsubsidized private enterprise show that an upswing in unsubsidized building began in 1929 and was temporarily interrupted in 1931; and

(2) although the first falls in building society mortgage rates took place in the autumn of 1932, it was not until the summer of 1933 that a reduction of 1% became general.

They also claim that the weekly cost of buying houses was falling well before the conversion to cheap money, because of the fall in building costs which had begun in the late 1920s.

Table 17 *Bowley's estimates of cost of buying houses*

Year	Average capital cost (£)	Building Society rates of interest (%)	Weekly cost of buying (s. d.)
1925	510	6	12 1
1926	510	6	12 1
1927	481	6	11 4
1928	432	6	10 0½
1929	416	6	9 9
1930	411	6	9 9
1931	404	5.9	9 4
1932	375	5.9	8 7
1933	362	4.9	7 8
1934	361	5.2	7 10
1935	371	4.5	7 8
1936	384	4.5	7 11
1937	427	4.5	8 10

Source: Housing and the State 1919–44, Table 6, p. 278, cols. 1, 2, 8 and 9

The most widely used estimates of the cost of buying houses are Marian Bowley's (Table 17). These do indeed show a fall in building costs and buying costs from 1927 onwards, and they do not show, as Nevin claims they do, "the important influence which an apparently trivial reduction in the mortgage rate may have upon the weekly cost of house purchase"[145] particularly since the mortgage rates with which Nevin compares the weekly cost figures are not the rates Bowley used to calculate the weekly buying costs. Marian Bowley used "the average rates of interest charged by building societies on new advances (slightly rounded off), as given in the Annual Reports of the Chief Registrar of Friendly Societies".[146] Nevin used the figures for average rate of interest charged given in the *BESS*, which are rather different (see Table 15). These are the figures given in the annual reports of the Chief Registrar of Friendly Societies as the "average rate of interest charged to borrowers on the mean mortgage balances outstanding". Nevin's inference is therefore illegitimate and the rates he uses are not suitable for working out what the weekly cost of buying a house would be for a *new* purchaser in the early 1930s.

Marian Bowley's figures are not ideal for the present purpose either. As she says, they were "calculated solely for the purpose of comparison between the economic and/or subsidized rents of local authority houses and the cheapest terms on an average of buying such a house. In practice, people starting out to buy houses tended to buy rather more elaborate houses, e.g. with parlours, gables, etc., and the terms on which advances were in fact obtained varied from those used as the basis of calculations with the variations in the practice of different building societies".[147]

Fortunately, however, there is no need to use Bowley's figures because MacIntosh has worked out the weekly carrying charges for a new house using information on the average new mortgage loans of all building societies, and not the average cost of a local authority-built three-bedroom, non-parlour house that Bowley used (see Table 18).

Table 18 *MacIntosh's estimates of cost of buying houses*

Year	Average new mortgage loan (£)	Estimated typical lending rates (%)	Assumed length of repayment (years)	Weekly carrying charges (s. d.)
1930	558	6	20	18 9
1931	557	6	20	18 8
1932	517	6	20	17 4
1933	529	5.5	20	17 0
1934	523	5.0	20	16 2
1935	543	4.5	20	16 1
1936	557	4.5	20	16 6
1937	569	4.5	20	16 10

Source: "A Note on Cheap Money and the British Housing Boom", *EJ*, March 1951, Table II
Note: The assumed length of repayment is the terms on which a marginal buyer could reasonably expect to obtain a loan, not the actual average loan's life, which was about ten years at the time.

The reduction in the weekly carrying charges assumes a rather more significant magnitude, especially in relation to the current average salary, when MacIntosh's figures are used.[148] Richardson and Aldcroft admit this,[149] but continue:

"It still remains true that as far as new mortgages were concerned the average weekly carrying charges fell considerably in 1931–2, before the new mortgage rates became effective, and that in the following year the reduction was quite small. This could only have been brought about by the fall in the capital cost of houses and at this point the level of building costs becomes important. These had been falling slowly in the late 1920s and between 1930 and 1933 the cost of materials fell by nearly 13% and the overall index of building costs by nearly 10%. . . . Since these changes took place before the first 1% reduction in mortgage rates became operative, it suggests that the initial upswing in building was a reaction to a fall in building costs, which was sufficiently sharp to produce a response."[150]

With the first sentence I would not disagree, but before accepting the rest, one must remember the point emphasized by Bowley,[151] that falling building costs are, if they are expected to continue falling, not much of an incentive to builders to start building. One would expect a large increase in building due to a fall in building costs to occur when it was believed that bottom had been reached and costs would not fall further. Therefore, on this hypothesis, the great upswing in 1932–3 is to be explained by a change in expectations with respect to costs in 1932. Why should there have been such a change? The only candidate is that the introduction of a liberal monetary policy by the authorities gave people reason to believe that the bottom of the slump, and hence the end of falling prices, would shortly be reached. The indices in Richardson's and Aldcroft's *Building in the British Economy* show that the total of houses built and gross domestic capital formation in building shot up when building costs had reached bottom.[152]

As I have said before, the weakness of the monetary explanation that has encouraged the search for alternative explanations is the lag problem. What, therefore, do the series show?

For private unsubsidized building Richardson and Aldcroft use the Ministry of Health's annual figures for years ending 31 March.[153] These do indeed show a big jump in 1932 over 1931, but that does not lend much support to Richardson's and Aldcroft's claims when one remembers that the figure for 1932 includes the first quarter of 1933. These figures are also available half-yearly; they show that the significant increase is between the half year ending in September 1932 and that ending in March 1933 (Table 19).

Table 19 *Private unsubsidized building (Ministry of Health figures)*

Half year ending	Total no. of houses built without State assistance
March 1930	53,393
September 1930	56,982
March 1931	71,746
September 1931	61,163
March 1932	69,740
September 1932	63,146
March 1933	80,291
September 1933	87,589
March 1934	122,247
September 1934	139,162
March 1935	154,382
September 1935	131,377
March 1936	147,529
September 1936	127,944
March 1937	146,139
September 1937	118,801
March 1938	139,980
September 1938	110,821

Source: Stolper, "British Monetary Policy and the Housing Boom", *QJE*, 1941, p. 5.

Two other series can be used to indicate building activity:

(1) *The Economist* index of building activity, available monthly;
(2) Building plans approved by 146 local authorities in England and Wales, also available monthly.[154]

(1) This is not particularly useful for the present purpose, because it includes all building. It is worth noting, however, that it shows a sustained rise from October 1932.

(2) MacIntosh observed of these figures (seasonably adjusted):

> "Building plans approved (which is an index of planned investment in housing) tended to decline during 1930–31, and reached their trough in November 1931. But an uninterrupted rise did not occur until after July 1932, and it is more plausible to select the latter date as the true turning point. The apparent upward movement in the first half of 1932 can be explained as an irregular movement not unlike similar random fluctuations during the previous two years. After the war-loan conversion on July 1, 1932, plans rose to a high level in October 1932. The significant fact is that they now remained at this level for the first time in three years."

He continued:

> "Recovery in building plans was initially due to the conversion operation, which had two effects: on the supply side of the market for funds, the building societies were feeling the heavy influx of savings, and knowing that mortgage rates would eventually have to be reduced, they encouraged builders to start construction. On the demand side, the builders also felt pressure from prospective home-owners, who were motivated by a prospective reduction in carrying charges. This anticipated decline in mortgage rates was confirmed in September, when most of the large building societies reduced their lending rates by ½%. The conditions for a boom were now satisfied, and building plans rose steadily until mid-1934." [155]

Bellman, looking at the same series, came to exactly the same conclusion. [156] The lag can be lengthened by taking account of the fact that the change in monetary conditions generally occurred in March–April 1932 [157] and from this point on people were expecting the conversion of War Loan.

The increase in planned housebuilding soon showed itself in an increase in employment in certain trades associated with housebuilding, an increase that was in advance of increases in employment generally. [158] The upswing in housebuilding was followed in 1933 by an increase in industrial production and investment. The recovery then began to make some impression on prices and unemployment (see Table 20).

There was a slight pause in recovery in mid-1934, which has been attributed to monetary factors, namely the fall in bank deposits and the money supply between June 1933 and March 1934. [159] If the monetary lag is taken to be 3–12 months, [160] this is plausible, but several non-monetary factors were operating in the same direction. The area of greatest expansion in investment changed from housebuilding to other industries in 1934 and the effects of the latter investment showed up in output and employment the following year. Phelps Brown's and Shackle's series for employment in the non-export industries shows a sudden horizontal segment beginning in the middle of 1934; at the same time "export-sensitive" employment, which had been rising in 1933, dropped quite sharply, and did not recover its end-1933 level until late 1936. Given the general pattern of fluctuations in these series, it is "especially . . . probable that in the fall of export-sensitive employment from the peak reached at the end of 1933, we have an explanation of 'the half in recovery' . . . in 1934". [161] Furthermore, while deposits and the money supply resumed their growth in mid-1934, the factors responsible for their setback of the previous nine months remained (Appendix 2, Table 3), being offset by the banks' response to the state of trade (above p. 102).

116

Table 20 *Investment, income, prices, 1930–8*

	Industrial Production Index (1913 = 100)	Investment G.D.F.C.F. at constant prices £m	N.D.F.C.F. at constant prices Dwellings £m	Total £m	Income G.D.P. at constant prices £m	Prices Board of Trade Wholesale price indices (1913 = 100)	Wholesale (1930 = 100)	Cost of living index (1914 = 100)	Wages average weekly wage rates (1913 = 100)	Unemployment among insured workers (annual averages of monthly figures) %
1930	120.1	463	81	146	4,720	120	100	158	175	16.0
1931	112.3	454	85	128	4,480	104	88	148	173	21.3
1932	111.9	396	85	65	4,493	102	86	144	170	22.1
1933	119.3	409	124	74	4,544	101	86	140	168	19.9
1934	131.2	498	143	163	4,851	104	88	141	168	16.7
1935	141.2	518	132	176	5,033		89	143	170	15.5
1936	153.9	565	129	215	5,190		94	147	173	13.1
1937	163.1	584	117	218	5,411		109	154	180	10.8
1938	158.7	592	113	219	5,572		101	156	185	13.5

Sources: Feinstein, *National Income*, Tables 51, 40, 48, 5 and 65; Mitchell and Deans, *Abstract of British Historical Statistics*, pp. 477–8; L.C.E.S., *Key Statistics*, Table E.

The Authorities' Reaction to Recovery

On 8 November 1933 the Cabinet was informed, by means of a Committee on Economic Information report backed up by comments on it from the Chancellor of the Exchequer and the President of the Board of Trade, that recovery had now come about and that it was due to the cheap money policy.[162] The Committee had first noted signs of recovery (and had wanted to see an end to the economy policy and an expansion of public works schemes in order to help the budding revival on its way) back in November 1932.[163] The Treasury had been more cautious, Hopkins telling Chamberlain in February 1933:

> "Whether we really are at the present time past the turning point and beginning to climb again to prosperity is very difficult to say. There are a certain number of indications in that direction . . . [but] it seems a doubtful assumption on which to base any large departure in policy." [164]

By September 1933, however, the Treasury noted:

> "Practically every economic signpost in this country now points to a slow but steady and sustained recovery . . . Despite the rejection of the public works programmes put forward by Mr. Keynes in . . . ["The Means to Prosperity" in March] the building industry is . . . doing very well." [165]

The government therefore saw no reason to change the economic policies it had adopted early in 1932. Cheap money continued through 1934 and 1935, while Chamberlain pressed on with his budgetary aims. By 1935 most of the Treasury's predictions in its "Old Moore's Almanack" of 1932 had been fulfilled. The officials had been right in predicting that by 1935 exports would not have recovered their 1929 level, that the gilt-edged rate of interest would be approximately the same as it would be when War Loan was converted, and that wage rates would be unaltered from their 1929 level. Hopkins and his colleagues had, however, been too optimistic about prices and unemployment. In consequence they raised their minimum unemployment figure upwards in mid-1934, when they put it, in the absence of a marked revival of international trade, at 1,500,000.[166]

Another consequence was a small change in the attitude of some of the Treasury officials to public works. Early in 1935 Fergusson, the Chancellor's Secretary, had after a meeting of several Treasury officials to explain to Chamberlain that Phillips and Hopkins had come to believe public works could have a part to play in the government's recovery policy. Hopkins thought that "the stage now reached in the general recovery is one at which an expansion of public borrowing would be useful for keeping up the impetus." According to Phillips, "the argument for public works [in the expanding areas of the country] is that the Government intervention on a limited scale may do something to accelerate recovery. Apart from certain industries such as housebuilding and the iron and steel industry the response to cheap money has lagged a little". Phillips also suggested public investment in the depressed areas, which were suffering from the permanent loss of exports, in order to "spread . . . over the whole country . . . a burden which has fallen with peculiar force on certain districts".[167] Although there was a small increase in 1935 in government assistance for investment in, for instance, suburban railways and shipbuilding,[168] cheap money naturally remained the dominant element in British economic policy. The Treasury would not contemplate a return to the gold standard or even temporary exchange stabilization in mid-1935 because:

"We have far more to lose, and are more likely to lose, from a setback in our internal recovery than we are likely to gain in the field of foreign trade."

. . .

"The country has, in the last two or three years, benefitted enormously from the liberal credit policy pursued by the Bank of England . . . having had to deal pretty closely with the people at the Bank for a long time, I am of opinion that once a definite exchange figure is named . . . their management of credit will be likely to become decidedly less liberal than at present."[169]

6

Rearmament and Recession

In 1935 the Committee on Economic Information wrote:

> "The whole fabric of our present prosperity is threatened by the likelihood
> of a decline culminating possibly in a virtual collapse of activity in the con-
> struction of new dwelling houses. . . . We may predict with confidence that
> before the end of 1938 Great Britain will again be faced with the problem
> of dealing with an apparently inevitable increase in unemployment . . . A
> substantial decline in building activity before the end of 1936 . . . will . . .
> become general before the end of 1937."[1]

In fact,

> "In . . . 1935–7, the pace of recovery was supported by its spread in the
> iron and steel industry and the addition of aircraft manufacture to the list
> of rapidly expanding new industries. These . . . changes were partly but not
> entirely due to the rearmament policy then becoming effective, an impetus
> that continued, and was indeed strengthened, after the general ebb of
> activity in 1937–8."[2]

This chapter will deal with rearmament, the recession, both predicted and actual, and
their implications for monetary policy 1936–8.

Rearmament Finance

Britain's rearmament in the 1930s was delayed by "the [government's] opinion that
the 'financial risks' already besetting the nation were more dangerous than the military
risks hanging over its head."[3] * A short White Paper on 4 March 1935[4] announced
the official policy of rearmament, but it went into practice only slowly, its first
effects being on the 1936 budget. When the Treasury officials began to prepare this
budget, they had to face the problem of financing the five-year rearmament programme, and their attempt to deal with this problem over the years 1936–8 sheds a

---

* Defence expenditure was at its lowest in 1932/3, £103m. In 1932 the Cabinet rescinded
the "ten-year rule" (that defence planning should assume there would be no major war
for ten years) but two years elapsed before, at the prompting of officials, it appointed
a Defence Requirements Committee of officials to "prepare a programme for meeting
our worst deficiencies". The Committee first recommended a programme costing a bare
£82m, and the estimates for the Forces in 1935/6 rose to all of £124¼m. It was not
until July 1935 that the government recognized this was not enough and allowed the
Committee to prepare a larger programme in which "financial considerations [were] to
be of secondary importance to the earliest possible security". It was not until 22 March
1938 that the Cabinet cancelled the assumption on which rearmament had hitherto

good deal of light on their attitude towards budgetary policy in the later 1930s. In December 1935 Warren Fisher, on reading the first memoranda on the problem by Phillips and Hopkins, noted: "It would seem . . . that 'sound finance' includes some regard for expediency, and is something short of the absolute law and prophets."[5] At this time the problem was the financing of a programme which was estimated to cost £1,038.5m over the five years 1936/7 to 1940/1.[6] Hopkins and Phillips advocated increasing taxation in 1936 and subsequent years so as to be able to provide from revenue in each year at least a sum equal to what would be the normal annual expenditure on defence after the rearmament programme had been completed in five years' time and the extra annual expense of the additional debt incurred during the five years. This was in the interests of "sound finance"[7] and was in the tradition of the McKenna rule of 1916, i.e. "we never borrow a pound without making provision by new taxation sufficient to cover both interest and sinking fund".[8] Fisher (who was a leading member of the Defence Requirements Committee) argued against increasing taxation in 1936 on the grounds that this might prejudice the public, dangerously blind to the menace of Hitler, against increased defence expenditure and thus jeopardise the rearmament the country desperately needed.[9]

In the 1936 budget Chamberlain, who had completed his 1932 budgetary plans the previous year, raised the standard rate of income tax from 4s 6d to 4s 9d, increased the tea duty by 2d and raised the Road Fund, and thus managed to balance (nominally) this budget.[10] This was, however, the last of his nominally balanced budgets, which had really only been attained by "abandoning every canon of Gladstonian finance, by reverting to a tariff system, by virtually suspending the sinking fund, by ingenious conversions of the National Debt, by non-payment of the loans from the U.S. and by such fiscal devices as the raiding of the Road Fund",[11] and which had in fact resulted, like Churchill's budgets in the 1920s, in small deficits. Rearmament was to increase these deficits in the following three years, despite further increases in taxation (see Tables 21 and 22, and Appendix 1, Tables 4A and 4B). Chamberlain in his 1937 budget raised the standard rate of income tax by a further 3d, and suggested a complicated new tax of his own devising on the growth of profits, the National Defence Contribution, which had to be abandoned in favour of a simple percentage tax on profits because of strong opposition in and out of the Commons.[12] Sir John Simon, who took over from Chamberlain as Chancellor of the Exchequer during the debates on the 1937 Finance Bill, increased the standard rate of income tax yet again in 1938, this time by 6d, and increased the oil and tea duties.[13]

As the estimates of the cost of adequate rearmament rose, for political and economic reasons, the Treasury's views on defence borrowing changed. In December 1935 the officials "contemplated that we should borrow for armaments as we went along

been based, that the course of normal trade should not be impeded. In October 1938 Chamberlain (now Prime Minister) and Simon (Chancellor) were still "suspect[ed of being] against thorough-going rearmament because of its effect on our foreign trade", and as late as January 1939 Fisher thought it necessary to remind Simon of "the grim realities" of Hitler's "reincarnation of Prussianism in the most sinister form that devil's creed has ever assumed".
(Hancock and Gowing, *British War Economy*, pp. 62–3, 68, 70; Hawtrey, "Defence Expenditure and the Budget"; T. Jones, *A Diary with Letters*, p. 418; T. 171/341, Fisher to Chancellor, "Budget 1939–40", 3 January 1939)

Table 21 *The problem for the Treasury*

	Defence expenditure		Changes in taxation		Total tax revenue	Surplus or deficit
	From revenue	under Defence Loans Act	First year	Full year		
1935/6	137	–	−6	−12	739	+3
1936/7	186	–	+16	+23	783	−6
1937/8	197	65	+15	+36	841	+29
1938/9	272	128	+30	+35	896	−13
1939/40 (estimated)	248	502	+24	+34	917	–

Source: Hawtrey, "Defence Expenditure & the Budget". The same table, with a couple of small alterations and the last line omitted, appears in Hancock & Gowing, *British War Economy*, p. 68.

Table 22 *The outcome for the economy*

	Defence expenditure at current prices £m	Defence expenditure as % of total government expenditure	Defence expenditure as % of G.N.P.	Government expenditure as % of G.N.P.
1930	119.2	10.4	2.7	26.1
1931	115.4	9.8	2.8	28.8
1932	110.4	9.7	2.8	28.6
1933	112.4	10.5	2.7	25.7
1934	118.9	11.2	2.7	24.5
1935	140.8	12.6	3.1	24.4
1936	183.0	15.4	3.8	24.7
1937	254.7	19.5	5.0	25.7
1938	473.2	29.8	8.9	30.0

Source: Peacock and Wiseman, *The Growth of Public Expenditure in the U.K.*, Tables A-15, A-17, and A-6.

	Total government revenue £m	Total government expenditure £m	Deficit or surplus £m
1930	872	882	−10
1931	874	906	−32
1932	912	886	+26
1933	881	836	+45
1934	878	828	+50
1935	890	867	+23
1936	921	907	+14
1937	987	989	−2
1938	1,036	1,145	−109

Source: Feinstein, *National Income*, Tables 12 and 34.

on Treasury Bills or other short-term securities, funding these into longer-term debt as it seemed expedient".[14] They also thought that if taxes were increased in the 1936 budget, borrowing could be postponed till 1937.[15] Hopkins explained the policy to the Chancellor in the following terms, first asking him to ask the rest of the Cabinet "to be careful to give no further currency to the talk which is going on about a Defence Loan".[16]

"In the first place we should delude ourselves if we looked upon the expenditure facing us as capital in nature. . . . So far as I can see the only ground for borrowing—though it may be a sufficient one—is that the expenditure places the Exchequer seriously in deficit *when the country is taxed to full capacity*, and the measure of the reasonable borrowing is provided by the amount of the deficit. It would be unfortunate if the Country began to think of a Defence Loan as a comfortable Lloyd Georgian device for securing not only larger forces but also lower estimates, Budget surpluses and diminishing taxation.

"In addition I doubt very much whether we shall ever see a Defence Loan of the kind which is discussed. When the Exchequer is short of money . . . [for any reason] . . . it borrows what it needs from week to week on Treasury Bills. When Treasury Bills become too numerous it makes a prosaic new issue of say 4% Consols and thereby converts some of its floating into long-term debt. This is the natural procedure: . . . there is no more case for the prior issue of a Defence Loan than there was a case for a National Prosperity Loan to finance another scheme recently in the public eye.

. . .

"In any event it would certainly be necessary that the whole of the expenditure should be voted in the ordinary way. If the Government had a general authority to spend a certain amount of borrowed money on Defence as it pleased without a Vote all Parliamentary control goes by the board."[17]

A year later, "[the] need to re-arm [was] already causing certain difficulties in connection with the Budget, the balance of payments, a shortage of certain kinds of skilled labour and of certain kinds of materials".[18] With respect to the budget, Phillips noted:

"The position is that we are budgeting for a deficit, that the pretence of producing a balanced budget is a fiction, and that there is no great technical difficulty in producing for a series of years budgets which are balanced at the end of the year to the nearest penny . . . Perhaps half a dozen financial writers in the country would understand from published accounts what was happening, but I doubt if any one of the half dozen is capable of making the position clear to the public.

"Nevertheless the fact remains that the unsoundness of the Budget exists only in that part of the Budget which relates to Defence expenditure. We do not want financial control weakened in respect of the non-defence services; on the contrary we want it to be stricter than ever. A series of completed Budgets which never showed a sizeable surplus (though they might show deficits due to failure to realise revenue estimates) would be very discouraging."[19]

The solution was (1) to make sure that the non-defence expenditure was covered by revenue, and to raise taxation for that purpose; and (2) to cover some of the defence expenditure by long-term borrowing. As for the balance of payments the Prime Minister (Baldwin) had in November asked Leith-Ross for a memorandum on the subject.[20] During its preparation Phillips made his views known. Unlike 1931 when an adverse balance of payments was "an extremely grave phenomenon because our gold reserves were very low", we could now, given our large gold holdings, "contemplate an adverse balance . . . of the order of £10m for ten years on end without turning a hair". Nonetheless, "there [was] a very strong case for taking any practicable measures to encourage exports" because healthy export industries would be needed to maintain employment once rearmament and the housing boom were over.[21] Leith-Ross also thought, and the Cabinet agreed, that the remedy for the adverse balance should be sought in increased exports. The Minister for Coordination of Defence (Inskip) told the Cabinet that he had been encouraging manufacturers of machine tools to maintain their exports to a considerable extent, and in cooperation with them had obtained some of our defence requirements from overseas suppliers.[22]

By this time the estimated cost of the five years' rearmament programme was up to £1,500m and Phillips thought the time had come to contemplate a fairly large long-term loan, £100m or £150m, early in 1937.[23] The Treasury began to prepare a Defence Loans Bill to enable it to borrow £400m of the £1,500m over the next five years.[24] The Governor of the Bank was not enthusiastic about borrowing specifically for defence: the market was not bright at that time (above p. 99) and he thought that the announcement in the Treasury's proposed Defence Loans Bill that the government was going to have to borrow £400m for defence "would have a depressing effect upon our credit". He saw Chamberlain on 4 February 1937 and told him:

> "He thought it most undesirable to state in advance the amount of money we proposed to borrow next year. This would have, he thought, the most damaging effects upon the market which would go utterly stale. The Chancellor told the Governor that for Parliamentary reasons it was absolutely essential to disclose the figure, and after a long debate there the matter was left."[25]

The Defence Loans Bill was introduced on 11 February 1937, and passed on 19 March. Under its authority the Treasury issued £100m 2½% National Defence Bonds 1944/48 in April 1937 and £81m 3% National Defence Loan 1954/58 in June 1938.

In December Phillips, fearing that interest rates would rise in the near future, had thought it "probably unwise to postpone borrowing unduly since we shall have to pay more for our borrowings later on".[26] In April the Governor told the Treasury that he thought that the present was not a bad time, because "the gilt edged market is bright following the Budget and would be better if the threat of Defence borrowing were out of the way".[27] The Chancellor agreed, on the advice of his officials, who thought "the Governor's advice must be taken on the point whether we borrow now or wait till autumn when the Governor thinks gilt edged prices may be worse".[28]

The second defence loan was suggested by the Governor in June 1938, but this time the Treasury quibbled over the amount of the loan. The Governor and Deputy Governor wanted £100m, the Treasury only £70 or £80m, because

> "It is true that other things being equal we always like to reduce the total of the Floating Debt and if we borrowed considerably in excess of requirements the surplus would simply decrease Treasury Bills. But with a decided recession in trade a reduction in the floating debt—which is taken by the market as a deflationary influence—is not very attractive."

Another reason against the larger issue was that it would cause a sizeable loss to the Issue Department of the Bank which would have to take up most of the stock initially.[29] Hopkins agreed with Phillips,[30] and Fisher added: "This is a question of the extent of borrowing by Government—not a matter for direction by the Bank."[31] The Chancellor opted for the smaller sum.

In the meantime the defence estimates had continued to rise, in spite of a review of the whole defence programme in June–October 1937 proposed by Simon at Chamberlain's instigation, and much talk in the Cabinet of dire consequences for the economy.[32] By June 1938 Phillips was warning:

"A short time ago we seemed at last to be getting a firm hold upon a ration, but it has slipped its leash once more and is for the moment almost lost to view. Very soon we shall have to renew the pursuit in earnest, but it is certain that Defence expenditure in 1939/40 will rise to a very high figure and probable that the £1,650 million for the five years will swell to some far greater amount. How we are going to finance it, and equally how we are going to finance the immensely increased cost of maintenance of the Forces after 1942, remains obscure."

He recommended the Chancellor ask other ministers to try to keep down civil expenditure.[33] The Chancellor did so on 20 July 1938, saying:

"It was clear that we could not continue indefinitely to borrow for defence. It followed that we could maintain our financial stability only in one or other of the following ways:

"First, that we should obtain an increase in the yield from taxation on the existing basis and no-one could reckon on this happening.

"Secondly, that we should obtain additional revenue by an increase in the rate of taxation, or by putting on new taxes.

"Thirdly, that we should reduce Civil Expenditure.

"He was deeply concerned lest our finances should become unmanageable as a result of the growth of expenditure.

"He suggested that when proposals for new expenditure were submitted, they should be considered from the point of view that another £25 millions represented 6d on the income tax."[34]

After the Munich crisis of September 1938 rearmament was accelerated and, as the Chancellor acknowledged, "it was clear that we should have to be prepared to face financial arrangements which we should not ordinarily contemplate as tolerable".[35] The 1939 budget was prepared accordingly,[36] and since the total sum needed to be borrowed was now £903m compared with the £400m authorized by the 1937 Defence Loans Act, another Bill to authorize the borrowing of another £400m (with the Treasury facing the "horrible prospect" of repeating the measure again in two years' time) was introduced.[37]

Before this last prewar stage was reached, the Treasury regarded the financing of the permanent charge for defence after the completion of the rearmament programme as more worrying than the present financing of the programme. This would mean "the work of balancing the budget [would] have to be done all over again". Balance in 1933–5 had only been achieved because taxation was high, interest rates and hence debt service was low, and there was no sinking fund.[38] Two things made this particularly worrying. One was the absence of a sinking fund since 1931:

"The unexampled difficulties of 1931 excused the abandonment of the sinking fund in that year and the solid rebuilding of our finances at a time when the finances of most other States remained in ruins has thus far excused its continued suspension. But it cannot remain indefinitely suspended without grave risks alike in peace and war. The end of the period of borrowing should be the beginning of the period of normal finance."[39]

The other was the severe slump that was forecast for the late 1930s and early 1940s·

> "So long as revenue is rising and unemployment is sinking and we can
> borrow what in reason we please, the real Budget problem is pushed into the
> background. But in four years borrowing powers will have lapsed, and one
> day (whether before or after that time) revenue will be falling, not rising,
> and unemployment will be rising, not falling. Then will come the day of
> reckoning."[40]

In the last stage what the Treasury was worried about was the effect on the pound,[41] a fear that was aggravated by the outflow of gold from the E.E.A. since May 1938.[42] However, though the Treasury was thus on the eve of the Second World War apparently still preoccupied with balancing the budget and with the effect of unbalanced budgets on government credit, there had been at least a change of emphasis, toward macroeconomic management and away from Gladstonian housekeeping. This becomes clearer when one considers the development of monetary policy in these years.

Monetary Policy 1936–8

For the first three or four years after the War Loan conversion and the related operations of 1932, the monetary authorities did not have to do anything to maintain cheap money except state their intention to do so. After 1935, however, the authorities were obliged, if they wished low interest rates and expansion of the money supply to continue, to be more active. This was the case partly for domestic reasons and partly because of events abroad and their repercussions on the Exchange Equalization Account.

On 25 September 1936 the French devalued the franc and the British, French and U.S. Treasuries announced their Tripartite Agreement. This failed, however, to stop the flight of capital from France which had begun when the left-wing Blum Government was elected in the spring of 1936. As a result of this and of the French repayment in gold of a £40m banking credit they had obtained earlier in the year to help support the franc, the E.E.A. had by the end of November 1936 gained so much gold that its sterling resources were threatening to run out by January 1937.[43] In order to avoid this, Phillips suggested reducing the fiduciary issue so that the E.E.A. could sell gold to the Bank of England without obliging the Bank to increase the note issue.[44] Selling gold to the Bank in order to obtain more sterling also avoided, of course, increasing the volume of Treasury bills.[45] The Governor wanted to solve the problem by letting the pound appreciate (which it would it the E.E.A. refused to buy any more gold).[46] The Treasury opposed this, so Hopkins told the Chancellor, because:

> "[It] . . . quite overlooks the effect on trade and on traders. To us it seems
> that it would be altogether wrong at this time to give a new impetus to im-
> ports and to impose further difficulties on exports because of a temporary
> crisis in regard to the movement of bad capital money . . . I am convinced
> that on economic no less than political grounds it is wrong to contemplate
> any serious increase in the value of the pound with unemployment at the
> present level. If unemployment were down to half its present level and cost
> of living and wages were rising inconveniently fast and gold were flowing
> into this country in a stream really beyond our capacity to manage, we
> might have to think about something of the sort. But we are no where near

that point and we may never come to it, and, if we did, there would be other measures to tackle first such as a real attempt to get foreign investment going again."[47]

On the other hand, Phillips was not in favour of increasing the resources of the E.E.A. (by selling gold to the Issue Department of the Bank) at the cost of expanding the note issue because the Bank had already taken £48½m of gold in this way since the beginning of the year and "that process cannot be repeated indefinitely without risking an over-issue of notes with the usual concomitant of sharply rising costs and prices". Another possibility, increasing the size of the E.E.A. by legislation, was ruled out simply because it "would be like taking a sledgehammer to a nut".[48] The Governor and the Chancellor agreed on Phillips' solution when they met to discuss the problem on 7 December 1936.[49]

The conflict for policy posed by the existence of unemployment and inflation was resolved for the Treasury by the forecast of a slump. The Committee on Economic Information and the Treasury both believed recovery had been initiated and sustained by cheap money and was dependent on the housing boom (above p. 118). In July 1934 Phillips wrote: "Our internal recovery has . . . been rather dangerously dependent on one single cause, the revival of private enterprise in building".[50] A year later the Committee on Economic Information, when trying to assess the economic outlook for the next few years, warned:

"No prediction can be made with greater confidence than that the present rate of housebuilding cannot be maintained . . . . Just as at one time an expansion of housebuilding offered the greatest hope for Great Britain's recovery from depression, so to-day the possibility of a decline in housebuilding must be one of the major sources of anxiety as to the continuation of the present recovery.

". . . It is extremely unlikely that the building of new houses can continue at its present rate for as long as three years . . .

"There is a grave danger that in 1937 or thereabouts this country may be faced with a crisis of the same magnitude as the last, but with one serious disadvantage in addition, namely, the saturation of that field of demand, which is most quickly responsive to a reduction in the rate of interest."[51]

On the basis of these predictions about housebuilding, the Committee's subcommittee on the Trend of Unemployment forecast an average unemployment percentage for the ten years 1936–45 of 15½–16.[52] Phillips, who had become a member of the Committee in October,

"thought that, at any rate as regards the next few years, the sub-committee were unduly pessimistic, and suggested that the results of the expansionist policy being pursued in America might lead to a considerable growth in the demand for labour in this country. Moreover, he was of opinion that there might be a tendency for expenditure in other branches of capital development in a manner which would compensate for any falling off in expenditure on housebuilding."[53]

Nonetheless, Phillips was in favour of the same advance measures to combat recession that the Committee recommended in its 18th and later reports, particularly the maintenance of cheap money throughout the upswing, the slowing-down of public investment in the upswing and the preparation of additional public works schemes to be put into operation as soon as the forecast recession began. At the end of 1936 and throughout 1937 Phillips advocated such measures to his Treasury colleagues, the Chancellor and the Cabinet. When the Committee on Economic Information, thanks to Keynes and over the objections of D.H. Robertson, advocated these measures most strongly in its 22nd report in February 1937, Phillips commented:

"This report raises in a definite manner questions of great importance. Broadly, the issues at stake are what we can do to prevent excesses during the boom period into which we are entering and what precautions we can take in advance with a view to mitigating the slump which we must in reason anticipate will follow the boom.

". . . The Committee produce a series of arguments, with which the Chancellor will be already familiar, to the effect that *the postponement at the present time of investment activity not of an urgent character would, on balance, prove beneficial to the average level of employment over a period of years.*

. . .

"The action that seems to be required is . . . the setting up of some interdepartmental machinery which can examine at once what the E.A.C. have said as to checking down capital expenditure other than expenditure on rearmaments, and report what measures in the field can be regarded as practicable." [54]

Hopkins, Fisher and Leith-Ross all supported Phillips' proposals and an interdepartmental committee under Phillips' chairmanship was set up. Unfortunately by the time it reported in August 1937 in favour of postponing appropriate public works schemes, recession was threatening to spread to Britain from America. A revised report by Phillips' Committee, advocating the preparation of additional public works schemes, then went to the Cabinet which agreed in January 1938 to act on the recommendations. [55]

One reason that the arguments of the Committee on Economic Information were familiar to the Chancellor was that Phillips had produced them in a memorandum he wrote at the end of 1936. This memorandum, which I have mentioned already (above pp. 123–4), began with the difficulties rearmament was causing for the budget, but in fact concentrated on the question of what to do, if anything, about the substantial rise in prices, particularly of raw materials, that had taken place during the year.

"Serious attention must . . . be drawn to the movements in the price level.

. . .

"We are now back to the average price level of 1930 and the present rate of increase would take us back within a year to a price level similar to that of 1928 or 1929, say 40 per cent higher than the price level of 1931, or even that of 1926 which was 48 per cent higher than 1931.

. . .

"The disadvantages of a great rise in prices are fairly obvious. It is gravely unjust to the owners of fixed incomes . . . The rising cost of living is almost as potent a factor as unemployment itself in producing social unrest and in providing a field for subversive propaganda . . .

"How far our export industries will be handicapped by rising prices will depend on the relative movement of prices in other countries . . .

"But the strongest objection to an unchecked rise in prices remains to be stated . . . The best precaution that can be taken against a slump is to secure that the previous boom is not allowed to reach a dangerous level.

". . . There is no reason why we should want to prevent prices rising to say 40% or perhaps even 50% over the 1931 level. But the dangers of an unchecked rise have been pointed out and we shall be very naive if we think that the rise will proceed up to the level we want and then stop . . .

"If we ever get fairly caught up in the vicious spiral of price rises continually forcing up wages and wage increases continually forcing up prices the only certain remedy would be to appreciate the pound i.e. by severe credit contraction to make the pound more valuable in terms of gold . . . This is the last remedy to be tried and it is to be hoped we shall never come to it.

"An increase of bank rate stands on a different footing. A normal level for the Bank rate is say 3½ per cent, anything much higher tending to have a depressing effect on industrial activity and prices. At present we have a Bank rate of 2 per cent, and even that is not made effective, the real short term interest rate being 1 per cent or less. This is an active element in raising prices rapidly. The first step will clearly be the return of bank rate to a normal level. It is quite true that a higher bank rate will check building and construction, tend to enrich the banks and cost the Government money. But when it is necessary to check expansion, a check there must be.

"The conclusion to be drawn from these considerations is as follows.

"Prices are now rising with some rapidity which is all to the good for the moment. But it is probable that the price level may be as high as we care to see it within twelve months and it is very highly probable that that will happen within two years. We must then face a rise in interest rates as not only necessary but desirable. I think that some step to increase bank rate will be needed by next Autumn and that it is likely to be up to 3½% or 4% in 1938.

"Nothing is certain but we have got to consider facts as they are, and this seems the rational conclusion from what we know at present."

However, though Phillips was thus contemplating the end of cheap money, he wished to postpone it for as long as possible because

"it is to be feared that the check when it comes may be most felt by the ordinary export industries associated with areas already suffering from depression. To serve those particular interests we should want cheap money indefinitely, but if we try to provide that the price situation in the country at large will get entirely out of hand. However necessary it may be to rearm quickly, it is clearly a most important factor in accelerating the rate at which prices are rising. It will force us quicker than would otherwise be the case to choose between continuing cheap money which is what the depressed areas want, and returning to normal methods of credit control which the condition of the country as a whole will certainly call [for] at not so distant a date."

The actual policy he recommended, therefore, was:

"So far as is practicable additional money should be raised for armaments by taxation."

and

". . . damping down all capital expenditure by public authorities except for urgent current needs or for depressed area development,"

because

(1) "the more we can deal with the possible dangers of rising prices and expanding activity by selective ad hoc measures the less need there will be of applying the harsh brake of a severe general credit contraction later," and

(2) "in any case one must expect some setback after the rearmament programme is completed and the building boom is over and it may not be too early to be thinking about the measures that will then be needed to maintain the volume of economic activity and the money income of the country." [56]

At the same time that Phillips's ideas were developing, interest rates were in fact rising *and* the Treasury was funding (above pp. 98–9, 101). Why, given there was, as Phillips admitted, "no case for raising interest rates at the moment or perhaps for almost a year to come",[57] did the Treasury persist in funding after interest rates had begun to rise? The answer is that the Treasury still, as late as 1939, "had no coherent theory of any relation between short and long rates".[58] This is very clear from several Treasury memoranda written at this time (early 1937). In July 1937 Phillips tried to explain to Neville Chamberlain what he thought determined interest rates.

"It is very difficult to set out the factors determining the rate of interest because so much of this business is irrational. For example (a) the business man looking to a profit of say 10 per cent on a new enterprise is not influenced much in his decisions by a change of ½, 1 or even 2 per cent in the gilt edged rate (b) interest rates are governed by what is in people's minds so that although the current rate may really be out of touch with current conditions it may be years and years before the adjustment comes.

"If there were no other disturbing factors the rate of interest, given the volume of savings, would be determined by the competition of general industry with State authorities, foreign borrowers and the building trade. The building trade *is* sensitive to movements in the gilt edged rate and cannot afford to pay more than a certain rate of interest. Thus if industry is prosperous what happens is that it bids the rate of interest high enough to make sure that it gets what capital it needs whoever else goes short.

"The interest rate is also affected by the trade cycle; subject to a time lag interest rates fall in a slump and rise in a boom. Taking the gilt-edged rate as 3¼ in 1875, it fell steadily with falling commodity prices to not much over 2¼ in 1897. Prices then rose with the greater gold output from the Transvaal and interest rates rose to something like 3½ in 1913. They were forced sky high by the War and did not really drop below 4½ until 1932.

"The great drop from that figure to say 3 per cent in January 1935 was due to the slump. Business was unprofitable, no one wanted to expand, and every important enterprise found itself with substantial working capital idle on its hands. It invested this money in gilt edged securities or alternatively kept it on deposit with its bankers (forcing those bankers to invest it in gilt edged). Since January 1935 the gilt edged rate has risen to about 3½%. Firms can use their working capital and have sold Government securities. The Banks are putting any new resources they get into advances to trade and not into gilt-edged securities. It is true that the Banks, being pretty flush with money, have not to any important extent liquidated the stock of gilt-edged securities they had already acquired but that will come along later. The depression continued so long that the appetite of industry for new capital for restoring, maintaining, and adding to its technical equipment will take a lot of satisfying.

"Prophecy about the future of interest rates is a rather gratuitous form of folly since as already noted the movements are often irrational. But there is a pretty strong presumption that the rate will get up to 4 per cent and it may go higher if there is anything in the way of an inflationary rise in prices." [59]

Therefore, when Keynes expressed concern for the effects of defence borrowing on interest rates,[60] Phillips wrote to the Chancellor:

"He [Keynes] argues that it is entirely a question of *management* at what interest rate the Government can borrow.

"On the whole we disagree with him. We do not think that experience during a boom will follow experience during a slump. In a great slump such as the 1931/32 period the effect of pumping money into the banks is that they are compelled to use it to buy gilt edged securities (having no other suitable outlet for their funds). This forces down the interest rate on gilt edged. But a similar experiment during a boom might have quite other effects, since there are then other profitable outlets for money, e.g. trade advances. That is not to say that we should not be glad to keep interest rates down if we saw a safe way but we doubt the possibility.

"He thinks we issue too many long term irredeemable stocks . . . . and that we should do better with redeemable stocks for periods up to say 15 years.

"It is quite arguable that he may be right *at the moment* but of course we can't indicate how we intend to borrow. As a general proposition, in view of the enormous *size* of our debt . . . , it is obvious that the only sound long term policy is the issue of the irredeemable stocks of which Keynes complains. If our debt fell due on the average once in say 15 years, we should have annual maturities to meet of over £400 millions, an appalling prospect.

"He argues that over a long future period, we ought not to expect the long term gilt edged rate of interest to be higher than 3 per cent, 'and, indeed, it should be lower'.

"Assuming there are no wars, this is quite an arguable proposition: it is much more likely to be true than his other proposition that the gilt edged rate can be kept down to 3 per cent in the few years covered by the armaments scheme." [61]

Before turning to the question of what actually happened to interest rates and the money supply in the years 1936–8, one should inquire into what the Bank was doing at this time. According to Clay,

"Until then [April 1937] Norman had taken advantage of the opportunity market conditions gave him to press on with the reduction by funding of the

Floating Debt. He had been concerned to preserve control of the volume of money, although the automatic safeguards provided by a fixed parity with an international standard had been lost. He had drawn the Committee of Treasury's attention to every symptom of incipient inflation—the danger of a multiplication of small industrial new issues which the abundance of money encouraged. He urged his friend the Chairman of the Stock Exchange to bring all the security business into his own recognised and properly organised market and to apply for a charter for the Stock Exchange."[62]

He also wrote to the Chairman of the Committee of London Clearing Bankers on 28 December 1936:

"I wish, if you please, to return to the subject [of the trend of Stock Exchange prices and the possible approach of overspeculation in London] because . . . I have noticed that during each of the last four months the aggregate figures for Bankers Loans to the Stock Exchange have shown a progressive and indeed disquieting increase.

"I suggest that the time has now come when this position should be considered by your Committee with a view to taking action. Your Committee would, I further suggest, be well advised to consider inter alia an increase by agreement in the margin for such loans, say, on industrial shares to 30% minimum and, say, on speculative (e.g. metal mining and oil) shares to 50% minimum.

"After consideration by your Committee will you kindly let me hear from you."[63]

He also kept Bankers Deposits at the Bank at the £100m at which they had been since the beginning of 1933.[64] In August 1936, the London and Cambridge Economic Service, observing some rise in Bankers Deposits and in the note reserve of the Banking Department of the Bank, thought it

"probable that we are witnessing another deliberate expansion of the cash base of the banking system, comparable to that which occurred in 1932 and 1933, and it seems that the Government, faced with the necessity of financing its increased expenditure, has no intention of allowing the rise in the note circulation to have any effect on the supply of credit. The 'cheap money policy' is still being energetically pursued."[65]

A month later they were forced to conclude that "the Bank of England evidently considers that Bankers' Deposits in the vicinity of £100m are adequate",[66] and at the end of the year they predicted that interest rates would rise in the coming year.[67] According to Clay, "The issue of the first National Defence Bonds in April 1937 marked a turning-point [in the Bank's policy]",[68] but though the need to finance rearmament may have caused Norman to consider a new government issue (above p. 124) there was apparently no change in his attitude to the cash base. By October 1938,

". . . bankers deposits are slightly higher than in 1937, but the increase is not very marked. A fair comment is that the cheap and plentiful money regime has been maintained, but no attempt has been made to counteract the recession by a fresh enlargement of the credit base."[69]

By this time the Bank like the Treasury was preoccupied with the problems of war finance.[70] The problem of the outflow of gold from the E.E.A. since May 1938 was

Chart 6 *Monetary series, monthly, 1935–8*
Source: See Appendix 1

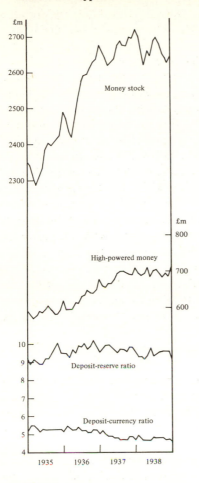

solved by the transference under the Currency and Bank Notes Act 1939 of the bulk of the Issue Department's gold to the E.E.A. (£200m on 6 January 1939 and the rest on the outbreak of the War), thus carrying "the revolution initiated by the suspension of the Gold Standard in 1931 . . . to its logical conclusion".[71]

Monetary Statistics and Interest Rates

These years saw a reversal of the trends in monetary statistics and interest rates that had characterized these series since 1932 (see Chart 6). Toward the end of 1936 the growth of the money supply began to slow down. In the first quarter of 1937 it fell quite sharply and though it recovered its December 1936 level by mid-1937, it grew little in the rest of the year, and fell over 1938. The result, in terms of quarterly averages, of these changes observed in the monthly figures, was that the money supply in the last quarter of 1938 was approximately the same as it had been in the last quarter of 1936 and the first two quarters of 1937, and at the end of 1937 it had

133

been only 3% higher than that level. High-powered money, however, continued to grow through the first half of 1937 and then just stopped growing. There was no decline, and then not a large one, until the third quarter of 1938. The deposit-reserve ratio, which had been growing through 1934, 1935 and the first half of 1936, fell slowly through the second half of 1936, 1937 and the first half of 1938. In July 1936 it was 10.0; in July 1938 it was 9.5. The deposit-currency ratio declined fairly steadily from a peak of 5.7 in January 1936 to 4.8 in August 1937 and then averaged, with little fluctuation, 4.9 for the rest of that year and the next. The behaviour of bank deposits was similar to that of the money supply. The growth of currency began to slow down in the second half of 1936; it continued to grow until the third quarter of 1937, after which it fell, but not by much, and the average for 1938 was £463m compared with £468m for the second half of 1937. Reserves continued to grow through 1936 and 1937 and the first quarter of 1938. Thereafter they fell, though not below the level of the second half of 1937. Therefore, the fall off in the growth of high-powered money was initially due to a fall in currency, which was only later, towards the end of 1938, reinforced by a fall in reserves, but the fall in the money supply, on the other hand, reflects both the slowdown in the growth of currency and deposits, and the falls in the deposit-currency and deposit-reserve ratios.

These developments all began well before the recession which occurred in the autumn of 1937. Long-term interest rates also began to rise slowly in 1936; short-term rates remained low. Two questions arise: Were the authorities responsible for these developments? Did these monetary developments have anything to do with the recession?

The most fundamental cause of the rise in interest rates in and after 1936 has been stressed by Nevin:

> "Although a very substantial credit expansion had been countenanced in 1932 in order to establish cheap money, credit was not subsequently expanded *pari passu* with the rise in the demand for active [money] balances so as to maintain the level of interest rates which had been achieved by the conversion operation of 1932." [72]

A major reason, again stressed by Nevin, why bank credit did not expand was the chronic shortage of bills, largely the result of the authorities' policy with respect to Treasury bills. In the second half of 1938 the banks faced the same difficulties with respect to secondary reserves as they had in 1933–4 and for the same reasons. [73] In between these times, the funding loans of 1936 and the defence loans of 1937 and 1938 had been keeping the volume of bills down. The authorities' policies can, therefore, explain the decline in the deposit-currency and deposit-reserve ratios in these years. What remains to be accounted for is the behaviour of currency.

I have described above (pp. 102–3) how, although the authorities may have wanted to maintain cheap money through the 1930s, even partly as a countercyclical policy, they had little or no wish to *extend* it in any way. The consequences of the Bank's non-expansionary policy with respect to the cash base eventually showed themselves in 1937. "The factor which eventually checked and reversed the accumulation of securities by the clearing banks appears to have been a shortage of cash rather than of liquid assets". [74] Nevin argues that this is shown by the following facts about the banks' behaviour:

(1) their investments fell in 1937 after rising since 1932;

134

(2) their advances continued to rise;

(3) their published cash ratio was close to the minimum throughout 1937;

(4) there was an increase in window-dressing.

As Nevin says,

> "The tightness of the bank's cash reserves, in other words, was forcing the banks to expand their advances only, firstly, by selling securities on a substantial scale, and secondly by operating on smaller reserves than the already hard-pressed reserves shown in the returns. The former action naturally affected the level of interest rates adversely; during 1937 Consols fell by more than 12%." [75]

The 1937–8 Recession

In 1936 the recovery from the slump changed its character, as contemporary commentators were quick to point out. In the early part of the year the London and Cambridge Economic Service was watching for signs of a collapse in building[76] but by June it could write:

> "The future of building remains a little obscure, since the statistics for successive months give different indications . . . [But] since the effect of the armament programme is still to be felt in industry, we may anticipate more confidently than before that employment as a whole will not fall, except for slight seasonal movements, during the next few months." [77]

Two months later, it observed: "The statistics of building plans indicate a check in the expansion of housebuilding, but a substantial increase in factory and other erections . . . The figures suggest a continuance of relatively high prices, and generally at least a partial approach to boom conditions".[78] *The Economist* summed up the year as the one in which "recovery bec[ame] worldwide"; for the U.K. it noted that "business activity . . . continued to expand rapidly, surpassing all previous records of aggregate production and employment". Both investment and consumer demand had increased markedly, and recovery was helped further on its way by an expansion in overseas trade, though imports had increased faster than exports so the trade balance became more adverse than it had been since 1931.[79]

A worldwide speculative commodity boom added to the pressure on prices in this year and the first quarter of 1937, but after March 1937 there was a sharp recession in wholesale prices all over the world, followed by a downturn in activity in the U.S.A. in the early summer.[80] In the U.K. recovery continued until the last quarter of the year. The National Bureau reference dates are May and September for the U.S. and the U.K. respectively. The British recession was preceded by both falls in wholesale prices and in share values in the early summer and a fall in exports later in the summer.

In June the "signs of hesitancy in recovery" in Britain[81] had caused the L.C.E.S. to write:

> "The most evident movement in recent months is the rapid fall in the value of stock exchange securities; since January our index has fallen about 12% back to its level at the end of 1935. In successive months the decline has been attributed to the Rearmaments Loan, to the belief that securities had been overvalued in anticipation of profits, to the National Defence

Contribution and its successor, and to the ambiguous position of gold. There has been no definite crisis and there is no expectation of a general collapse of values, but there is danger that if the present uncertainties continue there may be some slackening of investment and business."[82]

The fall in share prices in London in April 1937 came one month after the sharp fall in American stock prices and after a marked fall in the price of British government securities earlier in 1937. It coincided with the sharp fall in world commodity prices, precipitated by the "gold scare", i.e. the fears that U.S. President Roosevelt might lower the price of gold, and reaction to the preceding speculative boom.[83] The change in expectations undoubtedly affected the stock markets; in Britain there was also the effects of funding and a non-expansionary monetary policy on interest rates on long-term government securities and hence on other interest rates. The theory of the term structure and the data available certainly suggest funding was an influence (see Table 23 and Appendix 3). One has also to recognize that, as Clay puts it, although "the last of the funding issues, in November 1936, no doubt helped to depress long-dated issues . . . it was only one influence among others, the reaction from the new-issue boom of 1936 and the deterioration of international relations having also their effect".[84] The selling of securities by the banks in order to expand advances on low reserves (above p. 135) and the announcement of defence borrowing (above p. 124) were other contributory factors. In other words, there was an increase in the supply of long-term bonds at the same time as there was a fall in the demand for bonds, the increase in liquidity preference being the result of both monetary policy and a change in expectations. Expectations may also have been further hit by the announcement of the National Defence Contribution in the April 1937 budget.[85]

Table 23 *Estimated private sector holdings of national debt, by maturity class, as % of total private sector holdings, 31 March, selected years*

	Floating debt and debt under 5 years	Debt with maximum life of 5–15 years	Debt with maxium life of over 15 years or redeemable only at government option
1932	13.1	4.8	60.8
1933	10.7	7.8	61.2
1937	8.8	12.6	65.1

Source: Appendix 2, Table 2.

In mid-summer there was a fall in the sales of consumer durables in the U.K. One observer has suggested the reason was that consumers whose wealth had fallen as a result of the stock market decline became reluctant to purchase durables.[86] If this "wealth effect" on consumption of monetary factors contributed to a significant extent to the subsequent recession, then we have a monetary explanation of the 1937–8 recession. This is probably the only possible *monetary* explanation of the recession as the monetary developments of 1936 (above pp. 133–4) preceded the onset of the recession by a fairly long lag, longer than those found earlier in this study. Since expenditure on consumer durables had grown greatly over the preceding fifteen years,[87] it is possible that the size of such expenditure was by 1937 large enough that changes in it could have significant effects on the rest of the economy. By 1937 employment in the production of such goods also occupied a greater proportion of the total insured employed than ever before.[88] Stone's and Rowe's estimates of consumers' "net investment" in durable household equipment dropped in 1937 and the interwar peak in car sales in 1937 was followed by a severe recession in the car industry in 1938.[89] The fall in total expenditure on consumer durables from 1937 to 1938 was, however, less than the rise in 1936–7. Total expenditure on consumer durables was in the three years £387.4m, £412.3m and £398.9m.[90] More importantly, the fall in consumer durables expenditure was overshadowed by the fall in exports (see Table 24).

Table 24 *G.D.P. by category of expenditure, at constant prices, £m*

	Consumers expenditure	Public authorities current expenditure on goods & services	G.D.F.C.F.	Value of physical increase in stocks	Exports of goods and services	Total final expen- diture	Imports of goods and services	G.D.P.
1936	4,285	562	565	−6	771	6,177	987	5,190
1937	4,357	627	584	56	810	6,434	1,003	5,411
1938	4,392	749	592	83	757	6,573	1,001	5,572

Source: Feinstein, *National Income*, Table 5

In the textile industry "a few were cognizant that in the summer of 1937 productive activity was running well ahead of new orders, and anticipated that a downturn would occur soon. Their expectations materialized in the late summer."[91] The L.C.E.S. noted a fall in exports in August[92] and then "the October statistics . . . indicate[d] a slight recession" because unemployment was slightly up and imports and exports were both down.[93] Quarterly export figures show a fall off in exports to the U.S.A. in the third quarter and in total exports in the fourth quarter of 1937. In other series indicative of domestic activity the downturn came later, e.g. pig iron production in January 1938, electricity usage in February 1938, and steel output in March 1938.[94] Phelps Brown's and Shackle's series for employment in various groups of industries show that export-sensitive employment reached its highest point and began to fall sharply in the spring, while other employment had its highest point in late summer. Employment in consumer durables industries did not reach its peak until almost the end of 1937.[95] One thus does not see in the data what one should see if a fall in expenditure on consumer durables was a cause of the onset of the recession, namely an early fall in employment in consumer durables production. Phelps Brown and Shackle compared the turning-points in different categories of employment in 1929 and 1937:

1929	1937
March: export-sensitive	April: export-sensitive
July: consumers durable	September: consumers non-durable
October: producers durable and consumers non-durable	October: producers durable
	October–November: consumers durable

As they remark, "the lags between export-sensitive and producers durable are remarkably similar . . . in length" in 1929 and 1937.[96] So it would seem that the hypothesis that the 1937–8 recession originated in America and spread to Britain via its direct and indirect repercussions on British exports is better supported than the "monetary" hypothesis.

Richardson has argued that "the recession of 1937–8 was as much due to internal causes as to depression abroad". He is not, however, thinking of a monetary explanation on the grounds that "obviously [?] because money remained cheap despite the slight hardening of interest rates, the ceiling could not be a monetary one". In support of his thesis he cites (1) the behaviour of import prices, (2) labour shortages in key investment and heavy industries, (3) rising labour costs and falling profits, and (4) a change in expectations. However, as he admits, the causes of (1), (2) and (4) were the worldwide commodity boom and rearmament at home and abroad.[97] As for (3), the fact that annual figures show a fall in profits in 1938 over 1937 does not tell us anything about the causes of the recession: since nine months of 1938 and only three months of 1937 were periods of recession one is bound to observe lower profits in 1938. Similarly, at least some of the smaller increase in the % year-over-year changes in profits in 1936–7 compared with 1937–8[98] can be put down to the fact that 1936 was all boom and some of 1937 was recession. More of this fall in the rate of growth of profits can be accounted for by the rapid rise in prices in 1936 compared with 1937. The difference between the year-over-year profit changes in % terms is actually not as marked in Feinstein's figures as it is in the ones (Hart's) that Richardson uses.[99] Feinstein's figures also show that the share of profits in income continued to rise, and the share of wages continued to fall, until 1938.[100] The rate of growth of the share may have been declining, but it is difficult to argue on the basis of the available profit figures that the boom could not have continued beyond the end of 1937 if the American recession had not occurred.

The recession was both mild and shortlived. Some sectors were hit harder than others,[101] but there was no fall in real gross domestic product from 1937 to 1938, and the only falls in the annual aggregates were in exports and imports (see Table 24).

By April 1938 a slowing down of the decline in activity was observed[102] and though there were few signs of a definite upturn before the end of the year, there were few signs of any further deterioration either. In December there was still "no indication of any rapid change for the better or for the worse",[103] but looking back one can locate a lower turning point in or about September 1938. It was in 1938 that rearmament expenditure began to exert its full impact on the economy (see Table 20), and in February 1939 *The Economist* recorded:

> "The recession in progress at the beginning of 1938 has . . . been checked in most countries in the course of the year. In the United States public spending on a large scale made the wheels of commerce turn faster; in the United Kingdom and many other European countries deterioration was checked by increased public spending but on guns instead of butter."[104]

By assuming that £1m expenditure on capital goods would provide about 4,000 to 5,000 man-years direct and indirect employment Bretherton, Burchardt and Rutherford estimated that loan-financed defence expenditure provided 300,000 man-years of additional primary employment in 1937 and almost double that figure in 1938. Assuming further a multiplier of 1.5 or 2, they estimated that if deficit-financed defence expenditure had been the same in 1938 as in 1937, unemployment would have been in the neighbourhood of 2½ million rather than the 1.8 million that actually occurred. If there had been *no* deficit-financed defence expenditure in 1938 unemployment would on their assumptions have been as high as three million. "The depression would thus have become more severe than that of 1932 and presumably would have been increased in length too."[105]

Although the U.S. economy began to revive in the summer of 1938, U.K. exports did not show any marked improvement, for in a "disintegrating world economy"[106] there was little scope for an increase in international trade. Although cheap money was maintained at least partly because of the recession, it did not in fact do much to mitigate the recession, for just as the authorities had allowed bank deposits and the money supply to fall before the recession, so they allowed further falls during the recession, and at the time that economic activity was picking up again they were letting reserves and hence high-powered money fall too (above p. 134). In justification of the authorities' attitude it can be said that the Treasury did not expect cheap money to bring about recovery from a slump in the late 1930s, for, anticipating an end to the building boom and thus a situation in which housing investment could not be stimulated much by cheap money, it believed, as the Committee on Economic Information did, that increased government expenditure would be necessary to combat the slump that would ensue when housebuilding fell off (above pp. 127–30). Appropriate countercyclical public works, though eventually accepted by the Cabinet (above p. 128) did not in fact get under way during the recession, rearmament having put an end to the recession first. Thus increased public expenditure, albeit not the kind advocated by the economists, did indeed combat the slump.

7

Conclusions

In this study I have attempted both to explain why the authorities adopted particular monetary policies and to analyse the effects of their policies. The conclusions therefore relate to both sets of questions.

First of all, one of the most notable features of British monetary policy in the interwar years is that the authorities' conception of monetary management changed over the two decades. This is reflected in the reorientation of monetary policy immediately after the abandonment of the gold standard. Another notable feature is the persistence of the Treasury's "funding complex" throughout the same period.

In the 1920s the dominant objective of monetary policy was the restoration, and then the retention, of the gold standard at prewar parity. Believing that this one policy would achieve several objectives simultaneously, the authorities elevated this policy instrument into the object of policy. In the policy documents of the 1920s the monetary authorities were not inclined to make their goals explicit, but as Moggridge points out, the evidence suggests that their implicit goals were:

(1) prewar average employment;
(2) a surplus on the current account of the balance of payments in order to allow unrestricted overseas lending and the maintenance of Imperial commitments;
(3) free trade with the minimal pre-1931 exceptions;
(4) the maintenance of London as a leading international financial centre.[1]

To this one should add the avoidance of inflation, since this was very important in the immediate postwar years. Thus "the overall goal of the authorities might be accurately summarised as the maintenance, as far as possible, of the pre-1914 position".[2] The smooth working of the international gold standard with London at its centre had been an essential element in the maintenance of Britain's prewar prosperity, so the authorities (and others) took it for granted that the restoration of the gold standard was a prerequisite for the restoration of prewar standards of prosperity.[3] They saw the problems of the British economy in the early 1920s as stemming primarily from the disruptions caused by the Great War, and the appropriate monetary policy as one which would contribute most to removing war-induced obstacles, rather than one designed to cope with a permanently changed situation.

The long-run nature of the economic theories held by, for instance, Niemeyer reinforced this attitude on the part of the policy makers. Thinking in terms of a simple quantity theory of money and initially ignoring the adjustment problems of the short run, the policy implication of the proposition that output and employment were determined in the long run by real forces—the productivity of labour, the volume of saving, etc.—was that the government and the monetary authorities should

140

provide a stable framework within which these forces could be allowed free play. Given Britain's dependence on foreign trade this also meant helping to create a stable international system and prosperity for Britain's customers. Inflation was a source of instability (and social unrest) and it would also reduce Britain's competitiveness. It was also a monetary phenomenon, that is, while "real" variables such as output and employment were determined by the "real" forces of productivity and thrift, the price level of output as a whole was determined in the long run by the quantity of money in existence. The task of monetary policy was, therefore, to prevent inflation. The gold standard would assist in this since the use of Bank rate to keep the exchanges at par would nip incipient domestic inflationary tendencies in the bud. It would not prevent a rise in domestic prices if world prices were increasing, which they would be if the world supply of gold (or reserve currencies) were increasing. Furthermore, if Britain adopted the gold exchange standard and sterling were a reserve currency, then in situations where domestic deflation was required the short-run problems of adjustment would be lessened. The short-run problems involved in the restoration of the gold standard were not, therefore, regarded as necessarily severe.

As for the trade cycle, trade depressions would occur from time to time, as they had done before the War. But these too, given the appropriate institutional arrangements, in particular "the discipline of the gold standard" backed up by sound government finance, would go away of their own accord, that is *without a specifically countercyclical policy*. Given that Bank rate was used to protect the exchanges, money could be cheapened in times of depression if the exchange situation permitted, but this was not actually necessary since interest rates would fall in depression anyway and Bank rate would probably be merely following other rates down. Niemeyer could, therefore, at the bottom of the postwar slump argue that

> "The best assistance the State can give to the unemployed . . . is . . . to reduce its expenditure and . . . to repay its debts.
>
> . . .
>
> "The problem is while giving the minimum assistance necessary to prevent starvation to do as little as possible to create permanent employment by maintaining uneconomic prices."[4]

Whereas prewar unemployment policy proposals such as the Liberals' Development Act of 1909 "rarely came into collision . . . with a conscious and articulate Treasury point of view",[5] in the 1920s the Treasury men were certainly articulate and used their "view" to oppose active unemployment policies.[6]

Thus not only did the restoration of the gold standard close many avenues to policy makers,[7] but also the adoption of that aim meant that the authorities saw no need for any policies other than the "sound finance" needed to achieve that aim. With such an all-powerful instrument, it is hardly surprising that it should become an end in itself.

However, thanks to the overvaluation of the pound (at least relative to the authorities' goals).[8] things did not turn out as the policy makers hoped or expected. After the return to gold, "unemployment remained stubbornly high, at levels well above the prewar average, sterling suffered from fairly continuous exchange pressure, London's short-term financial position deteriorated . . . and Britain's international competitive position weakened as unit costs fell as fast or even faster abroad".[9] The authorities had to make the best of this situation. Under the gold standard regime the relevant authority was the Bank of England, the Treasury's role being to look after the government's finances. The Bank was, however, imperfectly insulated from political pressures, and the Treasury's increasing concern with the problem of unemployment resulted in Norman's sparing use of Bank rate and his experimenting with short-term palliatives. In other words by the end of the decade the authorities had manoeuvred themselves into a position where not only had their major policy instrument become the goal but also they had few instruments available to help them in achieving this goal, let alone others.

The monetary authorities' dilemma became acute when the world slump hit the British economy. The Bank tentatively tried the one measure consistent with its principles, cheaper money, but the attempt could only be half-hearted with an over-valued pound and a commitment to defend the pound at that rate. The Treasury could only attempt to make finance even sounder while the official policy was to stay on the gold standard.

In September 1931 the authorities gave up the struggle. The Treasury then came into its own. Responsibility for monetary policy initially reverted to it automatically, since only the government could take Britain off gold, but the Treasury retained responsibility thereafter, since by then under the impact of events and also partly because of a change in personnel, the Treasury view of the role of monetary policy had changed radically. The officials immediately began to consider the very matters that had not been important considerations in 1925, the choice of an exchange rate and criteria for the management of sterling.[10] The new attitude also manifested itself in a willingness to consider Keynes's views seriously and sympathetically. The results of the discussions of the winter of 1931−2 were the recommendation that the government not commit itself to a return to gold, the setting up of the Exchange Equalization Account, and the introduction of cheap money. The last was essentially a countercyclical policy: the currency was going to be managed, externally and internally, so as to get Britain out of the depression. Even if long-term interest rates would eventually fall of their own accord, the Treasury was determined that it would do all it could to get them down quickly.

The Treasury was thus aware that as the Macmillan Committee suggested, "in the case of our financial, as in the case of our political and social, institutions we may well have reached the stage when an era of conscious and deliberate management" was essential.[11] While the currency had been managed in practice in the 1920s, the principle was not then accepted, as the gold standard was supposed to be "automatic". In line with this acceptance of the principle of a managed currency went an awareness of the distinction between goals and instruments. This was initially largely a reaction to the mistaken optimism of the 1920s. The Treasury officials were now not only quite justifiably pessimistic about the efficacy of using one instrument but also, less justifiably, about the attainable goals, setting themselves targets which were low not only in relation to post-1945 experience but also pre-1914 experience.

Early in 1932 the Treasury officials explicitly stated the goals of their monetary policy and the targets they expected to reach by 1935. They wished to: (1) raise prices to their 1929 level, on the assumption that wages would remain at their 1924 level, so as to increase profits and hence output and employment; (2) reduce unemployment to its 1927 "level" of 1,200,000 on the assumption that British exports would not have recovered to their pre-depression levels; and (3) arrest the decline in exports. The means they chose to promote these ends were cheap money for (1) and keeping the pound down for (3); these together, in conjunction with first a confidence-creating balanced budget and (later) suitably restrained public works, would bring about (2). The remaining unemployment was not cyclical in character and would need further measures. For instance, early in 1935, after the Treasury had revised the estimate of "permanent" unemployment upwards, Phillips suggested public works in the depressed areas; in other years he and his colleagues advocated relaxation of the embargo on overseas loans to promote exports.

Although the Treasury officials became more pessimistic about future levels of unemployment as the 1930s went on, they became more willing to try different policy instruments. This reflected important changes of view on what monetary and fiscal policy could be expected to achieve, changes which are particularly apparent in the documents relating to the issue of public works. In 1930 Hopkins provided a classic statement of the "Treasury view" of public works to the Macmillan Committee; in 1932-3 the Treasury position on the issue was similar but less dogmatic. Although at this time they rejected the suggestion of economists such as Keynes, Henderson and Pigou that additional public expenditure be encouraged in order to back up the cheap money policy, Phillips and Hopkins were a little over a year later prepared to recommend such a step.[12] By the end of 1936, when another slump was widely forecast to begin within a year, Phillips, like Keynes, wanted to maintain cheap money as a weapon for the slump, to cope with the current inflationary tendencies by other measures such as raising taxes, and to prepare a countercyclical public works programme.[13] The arguments Phillips and Hopkins used reflect a belief that the government should assume some responsibility for maintaining aggregate demand; the government was urged not only to postpone non-urgent capital expenditure in the boom but also to endeavour to find new projects to be started in the slump.[14] Phillips and Hopkins are the important figures in this development. Phillips began to be the major author of the (new) "Treasury view" during the discussions on exchange policy in 1931-2; Hopkins was perhaps less of a "theoretician" than Phillips, but he had a pragmatic approach[15] and was prepared to be persuaded by Phillips' arguments, and once persuaded, to advocate policy innovations to the Chancellor. Phillips' solutions to the problems that the Treasury was set by the events of the 1930s included some of the major innovations in Treasury policy. Although at the time "there was no great confidence that any of the measures so far devised would do more than lead to some mitigation of the evil of severe unemployment",[16] these innovations were to be built on during and after the Second World War as the Treasury developed economic management on Keynesian principles.[17]

The new measures devised lay in the field of debt management as well as in monetary and budgetary policy. In this field, however, the development of new technical skills was in pursuit of the traditional objective, funding the debt at all opportune times. The departmental "underwriting" of new issues, for instance, served to make more times opportune, which was unfortunate given the impact that most of the government issues had on the economy. In the immediate postwar years debt management reinforced the Bank's (and the Treasury's) deflationary monetary policy. In the gold standard years, while the Bank was unable to carry out a strongly deflationary monetary policy, the Treasury's policy with respect to the debt served to exert a deflationary impact by keeping interest rates high, although at the same time the Treasury wanted to see rates come down. The authorities managed to use debt management to bring interest rates down in 1932 by converting 5% War Loan but thereafter they took the opportunity of low interest rates to fund short-term debt and reduce the amount of Treasury bills held by the market, thereby helping to raise interest rates again.

This brings me to the second set of questions, the impact of interwar monetary policy on the economy. I can summarise the findings about the causes of the interwar business cycles in Britain very briefly: while the first postwar cycle was domestically but not solely monetarily determined, the slump of 1929 and probably the recession of 1937 came from abroad. Both were eventually counteracted by government policy, the first by monetary policy, the second by increased government expenditure (on rearmament). The causal role of monetary policy in the cycles depended, not surprisingly, on the way in which it was being used. In 1920 though the authorities imposed dear money in an attempt to curb the boom, their hesitation meant that it failed to do that because it came too late. In the second chapter of this study I attempted to explain the reasons for and the immediate consequences of the dear money policy adopted at the end of 1919. Although I argued there that the Bank rate rise did not cause the boom to break in April 1920, and that it was only one of many factors contributing to the severity of the ensuing slump, one cannot judge the full effects of the policy without taking into account the effects of its continuation throughout the 1920s and its effect on the Treasury's attitude to the debt in both interwar decades.

In the early 1920s the dear money policy was intended to assist in the restoration of the gold standard. If one regards the restoration as "hasty" and/or ill-conceived, and if the pre-1925 monetary policy hastened the restoration, then one could argue that a less restrictive monetary policy would have been a "good thing" on those grounds alone. There are some difficulties with this line of argument, however, in particular the other developments which hastened the restoration,[18] but if the authorities could have regained the gold standard with a less restrictive monetary policy, then at least the economy would have been spared the deflationary influence of the policy actually pursued.

As well as aggravating the postwar slump, monetary policy *plus* debt management helped to keep the economy in the doldrums for the rest of the decade. There were of course other depressing factors, notably the consequences of the gold standard for the balance of payments, which at the least exacerbated the long standing difficulties of the staple export trades, but the evidence suggests a more expansionary monetary policy might have mitigated some of the other factors. Even if the Bank of England did not manage to control the money supply because its pressure on high-powered money was offset by rises in the banks' deposit-reserve ratios, it did keep short-term interest rates high, and even if these did not keep long rates up, the Treasury's debt operations would have tended to work in that direction. The persistently high interest rates were unfavourable to investment, particularly in a situation where a fall was expected. One result was that long-term investment in, for instance, housing was effectively postponed until the 1930s. This does not mean, however, that an aggressively expansionary policy ought to have been instituted in, say, 1927 or 1928. There is the problem that the effect of the world slump on the expectations of entrepreneurs encouraged to be optimistic only two years earlier might have been so shattering that investment would not subsequently have revived to the extent that it did with cheap money after 1932; there is also the problem of the balance of payments constraints that expansion might have run into.[19] But these problems do not justify the addition to the high Bank rate policy of a debt management policy which would of itself raise long-term interest rates.

In the 1930s, once the government had thrown off the shackles of the gold standard, the Treasury's cheap money policy fulfilled its intended purpose and served to initiate the housing boom and hence general recovery. Again, there were other factors operating, which could have set off recovery in other sectors in 1933–4, but in fact the first impulse was a substantial increase in housing starts, which occurred in 1932 in response to the change in expectations engendered by the new monetary policy.

In the initial phase of recovery debt management was working in the same direction as monetary policy. As the Treasury pressed on with funding this ceased to be the case, and the maintenance of cheap money was threatened by the Treasury's "counter liquidity preference"[20] even when the Treasury had accepted the idea of countercyclical economic management. The experience of 1920 can indeed be said to have cast a long shadow over interwar economic policy. The cheap money policy was also left to operate in nonexpansionary fiscal conditions: some of the blame for the very high levels of unemployment must be laid on the budgets of the 1930s. Although economic management in the 1930s was a considerable improvement over that in the 1920s, and a wider range of instruments was used, its potential was not fully utilized because policy instruments were not coordinated with one another.

Appendix 1

Statistics

1. Currency in Circulation

A consistent series of monthly figures for notes and coin in circulation in Great Britain and Ireland 1919–38 has been provided by the Bank of England. The figures for 1919–25 have previously been published in Pigou, *Aspects of British Economic History 1918–1925*, pp. 241–2; those for 1931–8 in *BESS*, January 1939. The annual averages of these figures differ from the annual figures for currency in circulation in the U.K. given by Sheppard, *The Growth and Role of U.K. Financial Institutions 1880–1962*, Table (A) 3.2, because they cover Southern Ireland as well as Great Britain and Northern Ireland.

2. Bank Deposits and Reserves

The monthly figures for ten London Clearing Banks 1919–30 come from the Macmillan Report, Appendix 1, Table 1; those for 1931–8 from the *BESS*. The *BESS* figures for 1937 and 1938 cover eleven banks because the District Bank joined the London Clearing House on 1 January 1936. The 1937 and 1938 figures used here have, therefore, been reduced by an estimate of the District Bank's deposits and reserves formed on the basis that in 1936, for which the *BESS* gives figures for both ten and eleven banks, the ten banks' average reserves and deposits amounted to 97% of those of the eleven banks. Deposits include both current and deposit accounts. The latter are "a curious species: they are like short-term loans because they pay interest, but with continuous recontract, and they are like money because they can be used to purchase things at any time, the usual custom being to deduct seven days' interest" (Goodwin, "Studies in Money", p. 157). They are included here because the banks make no distinction between the two classes of deposits for reserve purposes. The two classes behave differently over the cycle, but where I have wished to take this into account (above pp. 46–7, 67, 99) I have relied on Goodwin's study which has separate series. The data here are not seasonally adjusted; again Goodwin does provide such series. The reserve figures are "window-dressed"; on this see above pp. 45–6.

  My "money supply" is the sum of the monthly figures for currency in circulation and the monthly figures for the total deposits of ten London Clearing Banks, and is therefore only a proxy for the true money supply of the U.K. Sheppard's annual money supply series is superior because his currency figures are for the U.K. and his figures for bank deposits cover all U.K. commercial banks plus private deposits at the Bank of England and minus an estimate of interbank deposits (*The Growth and Role of U.K. Financial Institutions*, Table (A) 3.3). His data thus have the advantage of covering the same geographical area as the national income accounts for 1920–38. I have chosen to use the available monthly data because the London Clearing Banks accounted for, on average, 78% of total bank deposits in the U.K. in the interwar years, because I am not using econometric techniques, and most importantly because monthly data are more useful in the study of business cycles.

The "money supply" and its proximate determinants, high-powered money and the deposit-reserve and deposit-currency ratios (see p. 7), are plotted monthly in Charts 1, 2, 5, 6 and 7; quarterly averages of these monthly figures and their components are given in Table 1 below. The charts show the discrepancy between the figures for bank deposits in 1931 given to the Macmillan Committee and the figures for the same year published later in the *BESS*. There is unfortunately no obvious way of making the series consistent.

3. Interest Rates

A wide variety of series are available, of which I have tried to provide a reasonable selection. Table 2 below gives quarterly averages of the yield on 2½% Consols (the "long rate"), the three months Treasury bill rate, an average of the three months commercial bill rate and the rate on day-to-day money (the "average short rate"), and the "yield gap" calculated as the difference between the average short rate and the long rate. Tables 3A and 3B give quarterly averages of the indices of security prices and yields published monthly in the L.C.E.S. *Bulletin*. In the text tables will be found annual figures for Bank rate, Treasury bill rate, average short rate, the yields on short-term government securities as given in the L.C.E.S., *Key Statistics 1900−1970*, the yield of 2½% Consols, the yields on new debenture and preference share issues, and building society deposit and mortgage rates. The rates are all nominal rates; I have not attempted to estimate real rates because of the difficulty of estimating expected rates of change of prices.

4. Government Accounts

I have used Feinstein's figures for central government current and capital accounts and local authority current accounts for calendar years (*National Income, Output and Expenditure of the U.K. 1855−1965*, Tables 12, 13, 14 and 34). I have also provided Table 4B below to indicate the magnitude of sinking fund operations in the interwar years. The sources of information for other debt management operations are the indispensable Pember and Boyle, *British Government Securities in the Twentieth Century*, and the Treasury records (see Tables 1 and 11 in the text and Appendix 2).

5. National Income Accounts

Data on the components of national income and on industrial production comes from Feinstein, *National Income, Output and Expenditure of the U.K. 1855−1965*; details of investment and consumption from Feinstein, *Domestic Capital Formation in the U.K. 1920−1938*, and from Stone and Rowe, *The Measurement of Consumers' Expenditure and Behaviour in the U.K. 1920−1938*.

6. Prices, Wages, Unemployment

I have used the Board of Trade wholesale price indices for 1920−34 (1913 = 100) and 1930−8 (1930 = 100), the index of wage rates given in Feinstein, *National Income*, Table 65, and the Ministry of Labour figure for the percentage unemployed among workers insured under the government unemployment insurance scheme. The first and last of these four series begin in 1920 and 1922 respectively; for the earlier years I have used the information in Pigou, *Aspects of British Economic History 1918−1925*, pp. 234 and 221.

Table 1 *Monetary statistics, quarterly averages of monthly figures, 1919–38*

		M £m	D £m	C £m	R £m	H £m	D/C	D/R
1919	I	1,800	1,406	394	193	587	3.6	7.3
	II	1,928	1,505	423	254	675	3.6	6.7
	III	1,934	1,517	418	206	624	3.6	7.7
	IV	2,039	1,615	424	212	636	3.8	7.8
1920	I	2,111	1,695	416	183	599	4.1	9.3
	II	2,129	1,699	430	191	624	3.9	9.1
	III	2,154	1,718	436	181	616	3.9	9.5
	IV	2,198	1,766	432	204	630	4.1	8.8
1921	I	2,162	1,744	418	194	613	4.2	8.9
	II	2,132	1,726	406	210	616	4.2	8.3
	III	2,147	1,756	391	202	593	4.5	8.7
	IV	2,182	1,789	393	222	609	4.5	8.0
1922	I	2,138	1,766	372	201	573	4.8	8.2
	II	2,098	1,729	369	205	574	4.7	8.5
	III	2,031	1,672	359	193	555	4.6	8.7
	IV	2,021	1,663	358	203	561	4.7	8.2
1923	I	1,973	1,625	348	187	534	4.7	8.7
	II	1,927	1,571	356	191	547	4.5	8.4
	III	1,955	1,600	355	188	543	4.5	8.5
	IV	1,981	1,628	353	196	553	4.6	8.2
1924	I	1,965	1,616	349	188	537	4.6	8.6
	II	1,976	1,616	360	196	552	4.5	8.3
	III	1,967	1,606	361	184	545	4.5	8.7
	IV	1,979	1,623	356	201	557	4.5	8.1
1925	I	1,954	1,607	347	184	532	4.6	8.6
	II	1,949	1,595	354	193	547	4.5	8.2
	III	1,938	1,597	351	184	535	4.5	8.7
	IV	1,962	1,612	350	196	546	4.6	8.2
1926	I	1,926	1,585	341	183	524	4.5	8.7
	II	1,940	1,588	352	193	544	4.5	8.3
	III	1,959	1,612	347	186	536	4.6	8.7
	IV	1,994	1,650	344	194	539	4.8	8.5
1927	I	1,970	1,635	335	184	519	4.9	8.9
	II	1,993	1,648	345	198	543	4.8	8.7
	III	1,998	1,653	345	184	530	4.8	9.0
	IV	2,048	1,699	349	196	548	4.9	8.8
1928	I	2,012	1,678	334	179	516	5.0	9.4
	II	2,034	1,687	347	186	523	4.9	9.1
	III	2,059	1,715	344	185	529	5.0	9.3
	IV	2,098	1,757	341	206	544	5.2	8.7
1929	I	2,078	1,744	334	186	520	5.2	9.4
	II	2,075	1,731	344	186	530	5.0	9.1
	III	2,078	1,735	343	178	522	5.0	9.8
	IV	2,083	1,743	340	199	539	5.1	8.9
1930	I	2,022	1,690	332	176	508	5.1	9.6
	II	2,074	1,732	342	190	532	5.1	9.1
	III	2,092	1,750	342	184	526	5.1	9.6
	IV	2,131	1,791	340	203	543	5.3	8.9
1931	I	2,151	1,819	332	191	522	5.5	9.6
	II	2,092	1,752	340	182	521	5.2	9.7
	III	2,090	1,745	345	179	524	5.1	9.7
	IV	2,073	1,722	351	177	525	5.9	9.7

Table 1 (*continued*)

	M £m	D £m	C £m	R £m	H £m	D/C	D/R
1932 I	2,027	1,683	344	176	520	4.9	9.6
II	2,064	1,715	349	181	530	4.9	9.5
III	2,191	1,840	351	193	544	5.2	9.6
IV	2,274	1,925	349	198	546	5.5	9.7
1933 I	2,303	1,955	348	209	558	5.7	9.3
II	2,308	1,951	357	213	569	5.5	9.2
III	2,324	1,966	358	209	567	5.5	9.4
IV	2,298	1,940	358	216	574	5.4	9.0
1934 I	2,226	1,873	353	217	570	5.3	8.6
II	2,222	1,860	362	220	574	5.1	8.7
III	2,228	1,862	366	204	570	5.1	9.3
IV	2,296	1,928	368	220	581	5.2	9.0
1935 I	2,314	1,953	361	217	585	5.4	9.0
II	2,343	1,968	375	218	593	5.3	9.0
III	2,401	2,019	382	213	596	5.3	9.4
IV	2,443	2,055	388	213	601	5.3	9.7
1936 I	2,442	2,061	381	217	598	5.4	9.5
II	2,520	2,117	403	217	620	5.3	9.8
III	2,596	2,174	422	222	644	5.1	9.8
IV	2,645	2,216	430	227	656	5.1	9.8
1937 I	2,637	2,199	438	224	662	5.0	9.8
II	2,644	2,191	453	228	680	4.8	9.6
III	2,679	2,210	469	229	698	4.7	9.7
IV	2,706	2,238	467	231	698	4.8	9.7
1938 I	2,665	2,208	457	239	696	4.8	9.3
II	2,665	2,199	466	234	701	4.7	9.4
III	2,676	2,213	463	233	696	4.8	9.5
IV	2,638	2,172	466	230	696	4.7	9.5

Sources: M = D + C

D = total deposits of ten London Clearing Banks from Committee on Finance and Industry, *Report*, Appendix 1, Table 1 (1919–30), and *BESS*, selected issues (1931–8).

C = currency in circulation, Bank of England figures

R = reserves of ten London Clearing Banks from same sources as D

H = C + R

Table 2 *Some interest rates, quarterly averages, 1919–38, % p.a.*

		(1) 2½% Consols	(2) Treasury Bill rate	(3) Average Short rate	(4) Yield gap
1919	I	4.27	3.53	3.23	1.04
	II	4.54	3.53	3.11	1.43
	III	4.86	3.53	3.23	1.63
	IV	4.88	4.98	4.37	.51
1920	I	5.03	5.58	4.79	.24
	II	5.31	6.56	5.30	.01
	III	5.38	6.61	5.75	−.37
	IV	5.57	6.61	5.83	−.26
1921	I	5.29	6.50	6.14	−.85
	II	5.31	5.84	5.22	.09
	III	5.19	4.70	4.17	1.02
	IV	5.07	3.81	3.52	1.55
1922	I	4.67	3.36	2.96	1.71
	II	4.33	2.48	2.21	2.12
	III	4.32	2.16	1.97	2.35
	IV	4.41	2.45	2.07	2.34
1923	I	4.36	2.26	2.03	2.33
	II	4.24	2.02	1.88	2.36
	III	4.28	3.10	2.55	1.73
	IV	4.36	3.20	2.74	1.62
1924	I	4.38	3.32	2.82	1.56
	II	4.36	2.99	2.55	1.81
	III	4.37	3.64	3.20	1.17
	IV	4.33	3.72	3.21	1.12
1925	I	4.34	3.99	3.57	.77
	II	4.42	4.32	4.21	.21
	III	4.46	3.92	3.75	.71
	IV	4.53	4.21	3.22	1.31
1926	I	4.53	4.46	4.35	.18
	II	4.54	4.35	4.15	.39
	III	4.53	4.50	4.18	.35
	IV	4.60	4.73	4.33	.27
1927	I	4.53	4.30	4.07	.46
	II	4.57	4.08	3.88	.69
	III	4.58	4.34	4.00	.58
	IV	4.55	4.33	3.96	.59
1928	I	4.54	4.13	3.90	.64
	II	4.43	3.92	3.72	.71
	III	4.47	4.14	3.84	.63
	IV	4.47	4.35	3.99	.48
1929	I	4.49	4.85	4.68	−.19
	II	4.56	5.25	4.86	−.30
	III	4.64	5.50	4.90	−.26
	IV	4.70	5.41	5.33	−.63
1930	I	4.59	3.44	3.73	.86
	II	4.52	2.30	2.21	2.31
	III	4.50	2.20	2.05	2.45
	IV	4.33	2.21	1.98	2.35
1931	I	4.39	2.39	2.32	2.07
	II	4.24	2.29	2.14	2.10
	III	4.36	3.74	3.30	1.06
	IV	4.61	5.54	5.14	−.53

Table 2 (*continued*)

		(1)	(2)	(3)	(4)
1932	I	4.41	3.77	4.11	.30
	II	3.99	1.34	1.72	2.27
	III	3.47	.60	.74	2.73
	IV	3.35	.86	.79	2.56
1933	I	3.37	.67	.76	2.61
	II	3.38	.42	.58	2.80
	III	3.43	.35	.53	2.90
	IV	3.39	.94	.88	2.51
1934	I	3.24	.87	.92	2.32
	II	3.18	.86	.89	2.29
	III	3.11	.70	.81	2.30
	IV	2.89	.48	.64	2.25
1935	I	2.79	.35	.55	2.24
	II	2.88	.55	.69	2.19
	III	2.96	.57	.68	2.28
	IV	2.96	.62	.69	2.29
1936	I	2.93	.53	.66	2.27
	II	2.94	.61	.71	2.23
	III	2.94	.55	.66	2.28
	IV	2.94	.64	.71	2.23
1937	I	3.13	.53	.65	2.48
	II	3.29	.57	.68	2.61
	III	3.37	.52	.65	2.72
	IV	3.34	.63	.69	2.65
1938	I	3.29	.50	.65	2.64
	II	3.36	.54	.66	2.70
	III	3.37	.63	.67	2.70
	IV	3.49	.76	.75	2.74

Sources: Cols. (1), (3) and (4): Goodwin, "Studies in Money", Table XII. The average short
rate is the average of three-months bill rate and the rate on day-to-day money;
(4) = (1) − (3).
Col. (2): Morgan, *Studies in British Financial Policy*, p. 153 (1919–24); Federal
Reserve, *Banking & Monetary Statistics*, pp. 656, 658 and 660 (1924–38).

Table 3A *L.C.E.S. Indices of security prices and yields, quarterly, 1919–29, 1913 = 100*

		Price of twenty industrial ordinary shares	Price of four fixed-interest stocks	Yield of four fixed-interest stocks
1919	I	155	78.5	128
	II	162	76.0	132
	III	169	70.3	142
	IV	188	69.8	143
1920	I	206	66.5	151
	II	175	63.1	158
	III	156	63.7	157
	IV	141	61.7	162
1921	I	120	64.4	155
	II	122	66.2	151
	III	116	65.8	152
	IV	106	67.5	147
1922	I	116	75.9	133
	II	132	80.9	124
	III	137	79.6	126
	IV	144	78.9	127
1923	I	157	80.9	124
	II	167	84.6	118
	III	163	83.1	121
	IV	162	81.2	124
1924	I	159	78.3	127
	II	158	81.3	123
	III	157	81.0	124
	IV	168	82.2	122
1925	I	179	81.9	122
	II	179	80.3	124
	III	176	80.2	125
	IV	188	78.8	126
1926	I	187	78.6	127
	II	182	78.5	127
	III	184	78.6	127
	IV	193	77.4	129
1927	I	193	79.4	126
	II	199	79.0	127
	III	202	79.0	127
	IV	211	78.9	127
1928	I	219	80.4	124
	II	242	81.6	123
	III	244	80.9	124
	IV	244	81.0	123
1929	I	256	80.6	124
	II	241	78.9	127
	III	236	77.1	130
	IV	213	76.8	130

Source: L.C.E.S. *Bulletin*, selected issues. The four fixed-interest stocks were:
    4% Funding Loan 1960/90
    3% Local Loans 1912
    Metropolitan Water Board 1934–2003
    2½% L.C.C. 1929
  (L.C.E.S. *Bulletin*, Introductory number, January 1923).

Table 3B *L.C.E.S. indices of security prices and yields, quarterly, 1925–38, 1924 = 100*

		Price of industrial ordinary shares	Price of four fixed-interest stocks	Yield of four fixed-interest stocks
1925	I	109	110.3	99.7
	II	107	98.5	101.5
	III	109	98.0	102.2
	IV	116	96.3	103.9
1926	I	118	96.8	103.3
	II	116	97.0	103.1
	III	117	96.2	103.9
	IV	119	95.5	104.7
1927	I	119	97.0	102.9
	II	122	96.6	103.5
	III	124	96.6	103.5
	IV	131	97.3	102.8
1928	I	138	98.6	101.4
	II	145	100.4	99.6
	III	141	98.9	101.2
	IV	143	99.0	101.0
1929	I	147	98.8	101.2
	II	143	97.5	103.9
	III	141	94.6	105.7
	IV	126	94.2	106.2
1930	I	120	96.6	103.6
	II	117	98.8	101.3
	III	109	99.5	100.6
	IV	102	102.8	97.3
1931	I	95	100.5	99.7
	II	85	102.6	97.8
	III	82	99.5	101.0
	IV	87	92.3	108.6
1932	I	83	96.8	103.9
	II	78	107.6	93.4
	III	86	121.1	83.1
	IV	91	124.1	80.9
1933	I	94	122.8	81.9
	II	97	123.8	81.1
	III	108	124.0	80.8
	IV	114	126.7	79.0
1934	I	119	129.7	77.2
	II	125	130.6	76.7
	III	125	132.2	75.8
	IV	130	137.6	72.9
1935	I	133	137.9	72.8
	II	136	136.3	73.6
	III	143	135.9	73.6
	IV	145	134.6	74.5
1936	I	156	136.9	73.3
	II	156	136.9	73.2
	III	163	136.6	73.4
	IV	169	137.2	73.1
1937	I	163	130.0	77.1
	II	153	127.3	78.6
	III	149	125.8	79.6
	IV	137	127.8	78.3

Table 3B (*continued*)

		Price of industrial ordinary shares	Price of four fixed-interest stocks	Yield of four fixed-interest stocks
1938	I	128	128.9	77.7
	II	123	127.9	78.2
	III	121	126.6	78.6
	IV	119	123.1	81.4

Source: L.C.E.S. *Bulletin*, selected issues. The four fixed-interest stocks were:

    3% L.C.C.
    4% L.M.S. Debentures
    3½% Conversion Loan
    4% Funding Loan

(L.C.E.S. Special Memorandum no. 33, A.L. Bowley, G.L. Schwartz and K.C. Smith, "A New Index of Price of Securities", January 1931).

Table 4A *Central Government Accounts, calendar years, 1920–38, £m*

	Receipts						Expenditure							Deficit − Surplus +
	Taxes on income	Taxes on expenditure	Taxes on capital	National Insurance cont.	Other	Total	Current expenditure on goods and services	National Insurance benefits	Current grants to local authorities	Debt interest	Other grants and subsidies	Capital formation	Total	
1920	609	334	50	28	32	1053	277	15	66	320	271	15	964	+ 89
1921	503	343	48	47	79	1020	259	71	77	303	252	20	982	+ 38
1922	431	331	59	59	54	934	214	64	77	307	189	14	865	+ 69
1923	377	313	54	62	53	859	181	56	77	315	138	16	783	+ 76
1924	351	381	62	64	45	803	180	59	79	315	118	18	769	+ 34
1925	344	289	58	65	60	816	186	65	82	313	126	22	794	+ 20
1926	308	293	65	75	71	812	187	80	84	328	121	20	820	− 8
1927	296	309	76	80	80	841	185	78	87	303	116	20	789	+ 52
1928	286	321	83	82	85	857	181	88	88	312	116	19	804	+ 53
1929	295	317	79	82	91	864	182	98	104	316	118	20	838	+ 26
1930	303	308	81	81	99	872	180	130	128	304	117	23	882	− 10
1931	328	312	72	82	80	874	181	154	132	283	134	22	906	− 32
1932	352	348	73	89	50	912	177	125	125	279	162	18	886	+ 26
1933	310	346	87	90	48	881	176	108	124	243	171	14	836	+ 45
1934	291	365	78	94	50	878	184	108	126	226	169	15	828	+ 50
1935	284	373	87	98	48	890	209	110	134	227	171	16	867	+ 23
1936	288	396	86	104	47	921	252	105	139	223	166	22	907	+ 14
1937	326	413	93	107	48	987	322	107	139	228	164	29	989	− 2
1938	383	415	78	109	50	1036	439	122	142	232	175	35	1145	109

Source: Feinstein, *National Income*, Tables 12 and 34.

Table 4B *Budget and Sinking Fund payments, financial years, 1919–38, £m*

Financial year ending 31 March	Published deficit (−) or surplus (+)	Total debt charges	Interest and management	Debt redeemed out of revenue
1919	−1691	270	267	–
1920	−326	332	325	–
1921	+231	350	328	21
1922	+46	332	304	25
1923	+102	324	300	25
1924	+48	347	306	40
1925	+4	357	309	45
1926	−14	358	307	50
1927	−37	379	316	60
1928	+4	379	312	65
1929	+18	369	310	58
1930	−15	360	310	48
1931	−23	360	292	67
1932	+0.4	330	296	33
1933	−32	311	283	26
1934	+31	224	215	8
1935	+8	224	211	12
1936	+3	224	210	13
1937	−6	224	210	13
1938	+29	227	215	11

Sources: T. 171/371, Barlow to Trend, 10 October 1945; T. 175/15, "Debt payments since the War", undated but 1927; Pember and Boyle, *British Government Securities in the Twentieth Century*, pp. 522–3.

Table 5 *Components of G.N.P., at constant market prices, 1929–38, £m*

	Consumers expenditure	Public authorities current expenditure	Gross domestic fixed capital formation	Value of physical increase in stocks etc.	Exports of goods and services	Total final expenditure	Imports of goods and services	Gross domestic product	Net property income from abroad	Gross national product
1919	3485	830	172	80	728	5295	715	4580	72	4652
1920	3493	475	295	−60	781	4984	711	4273	73	4346
1920	3343	446	284	−60	813	4826	730	4096	70	4166
1921	3143	452	326	−70	648	4499	642	3857	96	3953
1922	3254	424	300	−63	816	4731	739	3992	102	4094
1923	3349	400	308	−45	895	4907	792	4115	121	4236
1924	3428	403	359	−4	923	5109	871	4238	129	4367
1925	3508	417	410	88	919	5342	893	4449	153	4602
1926	3496	424	397	12	843	5172	929	4243	170	4413
1927	3631	430	442	33	948	5484	945	4539	180	4719
1928	3690	435	438	14	955	5532	915	4617	178	4795
1929	3765	444	461	31	986	5687	961	4726	184	4910
1930	3822	455	463	79	849	5668	948	4720	185	4905
1931	3863	466	454	−3	684	5464	984	4480	173	4653
1932	3839	466	396	1	669	5371	878	4493	146	4639
1933	3937	471	409	−72	678	5423	879	4544	183	4727
1934	4051	482	498	34	704	5769	918	4851	192	5043
1935	4163	515	518	6	794	5996	963	5033	206	5239
1936	4285	562	565	−6	771	6177	987	5190	210	5400
1937	4357	627	584	56	810	6343	1023	5411	192	5603
1938	4392	749	592	83	757	6573	1001	5572	192	5764

Source: Feinstein, *National Income*, Table 5.
Note: From the lower figure for 1920 the estimates exclude Southern Ireland.

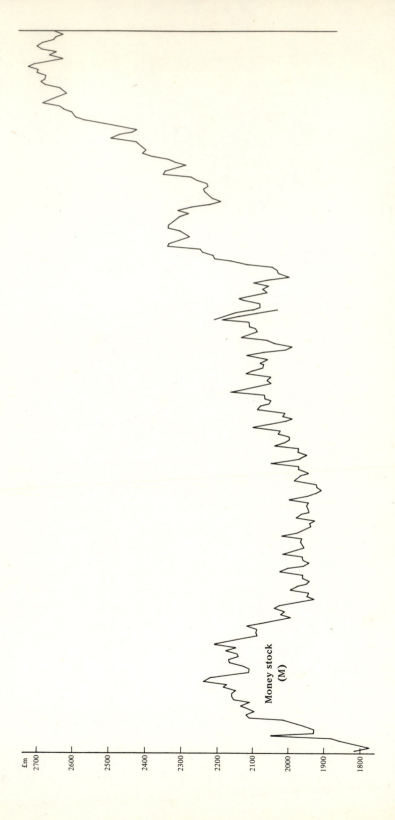

Chart 7 *Monetary series, monthly, 1919–38*

£m
2700
2600
2500
2400
2300
2200
2100
2000
1900
1800

Money stock
(M)

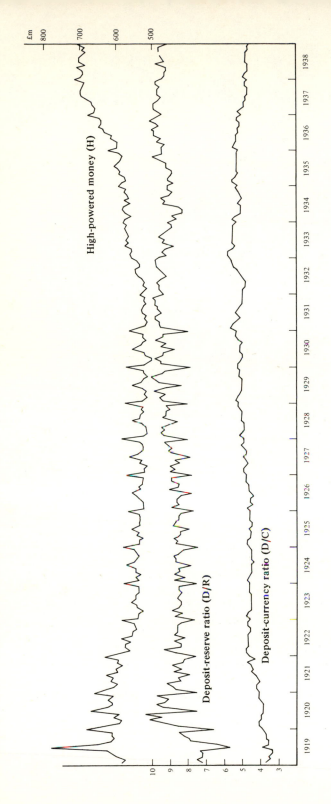

Appendix 2

Official Holdings of the National Debt

1. Estimates of Private Sector Holdings

The total outstanding debt in various classes of maturities and the holdings of the National Debt Commissioners, as of 31 March of each year, are given in Pember and Boyle, *British Government Securities in the Twentieth Century*. The total includes foreign holdings and the holdings of the Currency Note Redemption Account (1914–28), the Issue and Banking Departments of the Bank of England, the Exchange Equalization Account (from 1932), and other government departments. There is little or no information on the first and last of these (see Moggridge, *British Monetary Policy*, pp. 254–7). Inland Revenue estimates of total foreign holdings of British government securities are available only for January 1926 and January 1930 (T. 160/398/F 12394, Grigg to Leith-Ross, 10 May 1927 and 4 February 1931) and departmental Treasury bill holdings can be estimated for 1922–36 only (see below). For the Banking Department only total security holdings are given in the weekly return. The CNRA and Issue Department holdings have been obtained from the CNRA ledger and the monthly Issue Department statements in the Treasury. Therefore, the estimated private sector holdings in each maturity class (Tables 1 and 2) equal the total outstanding minus the CNRA, Issue Department and NDC holdings.

2. Market Treasury Bills

The Treasury did not know the composition of the security holdings of the Banking Department of the Bank of England, but various Treasury memoranda in the Public Record Office give Treasury bills available to the market or held by the Banking Department at the end of most quarters from September 1922 to September 1936 and the EEA holdings at the end of each month or fortnight from June 1932 to September 1936. The available information has been put together in Table 3, and the 31 March and 31 December figures for market holdings plotted against the total of Treasury bills outstanding in Chart 8. The volume of Treasury bills reaches its minimum in March and its maximum in December each year (Balogh, *Studies in Financial Organization*, p. 66).

The difference between the total and market series is, to say the least, marked, particularly in 1929 and after 1932. The market Treasury bill series also differs from the Treasury bill series in Table 1 because of the departmental holdings (other than those of the NDC); the error in the estimates of private sector holdings of other debt is not, however, likely to be so large since the departments' holdings were probably mainly of Treasury bills and Ways and Means (Moggridge, *British Monetary Policy*, p. 257).

3. The Role of the CNRA and the Issue Department in debt management

It has been known since 1938 that the authorities used the departmental funds to

Table 1 *Private sector holdings of national debt, by maturity class, 31 March, 1919–38, £m*

	With a maximum life of:				Repayable only by government option	Floating debt (Treasury bills)	Other internal debt	External debt	Total
	Under 5 years	5–15 years	15–25 years	over 25 years					
1919	937	1,027	56	1,954	237	865	248	1,293	6,617
1920	861	860	64	2,648	236	901	300	1,222	7,092
1921	841	811	79	2,593	236	935	309	1,129	6,092
1922	572	1,167	77	2,545	486	762	373	1,085	7,067
1923	693	774	2,067	686	905	514	375	1,156	7,170
1924	1,053	312	2,142	672	890	483	385	1,126	7,063
1925	951	292	2,213	657	914	486	390	1,122	7,025
1926	1,000	155	2,283	643	974	487	396	1,111	7,049
1927	733	212	2,352	631	1,097	535	396	1,101	7,067
1928	502	344	2,386	641	1,225	474	385	1,095	7,052
1929	472	194	2,402	613	1,360	507	388	1,085	7,021
1930	443	307	2,099	905	1,346	426	380	1,074	6,980
1931	366	397	2,070	897	1,323	446	409	1,067	6,975
1932	399	337	2,073	891	1,310	520	409	1,091	7,030
1933	112	558	259	885	3,263	654	409	1,060	7,200
1934	276	553	474	879	3,229	644	419	1,037	7,511
1935	184	557	284	1,008	3,191	612	311	1,037	7,184
1936	101	549	281	958	3,522	660	311	1,037	7,419
1937	67	533	732	754	3,163	561	303	1,033	7,146
1938	65	900	464	753	3,156	683	313	1,032	7,366

Source: Pember and Boyle, *British Government Securities in the Twentieth Century*, pp. 395–433 (odd numbers), 483–502. H.M. Treasury, CNRA ledger and monthly Issue Department statements.

Table 2 *Private sector holdings of national debt, by maturity class, as % of total private sector holdings, 31 March, selected years*

| | Treasury bills | With a maximum life of: | | | | Repayable only by government option |
		Under 5 years	5–15 years	15–25 years	Over 25 years	
1920	12.7	12.1	12.1	0.9	37.3	3.3
1924	6.8	14.9	4.4	30.3	9.5	12.6
1929	7.2	6.7	2.8	34.2	8.7	19.4
1932	7.4	5.7	4.8	29.5	12.7	18.6
1933	9.1	1.6	7.8	3.6	12.3	45.3
1937	7.9	0.9	12.6	10.2	10.6	44.3

Source: As Table 1

Chart 8 *Treasury bills*
 (1) Monthly averages of total amounts outstanding, 1919–36
 (2) Market holdings on 31 March and 31 December, 1922–36
 Sources: (1) U.K. Hicks, *The Finance of British Government*, p. 335
     (2) Table 3

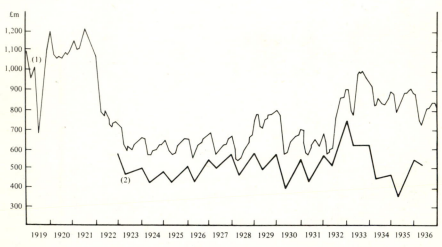

support the market for government securities and the Issue Department, in particular, to "underwrite" debt operations in the 1930s (Sayers, *Financial Policy 1939–45* pp. 150–1; Nevin, *The Mechanism of Cheap Money*, pp. 189–97; D.S. Lees, "Public Departments and Cheap Money, 1932–38", *Economica*, February 1955; Nevin, "Estimating Departmental Invervention", *Review of Economic Studies*, 1952). The statements of the security holdings of the CNRA and the Issue Department not only enable one to estimate departmental holdings of Treasury bills which differ substantially from the ingenious estimates of Nevin and Lees, but also to see the development of departmental intervention.

The practice seems to have started in a small way as far back as 1917, with the issue of 5% War Loan, since at the end of March 1919 three-quarters of the CNRA's assets was floating debt, namely £160m Ways and Means and £81m Treasury bills, and the remaining quarter consisted of £33m of short bonds with under five years to run and £38m 5% War Loan. This holding of War Loan was gradually sold off. It was down to £11m by June 1921 when the CNRA took up £86m of the 3½% Conversion Loan. The Account took more of the 1922 and 1925 issues of this stock and gradually sold it off. It also subscribed to the issues of 4½% Conversion Loan 1940/44 in

Table 3 *Distribution of outstanding Treasury Bills, "quarterly", 1922–36, £m (0 = <½m)*

End of quarter		Total out-standing (1)	Held by CNRA or Issue Department (2)	Held by NDC (3)	Held by other government departments (4)	Held by EEA (5)	Held by market and Banking Department (6)
1922	III	724	195	1	53		565
	IV	719	97	1	65		565
1923	I	616	102	0	46		468
	II	604	87				
	III	626	104	0	68		454
	IV	652	95	0	61		496
1924	I	588	105	0	59		424
	II	599	101				
	III	619	107	0	56		455
	IV	626	95	0	60		471
1925	I	576	87	3	59		427
	II	605	89				
	III	644	100	3	54		485
	IV	636	79	3	49		505
1926	I	665	78	0	44		436
	II	619	87				
	III	664	94	0	40		531
	IV	663	63	0	55		545
1927	I	599	64	0	35		501
	II	597	65				
	III	630	76	0	29		525
	IV	651	58	0	24		569
1928	I	527	53	0	16		458
	II	581	55				
	III	636	103	0	25		508
	IV	788	189	0	21		578
1929	I	700	193	0	23		485
	II	757	207				
	III	792	208	0	20		564
	IV	780	183	0	19		579
1930	I	589	163	0	21		405
	II	629	154				
	III	656	154				
	IV	718	127	0	41		550
1931	I	570	124	0	12		434
	II	617	110	0	11		496
	III	618	95	0	26		497
	IV	654	79	0	11		574
1932	I	604	81	2	11		511
	II	719	57	2	11	130	519
	III	866	120	2	13	102	629
	IV	928	70	2	17	93	749
1933	I	776	118	4	12	24	619
	II	970	155	4	12	214	585
	III	988	147	4	22	254	561
	IV	939	78	4	17	213	627
1934	I	800	129	7	13	200	451
	II	848	143	7	14	202	482
	III	823	171	7	6	209	420
	IV	892	186	7	8	231	460

Table 3 (*continued*)

	(1)	(2)	(3)	(4)	(5)	(6)
1935 I	799	179	8	19	222	371
II	877	172	8	16	200	481
III	899	171	8	2	140	578
IV	898	144	8	42	157	547
1936 I	763	95	8	14	125	521
II	805	85	8	57	42	613
III		151			48	642

Sources: Col. (1): Treasury memoranda as col. (6); Paish, "The Floating Debt, 1914–39, and its effect on the British Banking System", in Balogh, *Studies in Financial Organization*, pp. 206–7.

Col. (2): H.M. Treasury, CNRA ledger and monthly Issue Department statements.

Col. (3): Pember and Boyle, *British Government Securities in the Twentieth Century*, pp. 486–500. The published figures do not in fact all refer to 31 March of each year (Nevin, *The Mechanism of Cheap Money*, pp. 177–8) and the figure for each year has been taken to apply to all quarters for the purpose of calculating col. (4).

Col. (4) = Col. (1) − [Col. (2) + Col. (3) + Col. (5) + Col. (6)]

Col. (5): T. 160/538/F 13748, "Treasury Bills", n.d. but by file 1934;
T. 175/72, EEA Valuations;
T. 175/87, Daily Exchange Statements.

Col. (6): T. 175/46, Hopkins, "Treasury Bill Figures", n.d. but by file 1930;
T. 175/84, Phillips to Hopkins, "Funding Operation", 28 March 1934;
T. 160/538/F 13748, "Treasury Bills", 1934;
T. 160/633/F 18410, Memorandum by Phillips, 31 October 1936.

1925 and of 4% Consols in 1927. At the same time it was buying in short-dated bonds as they neared maturity. This increasing involvement in debt management shows up in the annual figures for its security holdings (Table 4).

It is, of course, not known whether other government departments assisted, but with respect to the NDC's holdings the Treasury's attitude on the occasion of its July 1929 offer of 4% Consols for 4½% Treasury Bonds probably illustrates the general situation. Phillips told Hopkins:

> "It seems to be in our general interest that he [Headlam, on behalf of the NDC] should convert [his holding of £25m Treasury Bonds] ... I have arranged for the Bank to report to Ismay [in the Treasury] Saturday morning to see if he has converted. If he hasn't acted by then perhaps you could have a word with him. I should much prefer that he converted on his own initiative without suggestion from us but if he doesn't do so we must try to persuade him"

(T. 160/551/F 9973, Phillips to Hopkins, 24 July 1929)

The conversion would involve some loss, and after discussions between Headlam, the Deputy Governor of the Bank, the Treasury officials and the Chancellor, the Chancellor suggested Headlam convert £7½m (T. 160/551/F 9973, Headlam to Chancellor, 26 July 1929; Hopkins to Chancellor, 27 July 1929; P.J. Grigg to Headlam, 29 July 1929).

After the passing of the Currency and Bank Notes Act of 1928 the Issue Department took over and extended the CNRA's role. Again even annual figures indicate the scale of operations (Table 5). The Issue Department's role in the 1930s shows up clearly in the changes in its holdings of 2½% Conversion Loan issued in 1933 and of the Funding Loans of April 1934, December 1935 and November 1936. The Department took nearly half of the spring 1933 issue of 2½% Conversion Loan 1944/49. Having sold most of this off, it took initially almost two-thirds of the September 1933

Table 4 *CNRA Holdings of Government Securities, 31 March, 1919–28, £000*

	With a maximum life of:				Repayable only by government option	Floating debt		Anglo-French Loan	Total
	Under 5 years	5–15 years	15–25 years	over 25 years		Treasury bills	Ways & Means		
1919	32,789	–	–	37,615	–	81,500	160,250		312,514
1920	34,673	–	–	37,087	–	186,663	52,950	7,809	319,182
1921	43,740	3,338	–	14,565	–	197,673	53,250		309,560
1922	57,193	23,769	–	6,151	14,184	113,785	48,600		263,682
1923	25,471	2,138	4,648	–	10,396	102,290	94,770		239,713
1924	18,874	4,904	1,910	–	8,457	105,025	96,870		236,040
1925	2,086	4,647	22,459	–	7,408	87,150	107,420		231,170
1926	6,392	152	7,309	300	16,119	77,825	121,820		229,917
1927	21,469	19,632	2,119	500	39,431	64,485	110,430		258,066
1928	3,848	24,971	4,832	2,334	15,746	53,230	42,450		147,411

Source: H.M. Treasury, CNRA Ledger.

Table 5 *Issue Department Holdings of Government Securities, 31 March, 1929–38, £000*

	With a maximum life of:				Repayable only by government option	Floating debt		Other internal debt	Foreign exchange	Total
	Under 5 years	5–15 years	15–25 years	Over 25 years		Treasury bills	Ways & Means			
1929	28,742	–	442	4,664	4,932	193,435	–	11,015	7,594	260,000
1930	14,038	19,381	8,648	18,490	6,170	162,930	–	11,015	11,379	260,000
1931	45,533	22,964	15,616	9,133	7,194	123,840	–	11,015	13,388	260,000
1932	49,017	34,486	10,910	3,752	52,827	81,838	–	11,015	17,159	275,000
1933	19,522	44,952	36,305	1,073	15,096	117,625	–	11,015	8,823	260,000
1934	91,556	4,825	8,675	1,950	5,300	129,295	–	11,015	–	260,000
1935	26,473	7,005	2,900	12,015	11,340	178,750	–	11,015	–	260,000
1936	41,002	2,800	1,850	156,760	7,310	95,220	–	11,015	–	260,000
1937	–	9,265	42,290	8,561	10,743	109,685	–	11,015	–	200,000
1938	10,785	12,001	1,000	5,016	4,250	144,345	–	11,015	–	200,000

Source: H.M. Treasury, monthly Issue Department statements.

issue of the same stock. Having reduced its holding of that stock from £98m
(31 October 1933) to £6m (April 1934) it then took £96m of the 3% Funding Loan
of April 1934.Twenty one months later it was ready to pick up three-quarters of the
issue of 2% Funding Loan and eleven months further on over half the 2¾% Funding
Loan (H.M. Treasury, Issue Department monthly statements). As Hopkins had to
explain to the Chancellor when these operations had involved the Issue Department
in a substantial loss:

> "The Currency Note Account while it existed and since 1928 the Issue
> Department has been regularly but secretly used to subscribe to new
> Government issues (whether for new money or for conversions) to such an
> extent as ordinary public subscriptions might be expected to fall short of
> the desired amount. The Issue Department places itself in funds by selling
> its holdings of Treasury Bills and uses the cash to buy the new issue. The
> securities thus acquired are subsequently peddled out to the public as a
> demand for them arises, as it always does in the end. As the securities are
> sold, the cash realised is reinvested in Treasury Bills. This entirely secret pro-
> cedure is the means by which the vast requirements of the Treasury have
> been and can be successfully met from time to time."
> (T. 175/100, Hopkins to Fisher and Chancellor, "The Loss in the Issue
> Department of the Bank of England", 21 February 1938)

The Bank complained about this loss (T. 175/95, Catterns to Hopkins, 26 July 1937).
It created a problem for the authorities because previous legislation only provided
for the payment of the profits of the Issue Department to the Treasury, and the
Government could not pass special legislation to provide for a loss because it would
then disclose its secret operations. The problem was eventually solved by a clause in
the Currency and Bank Notes Act 1939 (Sayers, *Financial Policy 1939–45*,
pp. 150–1).

Appendix 3

The Term Structure of Interest Rates

This appendix surveys the literature on the determinants of the relation between short- and long-term interest rates. There are three main theories of the term structure of interest rates. According to the (pure) expectations hypothesis, long-term rates of interest are an average of expected future short rates, of which forward rates constitute unbiased estimates. The hypothesis is based on the assumption that short- and long-term securities can (ignoring default risks) be treated as identical in all respects except term to maturity, and implies that the expected value of the returns from holding long- and short-term securities for identical time periods are the same. It also implies that the interest rate structure can be changed only by altering the market's expectations of future short rates. It allows that the authorities can, primarily by changing Bank rate and/or open-market operations, determine money market rates (i.e. the shortest interest rates) and affect the absolute level of interest rates (the height of the yield curve), but not the term structure (the shape of the yield curve): "for given expectations, the entire brunt of an unanticipated change in 'the interest rate' will be felt on the shortest end of the yield curve, regardless of the source of the disturbance" (Meiselman, *The Term Structure of Interest Rates*, p. 31). This is because if the long-term rate were initially affected by an increase in bonds outstanding, speculation in the form of a movement out of short-term and into long-term securities would force bond prices to return to their original positions. This movement would increase actual and hence expected short-term rates, and the entire yield curve would tend to rise. Thus the expectations hypothesis implies that changes in the maturity composition of outstanding debt, when total debt is given, will not have any long-run effect on the term structure, except in so far as the changes in the supplies of or demands for securities of different maturities affect expectations of future rates. Hence the authorities' debt management policy will have no long-run effect on the yield curve, unless the initial disturbance alters expectations of 'the interest rate' (ibid., pp. 31–2, 49–51; Kessel, *The Cyclical Behaviour of the Term Structure of Interest Rates*, pp. 40–58).

The second theory of the term structure is the Keynes–Hicks liquidity-premium hypothesis. According to it, forward short rates and hence the long rate can normally be expected to exceed the current short rate by a risk premium which the holder of a bond must be offered in order to compensate him for assuming the risks of price fluctuations. The assumptions are:

    (i) Many borrowers need funds over extensive future periods and will therefore have a strong propensity to borrow long.

    (ii) Lenders have the opposite propensity, preferring to lend short in order to minimize the variance in the money value of their portfolios. The resulting "constitutional weakness" in the pattern of supply and demand for loanable funds could be expected to be offset by speculators, but

(iii) Speculators are also averse to risk and must be offered a premium to induce them to purchase long-term securities.

Then in equilibrium implicit or forward rates will exceed expected rates, and the normal relationship is for long rates (average of current and forward short rates) to exceed short rates. Only if the short rate is considered abnormally high can long rates fall below short rates.

The expectations hypothesis, except in its "pure" form, is not inconsistent with this liquidity-premium theory, and as is mentioned below the evidence for this theory also suggests that the market's expectations of future interest rates are a very important determinant of the term structure.

In this liquidity-premium theory speculative shifts can no longer be assumed to offset the effect of changes in the supplies of securities of different maturities on interest rates to the extent of restoring an expectations-determined equilibrium pattern of interest rates. An increase in the supply of long-term bonds will tend to increase the long rate relative to the short rate because of the necessity to tempt more investors to hold larger quantities of long-term debt in their portfolios.

A third theory is the market segmentation theory (also known as the hedging-pressure theory, the preferred habitat theory and the institutional theory). As in the second theory, investors are assumed to be risk-averters, but this leads them to hedge against possible fluctuations in interest rates rather than to speculate, for investors are assumed to have definite preferences for different maturities depending on the maturity structure of their liabilities. Some investors such as insurance companies who lend long will prefer to borrow long, others, for example banks to borrow short, and there will be little or no switching between securities of different maturities in response to changes in interest-rate differentials. The yield structure is then determined not by expectations but by the pressure of supply and demand within each of the segmented markets. There is no presumption that the yield curve will be positively sloping: since some investors prefer to hold long securities the net effect of lenders' risk aversion on the yield curve is an empirical question. Such a theory therefore allows a greater role to debt management in determining the term structure than do the other two theories: but both the liquidity premium and market segmentation theories have the same implications for the effects of debt management on the term structure, in particular that the lengthening of the outstanding debt would tend to increase the spread between short and long rates.

Evidence for the expectations hypothesis has been provided by Meiselman, who got round the problem of unobservable expectations by incorporating into his model the hypothesis that expectations tend to be related to a weighted average of past interest rates and tend to be altered on the basis of new experience whenever actual interest rates turn out to be different from anticipated. It is generally agreed that Meiselman's results "constitute striking evidence that the expectations hypothesis has empirical validity" (Kessel, *The Cyclical Behaviour of the Term Structure of Interest Rates*, p. 12). Further evidence for the importance of expectations has been provided by Malkiel who formulated and tested an alternative expectations hypothesis. To take account of the criticisms of the pure expectations hypothesis on the grounds that investors cannot be expected to forecast the whole future pattern of interest rates, he incorporated expectations through explicit expected security price changes rather than expected future short interest rates and substituted a short planning period for the long-run horizon implicit in traditional expectations theories (Malkiel, *The Term Structure of Interest Rates*, Chapters 3 and 4).

Meiselman thought he had produced evidence for the *pure* expectations hypothesis since he believed that his finding of a constant term not significantly different from zero in his regression of errors (i.e. difference between acutal and predicted rates) against forecast revisions implied the liquidity premium must be zero. Kessel has shown this inference is invalid (*The Cyclical Behaviour*, pp. 16–17; see also Wood, "Expectations, Errors and the Term Structure of Interest Rates", *JPE*, April 1963, p. 166, and Malkiel, *The Term Structure*, pp. 32–3) and furthermore he has, by examining Meiselman's evidence, that of earlier writers on the subject, and further evidence provided by himself, shown that the expectations hypothesis is not by itself sufficient to explain the term structure of interest rates in the U.S.A. over the past century. "The evidence presented supports the Hicksian theory . . . that both expectations and liquidity preference determine the term structure of interest rates . . . [and] shows that forward rates must be interpreted as expected rates plus a liquidity premium." (Kessel, *The Cyclical Behaviour*, p. 42). Critics have also pointed to defects in Meiselman's methods of testing his hypothesis (Malkiel, *The Term Structure*, pp. 34–5).

On the market segmentation hypothesis, Kessel's evidence is, as he admits, less clear and he therefore dismisses the theory as "not of the same magnitude as liquidity preference and expectations in the determination of the term structure of interest rates" (*The Cyclical Behaviour*, p. 42). Malkiel has taken it rather more seriously and produced both aggregate and microeconomic evidence bearing on the hypothesis. His aggregate cross section data on ownership of government debt, showing shifts in the maturity composition of the holdings of financial institutions, "appear to be patently inconsistent with the extreme institutional hypothesis" (*The Term Structure*, p. 151). He also finds evidence that, on the supply side of the bond market, while transactions costs may prevent issuers wanting long-term funds from borrowing perpetually at short-term, these costs will not prevent *some* borrowing at short-term for a limited period until conditions become more favourable for the flotation of long issues. In periods of high interest rates new long-term issues will tend to be postponed. On the demand side of the market, his interviews with portfolio managers of several banks and insurance companies showed that there is considerable profit-motivated speculative movement between maturities. However, portfolio managers are risk-averters with definite maturity preferences and will lengthen the average maturity of their portfolios only if this promises extraordinary opportunity for capital gain. Thus he concludes that "we must reinterpret segmentation to mean simply that many buyers and sellers have habitual maturity preferences and require differential premiums to induce them to move from their preferred maturities" (ibid., p. 166).*

Malkiel's conclusion from his comprehensive study of the problem of the determinants of the term structure of interest rates is that though "this study . . . reaffirms the importance of expectations in the determination of the term structure", "the major finding . . . is that exogenous changes in the relative supplies of debt instruments of different maturities will influence the interest-rate structure of different

---

*   Meiselman has attempted to reconcile the market segmentation theory with the expectations hypothesis. He accepted that some investors, because of risk aversion and other impediments to mobility, may be rigidly committed to certain maturity areas, but he argued that "as a matter of descriptive reality . . . speculators who are indifferent to uncertainty will bulk sufficiently large to determine market rates on the basis of their mathematical expectations alone" (*The Term Structure*, p. 10). The microeconomic evidence produced by Malkiel, of diverse expectations on the part of investors and institutional factors circumscribing the volume of professional speculative activity in the government securities market, suggests that Meiselman's reconciliation will not work (Malkiel, *The Term Structure*, pp. 169–79).

maturities". Indeed, Malkiel believes that his "theoretical and empirical findings suggest that the degree of sensitivity of the rate structure to changes in relative supplies may be greater than many economists believe" (ibid., p. 219). The rather discouraging results of attempts, such as those by Modigliani and Sutch ("Innovations in Interest Rate Policy", *AER*, 1966, and "Debt Management and the term structure of interest rates: an empirical analysis of recent experience", *JPE*, 1967), to assess the degree of sensitivity can be explained in terms of the statistical difficulties involved (*The Term Structure*, pp. 221–32).

The same conclusion, that the authorities' policy with respect to the national debt can significantly affect the relation between long and short rates of interest, follows from the work of Wood and of Hamburger and Latta. Wood pointed out that the implication of the pure expectations model that debt management has no effect on the term structure only follows if expectations of future short rates are assumed to be inelastic with respect to changes in current short rates (Wood, "The expectations hypothesis, the yield curve and monetary policy", *QJE*, 1964). Hamburger and Latta compared empirically Wood's elastic-expectations model with Modligliani's model, between which the major difference is the importance attached to past interest rates as an indicator of expected future rates. Their results from U.S. data on yields on Treasury bills and long-term government bonds 1951–65 clearly favoured Wood's model. They then tested to see if the relationship obtained from that data held over a longer period, 1920–65. It did: "thus it appears that since the establishment of the Federal Reserve System the effects of open market operations in either short-term or long-term government securities have been transmitted to the other end of the yield curve in a very prompt and predictable way" ("The Term Structure of Interest Rates: some additional evidence", *JMCB*, 1969, pp. 71–83).

All the evidence mentioned so far is for the U.S.A.; but there is also evidence for the applicability of the conclusions reached for the U.S. to the U.K. Firstly, data on interest rates in the U.K. over a long period show that short rates were on average less than long rates and that the cyclical behaviour of the term structure is similar to that observed for the U.S. by Kessel and others (Hawtrey, *A Century of Bank Rate*; J.R. Hicks, "Mr. Hawtrey on Bank Rate and the Long-term Rate of Interest", *Manchester School*, 1939; Kessel, *The Cyclical Behaviour*; Malkiel, *The Term Structure*, pp. 14–15).

Meiselman's test has been run on British data for 1924–61 by J.A.G. Grant who reached a conclusion similar to Kessel's: "The usefulness of Meiselman's hypothesis when applied to . . . the market for British government securities is called in question"; "the determination of interest rates cannot be traced to one factor alone . . . Meiselman's hypothesis is not in itself a satisfactory explanation of the structure of rates" ("Meiselman on the Structure of Interest Rates: a British test", *Economica*, 1964, pp. 51–66). The additional independent determinant that Grant regards as most worthy of consideration is debt management: "The Bank of England operating through the Government broker is perhaps the most powerful single influence on prices, and it is clear from published evidence that it is not an 'error-learner'" (ibid., p. 66). Another feature of Grant's data is that the yield curves he constructed show 'humps' in the early maturities, a phenomenon which cannot be satisfactorily explained on the (pure) expectations hypothesis (see Malkiel, *The Term Structure*, pp. 31–5, 201–2, and Kessel, *The Cyclical Behaviour*, pp. 84, 89–90).

Grant's tests prompted further work on British data (for 1951–63) by Douglas Fisher. Although Fisher's results were in one sense more favourable to Meiselman's hypothesis than Grant's, he also found that "it appears as if relative quantities sometimes do contribute significantly to the variance explained, as the segmentation

Chart 9 *Yield curves for British government securities, 1925–39*
Source: Grant, "Meiselman on the structure of interest rates: a British test", *Economica*, February 1964

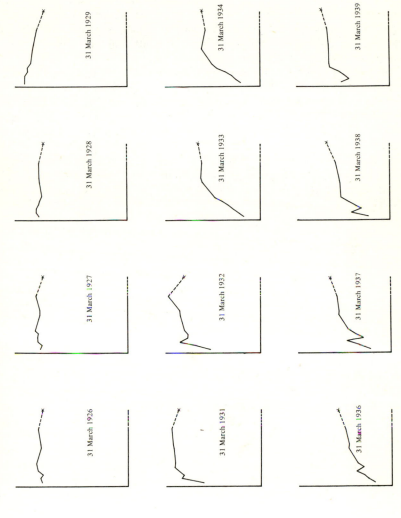

hypothesis maintains . . . [although] the empirical magnitude . . . tends to be small compared to expectations" (D. Fisher, "Expectations, the Term-Structure of Interest Rates and recent British experience", *Economica*, August 1966).

Another set of tests on British data (for 1959–68) was carried out by Rowan and O'Brien. They wished, like Modigliani and Sutch, to test the hypothesis that debt management can change the term structure of interest rates. Although "it was not possible to argue that the results confirm[ed] the typical theory of the way in which changes in the debt structure influence the rate curve . . . they certainly [did] not produce strong evidence against it". Insofar as they supported any particular theory, the results tended to support the proposition that the maturity composition of the debt influences the rate structure (Rowan and O'Brien, "Expectations, the Interest Rate Structure and Debt Policy", in Hilton and Heathfield (eds.), *The Econometric Study of the U.K.*, pp. 275–316).

The most recent work in this area is by Dodds and Ford. Their quarterly econometric model for the U.K. financial sector 1963–72 provides the strongest evidence yet that changes in the relative supplies of debt of different maturities do affect the term structure of interest rates. They emphasize, however, the limitations of their model (Dodds and Ford, *Expectations, Uncertainty and the Term Structure of Interest Rates*, pp. 269–92).

The only yield curves so far constructed for the U.K. in the interwar period are Grant's. I have plotted the yields he has calculated for British government securities of 1–6, 10, 11 and 15 years' maturity and for 2½% Consols, for 31 March 1925–39, in Chart 9.

Appendix 4

Treasury Discussions on Sterling Policy, September 1931–March 1932

1. The first discussions in Whitehall in September and October 1931 involved mainly Phillips, Hawtrey and Henderson, who recorded the arguments they used in the following memoranda:

> T. 188/20, Memorandum by Phillips, n.d. but by internal evidence between 26 and 28 September 1931;
>
> T. 188/20, Phillips to Leith-Ross, 30 September 1931;
>
> T. 188/20 and T. 175/56, Hawtrey, "Pegging the Pound. I", 28 September 1931;
>
> T. 188/29, Hawtrey, "Pegging the Pound – II", 2 October 1931;
>
> T. 188/20, Henderson, "Comments on Mr Hawtrey's Memorandum, Pegging the Pound – II", 6 October 1931.

Leith-Ross's views appear in, for example, T. 188/20, Memorandum by Leith-Ross, n.d. but between 21 and 26 September 1931, and T. 188/20, Leith-Ross to Hopkins, 2 December 1931. (See above pp. 83–5)

2. On 9 and 13 December, Leith-Ross wrote to Henderson and Keynes, respectively. He referred to the view, whose "wide acceptance" he attributed to Keynes—mentioning Keynes's 27 September article in the *Sunday Express* (reprinted in *Essays in Persuasion*, *JMK* Vol. IX, pp. 245–9)—that if France and America observed "the rules of the game" the international gold standard would work properly, and he asked for a statement of "the practical measures" that should be taken (T. 188/28, Leith-Ross to Henderson, 9 October 1931; Leith-Ross to Keynes, 13 October 1931). Keynes replied on 14 October that he would write a statement of his views for Leith-Ross as soon as he had made up his mind (T. 188/28, Keynes to Leith-Ross, 14 October 1931). Henderson sent his statement on 16 October, admitting it was "not very helpful" on the question of what France and America could be asked to do, but it did give his views about a tentative stabilization policy (T. 188/28, Henderson to Leith-Ross, 16 October 1931). Leith-Ross sent Henderson's memorandum (T. 188/28, "International Co-operation and the Gold Standard", 16 October 1931) to Hopkins, Phillips and Hawtrey for their comments (T. 188/28, Leith-Ross to Hopkins, Phillips and Hawtrey, 16 October 1931), and these comments (T. 188/28, Memorandum by Phillips, 20 October 1931; Hawtrey to Leith-Ross, 26 October 1931) continued their discussion on pegging the exchanges (above pp. 83–5).

3. Keynes's memorandum was ready by 20 November when he sent it to Leith-Ross and to the Prime Minister, who made him a member of his Advisory Committee on Financial Questions and also circulated the memorandum to some Cabinet ministers (T. 188/48, Keynes to Leith-Ross, 20 November 1931; Cab. 58/169, EAC Subcommittee on Financial Questions, 6th meeting, 26 November 1931). Keynes suggested an Imperial Currency Conference in order to form an Empire sterling standard (which other countries might later join). On the way this standard should be managed there were, said Keynes, three alternatives:

(1) To carry on as at present, allowing frequent moderate fluctuations in the exchange around $3.85 (the current level) with the Bank stepping in secretly to prevent extreme fluctuations;

(2) To decide upon a new parity and return to a strict gold standard at that parity;

(3) To fix sterling within not too narrow limits in terms of a price standard.

In favour of (1) and against (2) were the many uncertainties of the present situation; certainly no definite step could be taken until the reparations problem had been solved. The memorandum argued for (3) on the lines of *A Treatise on Money*, Book VIII (*JMK*, Vol. VI, pp. 189–367) and *A Tract on Monetary Reform* (*JMK*, Vol. IV), pp. 189–91.

In deciding the present and future value of sterling, four criteria were available:

(1) prevention of inflation, which would give a present rate of $3.75–$4;

(2) reduction of the burden of the national debt ($3);

(3) maximizing the benefit to the balance of payments ($3.50–$3.75);

(4) raising the prices of agricultural products and raw materials to at least their 1929 level, so as to bring prosperity back to primary-producing countries and hence increase Britain's trade and prosperity; this, particularly to be recommended if we were to form a sterling area, would require a present exchange rate of $3.40 to $3.50, and in future managing sterling on the basis of an index of prices of the main raw commodities of international trade.

The last was, of course, Keynes's recommendation (Cab. 58/169, Keynes, "Notes on the Currency Question", 16 November 1931).

On 15 December 1931 Hopkins told the Chancellor that he had written a paper on Keynes's memorandum and suggested that this might form the basis of the Treasury memorandum for the Cabinet Committee on Currency Questions (T. 175/57, Hopkins to Fergusson, 15 December 1931). Hopkin's memorandum, which incorporated some passages from a short memorandum by Leith-Ross, also has marginal comments by Phillips which show clearly the development of the Treasury's views.

The main point with respect to policy in the near future that Hopkins made against Keynes was that the Bank could not in fact control the pound. On the one hand, there were so many variables affecting the exchanges; on the other, the Bank's lack of reserves.

> "Not only is there the German riddle [Keynes's term for the reparations problem]: not only is there the problem of the balance of trade: not only is there the problem of the immediate fate of other countries now precariously clinging to the gold standard: not only are there the new exchange and other restrictions springing up in all quarters of the globe . . . the Bank of England and the Treasury . . . have short debts running to £m 100 which have to be met within the year . . . entail[ing] heavy purchases of foreign exchange or the export of practically all our present store of gold . . . [and] we are still the repositories of vast sums of short money left in London [which might be withdrawn at any time] . . . Even if it [the Bank] could be assured of a settled trade balance and a settled policy abroad toward sterling deposits and indeed a settled world, it would still need . . . the requisite resources."

At present the Bank could not prevent a fall in the exchanges because it had no foreign exchange reserves with which to buy sterling. (T. 175/57, Hopkins, "Note on Mr Keynes' Memorandum of 16 November", 15 December 1931, paras. 4–5).

However Hopkins thought it

> "legitimate to hope if other things go well and especially if there is a reasonable settlement of reparations that after a time, perhaps in a few months with the seasonal demand for imports abated, the pound will acquire a new

strength and the Bank, without unduly depressing sterling, will be able quietly to sell it and acquire that large reserve of foreign currencies that it requires. When that stage comes . . . we can be said to have entered upon the situation described in Mr. Keynes' first alternative, but not till then. But . . . it would be folly to turn that hope into an assumption." (Ibid., para. 6)

Hopkins was in favour of an ultimate return to gold, though not at the old parity, and certainly not in the current disordered state of world monetary affairs, which also in his view ruled out Keynes's suggestion of a managed price-index currency. There was still a large volume of foreign short-term money in London, which would be withdrawn if confidence were shaken which it certainly would be if the U.K. were to admit that it was not intent on returning to gold and/or if it were thought abroad that we were trying out "the doctrine of the managed currency" (ibid., paras. 7–10).*

Hopkins also thought Keynes's choice of index ill-judged, since wholesale primary commodity prices were more unstable than manufactured goods prices and labour costs;† they had fallen further in recent years and would probably rise sooner and quicker as recovery progressed; therefore though the exchange would start at a low point, say 3.40, it might rise within a short time to as high as 4.40,‡ which would be damaging to the export trades. This "risk of our suffering a second time so close an analogy to the past troubles of the export trades is surely conclusive against Mr Keynes' scheme" (ibid., paras. 12–16). However, "if a long period ensues before restabilisation upon gold becomes practicable, there may come a time during the intervening period when there will be some advantage in applying certain parts of Mr. Keynes' proposal in a modified form", namely in a period of *de facto* stabilization, exchange rates should be permitted to vary if substantial changes in world prices occur. But it "would be essential that the Bank of England should not be committed§ to . . . any single criterion laid down in advance".

Hopkins concluded:

"In brief then, we cannot now control the pound: we may hope, but we certainly cannot assume, that within a reasonably short time we shall be able to hold it fairly stable round some chosen point: our ultimate objective (unless world opinion greatly changes) must be re-stabilisation on gold: we fear that the attainment of this objective is as yet remote but we cannot afford to say openly: it is too early as yet to attempt any precise policy for the whole intervening period, for the world is subject to kaleidoscopic change." (Ibid., para. 18)

This negative conclusion disposed of Keynes's idea of an Imperial Currency Conference (ibid., para. 19).

A further section of the memorandum was concerned with the choice of an exchange rate for the immediate future. Hopkins "join[ed] issue with Mr Keynes when he places the point below 3.50", because of the effects on gold prices and the financial position of other countries, particularly those in debt to Britain. He said he was a $4 man but suggested giving his reasons orally to the Chancellor rather than lengthening the memorandum (ibid., paras. 21–26).¶

---

* Leith-Ross shared this view of the consequences of trying out Keynes's scheme (T. 188/48, Leith-Ross, "Note of Mr Keynes' Memorandum"); for Phillips' views, see below.
† Phillips, in his marginal comments, made the point that it was the only index available.
‡ For Phillips' alteration, see below.
§ Phillips added "publicly".
¶ He gave some reasons in T. 172/1768, Hopkins to Chancellor, 15 December 1931 (above p. 85).

Phillips' marginal comments show a significant shift of opinion away from the gold standard toward management of the currency. He crossed out the entire last section; he amended Hopkins' conclusion to read:

> "In brief then we cannot even yet control the pound *with precision; but we may hope* that within a reasonably short time we shall be able to hold it fairly stable round some chosen point; our ultimate objective (unless world opinion greatly changes) *may have to be* re-stabilisation on gold . . ." (Ibid., para. 18; my italics).

Whereas Leith-Ross wrote that it would be "impossible"* and Hopkins that it would be "a serious decision", for this country "so deeply committed to international trade" to abandon the gold standard for a currency managed with the objective of internal price stability, Phillips, while leaving Hopkins' statement, added "It may come that in the end" (ibid., para. 16).

With respect to Hopkins' contention that Keynes's scheme involved an initial "very low" exchange rate of 3.40 and then in all probability a rapid rise to 4.40 or more, Phillips crossed out the latter statement and wrote that an initial rate of 3.40 "is fairly in accordance with the Treasury view, but on the Treasury view the exchange should not be allowed to move upwards unless and until world prices have moved upwards quite substantially. On Mr Keynes's plan the exchange must move upward immediately the price of raw materials shows any recovery". He agreed with Hopkins that an Imperial Currency Conference was not feasible and suggested "we . . . keep in touch with Egypt, the Scandinavian countries and other countries similarly situated to ourselves . . . through the Bank of England" (ibid., para. 19).

4. The final Treasury memorandum, of which there is unfortunately no copy in the Treasury files or the Cabinet papers of the time, was circulated to the Cabinet Committee on Currency Questions on 8 March (T. 188/48, "Committee on Currency Questions, Note by Chancellor", 8 March 1932), and consisted of two parts, one on the present position of the pound and the other on future policy, the latter comprising several short memoranda on the utility of an international monetary conference, silver, "the goods or commodity standard", "Empire Currency and the Sterling Block", and a brief concluding section. The many drafts (at least three of each section) are to be found in T. 175/56, T. 175/57, T. 175/58 and T. 175/64. Hopkins wrote an outline and the earliest drafts; the later drafts were (mostly) Phillips' work.

Hopkins' outline was as follows:

"SKELETON OUTLINE

I.

The present position
Present inability to control the pound.
Action necessary to obtain control and to safeguard the repayment of the foreign loans.
What is the desirable level of the pound?
Existing restrictions and the criticisms directed against them.

II.

The Future of the Gold Standard
Better management (cf. for instance report of Macmillan Committee).
Estimate of prospects of foreign central banks coming into line.
Point out that gold prices are still falling—they have dropped 4½% since we left gold.

* T. 188/48, "Note of Mr Keynes' Memorandum".

176

Short reference to Cassel and Kitchin and their theories of effect of gold shortage on world prices.

End by noting that so long as we only tie ourselves to gold de facto we have a measure of assurance against the worst vagaries of gold. For instance a fresh calamitous fall in the future would be met by lowering the exchange value of the pound. Nevertheless it is a remedy that could not be adopted too often and would need to be reserved for emergencies—since fluctuations in the gold value of sterling would greatly interfere with international investment.

III.

Silver
(Short but fairly comprehensive)

IV.

Specific development of British Empire Currencies
(An Empire standard is probably visionary but subject would be treated sympathetically)

V.

Commodity standards generally
(Adapt from the note on Keynes' plan)

VI.

The Question of international or imperial currency conferences."
(T. 176/56, Hopkins, "Skeleton Outline", n.d. but it follows immediately after two drafts of Hopkins' "Note on Mr Keynes' memorandum of 16 November").

Hopkins' last version of "The Present Position of the Pound" dealt with the inability of the Bank to control the pound and its need of additional resources, on the lines of his earlier memorandum (as amended by Phillips), and the question of the proper level of the pound, which he thought should be $3.60–$3.70 (see above p. 85).

The draft ended with a few paragraphs on "The Future of Sterling":

"We have got through the first three or four months fairly well . . . Great problems, however, still remain in the international sphere. Our credit abroad does not stand high. Our short-term obligations abroad are very great. The short-term claims of foreign countries upon London, though somewhat reduced, are still of great magnitude. Our resources are low. The United States, France, Italy, Germany, Holland and Switzerland still remain on gold and we cannot afford to dissociate ourselves completely from the currency standard of the most important commercial nations. Constant and wide fluctuations in the gold value of our own currency would be a most serious obstacle to our traders.

"All these considerations point in one direction, namely, that our essential objective is to link sterling de facto to gold at such a level as is best consonant with our national interests and at the time to acquire the command of sufficient immediate resources to enable us to view with equanimity further withdrawals from London on whatever scale they may be attempted. No other aim however important should be allowed to interfere. Indeed it is obvious that whatever value we might attach to particular reforms in world currency matters our ability to help in securing such reforms must for practical purposes be ranked at nil, until we have escaped from the position when our own financial standing is dependent on the forbearance of foreign powers.

177

"Further it must never be forgotten that foreign opinion on some currency matters is very different to British opinion. Projects which British economists generally might accept as at least matters for serious study and consideration are regarded abroad as heresies. The greatest care is needed at the present time lest a belief that official support is given here to certain debatable doctrines should precipitate foreign withdrawals and prolong the period of our comparative impotence."

(T. 175/57, Hopkins, "The Present Position of the Pound", 12 January 1932)

The next, Phillips' first, draft of this section differed in its view of the desirable objectives of monetary policy. Phillips himself told Henderson:

"[Though] the first part of this memorandum was written some little time back . . . I propose to leave it as it is, with a note that the position has undergone a change for the better since.

"I am also going to work in an argument for keeping exchange low, that the most desired objective is a general rise in world gold prices and that the most powerful single force working to that end is the flow of gold from India. Now the volume of that flow depends other things being equal on the depreciation of the rupee, that is the depreciation of sterling. A rise in sterling would have a deadening effect which would be most unfortunate etc.

"As a matter of fact, I have heard estimates given which suggest that the flow would not be much checked if sterling rose to 3.60 or 3.70 I feel sure however that 3.90 would cut off most of it."

(T. 175/57, Phillips to Henderson, 26 February 1932)

Hopkins' concluding paragraphs and his section on the proper level of the pound went, to be replaced by a brief statement of the arguments for $3.90 and a longer statement of those for $3.40 (T. 175/57, Phillips, "The Present Position of the Pound", 24 February 1932; see above pp. 85–6).

The first drafts of section II and V, "The Future of the Gold Standard" and "The Goods or Commodity Standard" were written by Hopkins (T. 175/64, handwritten drafts). Section III, on silver, was based on a longer memorandum by Waley (T. 160/411/F 3420/02, Memorandum on "Silver", n.d., unsigned but on which Waley had written "Draft given to Phillips for general currency memo, 5/1/32") and recommends inaction with respect to the "silver question" on the part of the British Government. Section V, in all its drafts, followed Hopkins' original memorandum on Keynes closely. The section on Empire Currencies was apparently written by Phillips (T. 177/8, Henderson to Phillips, 12 February 1932); after discussing various schemes that had been put forward in the 1920s for a single Empire currency, it advocated the formation of a sterling area and discussion of that at Ottawa.

"The Future of the Gold Standard" changed its name to "Future Policy", and its contents accordingly, under Phillips' influence. In the drafts Hopkins and Phillips repeated their views as they had expressed them in the (annotated) "Note on Mr Keynes' Memorandum of 16 November". Hopkins' January draft has already been quoted; Phillips, a month later, wrote instead:

"Looking . . . ahead we may contemplate a period of elastic de facto stabilisation, sterling probably rising from time to time in rough conformity with the rise of gold prices which sooner or later should arrive.

"For the more distant future nothing has been found which the world would accept as a substitute for gold.

"Our ultimate objective has been stated to be to return to gold as soon as circumstances permit; on the question of the time when, and the parity at which, we have not spoken and cannot speak. We may secretly feel that the time may be long: we may even wonder whether in the end some alternative course for the world as a whole will prove to be both prefereable and acceptable. But these can only be private speculations and it is useless to pursue them now.

"In the period pending restabilisation this country's natural aim would be to become the leader of a sterling block. The aim cannot be gained by divided and uncertain counsels and this country be reason of its unique position must have the undivided leadership. Adherence must be sought, not by the method of conference, but by good management of sterling . . . and by consideration for the needs of others.

"In general the least said the soonest mended. An international monetary conference summoned by this country would be a fiasco. A special inter-Imperial Currency Conference . . . would be neither necessary nor useful. What rather is needed . . . is a discussion, not too formal and not too ambitious, at Ottawa. The necessary touch with foreign countries that look to sterling can for the present be best maintained . . . informally by the Central Banks concerned."

(T. 175/57, Phillips, "Future Policy", 24 February 1932)

Phillips sent drafts of his "treatise" to Henderson, who of course took issue with Phillips over the exchange rate. Phillips therefore added the following paragraph:

"It must be admitted that some economists would not accept the argument just set out. They would of course agree that the *direct* result of a rising exchange must be adverse to the export trades. But they hold the view that the present depreciation of the pound has itself played an important part in reducing world gold prices and incidentally in stimulating the adoption of the system of quotas and surtax abroad. Thus they would anticipate as an *indirect* result of a rising exchange an improvement in the world situation and some relaxation of the network of trade restrictions abroad. On the whole this possibility of indirect advantages to the export trades from a rising exchange appears to the Treasury too uncertain to outweigh the other arguments."

Henderson did not think this did justice to his view and suggested another version of this paragraph, but it is not known whether this appeared in the final memorandum (owing to its disappearance). (T. 175/57, Phillips to Henderson, 26 February 1932; T. 188/48, Henderson to Phillips, 29 February 1932, Henderson to Phillips, 3 March 1932; T. 175/57, "The Present Position of the Pound, Second Edition", 29 February 1932).

Leith-Ross returned from the visits to Paris and Berlin which had kept him out of the Treasury in the early months of 1932 (Leith-Ross, *Money Talks*, p. 143) to be "struck by the apparent alarm and despondency caused by the recent strength of sterling" (now around $3.80). He thought the rate should be allowed to go up to at least $4 (T. 188/48, Leith-Ross, "The Present Position of Sterling", March 1932). For Phillips' reply see above p. 86.

Abbreviations

The following abbreviations have been used in the Tables, the Appendices, the Notes and the Bibliography.

AER	American Economic Review
BEQB	Bank of England Quarterly Bulletin
BESS	Bank of England Statistical Summary
BOIS	Bulletin of the Oxford Insitute of Statistics
C.N.R.A.	Currency Note Redemption Account
E.A.C.	Economic Advisory Council
E.E.A.	Exchange Equalization Account
EHR	Economic History Review
EJ	Economic Journal
F.R.B.N.Y.	Federal Reserve Bank of New York
G.D.F.C.F.	gross domestic fixed capital formation
G.D.P.	gross domestic product
G.N.P.	gross national product
H.M.S.O.	Her Majesty's Stationery Office
JMCB	Journal of Money, Credit and Banking
JMK	The Collected Writings of John Maynard Keynes
JPE	Journal of Political Economy
JRSS	Journal of the Royal Statistical Society
L.C.E.S.	London and Cambridge Economic Service
N.B.E.R.	National Bureau of Economic Research
N.D.C.	National Debt Commissioners
N.D.F.C.F.	net domestic fixed capital formation
NIER	National Institute Economic Review
N.I.E.S.R.	National Institute of Economic and Social Research
O.E.C.D.	Organisation for Economic Cooperation and Development
OEP	Oxford Economic Papers
QJE	Quarterly Journal of Economics
REStats	Review of Economics and Statistics
REStudies	Review of Economic Studies
SJPE	Scottish Journal of Political Economy

Notes

Public Record Office documents are preceded by the call number of the file or volume. The call numbers of all the files/volumes used are listed in the Bibliography.

Chapter 1

1 R.S. Sayers, *The Bank of England 1891–1944* (1976).
2 K. Wicksell, *Interest and Prices*, p. xxviii; *Lectures on Political Economy*, Vol. II, pp. 190–208; J.M. Keynes, *A Treatise on Money* (*JMK*, Vols. V and VI), Chapters 13 and 37; *The General Theory of Employment Interest and Money* (*JMK*, Vol. VII), pp. 171–2, 197–201; M. Friedman, "Money and Business Cycles", in *The Optimum Quantity of Money and other Essays*, pp. 229–34.
3 Keynes, *General Theory*, Chapter 12 and pp. 315–20; "The 'Ex Ante' Theory of the Rate of Interest" in *JMK*, Vol. XIV, pp. 217–22; "The General Theory of Employment" in *JMK*, Vol. XIV, pp. 117–19; A.R. Roe, "The Case for Flow of Funds and National Balance Sheet Accounts", *EJ*, June 1973.
4 For a survey of the theories and evidence on the factors determining the relation between interest rates on short- and long-term securities see Appendix 3.
5 Goodhart, "The Importance of Money", *BEQB*, June 1970, p. 161.
6 Ibid., p. 161; Friedman and Meiselman, "The Relative Stability of Monetary Velocity and the Investment Multiplier in the U.S. 1897–1958", in Commission on Money and Credit, *Stabilization Policies*, pp. 213–22.
7 Fisher and Sheppard, *Effects of Monetary Policy on the United States Economy: A Survey of Econometric Evidence*, p. 3.
8 Meade and Andrews, "Summary of Replies to Questions on the Effects of Interest Rates" in Wilson and Andrews (eds.), *Oxford Studies in the Price Mechanism*.
9 Meyer and Kuh, *The Investment Decision* (1957); Eisner and Strotz, "Determinants of Business Investment", in Commission on Money and Credit, *Impacts of Monetary Policy* (1963); Jorgenson, "Econometric Studies of Investment Behaviour: a Survey", *Journal of Economic Literature*, 1971.
10 Ibid.
11 Fisher and Sheppard, *Effects of Monetary Policy on the U.S. Economy*, Chapter 3; de Leeuw and Gramlich, "The Federal Reserve-MIT Econometric Model", *Federal Reserve Bulletin*, January 1968; de Leeuw and Gramlich, "The Channels of Monetary Policy", *Federal Reserve Bulletin*, June 1969; Modigliani, "Monetary Policy and Consumption: Linkages via Interest Rate and Wealth Effects in the FMP Model", in Federal Reserve Bank of Boston Conference Series no. 5, *Consumer Spending and Monetary Policy: the Linkages*, June 1971, and "The Channels of Monetary Policy in the Federal Reserve-MIT-University of Pennsylvania Econometric Model of the United States", in G. Renton (ed.), *Modelling the Economy* (1975).
12 See the articles by Modigliani cited in previous note; and O.E.C.D., *Monetary Policy in the United States* (1974), pp. 80–4.
13 C.M.E. Whitehead, *The U.K. Housing Market: an Econometric Model* (1974); L.B. Smith, *The Postwar Canadian Housing and Residential Mortgage Markets and the Role of Government* (1974).
14 Tobin, "Monetary Semantics", in K. Brunner (ed.), *Targets and Indicators of Monetary Policy*.
15 See Friedman, "Money and Business Cycles" and "The Monetary Studies of the National Bureau" in *The Optimum Quantity of Money and other Essays*, pp. 189–90,

265, and "A Theoretical Framework for Monetary Analysis", *JPE*, April 1970.

16   See, for example, Keynes, "A Monetary Theory of Production", in *JMK*, Vol. XIII, and "The General Theory of Employment", in *JMK*, Vol. XIV; J. Robinson, "The Production Function and the Theory of Capital", *REStudies*, 1954; Samuelson, "The Paradoxes of Capital Theory: a summing up", *QJE*, November 1966; Hahn, "On some problems of proving the existence of equilibrium in a monetary economy", in Hahn and Brechling (eds.), *The Theory of Interest Rates* (1965).

17   Keynes, *The General Theory*, Chapter 22.

18   Hawtrey, *Currency and Credit*, Chapters I, III and IV; Kaldor, "Hawtrey on Short- and Long-term Investment" in *Essays on Economic Stability and Growth*, pp. 79–82; see below pp. 19, 23–4, 41.

19   Kavanagh and Walters, "The Demand for Money in the U.K. 1877–1961, Some Preliminary Findings", *BOIS*, 1966; Barratt and Walters, "The Stability of Keynesian and Monetary Multipliers in the U.K.", *REStats*, November 1966; Walters, "Monetary Multipliers in the U.K.", *OEP*, November 1966; Walters, "The Radcliffe Report – Ten Years After, A Survey of Empirical Evidence", in Croome and Johnson (eds.), *Money in Britain 1959–1969*; Goodhart and Crockett, "The Importance of Money", *BEQB*, June 1970; Laidler, "The Influence of Money on Economic Activity: some current problems", in Clayton, Gilbert and Sedgwick (eds.), *Monetary Theory and Monetary Policy in the 1970s*.

20   Walters, "Monetary Multipliers in the U.K." and "A Survey of Empirical Evidence", pp. 54–5.
Recent Bank of England studies on lags in monetary policy in Britain have also come up with similar results (Crockett, "Timing Relationships between Movements of Monetary and National Income Variables", *BEQB*, December 1970; L.L.D. Price, "The Demand for Money in the U.K.: a further investigation", *BEQB*, March 1972).

21   Sheppard, *The Growth and Role of U.K. Financial Institutions 1880–1962*, Chapters 3, 4 and 5.

22   Ibid., p. 39.

23   Ibid., p. 40.

24   Ibid., pp. 44, 46–7, 63–4. On the usefulness of the money supply model see Tobin, "The Monetary Interpretation of History", *AER*, June 1965, pp. 467–71. A simple multiplier theory of deposit creation would require D/R and D/C to be constant.

25   A.J. Brown, "The Liquidity-Preference Schedules of the London Clearing Banks", *OEP*, 1938.

26   Goodwin, "Studies in Money, England and Wales 1919–38", Unpublished Harvard Ph.D. thesis, 1941, Chapter I.

27   Ibid., pp. 68–9

28   Ibid., Chapter II; see also Goodwin, "The Supply of Bank Money in England and Wales", *OEP*, June 1941; below pp. 74–8.

29   Ibid., pp. 95–103.

30   Ibid., p. 107.

31   Ibid., pp. 154–71.

32   Laidler and Parkin, "Inflation: s Survey", *EJ*, December 1975.

Chapter 2

1   For example, Hawtrey, *Currency and Credit* (4th edition), pp. 372–3; *A Century of Bank Rate*, pp. 130–4; Keynes, *A Treatise on Money*, Vol. II (*JMK*, Vol. VI), p. 158; Pigou, *Aspects of British Economic History 1918–1925* (hereafter *Aspects*), pp. 196–7; Sayers, *Central Banking after Bagehot*, p. 70; Tawney, "Abolition of Economic Controls 1918–21", *EHR*, 1943, p. 15.
The same criticisms have been levelled at the U.S. authorities in 1919–21: Friedman and Schwartz, *A Monetary History of the United States 1867 1960*, pp. 229–34.

2   Pigou, *Aspects*, p. 5.

3   Ibid., pp. 5–7; Morgan, *Studies in British Financial Policy 1914–1925* (hereafter *Studies*), pp. 82–4.

4   The average trade union unemployment percentage for 1919 was 2.4 compared with the prewar average of 4.1 for 1900–13, while in the years 1921–6 the minimum percentage was 8.1 (1924); the Ministry of Labour figure for the percentage unemployed among insured workpeople for December 1919 was 6.6, the following December it was 7.9 and thereafter it averaged 14.1 (1921–38) for this time of year.

5   Feinstein, *National Income, Output and Expenditure of the U.K. 1855–1965*

(hereafter *National Income*), Tables 51 and 5. It should be remembered that the G.D.P. figures for these years are only rough estimates, with a margin of error of ± 15−25% (ibid., p. 22).

6   *Aspects*, pp. 154−60.
7   Aldcroft, *The Inter-War Economy: Britain 1919−1939*, p. 35; see also Pigou, *Aspects*, pp. 173−4.
8   Ibid., pp. 172−3.
9   Ibid., p. 172.
10   Keynes Papers, Unpublished Minutes of Committee on Finance and Industry, 31 October 1930.
11   Rothbarth's tables in Pigou, *Aspects*, p. 227.
12   Cab. 24/97, C.P. 564, Board of Trade Report, 23 January 1920.
13   *The Economist*, Commercial History and Review of 1919, 21 February 1920.
14   Cab. 24/86, G.T. 7905, Board of Trade Report, 16 June 1919.
15   It has sometimes been suggested, for example by Sayers, *A History of Economic Change in England 1880−1939*, p. 50, that the fall in export demand caused the boom to break when businessmen observed signs of a decline in orders. However, the evidence cited in notes 12 and 13 suggests a decline in home demand preceded that in export orders.
16   Pigou, *Aspects*, p. 7; Morgan suggests the end of 1921 (*Studies*, p. 85); the N.B.E.R. reference cycle date is June 1921, the last month of the coal strike.
17   Morgan, *Studies*, pp. 13−14, 166−9, 241.
18   This section is a shortened version of Howson, "The Origins of Dear Money, 1919−20", *EHR*, February 1974.
19   The U.K. had been legally on the gold standard throughout the War, and even after March 1919 notes and coin remained legally convertible into gold. However, the circulation of gold coin had fallen considerably during the War and immediately afterwards, and there was no later return to an internal gold circulation (Morgan, *Studies*, pp. 217−18). On the rate of wartime pegging, see Keynes, *A Treatise on Money*, Vol. I (*JMK*, Vol. V), p. 17; Keynes Papers L/29, Waley to Keynes, 19 and 26 April 1929.
20   *The Times*, 31 March 1919.
21   Committee on Currency and Foreign Exchanges after the War, *First Interim Report*, Cd. 9182 (1918). The prerequisites for the restoration were cessation of government borrowing, use of Bank rate to protect the exchanges, and limitation of the note issue (para. 47).
22   Pigou, *Aspects*, p. 148; W.A. Brown, Jr., *England and the New Gold Standard 1919−1926*, p. 8.
23   B.B. Gilbert, *British Social Policy 1914−1939*, pp. 17−18.
24   Cab. 24/75, G.T. 6820, "Minutes of a Conference . . . on Unemployment and the State of Trade", 17 February 1919.
25   Cab. 27/58, G. 237 and Appendices, and Cab. 24/75, G.T. 6887.
26   Cab. 24/75, G.T. 6887, "Shorthand notes of a Conference . . . 25 February 1919 on Unemployment and the State of Trade." The conference is discussed fully in P.B. Johnson, *Land Fit for Heroes: The Planning of British Reconstruction 1916−1919*, pp. 364−74.
27   Cab. 27/58, G. 237, Appendix VIII (G.T. 7002).
28   McFadyean of the Treasury, who attended the meeting, told ministers that Chamberlain would welcome a recommendation to end exchange support; see also Keynes, Letter to *The Times*, 27 February 1924, in *JMK*, Vol. XVI, p. 412.
29   T. 170/140, Note of meeting with bankers, 27 March 1919.
30   T. 170/125, "Reconstruction finance", 21 February 1918.
31   T. 185/1, Cunliffe Committee Minutes, Vol. I, pp. 93, 107.
32   Ibid., p. 340.
33   T. 185/2, Cunliffe Committee Minutes, Vol. II, p. 530.
34   T. 185/1, pp. 116−21.
35   Ibid., pp. 283−4.
36   Ibid., p. 95.
37   *Interim Report*, paras. 16, 17, 20, 21, 40, 41, 43, 44.
38   Clay, *Lord Norman*, p. 113.
39   T. 172/895, Cokayne to Chancellor, 16 October 1918.
40   Clay, *Lord Norman*, p. 114.
41   Boyle, *Montagu Norman*, pp. 124−5.

42 Clay, *Lord Norman*, p. 116.
43 Ibid., pp. 117–18; Boyle, *Montagu Norman*, pp. 125–6.
44 T. 172/1020, Cokayne to Chancellor, 12 February, Chancellor to Cokayne, 15 February 1919.
45 Morgan, *Studies*, p. 116.
46 T. 172/1059, Cokayne to Chancellor, 10 July 1919.
47 Cab. 27/71, F.C. 1.
48 Cab. 27/71, F.C. 1, Appendix, "Defence of Realm Regulations 41D and 30F and Customs Prohibition of Import of Securities".
49 Cab. 27/71, F.C. 1.
   On 18 August 1919 the Treasury permitted remittance abroad for the purchase of existing securities or new issues made outside the U.K. Control was maintained over issue for capital purposes abroad until 11 November 1919, controls over domestic new issues having been removed in March (Morgan, *Studies*, pp. 64–5).
50 Clay, *Lord Norman*, p. 120; H.M. Treasury, C.N.R.A. ledger.
51 Ibid.
52 Johnson, *Land Fit for Heroes*, pp. 350, 444–9.
53 Boyle, *Montagu Norman*, pp. 126–7; Clay, *Lord Norman*, p. 120.
54 Norman's diary, quoted in Boyle, *Montagu Norman*, p. 127.
55 Cab. 27/72, F.C. Paper 5.
56 Clay, *Lord Norman*, p. 121.
57 Pigou, *Aspects*, p. 148.
58 *Hansard* (Commons), 15 December 1919, cols. 43–5.
59 Morgan, *Studies*, p. 147.
60 Ibid., p. 250.
61 Clay, *Lord Norman*, p. 124.
62 T. 172/1384, Cokayne to Chancellor, 25 February 1920.
63 T. 172/1384, Bank memorandum, 10 February 1920.
64 T. 172/1384, Niemeyer to Blackett, 3 February 1920.
65 T. 172/1384, Hawtrey, "Cheap or Dear Money?", 4 February 1920.
   Therefore, although Hawtrey was strongly in favour of raising Bank rate early in 1920, by the summer he wanted it to be reduced, and he blamed the slump on the delay in reducing it (Hawtrey, "The Return to Gold in 1925", *Bankers Magazine*, August 1969; *A Century of Bank Rate*, pp. 132–3; T. 176/5, "The Credit Situation", 19 August 1921).
66 The two letters are in the Keynes Papers and will be published in *JMK*, Vol. XVII.
67 T. 172/1384, Note of Interview with Keynes, 4 February 1920.
68 T. 172/1384, Keynes to Chancellor, 15 February 1920.
   The file was collected together during the Second World War at Keynes's request and includes a comment by him in 1942. This shows he did not regret having given this advice in the circumstances. He wrote:
   > "What impresses me most is the complete hopelessness of the situation. All controls had been abandoned . . . With all the methods of control, then so unorthodox, excluded, I feel myself that I should give today exactly the same advice that I gave then, namely a swift and severe dose of dear money, sufficient to break the market, and quick enough to prevent at least some of the disastrous consequences which would otherwise ensue. In fact the remedies of the economists were taken, but too timidly."
   For further information on Keynes's views on monetary policy in 1920 and their relation to his later views, see Howson, " 'A Dear Money Man'?: Keynes on Monetary Policy, 1920", *EJ*, June 1973.
69 T. 172/1384, Blackett Memorandum on Dear Money, 19 February 1920.
70 T. 172/1384, Blackett to Chancellor, 21 February 1920.
71 T. 172/1384, Blackett to Chancellor, 4 March 1920.
72 Clay, *Lord Norman*, p. 126.
73 T. 172/1384, Notes on Conferences with Bankers, 9 and 11 March 1920.
74 T. 172/1384, Blackett to Chancellor, 11 March 1920.
75 Keynes Papers, to be published in *JMK*, Vol. XVII.
76 Clay, *Lord Norman*, pp. 127–8.
77 Pigou, *Aspects*, pp. 169–70.
78 Morgan, *Studies*, pp. 99–105.
79 *National Income*, Table 12.

80 Keynes, *A Treatise on Money*, Vol. II (*JMK*, Vol. VI), pp. 119–25; Kaldor, "Hawtrey on Short- and Long-term Investment", in *Essays on Economic Stability and Growth*.

81 Dow, *The Management of the British Economy 1945–1960*, pp. 293–5.

82 Keynes, *Treatise*, Vol. II, pp. 119–25; Kaldor, "Hawtrey on Short- and Long-term Investment".

83 Above, p. 6.

84 *The Economist*, 18 October 1919; Pigou, *Aspects*, p. 171.

85 Cab. 24/97, C.P.564, Board of Trade Report, 23 January 1920.

86 Private sector G.D.F.C.F. at current prices fell from £379m in 1920 to £299m in 1921 and £261m in 1922. Total G.D.F.C.F. did not fall as much because of the substantial increase in local authority investment, chiefly in housebuilding, from £90m in 1920 to £141m in 1921 (£109m in 1922) (Feinstein, *National Income*, Table 39).

87 Armitage, *The Politics of Decontrol*, pp. 13–15, 20; Johnson, *Land Fit for Heroes*, pp. 375, 394–402; Morgan, *Studies*, pp. 59–66.

88 Pigou, *Aspects*, pp. 169–70.

89 T. 172/1384, Note by Keynes, 7 January 1942; T. 160/1378/F 18064/04, Keynes, "New Issues Control", 29 January 1945.
Grant has suggested financial controls alone would have been sufficient in 1919–20 (*A Study of the Capital Market in Britain 1919–1936*, p. 85); experience in and after the Second World War indicates physical controls would have been needed as they were later (Dow, *The Management of the British Economy 1945–1960*, pp. 242–4).

90 Ibid., pp. 10–11, 27–9, 49, 54, 116.

91 T. 171/180, Blackett, "Present Conditions in Finance and Industry", 28 June 1920.

92 Clay, *Lord Norman*, p. 132.

93 Ibid., pp. 128–9.

94 Morgan, *Studies*, p. 146.

95 Ibid., pp. 210–1.

96 Grant, *A Study of the Capital Market*, p. 83.

97 Clay, *Lord Norman*, pp. 131–2.

98 Morgan, *Studies*, pp. 250–1.

99 Ibid., pp. 256–7.

100 Ibid., pp. 118–19.

101 T. 160/194/F 7380/02, Niemeyer to Chancellor, 5 December 1924; see also T. 171/196, Blackett to Chancellor, 14 March 1921, in which Blackett suggested the issue.

102 Morgan, *Studies*, p. 120.

103 Clay, *Lord Norman*, p. 133.

104 Chandler, *Benjamin Strong: Central Banker*, p. 174.

105 Clay, *Lord Norman*, pp. 132–3.

106 T. 175/5, Hawtrey, "The Credit Situation", 19 April 1921.

107 Clay, *Lord Norman*, pp. 135, 140–1; Letter Norman to Strong, 6 February 1922, quoted in Chandler, *Strong*, pp. 304–5.

108 Morgan, *Studies*, p. 209.

109 T. 176/5, Niemeyer Memorandum on Deflation, no date but position in file indicates 1921.

110 T. 176/5 and T. 172/1208, Blackett to Chancellor, 8 June 1921.

111 See, e.g., T. 176/5, Niemeyer to Chancellor, 5 October 1921.

112 T. 172/1208, Niemeyer to Colonial Secretary, 5 October 1921; Niemeyer to Chancellor, 7 October 1921; Note by Hilton Young (then Financial Secretary to the Treasury) of interview with Norman; Cab. 23/27, Cabinets 79(21) and 80(21), 14 and 17 October 1921.
The Treasury view prevailed more "successfully" in bringing about the end of Addison's housing scheme (Gilbert, *British Social Policy 1914–1939*, pp. 77, 151–2, 158–9; Johnson, *Land Fit for Heroes*, pp. 497–9). The Treasury was not alone in its desire for economy at all costs: the "Geddes axe" started to swing in February 1922. On the Geddes Committee, see, for example, U.K. Hicks, *The Finance of British Government 1920–1936*, pp. 5–6, 28, 63, 336.

113 *Studies*, p. 210.

114 Ibid., pp. 212–13.

115 *The Economist*, 16 February 1924.

116 *Studies*, p. 213; Sayers, *Central Banking after Bagehot*, p. 72.

117 T. 175/13, Niemeyer to Norman, 23 June 1923.

118   *Lord Norman*, pp. 145–6.
119   Sayers, *Central Banking after Bagehot*, p. 70.
120   T. 176/5, Niemeyer to Chancellor, March 1924.
121   Morgan, *Studies*, p. 255. On window-dressing see below, pp. 45–6.

Chapter 3

1   Pigou, *Aspects*, p. 7.
2   For example, by Sayers, *A History of Economic Change in England 1880–1939*, pp. 51–3.
3   Commercial Histories and Reviews of 1922–9.
4   *A Monetary History of the United States 1867–1960*, p. 41.
5   *A Century of Bank Rate*, p. 137.
6   *JMK*, Vol. VI, pp. 162–3, 165.
7   *Central Banking after Bagehot*, p. 79.
8   "The Return to Gold, 1925", in Pollard (ed.), *The Gold Standard and Employment Policies between the Wars*, p. 93. Sayers does, however, assign restrictive monetary policy a role in keeping the U.K. in the doldrums (see below pp. 56 and 93).
9   *British Monetary Policy 1924–1931*, p. 112.
10   Ibid., pp. 98–112.
11   Lomax, "Production and Productivity Movements in the U.K. since 1900", *JRSS*, 1959, and "Growth and Productivity in the U.K.", *Productivity Measurement Review*, 1964; Feinstein, *Domestic Capital Formation in the U.K. 1920–1938* (1965).
12   E.g., Aldcroft, "Economic Growth in Britain in the inter-war years: a Reassessment", in Aldcroft and Fearon (eds.), *Economic Growth in Twentieth-Century Britain*, and "Economic Progress in Britain in the 1920s", in Aldcroft and Richardson, *The British Economy 1870–1939*; Richardson, "The Basis of Economic Recovery in the 1930s", "Over-Commitment in Britain before 1930", and "The New Industries between the Wars", all in Aldcroft and Richardson, *The British Economy 1870–1939*.
13   *The British Economy 1870–1939*, p. 55; see also Aldcroft, "The Impact of British Monetary Policy, 1919–39", *Revue Internationale d'Histoire de la Banque*, 1970, and "British Monetary Policy and Economic Activity in the 1920s", *Revue Internationale d'Histoire de la Banque*, 1972.
14   See, e.g., T. 176/5, Niemeyer Memorandum on Deflation, 1921; T. 172/1384, Blackett Memorandum on Dear Money, 19 February 1920; T. 176/5, Hawtrey, "The Credit Situation", 19 April 1921 and "Bank Rate", 5 July 1921.
15   *JMK*, Vol. IV, pp. 63, 67.
16   *JMK*, Vol. V, p. 140.
17   Ibid., pp. 245–6.
18   *JMK*, Vol. VII, p. 291.
19   Ibid., pp. 118–19.
20   Ibid., p. 304.
21   H.G. Johnson, "A Survey of theories of inflation", in *Essays in Monetary Economics*, pp. 104, 106–7.
22   The discussion of Bank of England policy in 1924–31 is heavily dependent on Clay, *Lord Norman*, Chapters IV and VI, S.V.O. Clarke, *Central Bank Cooperation 1924–1931*, Chapters 7–9, and Moggridge, *British Monetary Policy 1924–1931*, Chapters 5–9.
23   Youngson, *Britain's Economic Growth 1920–1966*, p. 27.
24   Morgan, *Studies*, p. 214.
25   Clay, *Lord Norman*, p. 143; Clarke, *Central Bank Cooperation*, pp. 76–7, 85–7; Chandler, *Benjamin Strong*, pp. 241–3.
26   Clarke, *Central Bank Cooperation*, p. 86.
27   Moggridge, *British Monetary Policy*, pp. 54, 222.
28   Morgan, *Studies*, p. 215.
29   Moggridge, *British Monetary Policy*, p. 38.
30   Clay, *Lord Norman*, pp. 148, 164; Moggridge, *British Monetary Policy*, pp. 27–8, 50, 53.
31   Another way Norman assisted was his negotiation in New York of the Federal Reserve and Morgan credits (Clarke, *Central Bank Cooperation*, pp. 81–2; Chandler, *Strong*, pp. 308–21; Moggridge, *British Monetary Policy*, pp. 57–61, 79–83). Sterling was also, and probably more importantly, improved by speculative movements of funds to London in anticipation of an early return to gold (ibid., p. 87; Clarke, p. 93) and also by fortuitous developments (ibid., pp. 93–5).

32 Morgan, *Studies*, p. 215.
33 Clarke, *Central Bank Cooperation*, pp. 88–9; Moggridge, *British Monetary Policy*, p. 131.
34 Sayers, *Central Banking after Bagehot*, p. 73.
35 T. 176/13, Niemeyer to Norman, 21 July 1925.
36 T. 176/13, Norman to Niemeyer, 25 July 1925.
37 F.R.B.N.Y., Norman to Strong, 22 and 26 May 1925; Moggridge, *British Monetary Policy*, p. 131.
38 *Central Bank Cooperation*, p. 100.
39 Ibid., pp. 101–2; Moggridge, *British Monetary Policy*, p. 132.
40 Committee on Finance and Industry, *Minutes of Evidence*, Q. 7596. The Governor gave difficulties with Treasury bill sales as the reason to Leith-Ross at the Treasury the day before the increase (T. 176/13, Memorandum by Leith-Ross, 3 December 1925).
41 Moggridge, *British Monetary Policy*, pp. 132, 164.
42 Ibid., pp. 162–4; Clay, *Lord Norman*, pp. 221–2, 233.
43 Clarke, *Central Bank Cooperation*, p. 102; Moggridge, *British Monetary Policy*, pp. 162–3.
44 T. 176/13, Relations between Treasury and Bank of England – Testimony of former Permanent Secretaries and Controllers of Finance, December 1925.
45 Clay, *Lord Norman*, p. 225.
46 Moggridge, *British Monetary Policy*, pp. 132–3.
47 Clarke, *Central Bank Cooperation*, p. 103.
48 Clay, *Lord Norman*, p. 235; Moggridge, *British Monetary Policy*, p. 133.
49 Ibid., pp. 133–6; Clarke, *Central Bank Cooperation*, pp. 11–12, 115–30; Clay, *Lord Norman*, pp. 227–32, 235–7.
50 Ibid., pp. 238–53; Clarke, *Central Bank Cooperation*, pp. 147–64; Moggridge, *British Monetary Policy* pp. 136–9; Friedman and Schwartz, *A Monetary History of the U.S.*, pp. 254–68; Chandler, *American Monetary Policy 1928–1941*, pp. 46–70.
51 Several times in 1928 and 1929 the Treasury told the Bank that it did not want to see any increase in Bank rate (Moggridge, *British Monetary Policy*, p. 162).
52 Reserves hidden from the Treasury helped Norman in this (ibid., pp. 183–5; below p. 83).
53 Clay, *Lord Norman*, p. 238; below p. 36.
54 Moggridge, *British Monetary Policy*, p. 137.
55 Ibid., pp. 138–9, 163–4; Clarke, *Central Bank Cooperation*, p. 159.
56 According to Youngson, "Monetary policy after 1925 is inevitably simpler than before . . . There could no longer be vacillation or alternation between policies designed to facilitate government financing, policies designed to maintain the exchange value of the pound, and policies designed to improve the level of economic activity at home." (*Britain's Economic Growth 1920–1966*, pp. 31–2). The discussion of policy 1920–5 in this and the previous chapter shows that the Bank and the Treasury had clear aims and did not let others interfere. After 1925, the Bank faced a constant problem of reconciling conflicting aims (even if one set was "politically" inspired) and management was more necessary, not less.
57 *Minutes of Evidence*, Q. 7512.
58 Ibid., Q. 7597.
59 Moggridge, *British Monetary Policy*, Chapters 7–9.
60 Ibid., pp. 219–20.
61 Ibid., pp. 147–53; Clarke, *Central Bank Cooperation*, p. 103; Sayers, *Central Banking after Bagehot*, p. 52.
62 Moggridge, *British Monetary Policy*, pp. 147–53.
63 T. 176/13, Niemeyer to Norman, 23 June 1923.
64 Williams, "Montagu Norman and Banking Policy in the 1920s", *Yorkshire Bulletin of Economic and Social Research*, 1959.
65 T. 172/1499B, Niemeyer, "Notes on the Gold Standard", 29 April 1925; Hawtrey and Niemeyer, "The Gold Standard and American Influence", 13 May 1925; T. 176/16, Niemeyer, "Gold Standard Results", 4 August 1925; T. 175/11, Churchill to Niemeyer, 20 May, and Niemeyer to Churchill, 27 May 1927.
66 Moggridge, *British Monetary Policy*, pp. 162–3.
67 Sayers, *Central Banking after Bagehot*, p. 70.
68 T. 160/194/F 7380/02, "Ways and Means Advances and Treasury Bills".

69 Ibid.; the memorandum is a summary of Hawtrey, "Floating Debt", 23 October 1924, in the same file; see also Committee on National Debt and Taxation, *Minutes*, QQ. 8689–90.
70 Ibid., Keynes's Evidence-in-Chief, 1 October 1924, para. 2, and QQ. 3952–63.
71 The Treasury did run into this complication in 1928–30 (T. 175/40, Hopkins to Grigg, 21 October 1929).
72 T. 176/5 and T. 172/1208, Niemeyer to Colonial Secretary, 5 October 1921; above, pp. 12–13.
    To this argument it can be objected that owners of gilt-edged stocks are cautious and will reinvest in other gilt-edged stocks (Colwyn Committee, *Minutes*, Keynes's Evidence-in-Chief, para. 3, and QQ. 2974–8).
73 See Treasury files T. 160/226/F 8469, T. 160/551/F 9973, T. 175/15 and T. 175/25.
74 T. 160/198/F 5478, Niemeyer to Chancellor, 21 March 1924. The reasons given are very similar to those for the 1921 Conversion Loan (above p. 26).
75 T. 160/551/F 9973, Niemeyer to Chancellor, 23 November 1926.
76 T. 160/551/F 9973, Niemeyer to Churchill, 20 January 1927.
77 T. 160/239/F 8970, Niemeyer to Churchill, 17 September 1925. The timing of this issue, followed as it was by a rise in Bank rate, gave rise to criticism in the House of Commons the following March. In his brief for Churchill Niemeyer contended the Bank rate increase had been unexpected! (T. 160/239/F 8970, Niemeyer to Churchill, 18 March 1926).
78 T. 175/15, Hopkins to Churchill, 10 August 1928.
79 T. 175/15, Churchill to Hopkins, 14 August 1928.
80 T. 175/25, Hopkins to Chancellor, 10 January 1929.
    The two conversion issues of 4% Consols in July 1928 and July 1929 were consequences of the conversion rights offered in the prospectuses for 5% Treasury Bonds in December 1927 and 4½% Treasury Bonds in November 1928.
81 T. 175/15, Hopkins to Chancellor, 28 October 1929.
82 T. 160/429/F 11721, Hopkins to Chancellor, 6 February 1930.
83 *The Economist*, 9 November 1929.
84 T. 175/26, Hopkins, "Notes for Evidence. Conversion Loan and paying-off Treasury Bills", not dated but file indicates May or June 1929; see also later version of Notes in T. 176/46, and Committee on Finance and Industry, *Minutes of Evidence*, QQ. 5429–33, 16 May 1930.
85 T. 175/26, Hawtrey, "Floating Debt and Business Conditions", April 1930; "Debt Policy and Unemployment", 29 June 1929; "Debt Policy and Unemployment, II", 15 July 1929.
86 T. 172/1272, "Budgeting for a Deficit", 24 March 1922.
87 Niemeyer's evidence to the Colwyn Committee on National Debt and Taxation, *Minutes*, QQ. 8797, 8799, 3 November 1925, and Q. 68, 2 May 1924.
88 T. 175/40, Hopkins to Grigg, 21 October 1929.
89 U.K. Hicks, *The Finance of British Government 1920–1936*, pp. 7–11.
90 Ibid., pp. 6–7, 12; Morgan, *Studies*, p. 97.
91 *National Income,* Table 12.
92 Keynes, *A Treatise on Money*, Vol. II (*JMK*, Vol. VI), pp. 54, 65–6; Goodwin, "Studies in Money, England and Wales 1919–38", pp. 50–3.
93 Ibid., p. 52.
94 Sayers, *Modern Banking* (1st edition), pp. 36–40, 142–3; Morgan, *Studies*, pp. 229–38; Balogh, *Studies in Financial Organization*, pp. 45–56.
95 "Studies in Money", pp. 37–43.
96 Ibid., pp. 37–8.
97 Ibid., p. 40.
98 Ibid., p. 41.
99 Ibid., p. 35.
100 Ibid., p. 60.
101 Ibid., pp. 66, 75.
102 Keynes, *A Treatise on Money*, Vol. II (*JMK*, Vol. VI), p. 9.
103 Ibid., p. 9.
104 "Studies in Money", p. 72.
105 Ibid., pp. 73–5.
106 Sheppard, *The Growth and Role of U.K. Financial Institutions*, pp. 48–50.
107 Moggridge, *British Monetary Policy*, pp. 4, 164–5.

108 J.R. Hicks, "Mr Hawtrey on Bank Rate and the Long-term Rate of Interest", *The Manchester School*, 1939.

109 Moggridge, *British Monetary Policy*, pp. 221–4.

110 Morgan, "The Future of Interest Rates", *EJ*, 1944.

111 Hicks, "Mr Hawtrey on Bank Rate and the Long-term Rate of Interest", *The Manchester School*, 1939.

112 Williams, emphasizing the effect on expectations of high short rates, attributes high long rates primarily to Bank policy ("Montagu Norman and Banking Policy in the 1920s", *Yorkshire Bulletin of Economic and Social Research*, 1959).

113 The quoted expression is Niemeyer's: T. 188/14, Niemeyer to Churchill, April 1927.

114 Grant, *A Study of the Capital Market in Britian 1919–1936*, p. 115.

115 Ibid., p. 108.

116 Ibid., p. 143–4; Kindleberger, *Economic Growth in France and Britain 1860–1960*, pp. 87–8; Nevin, *The Mechanism of Cheap Money*, pp. 220–1.

117 *A Study of the Capital Market*, pp. 96–7.

118 *The Economist*, 10 November 1928, p. 854.

119 Grant, *A Study of the Capital Market*, pp. 143–6; R.A. Harris, "A Re-analysis of the 1928 New Issue Boom", *EJ*, September 1933.

120 U.K. Hicks, *The Finance of British Government*, pp. 352–3.

121 Kindleberger, *Economic Growth in France and Britain*, p. 67.

122 *The Mechanism of Cheap Money*, pp. 226–8.

123 Committee on Finance and Industry, *Report*, para. 404.

124 R.F. Henderson, *The New Issue Market*, pp. 39, 65–6, 129, 138–9; Balogh, *Studies in Financial Organization*, pp. 281–2; Frost, "The Macmillan Gap, 1931–53", *OEP*, 1954, p. 184.

125 Meyer and Kuh, *The Investment Decision*, p. 167.
The discrimination against the small firm in the capital market and the greater vulnerability of small firms in tight credit conditions has recently been strongly confirmed for the U.K. in the postwar period by Davis and Yeomans, *Company Finance and the Capital Market, A Study of the Effects of Firm Size* (1974).

126 Sayers, "The Rate of Interest as a Weapon of Economic Policy", in Wilson and Andrews (eds.), *Oxford Studies in the Price Mechanism*, p. 14.

127 Clay, "The Financing of Industrial Enterprise", *Transactions of the Manchester Statistical Society*, 1931–2; Balogh, *Studies in Financial Organization*, p. 278.

128 E.g., Meade and Andrews, "Summary of Replies to Questions on the Effects of Interest Rates", in *Oxford Studies in the Price Mechanism*; Meyer and Kuh, *The Investment Decision*; Eisner and Strotz, "Determinants of Business Investment", in Commission on Money and Credit, *Impacts of Monetary Policy*.
The findings of Lund and Holden for interwar Britain seem to be consistent with the above evidence, since profits are one of the more useful explanatory variables in their regression equations (P.J. Lund and K. Holden, "A Econometric Study of Private Sector Gross Fixed Capital Formation in the U.K., 1923–38", *OEP*, 1968).

129 Grant, *A Study of the Capital Market*, pp. 196–7.

130 Keynes, a shareholder in the company, wrote to one of the directors to warn him of the dangers of such investments (Keynes Papers L/23, Keynes to Sir John Wormald, 21 February 1923).

131 A formal model from which these propositions can be derived is given by Cunningham, "Business Investment and the Marginal Cost of Funds", *Metroeconomica*, 1958.

132 Meyer and Kuh, *The Investment Decision*, pp. 159–80, 94–100, 136–58, 116–53, 166–80; Davis and Yeomans, *Company Finance and the Capital Market*.

133 Schumpeter, *Business Cycles*, Vol. II, pp. 692–5; Sayers, *A History of Economic Change in England 1880–1939*, pp. 31–2; Feinstein, *National Income*, p. 18.

134 Burns and Mitchell, *Measuring Business Cycles*, p. 79.

135 *A Century of Bank Rate*, p. 134; *Currency and Crédit*, p. 395.

136 Commercial History and Review of 1922, 17 February 1923.

137 *The Economist*, Commercial History and Review of 1923, 16 February 1924.

138 L.C.E.S., *Key Statistics*, Tables K, L and C.

139 *The Economist*, Commercial History and Review of 1924, 14 February 1925.

140 Memorandum by Benjamin Strong, 24 December 1924, quoted by Chandler, *Strong*, p. 243.

141 Clarke, *Central Bank Cooperation*, p. 92.

142 Ibid., pp. 93–5.

143 Schumpeter, *Business Cycles*, Vol. II, p. 726.

144 *Central Bank Cooperation*, pp. 97–105.

145 Sayers, *A History of Economic Change in England*, p. 52.
Sayers, who is not one of the harshest critics of the return to gold (see his "The Return to Gold, 1925" in Pollard (ed.) *The Gold Standard and Employment Policies between the Wars*), even goes so far as to describe the years 1927–9 as follows: "With so much of the country's resources concentrated in . . . comparatively unwanted industries, and with their competitive position aggravated by monetary policy, the British economy was scarcely aware that a world boom was in progress" (*A History of Economic Change*, p. 52).
On the deteriorating state of U.K. trade in manufactures, see Moggridge, *British Monetary Policy*, pp. 123–5.

146 Ibid., p. 116; see also Phelps Brown and Shackle, "British Economic Fluctuations, 1924–38", *OEP*, May 1939, pp. 116–17.

147 Feinstein, *Domestic Capital Formation*, p. 47.

148 Ibid., pp. 41, 47; Bowley, *Housing and the State*, p. 45.

149 Feinstein, *Domestic Capital Formation*, p. 54.

150 Alford, *Depression and Recovery?*, pp. 26–8; Dowie, "Economic Growth in the Inter-War Period: some more arithmetic", in Aldcroft and Fearon (eds.), *Economic Growth in Twentieth-Century Britain*, pp. 56–60.

151 Ibid., pp. 56–7; Matthews, "Some Aspects of Post-War Growth in relation to Historical Experience", in Aldcroft and Fearon (eds.), *Economic Growth in Twentieth-Century Britain*, p. 90; Alford, *Depression and Recovery?*, pp. 19–20.

152 Ibid., pp. 22–5; Dowie, "Economic Growth in the Inter-War Period", pp. 57–60; Lomax, "Growth and Productivity in the U.K.", in Aldcroft and Fearon (eds.), *Economic Growth in Twentieth-Century Britain*, pp. 10–12; Feinstein, "Production and Productivity 1920–62", also in Aldcroft and Fearon (eds.), pp. 1–6.

153 Pollard, in Pollard (ed.), *The Gold Standard and Employment Policies between the Wars*, pp. 4–5.

154 The data come from Feinstein, *National Income*, Tables 6, 57 and 58.

155 "Why has Britain had Full Employment since the War?", *EJ*, September 1968.

156 Gordon, *Business Fluctuations*, p. 369.

157 Ibid., p. 371.

158 A.E. Kahn, *Great Britain in the World Economy*, p. 110.

159 Ibid., p. 100; Maxcy and Silberston, *The Motor Industry*, p. 14.

160 Aldcroft, *The Inter-War Economy: Britain, 1919–1939*, p. 185.

161 A.E. Kahn, *Great Britain in the World Economy*, p. 110; Maxcy and Silberston, *The Motor Industry*, pp. 38–41.

162 Nevin, *The Mechanism of Cheap Money*, pp. 234–5.

163 Kahn, *Great Britain in the World Economy*, p. 114.

164 Aldcroft, "Economic Growth in Britain in the inter-war years", in Aldcroft and Fearon (eds.), *Economic Growth in Twentieth-Century Britain*, pp. 47–9, and "Economic Progress in Britain in the 1920s", in Aldcroft and Richardson, *The British Economy 1870–1939*, pp. 227–9.

165 Aldcroft, "Economic Growth in Britain in the inter-war years", p. 47.

166 Aldcroft, "Economic Progress in Britain in the 1920s", p. 228.

167 Kahn, *Great Britain in the World Economy*, p. 107; Moggridge, *British Monetary Policy*, p. 116.

168 Sayers, "The Springs of Technical Progress in Britain 1919–39", *EJ*, 1950, p. 275.

169 Aldcroft, "Economic Growth in Britain in the inter-war years", pp. 44–7, and "Economic Progress in Britain in the 1920s", pp. 228–30.

170 Lomax, "Growth and Productivity in the U.K.", p. 26; Feinstein, "Production and Productivity 1920–62", pp. 6–7.

171 Lomax, "Growth and Productivity in the U.K.", pp. 26–8; Salter, *Productivity and Technical Change* (2nd edition, 1966), pp. 4, 122–7; Matthews, "Some Aspects of Britain's post-war growth in relation to Historical Experience", pp. 95–8.

172 *Productivity and Technical Change*, pp. 147–55.

173 Ibid., pp. 150–5.

174 Schmookler, *Invention and Economic Growth* (1966); see also Rosenberg, "Science, Invention and Economic Growth", *EJ*, March 1974.

175 Arrow, "The Economic Implications of Learning by Doing", *REStudies*, June 1962, pp. 155–6.

176 See also Kennedy and Thirlwall, "Technical Progress", in *Surveys of Applied Economics*, Vol. I.
177 Aldcroft and Richardson, *The British Economy 1870–1939*, pp. 37–8.
178 Richardson, "The Basis of Economic Recovery in the 1930s" and "Over-commitment in Britain before 1930", both in Aldcroft and Richardson, *The British Economy 1870–1939*.
179 "The Springs of Technical Progress", pp. 282–5, 287–8, 276–7; see also Landes, *The Unbound Prometheus*, pp. 428–30, 442–5, 454–9, 464; Phelps Brown and Shackle, "British Economic Fluctuations 1924–38", *OEP*, 1939, p. 123.
180 Kahn, *Great Britain in the World Economy*, p. 121.
181 Stolper, "British Monetary Policy and the Housing Boom", *QJE*, November 1941, pp. 4–9.
182 Bowley, *Housing and the State*, p. 45.
183 Stolper, "British Monetary Policy and the Housing Boom", pp. 4–7.
184 Bowley, *Housing and the State*, Chapter V and VI; Richardson and Aldcroft, *Building in the British Economy between the Wars*, pp. 164–79.
185 Bowley, *Housing and the State*, pp. 10–14.
186 Aldcroft, "Economic Progress in Britain in the 1920s", pp. 234, 237–8; see also the other references cited in note 12.
187 Landes, *The Unbound Prometheus*, p. 397.
188 Makower, Marshak and Robinson, "Studies in Mobility of Labour: Analysis for Great Britain Part I", *OEP*, May 1939.
189 Pigou, *Aspects*, pp. 53–4.
190 *A History of Economic Change in England*, pp. 52–3.

Chapter 4

1 Sayers, *A History of Economic Change in England 1880–1939*, p. 53.
2 *Slump and Recovery, 1929–37*, p. 53.
3 Ibid., pp. 34–41, 50–2, 56–7; see also W.A. Lewis, *Economic Survey 1919–1939*, pp. 45–6, 56–8.
4 *A History of Economic Change*, p. 53.
5 W.A. Brown, Jr., *The International Gold Standard Reinterpreted* (1940); Kindleberger, *The World in Depression* (1973).
6 Ibid., p. 22.
7 *A Monetary History of the United States*, Chapter 7.
8 "Exports and the British Trade Cycle: 1929", *The Manchester School*, 1958.
9 Ibid., p. 130.
10 Kindleberger, *The World in Depression*, p. 54.
11 Ibid., pp. 70–4; see also H. Fleisig, "The United States and the non-European Periphery during the Early Years of the Great Depression", in H. van der Wee (ed.), *The Great Depression Revisited*, pp. 149–54.
12 Hodson, *Slump and Recovery*, pp. 55–6, 58–9.
13 Corner, "Exports and the British Trade Cycle: 1929", p. 132.
14 Ibid., p. 136.
15 "British Economic Fluctuations 1924–38", *OEP*, May 1939, pp. 114, 127.
16 Moggridge, *British Monetary Policy 1924–1931*, pp. 153, 155–8.
    Rising interest rates, and the rising tide of speculation generally, probably had adverse effects on investment in the U.S.A. from 1928 on (Chandler, *American Monetary Policy 1928–41*, pp. 52–3, 83–4; Gordon, *Business Fluctuations*, pp. 377–9; Kindleberger, *The World in Depression*, pp. 75–6).
17 Clay, *Lord Norman*, p. 360.
18 *Financial Policy 1939–45*, p. 147; see also *A History of Economic Change*, p. 156.
19 Clarke, *Central Bank Cooperation 1924–31*, pp. 169–70.
20 Ibid., pp. 168–9..
21 Ibid., pp. 170–1.
22 Ibid., p. 170.
23 Goodwin, "Studies in Money", Table III and pp. 53–4, 61.
24 Ibid., p. 73.
25 Clay, *Lord Norman*, p. 363.
26 Ibid., p. 367.
27 Ibid., p. 369; Moggridge, *British Monetary Policy*, pp. 139–40.
28 F.R.B.N.Y., Cable 135/30, Harvey to Harrison, 18 June 1930.

29 F.R.B.N.Y., Cable 174/30, Norman to Harrison, 27 August 1930.
30 Moggridge, *British Monetary Policy*, p. 187.
31 F.R.B.N.Y., Cable 16/31, Norman to Harrison, 21 January 1931.
32 *Central Bank Cooperation*, p. 173.
33 Moggridge, *British Monetary Policy*, pp. 147, 151, 153.
34 Ibid., pp. 154–5.
35 Clarke, *Central Bank Cooperation*, p. 171.
36 Ibid., p. 173.
37 Kindleberger, *The World in Depression*, pp. 142–5.
38 *A History of Economic Change*, p. 53.
39 F.R.B.N.Y., Cable 121/31, Norman to Harrison, 5 May 1931.
40 F.R.B.N.Y., Cable 130/31, Norman to Harrison, 13 May 1931.
41 T. 175/46, Hopkins, "Plentiful Credit and Cheap Money", April 1930.
42 Cab. 27/435, Committee on Trade Policy, 1st meeting, 1 December 1930.
43 Leith-Ross, *Money Talks*, p. 129.
44 T. 172/1690, Snowden to Churchill, 23 January 1930; Snowden, *An Autobiography*, Vol. II, Chapters XLVIII and LXVII.
45 T. 172/1684, Grigg to Chancellor, 18 October 1929.
46 Mallett and George, *British Budgets 1921–1933*, pp. 284–5.
47 T. 171/279, Memorandum by Phillips, undated.
48 U.K. Hicks, *The Finance of British Government 1920–1936*, p. 12; Mallett and George, *British Budgets 1921–1933*, pp. 285–7.
49 T. 175/40, Hopkins to Chancellor, 21 October 1929.
50 Mallett and George, *British Budgets 1921–1933*, p. 282.
51 Cab. 24/219, C.P. 3(31), "The Financial Situation", paras. 2, 3, 4.
    At the Cabinet meeting the Cabinet, "recognising that the financial situation was serious and very urgent", appointed Alexander (First Lord of the Admiralty) and Graham (President of the Board of Trade) "to co-operate with the Chancellor of the Exchequer in a preliminary consideration of the situation" (Cab. 23/66, Cabinet 6(31)4, 14 January 1931).
52 Mallett and George, *British Budgets 1921–1933*, p. 318.
53 Ibid., p. 319.
54 Ibid., pp. 322–7.
55 T. 171/287, Hopkins to Snowden, 10 October 1930, and Fergusson to Chancellor, 19 March 1931.
56 T. 188/14, Niemeyer to Churchill, 27 April 1927.
57 T. 188/14, Leith-Ross to Hopkins, 3 October 1927; see also Phillips, "5% War Loan", 30 September 1927, in same file.
    Clay says that the Deputy Governor of the Bank, Harvey, was "mainly responsible" for the scheme finally adopted in June 1932 (*Lord Norman*, p. 457) but there is no evidence of this in the Treasury papers. Given the 1927 memoranda, it would seem that the main principles of the scheme were the responsibility of the Treasury. What I suspect the Bank was responsible for was the decision early in 1931 that War Loan could now be dealt with as a block and the rate of interest finally chosen: see T. 160/449/F 13047/1, Phillips, "Debt Schemes", 24 January 1931, and "5% War Loan", May 1931; Clay, *Lord Norman*, p. 457; and E.E. Jucker-Fleetwood, "Montagu Norman in the Per Jacobssen Diaries", *National Westminster Bank Quarterly Review*, November 1968, p. 66.
58 T. 171/293, Phillips, "Notes on 5% War Loan".
59 T. 160/449/F 13047/1, Phillips, "Debt Schemes", 24 January 1931.
60 T. 171/287, Notes by Snowden of Suggestions.
61 Another piece of evidence on Snowden's intentions at the end of 1930 is the fact that he asked Fergusson for a memorandum from the Treasury on the effect of price changes on the burden of the national debt (T. 171/287, Fergusson to Chancellor, 5 December 1930, and Hopkins to Fergusson, 4 December 1930; T. 175/57, Phillips, "The Effect of Price Changes on the Burden of the National Debt", 2 December 1930).
62 T. 160/449/F 13047/1, Phillips, "5% War Loan".
63 T. 171/293, Phillips, "Notes on 5% War Loan".
64 E.g., by the City and the Staff of the E.A.C. (*The Economist*, 9 November 1929 and Commercial History and Review of 1929, February 1930; Cab. 58/145, Henderson, "The Economic Outlook", April 1930).
65 Cab. 58/11, Henderson, "The State of Trade", 22 July 1930; Cab. 58/14, Reports by

E.A.C. Staff on "The Economic Situation", 8 September and 9 December 1930, 10 March, 13 April and 21 July 1931.

66 T. 175/70, Hawtrey, "The 1931 Financial Crisis", 11 July 1932.

67 Williams, "The 1931 Financial Crisis", *Yorkshire Bulletin of Economic and Social Research*, 1963, pp. 92, 100–5.

68 T. 175/70, Hawtrey, "The 1931 Financial Crisis", p. 3.

69 Clarke, *Central Bank Cooperation 1924–31*, pp. 202–3; see also Cab. 27/462, Harvey's statement to the Financial Situation Committee, 17 September 1931.

70 Clay, *Lord Norman*, p. 386.

71 On the fall of the Labour Government see Clay, *Lord Norman*, pp. 383–98; R. Bassett, *1931: Political Crisis*; and the following Public Record Office papers: Prem. 1/96, Duff to Prime Minister, "Diary of Events", 28 August 1931; Cab. 23/67, Cabinet 40(31)10, 30 July 1931; Cab. 24/222, C.P. 203(31), Report of Cabinet Committee on National Expenditure, 18 August 1931; Cab. 27/454, C.P. 203(31) Revise, 21 August 1931; and Cab. 23/67, Cabinets 41, 42, 43, 44, 45 and 46 of 1931, 19–23 August 1931.
In the consultations Harvey and Edward Peacock represented the Bank, as Norman was out of the country following his collapse in late July; Neville Chamberlain and Sir Samuel Hoare represented the Conservatives while Baldwin was in Aix-les-Bains; Sir Herbert Samuel and Sir Donald Maclean represented the Liberals as Lloyd George was ill; and Ernest Bevin and W.M. Citrine represented the T.U.C.

72 T. 171/288, Hopkins to Snowden, 20 August 1931.

73 The tax on the rentier had been discussed in February 1931, when the political difficulties were seen as "stupendous" (T. 171/287, Fergusson to Chancellor, 6 February 1931). The proposal was eventually rejected on the basis of an Inland Revenue memorandum (T. 171/288, Grigg to Chancellor, 17 August 1931). On new taxation see T. 171/288, Fisher, Hopkins, Grigg and A.J. Dyke to Chancellor, 18 August 1931.

74 Mallett and George, *British Budgets 1921–1933*, pp. 363–73; T. 171/288, "Budget Position", n.d. The economies were decided by a Cabinet Committee of MacDonald, Baldwin, Cunliffe-Lister and Maclean on 27 August (Cab. 27/456, C.P. 208(31)).

75 T. 171/293, "Finance (No. 2) Bill, 1931, Notes on Clauses (Treasury), Part III, Provisions as to 5% War Loan 1929/47", and "Treasury Finance Bill Clauses, Effect of Suspension of Gold Payments", Memorandum for Chancellor, n.d. but prepared during the House of Commons debates on the Finance Bill.

76 Clay says the financial crisis "postponed action in May and again in September" (*Lord Norman*, p. 457). A Treasury memorandum of the same time pointed out that Graham's speech on the budget on 10 September and his article in the *Daily Herald* on 3 September showed "he had a very good knowledge of the taxation proposals which [Snowden] had in mind": among the measures advocated by Graham in his article were suspension of the sinking fund and conversion of War Loan (T. 171/293, Fergusson to Chancellor, n.d. but probably 10 September 1931).

77 T. 175/70, Hawtrey, "The 1931 Financial Crisis", pp. 5–6.

78 E.g., Morton, *British Finance 1930–1940*, pp. 19–21, 57–70; Williams, "The 1931 Financial Crisis".

79 Moggridge has argued that the balance of payments figures show Britain would have been forced off the gold standard sometime in 1931–2 and that this was recognized by the authorities early in 1931 ("The 1931 Financial Crisis–a New View", *The Banker*, 1970). I have mentioned above (pp. 69–71) that the Treasury was aware of the effects of budgetary difficulties on confidence abroad; the authorities' awareness of the existence of a balance of payments problem appears in T. 160/430/F 12317/02, Discussions of January and February 1931 with French Treasury officials. Moggridge also records that Hopkins asked Hawtrey to make a case for defending the existing parity, and Hawtrey refused, early in 1931.

80 T. 175/70, Hawtrey, "the 1931 Financial Crisis", p. 6; Clay, *Lord Norman*, p. 308.

81 The Committee was set up at the Prime Minister's instigation following the National Government's decision on the economy measures, "to produce to the Cabinet at its next meeting a statement of the actual financial position, which, assuming the present crisis is allayed, will have to be faced and to make recommendations as to what, if anything, will have to be done by the Government in consequence" (Prem. 1/97, Letters from the Prime Minister to his colleagues, 10 September 1931). It consisted of MacDonald, Snowden, Lord Reading (Foreign Secretary) and Neville Chamberlain (Minister of Health) and first met on 14 September when it discussed the questions of the mobilization of foreign securities and prohibition of the import of luxuries

(Cab. 27/462, Cabinet Committee on Financial Situation, first meeting). Its fourth and last meeting was on 6 October when the Committee asked Harvey and Peacock for their advice on the effect on the pound of a general election (Cab. 27/462, Financial Situation Committee, fourth meeting, 6 October 1931; also in Prem. 1/97 as "Notes of a Conference on October 6th").

82 Cab. 27/462, Committee on the Financial Situation, second meeting, 17 September 1931.
83 Cab. 23/68, Cabinet 59(31).
84 T. 163/68/G 3788, Memorandum by Phillips, 17 September 1931.
85 Prem. 1/97, Duff, "Notes of a meeting on 18 September 1931", 20 September 1931; see also S. Roskill, *Hankey: Man of Secrets, Vol. II 1919–1931*, pp. 558–9.
86 Prem. 1/97, Notes of a conference on 19 September 1931; a copy is also in Cab. 27/462, Financial Situation Committee, third meeting.
87 Leith-Ross, *Money Talks*, p. 140.
88 Cab. 23/68, Cabinet 60(31); see also Roskill, *Hankey*, p. 558.
89 From, e.g., *The Economist* of 19 September, where devaluation is rejected and deflation recommended as a means of restoring both budgetary and international balance.
90 Clay, *Lord Norman*, pp. 399–400.
91 Ibid., p. 399.
92 T. 175/56, Memorandum by Niemeyer, 26 September 1931.
93 T. 175/56, Siepmann to Leith-Ross, 23 September 1931.
94 T. 175/51, Hopkins to Chancellor, 24 July 1931.
95 Cab. 24/223, C.P. 233(31), Fisher, "Financial and Economic Position of U.K.", 11 September 1931; Cab. 23/68, Cabinet 57(31)5.
96 T. 172/1775, Fisher to Chancellor, "Measures in existence or in Treasury view requisite for safeguarding pound", 30 September 1931.
97 Cab. 58/30, "The Balance of International Payments", 25 September 1931. The members of the committee were, besides Stamp, G.D.H. Cole, W.M. Citrine, Keynes, Sir Alfred Lewis, and H.D. Henderson.
98 Prem. 1/97, Henderson to MacDonald, 26 September 1931. The members of this committee were originally R.H. Brand, Walter Layton, Reginald McKenna, Lord Macmillan, Stamp and Henderson (Secretary). Sir Arthur Salter joined at the end of September and Keynes in November. The committee became known as the E.A.C. Subcommittee on Financial Questions and produced a report on sterling policy in March 1932 (below p. 86). On Keynes's views see below p. 84 and Appendix 4, para. 3.
99 Cab. 58/169, "The Problems arising from the suspension of gold payments", 24–25 September 1931.
100 Cab. 58/169, Financial Questions Committee, 4th meeting, 29 September 1931.
101 Cab. 58/169, Financial Questions Committee, meetings of 2 and 26 November and 3 December 1931.
102 Cab. 23/69, Cabinet 74(31)3.
103 T. 188/20, Leith-Ross to Hopkins, 2 December 1931; T. 175/56, "Agenda for discussion on Exchange Position", 8 December 1931.
104 Clay, *Lord Norman*, p. 401. The memorandum is not in the Treasury papers.
105 Ibid., p. 401.
106 T. 175/56, "The Exchange Position", 8 December 1931.
107 Cab. 23/69, Cabinet 87(31)7.
108 T. 188/20, Memorandum by Phillips, not dated but the file indicates between 26 and 28 September 1931.
109 T. 188/28, Hawtrey to Leith-Ross, 26 October 1931.
110 T. 175/56, Hawtrey to Hopkins, "Pegging the Pound, I", 28 September 1931.
111 T. 188/28, Henderson, "International Co-operation and the Gold Standard", 16 October 1931. Henderson was at this time secretary of the E.A.C.
112 T. 188/28, Hawtrey to Leith-Ross, 26 October 1931; Phillips to Hopkins, 28 October 1931.
113 Cab. 58/169, Keynes, "Notes on the Currency Question", 16 November 1931.
114 T. 188/29, Henderson, "Comments on Mr Hawtrey's Memorandum", 6 October 1931; T. 188/28, Henderson, "International Co-operation and the Gold Standard", 16 October 1931.
115 T. 175/57, Hopkins, "Note on Mr Keynes' Memorandum of 16 November",

15 December 1931; T. 172/1768, Hopkins to Chancellor, "Capital Items in the Balance of International Payments", 15 December 1931.

116 T. 175/57, Hopkins, "The Present Position of the Pound", 12 January 1932.

117 T. 175/57, Phillips, "The Present Position of the Pound", 24 February 1932.

118 T. 188/48, Phillips to Leith-Ross, 31 March 1932.

119 T. 175/57, Memorandum by Phillips, 5 March 1932.

120 On 9 March 1932 the Cabinet added the Secretary of State for India to the committee (Cab. 23/70, Cabinet 17(32)5) but there is no further reference to it.

121 Clay, *Lord Norman*, pp. 400–1. The Cabinet on 2 March "took note with satisfaction" of the large amount to be repaid, compared with the sum mentioned at an earlier meeting on 24 February (Cab. 23/70, Cabinets 15(32)10 and 16(32)12).

122 *The Mechanism of Cheap Money*, pp. 90–1; "The Origins of Cheap Money 1932–2" in Pollard (ed.), *The Gold Standard and Employment Policies between the Wars*, pp. 82–3.

123 T. 175/57 and T. 188/48, Hopkins to Chancellor, 24 February and 1 March 1932.

124 T. 175/57, Phillips, 5 March 1932.

125 Ibid.

126 Moggridge, *British Monetary Policy 1924–1931*, Chapter 8.

127 The relevant memoranda are: T. 175/57, Phillips, 5 March 1932; Phillips, "Objects Sought", 5 March 1932; Phillips, 22 March 1932; T. 188/48, Hopkins to Chancellor, 21 March 1932; Phillips to Leith-Ross, 22 March 1932; T. 175/57, T. 188/48 and T. 171/301, Hopkins to Chancellor, "Exchange Equalisation Account Proposals", 6 April 1932.
In the first of these Phillips recommended that the Bank should not only reduce Bank rate but also continue to purchase foreign exchange after the credits had been repaid. This would require an assurance for the Bank that any losses it incurred in carrying out this policy would be borne by the Treasury. "The technical form in which the undertaking will be given will need working out. A futher note on this is attached." The note attached was "Objects Sought", which was followed by two alternative plans for an E.E.A. The 22 March memorandum suggested the necessary legislation be included in the Finance Bill in April. The April memorandum told the Chancellor that the Bank had suggested the Treasury's original figure of £100m for the borrowing powers of the E.E.A. be raised to £150m; it also pointed out that the reason why an E.E.A. was needed when it had not been needed when Britain was last off gold, i.e. before 1925, was the "new . . . desire to keep *down* the pound". Hopkins continued: "We cannot however put it quite as bluntly as that, and the following notes have been compiled to serve as a defence if we are ever challenged along this line of argument".

128 See, e.g., T. 175/71, Hopkins to Fisher and Chancellor, 9 July 1932, Hopkins to Chancellor, 15 October 1932, Hopkins to Fisher and Chancellor, 30 January 1933; T. 175/94, Phillips, "Position of Exchange Equalisation Account", 1 December 1936, Hopkins to Chancellor, 2 December 1936.

129 T. Jones, *A Diary with Letters 1931–1950*, p. 358.

130 For further information on the E.E.A. see Clay, *Lord Norman*, pp. 402–6; "The Origins of the Exchange Equalisation Account", *BEQB*, December 1958; Sayers, *Modern Banking* (1st edition), pp. 195–210.
Clay records that foreign observers did not appreciate "the simple explanation of its origin–that the Bank itself had not resources of its own adequate to the task of preventing disconcerting fluctuations in sterling", and attributed "wider commercial and political aims to it", since "its declared object, to moderate fluctuations, did not seem sufficient to justify its establishment". From the Treasury papers one can only conclude that the foreign observers were to a large extent right, even though according to Clay such aims were repugnant to Norman (*Lord Norman*, p. 403).

131 Ibid., p. 402.

132 T. 160/449/F 13047/2, Note of discussion at Bank on 18 January 1932.

133 Clay, *Lord Norman*, p. 457.

134 Ibid., pp. 457–8.

135 Feiling, *Life of Neville Chamberlain*, p. 209; Cab. 23/72, Cabinet 41(32)3, 30 June 1932.

136 *Hansard* (Commons), 30 June 1932, cols. 2121–6.

137 Clay, *Lord Norman*, p. 458.

138 Ibid., p. 458.

After the conversion lists closed on 30 September, the ban on home and empire issues was removed except for certain optional conversions, a restriction made in order to keep down Australian demand. The embargo on overseas loans was retained, in order to help the balance of payments and protect the pound, and though by the end of 1933 the Treasury officials thought it was no longer necessary or desirable, it stayed for the rest of the 1930s.

See T. 160/533/F 13296/1 and T. 160/496/F 13228, Waterfield, "New Government Borrowings", 27 September 1932; T. 160/533/F 13296/1 and T. 175/70, Hopkins, "Note relating to the embargo on capital issues", 13 November 1932; Note by Chamberlain, 14 November 1932; Hopkins to Chancellor, 10 January 1933; T. 175/84, Hopkins, Phillips and Fisher to Chancellor, 30 November 1933; below notes 31 and 91 to Chapter 5.

139 Clay, *Lord Norman*, p. 458.
140 Chapter 5, pp. 99–101; Nevin, *The Mechanism of Cheap Money*, pp. 101–3.
141 Ibid., p. 107.
142 Clay, *Lord Norman*, p. 458; Nevin, *The Mechanism of Cheap Money*, pp. 80–1.
143 Ibid., pp. 98–101.
144 Ibid., pp. 95–6.
145 Ibid., pp. 76–82.
146 "The Origins of Cheap Money 1931–2" in Pollard (ed.), *The Gold Standard and Employment Policies between the Wars*, pp. 68, 84.
147 *The Mechanism of Cheap Money*, p. 92.
148 Chapter 3, pp. 37–41, 49–50.

Chapter 5

1 Clay, *Lord Norman*, p. 442.
2 T. 175/70, Phillips to Hopkins and Chancellor, 19 October 1932.
3 Cab. 58/183, "The foreign demand for the return of the United Kingdom to gold", memorandum by Treasury, October 1932. The memorandum was written by Phillips: see drafts in T. 175/93.
4 T. 175/83, Memorandum by Phillips, 30 September 1933.
   The memorandum was written as an argument against stabilization of the sterling exchange with the dollar and the franc. Phillips made two points against stabilization:
   (i) the maladies being suffered by, and hence the objectives of, the three countries were different (the U.S.A. had the problems of reconciling prices and debts, not prices and costs; the discrepancy between prices and costs in France had been complicated by years of continuous deflation);
   (ii) although the U.K. gap between prices and costs to be remedied was not as great as 66% because of increased productivity of labour as compared with prewar, the existence of over two millions unemployed was evidence of a gap and "we ought not to stabilise till employment is fairly good (below one million unemployed)".
5 Cab. 58/183, "The foreign demand for the return of the U.K. to gold", Treasury memorandum, October 1932; T. 172/1814, "The level of prices as affected by monetary policy", memorandum by Treasury, 29 September 1932. For the action of the Treasury with respect to the World Economic Conference see Howson and Winch, *The Economic Advisory Council 1930–1939*, Chapter 5.
6 T. 172/1821, Phillips to Chancellor, 3 July 1934.
7 T. 175/70, Phillips to Hopkins and Chancellor, 19 October 1932.
   Phillips was referring to letters in *The Times* from Gregory, Hayek, Plant and Robbins on 19 October and from Macgregor, Pigou, Keynes, Layton, Salter and Stamp on 17 October 1932.
8 T. 175/70, Hopkins to Chancellor, 20 October 1932.
9 T. 172/1814, "The level of prices as affected by monetary policy", Treasury memorandum, 29 September 1932; see also T. 175/17, Phillips, "Notes on Cheap Money", 15 February 1933; Phillips to Hopkins, 28 February 1933; Phillips, "The Question of Raising Prices", 15 May 1933; T. 188/72, Leith-Ross, "Money and Prices", September 1933.
10 T. 175/17, Memorandum by Phillips on Minister of Labour's memorandum on unemployment situation, 6 June 1932; see also T. 175/17, Phillips, "Notes on Cheap Money", 15 February 1933; T. 172/1814, "The level of prices as affected by monetary policy", 29 September 1932; T. 188/72, Leith-Ross, "Money and Prices", September 1933.

11   T. 172/1814, "The level of prices as affected by monetary policy", 29 September
      1932. Borrowing for the unemployment fund, which was advocated by Clay in the
      Report of the Royal Commission on Unemployment Insurance and by the Committee
      on Economic Information was also ruled out by the fear of the effect on opinion
      abroad (T. 175/93, Hopkins, "Committee on Economic Information Fifth Report
      (C.P. 422)", 8 December 1932).
12   Mallett and George, *British Budgets 1921–1933*, pp. 398–9, 402–3, 405–7.
13   Sabine, *British Budgets in Peace and War 1932–1945*, pp. 14–16, 30–1.
14   The argument appears in, e.g., T. 175/17, Phillips to Hopkins, 28 February 1933;
      Phillips and Hopkins to Chancellor, "Mr Keynes' First and Second Articles",
      17 March 1933; Phillips, "Mr Keynes' Articles", 21 March 1933.
15   T. 172/1814, "The level of prices as affected by monetary policy", 29 September
      1932.
16   T. 175/70, Phillips to Hopkins and Chancellor, 19 October 1932; Hopkins to
      Chancellor, 20 October 1932; T. 175/17, Gilbert, "The Means to Prosperity, Mr
      Keynes' First Article, Treasury Note", 14 March 1933; Phillips, "Gilbert on Keynes",
      14 March 1933; Phillips, "Mr Keynes' First and Second Articles", 17 March 1933;
      Hopkins, "Mr Keynes' First Article in the Times", 30 March 1933; T. 177/12,
      Phillips, "Public Works as a Method of Raising Price Levels", about 11 July 1933;
      T. 188/72, Phillips, "Recovery from the Trade Depression", 21 September 1933.
17   Ibid.
18   Cab. 27/503, Prime Minister's statement to first meeting of Panel on Trade and
      Employment, 23 November 1932; Cab. 23/75, Prime Minister's statement to Cabinet
      on 19 January 1933.
19   Sabine, *British Budgets in Peace and War*, pp. 36–7.
      Another reason for not reducing taxation earlier was that it would not be a good
      preface to a petition for remission of the American war debt (Feiling, *Life of Neville
      Chamberlain*, p. 221; T. 175/17, Phillips and Hopkins, "Mr Keynes' First and Second
      Articles", 17 March 1933).
20   Sabine, *British Budgets in Peace and War*, pp. 55–8.
21   T. 171/309, Hopkins to Fergusson, 22 April 1933.
22   T. 160/760/F 14596, "Sinking Funds Account", 2 March 1938.
23   T. 171/317, Phillips, "Budget Prospects", 11 February 1935; see also T. 175/94,
      Treasury note to Minister for Coordination of Defence, 22 October 1937; below p. 125.
24   Feiling, *Life of Neville Chamberlain*, pp. 201–4; Snowden, *An Autobiography*, Vol. II,
      pp. 988–1012; Cab. 23/69, Cabinet 88(31)4, 11 December 1931; Cab. 27/467, Balance
      of Trade Committee, minutes, memoranda and report; Cab. 24/227, C.P. 31(32),
      Committee on Balance of Trade, Memorandum of Dissent from the Committee's
      Report by Lord Privy Seal, 18 January 1932; C.P. 32(32), Committee on Balance of
      Trade, Memorandum by Home Secretary, 19 January 1932; Cab. 23/70, Cabinets 5, 6
      and 7 of 1932, 21 and 22 January 1932.
25   Cab. 23/77, Cabinet 68(33)5, 6 December 1933.
26   T. 171/296, Hopkins to Chancellor, 11 March 1932; T. 175/59, Hopkins to Forber,
      15 March 1932; T. 171/296 and T. 188/48, Hopkins to Chancellor, "Speculative fore-
      cast of 1935 on the basis of 'Old Moore's Almanack'", 21 March 1932.
27   T. 175/64, Memorandum by Hopkins, 26 February 1932.
28   T. Jones, *A Diary with Letters 1931–1950*, p. 31.
29   T. 177/12, Siepmann to Phillips, 9 July 1932 – this gives Norman's criticisms of the
      draft of the Chancellor's Ottawa statement; T. 175/70, Phillips to Chancellor, 29
      October 1932 – this is an account of a discussion between Hopkins, Phillips and
      Norman on the Treasury memorandum of October 1932.
      At Ottawa the Chancellor stated: "We do not see any prospect of a speedy return to
      the gold standard, nor are we prepared to say at the present time at what parity such a
      return should be effected if and when it takes place", and the U.K. delegation laid down
      the following conditions for a return: "(i) a rise in the general level of commodity
      prices in the various countries to a height more in keeping with the level of costs, in-
      cluding the burden of debt and other fixed and semi-fixed charges; and (ii) an adjust-
      ment of the factors political, economic, financial and monetary which have caused the
      breakdown of the gold standard in many countries and which if not adjusted would
      inevitably lead to another breakdown of whatever international standard may be
      adopted" (T. 175/70, "Ottawa resolutions and statements regarding monetary and
      financial questions", and "The foreign demand for the return of the U.K. to gold",
      Treasury memorandum, October 1932).

30 T. 177/12, Siepmann to Phillips, 9 July 1932; see also Clay, *Lord Norman*, pp. 419–21.

31 Ibid., p. 459.
The lack of "traditional warning signals" caused Norman to advocate some form (unspecified) of government control over all new issues in order to prevent speculation, a suggestion which the Treasury did not think was useful (T. 160/533/F 13296/01, Waterfield to Fisher, 10 November 1932; Fisher to Hopkins and Ferguson, "Capital Embargo", 11 November 1932; Phillips to Hopkins, 15 November 1932).
Norman remained "the most uncompromising advocate" of the embargo on overseas loans, while from at least late 1933 the Treasury officials favoured relaxation in the hope that a revival of foreign lending would help British exports (T. 160/533/F 13296/01, Hopkins, "Foreign Issues, Discussion with the Governor on the 9th February 1933", 10 February 1933; T. 175/84, Phillips to Hopkins, 7 June 1933; Hopkins, Phillips and Fisher to Chancellor, 30 November 1933; T. 175/94, Hopkins to Woods, 30 January 1937; Phillips to Hopkins, "The Kennet Committee and Investment Abroad", 17 November 1937; Hopkins to Fisher and Woods, 24 November 1937; Hopkins' note of discussion with Governor, December 1937). Chamberlain appears to have been in favour of the embargo for "political" reasons (T. 160/533/F 13296/02, Fisher to Chancellor, 16 December 1933) but the Treasury eventually managed to persuade Sir John Simon to permit some relaxation in 1938.
For more information on the Treasury and the embargo see Howson and Winch, *The Economic Advisory Council 1930–1939*, Chapter 5.

32 T. 175/70, Phillips to Chancellor, 29 October 1932.

33 Nevin, *The Mechanism of Cheap Money*, pp. 110–12; Clay, *Lord Norman*, pp. 436–8, 441.

34 Ibid., p. 435.

35 E.E. Jucker-Fleetwood, "Montagu Norman in the Per Jacobssen Diaries", *National Westminster Bank Quarterly Review*, November 1938, pp. 65–6.

36 Keynes Papers A/33, Henderson to Keynes, January 1933.

37 Keynes Papers L/33, Sprague to Keynes, 18 January 1933.

38 T. 177/12, Memorandum by Clay, 14 December 1932; T. 188/72, Siepmann to Leith-Ross, 25 September 1933; T. 172/1814, Phillips to Hopkins, "World Economic Conference", 10 December 1932.
The rationale for the Bank's advisers' advocacy of public works was that "when trade is depressed the trouble is not scarcity of money, but disinclination to use what money there is. I should expect more than is suggested [by the Treasury] from an expansion of public capital expenditure, because this would stimulate enterprise in the field of construction . . . [While] cheap money . . . [is] needed for the confidence on which lasting improvement is based, improvised public works . . . although they probably do nothing to assist permanent improvement may help a country through a bad winter" (T. 188/72, Note by either Clay or Sprague sent to Leith-Ross by Siepmann, 25 September 1933; see also T. 177/12, Memorandum by Clay, 14 December 1932).

39 Clay, *Lord Norman*, pp. 460–3; below pp. 98–9, 102–3.

40 T. 160/429/F 11721, 4½% Conversion Loan 1940/44; T. 160/551/F 9973/2, 4% Consols; T. 160/527/F 12995, 3% Treasury Bonds.

41 T. 160/496/F 13228, Waterfield to Fisher, 26 September 1932.

42 T. 160/496/F 13228, "New Government Borrowings", Note of meeting between Governor, Deputy Governor, Fisher, Leith-Ross and Waterfield, 27 September 1932, and Hopkins to Chancellor, 27 October 1932.

43 T. 160/496/F 13228, "New Government Borrowings", 27 September 1932.

44 T. 160/497/F 13380/1, Phillips, "Conversion of Treasury Bills", Phillips to Hopkins, and Hopkins to Fergusson, all 2 March 1933.
The scheme was suspended because the first offer had been tendered for at too high a price and most of the bonds offered in subsequent weeks had to be taken up by the Bank who could not resell them while the bonds were still on weekly offer, and it was not resumed.
See T. 160/497/F 13380/1, Hopkins to Chancellor, "2½% Conversion Bonds: weekly offer", 27 May 1933.

45 T. 160/497/F 13380/2, Note by Phillips of discussion with Fisher and Harvey, 18 September 1933.

46 T. 160/497/F 13380/2, Phillips to Hopkins, "Conversion Operation", 18 September 1933.

47 T. 160/538/F 13748, Waterfield to Hopkins, "4% Treasury Bonds 1934/36" 2 January 1934.

48   T. 160/538/F 13748, Hopkins to Chancellor, 12 March 1934.
49   T. 160/538/F 13748 and T. 175/84, Phillips to Hopkins, "Funding Operation", 13 March 1934.
50   T. 160/538/F 13748, Hopkins to Chancellor, 16 March 1934.
51   T. 160/538/F 13748, Fisher to Chancellor, and Note by Chancellor, 17 March 1934.
52   *Lord Norman*, p. 462.
53   T. 160/489/F 14370, Phillips to Chancellor, 21 November 1935.
54   T. 160/489/F 14370, Memorandum by Phillips, 22 November 1935.
55   T. 160/489/F 14370, Phillips to Hopkins and Fergusson, 26 November 1935; Hopkins to Fergusson and Chancellor, 26 November 1935.
56   T. 160/633/F 14810, Memorandum by Phillips, 31 October 1936.
57   T. 160/633/F 14810, Memorandum by Phillips, 4 November 1936.
58   *The Mechanism of Cheap Money*, p. 119.
59   Goodwin, "Studies in Money", Chart 15.
60   Ibid., Chart 3.
61   Ibid., pp. 63–4; Nevin, *The Mechanism of Cheap Money*, pp. 118–54.
62   Goodwin, "Studies in Money", Chart 19 and Table III.
63   Nevin, *The Mechanism of Cheap Money*, pp. 120–2; Balogh, *Studies in Financial Organization*, pp. 177–82.
64   *The Mechanism of Cheap Money*, pp. 126–42.
65   Ibid., p. 133.
66   H.G. Johnson, "Clearing Bank Holdings of Public Debt, 1930–50", L.C.E.S. *Bulletin*, November 1951.
67   Nevin, *The Mechanism of Cheap Money*, p. 135.
68   Ibid., pp. 132–3, 137–8.
69   Ibid., pp. 89–92; Clay, *Lord Norman*, pp. 458–9; W.A. Brown, Jr., *The International Gold Standard Reinterpreted*, Vol. II, pp. 1147–61.
70   Clay, *Lord Norman*, pp. 460, 459.
71   Brown, *The International Gold Standard Reinterpreted*, Vol. II, pp. 1147, 1154–5, 1149, 1156.
72   Ibid., p. 1148.
73   Clay, *Lord Norman*, p. 461.
74   Ibid., p. 461.
75   Ibid., p. 461.
76   Sayers, *Financial Policy 1939–45*, pp. 149–50.
77   "The Exchange Equalisation Account: its origins and development", *BEQB*, December 1968; Sayers, *Modern Banking* (1st edition), pp. 200–10.
78   Clay, *Lord Norman*, pp. 460–1.
79   Goodwin, "Studies in Money", p. 36.
80   Sayers, *Financial Policy 1939–45*, p. 149.
81   Williams, "Montagu Norman and Banking Policy in the 1920s", *Yorkshire Bulletin of Economic and Social Research*, 1959; Clay, *Lord Norman*, pp. 165–7.
82   T. 175/70, Phillips to Hopkins, 12 October, and Hopkins to Chancellor, 13 October 1932.
83   T. 175/70, Note by Hopkins, not dated but file indicates between 29 and 31 October 1932.
84   T. 175/17, Hopkins to Fergusson, 21 April 1933.
85   T. 175/17, Hopkins to Fergusson, and "Forced Reduction of Interest Rates", 21 April 1933.
86   T. 175/17, Hopkins to Fergusson, 21 April 1933.
87   Of, e.g., W.F. Crick, "British Monetary Policy 1931–7", *Bankers Magazine*, February 1938; U.K. Hicks, *The Finance of British Government*, pp. 374–7.
88   *The Mechanism of Cheap Money*, pp. 206–17.
89   Ibid., p. 217.
90   Ibid., pp. 218–9.
91   See Cairncross, *Control of Long-term International Capital Movements* (1973) and R.B. Stewart, "Great Britain's Foreign Loan Policy", *Economica*, 1938.
92   *The Mechanism of Cheap Money*, pp. 221–2.
93   Ibid., pp. 223–5.
94   Ibid., pp. 226–8; Grant, *A Study of the Capital Market in Britain 1919–36*, pp. 150–1.
95   Nevin, *The Mechanism of Cheap Money*, p. 228.
96   Ibid., pp. 226, 249–50.

97   Ibid., pp. 250–1.

98   Ibid., pp. 248, 247.

99   Sheppard, *The Growth and Role of U.K. Financial Institutions 1880–1962*, Chapters 1 and 2.

100   Ibid., pp. 3, 21–2; Nevin, *The Mechanism of Cheap Money*, p. 281.

101   Bellman, "The Building Trades", in British Association, *Britain in Recovery*, p. 419.

102   Ibid., p. 419; Nevin, *The Mechanism of Cheap Money*, pp. 258–60.

103   Ibid., pp. 257–67; Bellman, "The Building Trades", p. 419.

104   Ibid., pp. 420–2.

105   Nevin, *The Mechanism of Cheap Money*, pp. 283–8.

106   Ibid., pp. 290–5; Bellman, "The Building Trades", pp. 426–8; Stolper, "British Monetary Policy and the Housing Boom", *QJE*, November 1941, pp. 52–4.

107   Ibid., pp. 21–32; Nevin, *The Mechanism of Cheap Money*, pp. 271–2; Bellman, "The Building Trades", pp. 423–5.

108   Nevin, *The Mechanism of Cheap Money*, p. 267; see also Grant, *A Study of the Capital Market in Britain 1919–36*, pp. 191, 219.

109   Sayers, *A History of Economic Change in England*, p. 55.

110   *Economic Recovery in Britain 1932–39*, pp. 23–7.

111   Stolper, "British Monetary Policy and the Housing Boom", pp. 1–20, 25–7, 49–55, 112–22; Richardson and Aldcroft, *Building in the British Economy between the Wars*, pp. 204–6, 211–12; Nevin, *The Mechanism of Cheap Money*, p. 281; Feinstein, *Domestic Capital Formation in the U.K. 1920–1938*, pp. 41–3; Sayers, *A History of Economic Change in England*, pp. 55–6.

112   Before the First World War all imports and most exports were quoted in sterling (Balogh, *Studies in Financial Organization*, p. 234) and one would expect this to have remained largely the case while Britain was on the gold standard after the War. Further, it is a necessary condition for an initial decline in the trade balance in the currency contract period that U.K. *import* contracts are denominated in foreign currencies (Magee, "Currency Contracts, Pass-through and Devaluation", *Brookings Papers on Economic Activity*, 1:1973).

113   Ibid.

114   "The Effects of Devaluation on the Balance of Payments", *NIER*, November 1967, pp. 4–9. The effect on market shares could take up to five years (Junz and Rhomberg, "Price Competitiveness in Export Trade among Industrial Countries", *AER*, May 1973).

115   L.C.E.S. *Bulletin*, selected issues.

116   L.C.E.S. *Bulletin*, 23 January 1932.

117   L.C.E.S. *Bulletin*, 23 March 1932.

118   L.C.E.S. *Bulletin*, 23 July 1932.

119   L.C.E.S. *Bulletin*, 23 August 1932.

120   "The balance of payments in the inter-war period: further details", *BEQB*, March 1974.

121   Feinstein, *National Income*, Table 5. If the marginal propensity to import is taken as 0.3 (Chang, *Cyclical Movements in the Balance of Payments*, Chapter 6) then the fall in real income of £14m would imply a fall in imports of about £4m.

122   Richardson, *Economic Recovery in Britain*, Table 20.

123   Feinstein, *National Income*, Table 64.

124   L.C.E.S. *Bulletin*, selected issues.

125   Cab. 58/30, Committee on Economic Information, 2nd and 3rd Reports, March and May 1932.

126   Feinstein, *Domestic Capital Formation*, Table 8.01; Landes, *The Unbound Prometheus*, p. 475; Burn, *The Economic History of Steel-Making 1867–1939*, pp. 450–1.

127   E.g., "The Housing Boom – I", *The Economist*, 26 October 1935; Arndt, *The Economic Lessons of the Nineteen-Thirties*, p. 131; Richardson, *Economic Recovery in Britain*, Chapter 5; and the references cited in Nevin, *The Mechanism of Cheap Money*, pp. 272–3.

128   Feinstein, *Domestic Capital Formation*, p. 43.

129   Nevin, *The Mechanism of Cheap Money*, pp. 273–4.

130   Feinstein, *Domestic Capital Formation*, p. 43.

131   Richardson, *Economic Recovery in Britain*, pp. 164–5.

132   Feinstein, *Domestic Capital Formation*, p. 43; Nevin, *The Mechanism of Cheap Money*, pp. 273–4.

133   F. de Leeuw, "The Demand for Housing: a review of cross-section evidence", *REStats*, February 1971.

134   C.M.E. Whitehead, *The U.K. Housing Market: an Econometric Model* (1974), pp. 132–5, 153–5.
There is similar evidence for Canada in the postwar period where L.B. Smith found that while the trend could be explained in terms of an initial shortage of housing, favourable demographic factors and rising real incomes, observed fluctuations in housebuilding were "crucially" determined by fluctuations in the cost and availability of mortgage finance (L.B. Smith, *The Postwar Canadian Housing and Residential Mortgage Markets and the Role of Government* (1974), pp. 58–67).

135   "The Role of Consumption in Inter-war Fluctuations", in Aldcroft and Fearon (eds.), *British Economic Fluctuations 1790–1939*, p. 165.

136   Ibid., p. 187; *Economic Recovery in Britain*, p. 123.

137   Feinstein, *National Income*, Table 25.

138   Stone and Rowe, *The Measurement of Consumers' Expenditure and Behaviour in the U.K. 1920–1938*, Vol. II, pp. 14–15.

139   The "extremely successful" Ford 8 was introduced in the latter part of 1931 (Maxcy and Silbertson, *The Motor Industry*, p. 102).

140   Stone and Rowe, *The Measurement of Consumers' Expenditure*, pp. 52–3.

141   As Richardson notes (*Economic Recovery in Britain*, p. 123).

142   Feinstein, *Domestic Capital Formation*, pp. 40–1, 45–6, Table 8.01.
The exception is motor vehicles, where investment (at 1930 prices) went from £3.6m in 1930 to £5.2m in 1931 and £5.8m in 1932 and then dropped back to £3.1m in 1933 (ibid., Table 8.01). This is due to the Ford Motor Company's building its new factory at Dagenham, which began production in 1932 (Maxcy and Silbertson, *The Motor Industry*, pp. 14, 163).

143   Such factors as increase in population, changes in tastes, etc. explain the *potential* demand for housing but not how that demand became effective, for which the possible explanations are the rise in real incomes, the fall in building costs, and cheap money (Feinstein, *Domestic Capital Formation*, p. 42).

144   *Building in the British Economy between the Wars*, pp. 201–4.

145   *The Mechanism of Cheap Money*, pp. 288–9.

146   *Housing and the State 1919–1944*, p. 278, note (f) to Table 9.

147   Ibid., p. 278, note (f).

148   MacIntosh, "A Note on Cheap Money and the British Housing Boom", *EJ*, March 1951, pp. 168–9.

149   On p. 73 of *Building in the British Economy between the Wars* they say they will use the same rates as MacIntosh in the rest of the book, but in the chapter on "Housing and Monetary Policy" they use Bowley's calculations (p. 203).

150   Ibid., p. 204.

151   *Housing and the State*, pp. 78–81.

152   *Building in the British Economy*, p. 160.

153   Ibid., p. 156.

154   There are also the indices constructed from the primary data by, e.g., Braae, "Investment in Housing in the U.K. 1924–38", *The Manchester School*, 1964.

155   "A Note on Cheap Money and the British Housing Boom", p. 172.

156   "The Building Trades", in *Britain in Recovery*, pp. 402–4.

157   W.A. Brown, Jr., *The International Gold Standard Reinterpreted*, Vol. II, pp. 1095–6; above pp. 143–7. The lag is of the same order as that found by Whitehead for the postwar period (*The U.K. Housing Market*, pp. 153–5).

158   Bellman, "The Building Trades", pp. 412–5.

159   Goodwin, "Studies in Money", p. 106.

160   Above p. 6.

161   "British Economic Fluctuations 1924–38", *OEP*, 1939, pp. 113–15, 122–3.

162   Cab. 58/30, Committee on Economic Information, 9th Report, 24 October 1933; Cab. 23/77, Cabinet 61(33)10, 8 November 1933.

163   Cab. 58/30, Committee on Economic Information, 5th Report, 14 November 1932; see also Cab. 58/30, Letter from Committee on Economic Information to Prime Minister on Financial Policy, February 1933.

164   T. 175/93, Hopkins to Chancellor, 16 February 1933.

165   T. 188/72, Phillips, "Recovery from the Trade Depression", 21 September 1933.

166   T. 175/93, Phillips, "Committee on Economic Information – 11th Report", July 1934.

167   T. 172/1828, Fergusson to Chancellor, Hopkins to Chancellor, and Note by Phillips,

168   Bretherton, Burchardt and Rutherford, *Public Investment and the Trade Cycle in Great Britain*, pp. 211–4, 379–80; Cab. 27/640, Committee on Public Capital Expenditure, Report, 13 August 1937; see also Burn, *The Economic History of Steel-Making*, p. 467.

169   T. 175/88, Phillips, "Relations with U.S.A.", 4 June 1935.
Phillips gave two other reasons against stabilization: (1) exchange rates were out of equilibrium, and (2) the dangers of speculative movements of funds. Norman regarded the latter as the main reason for staying off gold (Clay, *Lord Norman*, pp. 419–21).

Chapter 6

1   Cab. 58/30, Committee on Economic Information, 18th Report, "The Economic Outlook for the Next Few Years", 29 July 1935, paras. 44, 23.
2   Sayers, *A History of Economic Change in England*, p. 55.
3   Hancock and Gowing, *British War Economy*, p. 63.
4   *Statement relating to Defence*, Cmd. 4827.
5   T. 160/688/F 14996/1, Fisher to Chancellor, "Defence (D.P.R. 52)", 2 December 1935.
6   The Defence Requirements Committee recommended a programme costing this amount on 21 November 1935 and the Defence Policy and Requirements Committee (a ministerial committee set up in July 1935 "to keep the defensive situation as a whole constantly under review") recommended the acceptance of a programme of this size, which the Cabinet agreed to on 25 February 1936 (Hawtrey, "Defence Expenditure and the Budget"; Hancock and Gowing, *British War Economy*, pp. 63, 69; Cab. 24/259, C.P. 26(36), Report of D.P.R. Committee, 12 February 1936, and Report of (official) D.R. Committee (D.R.C. 37/D.P.R. 52), 21 November 1935; Cab. 23/83, Cabinet 10(36), 25 February 1936).
7   T. 160/688/F 14996/1, Phillips, "General Note . . . on methods of financing the Defence Programme", 29 November 1935; Memorandum by Hopkins, 2 December 1935.
8   Hancock and Gowing, *British War Economy*, p. 6.
9   T. 160/688/F 14996/1, Fisher to Chancellor, "Defence (D.P.R. 52)", 2 December 1935.
10   Sabine, *British Budgets in Peace and War 1932–1945*, pp. 73, 79–80, 95.
11   Ibid., p. 95.
12   Ibid., pp. 98, 101–2, 101–11; Feiling, *Neville Chamberlain*, pp. 292–3.
13   Sabine, *British Budgets in Peace and War*, pp. 123–4.
14   T. 175/94, Phillips to Hopkins, 31 December 1936.
15   T. 160/688/F 14996/1, Hopkins to Chancellor, 2 December 1935.
16   The Chancellor did so on 9 October 1935 and again on 4 February 1936 (Cab. 23/82, Cabinet 45(35)7; Cab. 23/83, Cabinet 11(36)1.
17   T. 172/1832, Hopkins to Fisher and Chancellor, n.d. but by internal evidence 9 October 1935. The scheme Hopkins referred to was Lloyd George's "New Deal" which he had announced in January and sent as a memorandum to the Prime Minister in March 1935. The government had responded by setting up a General Purposes Committee of the Cabinet to consider the scheme in the light of departmental memoranda and conversations with Lloyd George. It published its reply (prepared by an official committee under Hopkins) on 22 July 1935 (Cab. 27/583, General Purposes Committee, Minutes; Cab. 24/254, C.P. 46(35), General Purposes Committee Interim Report, 1 March 1935; Cab. 27/584, G.P. (35)7, Lloyd George's Memorandum on Unemployment, 14 March 1935; C.P. 150(35), Statement by H.M. Government on Certain Proposals submitted to them by Mr Lloyd George, 18 July 1935).
18   T. 175/94, Phillips to Hopkins, 31 December 1936.
19   T. 177/25, Phillips to Fraser, 27 November 1936.
20   Leith-Ross, *Money Talks*, p. 228.
21   T. 177/24, Phillips to Hopkins, n.d.
22   Cab. 24/265, C.P. 339(36), Memorandum on the Balance of Payments by the Chief Economic Adviser to H.M. Government, 7 December 1936; Cab. 23/87, Cabinet 2(37)6, 20 January 1937.
23   T. 175/94, Phillips to Hopkins, 31 December 1936.
24   T. 160/688/F 14996/2, Phillips to Hopkins, 17 December 1936; Hopkins, "Notes on Sir F. Phillips' Memorandum", 17 December 1936; Hopkins to Phillips, 18 December 1936.

25   T. 172/1853, Woods to Hopkins, 5 February 1937.
26   T. 175/94, Phillips to Hopkins, 31 December 1936.
27   T. 160/691/F 15060, Phillips to Hopkins, 22 April 1937.
28   T. 160/691/F 15060, Phillips to Hopkins, 22 April 1937; Hopkins to Chancellor,
     22 April 1937; Note by Phillips, 23 April 1937.
29   T. 160/770/F 15551, Phillips, "Defence Borrowing", 8 June 1938; see also Phillips,
     "National Defence Loan", 10 June 1938, in same file.
30   T. 160/770/F 15551, Hopkins to Fisher and Woods, 9 June 1938; Hopkins to Fisher
     and Chancellor, 10 June 1938.
31   T. 160/770/F 15551, Fisher to Chancellor, 11 June 1938.
32   Cab. 24/270, C.P. 165(37), Defence Expenditure, Memorandum by Chancellor,
     25 June 1937; Cab. 23/88, Cabinet 27(37), 30 June 1937; Cab. 24/272, C.P. 256(37),
     Defence Expenditure in Future Years, Estimates submitted by Defence Departments
     and Home Office, October 1937; and C.P. 257(37), Defence Expenditure in Future
     Years, Memorandum by Chancellor, 22 October 1937; Cab. 23/90, Cabinet 39(37),
     27 October 1937; Cab. 24/273, C.P. 316(37), Defence Expenditure in Future Years,
     Interim Report by Minister for Coordination of Defence; Cab. 23/90, Cabinets 48(37)
     and 49(37), 22 December 1937; Cab. 24/274, C.P. 24(38), Defence Expenditure in
     Future Years, Further Report by Minister for Coordination of Defence.
33   T. 177/42, Phillips to Fisher and Chancellor, n.d. but internal evidence indicates June
     1938.
34   Cab. 23/94, Cabinet 33(38)6, 20 July 1938.
35   Cab. 23/96, Cabinet 53(38)2, 7 November 1938.
36   T. 171/341, Fisher to Chancellor, "Budget 1939–40", and memoranda by Phillips
     and Hopkins, 3 January 1939.
37   T. 175/112, Hopkins to Fisher and Chancellor, 6 January 1939.
38   T. 175/94, Phillips to Hopkins, 31 December 1936.
39   T. 175/94, Treasury Note to Minister for Coordination of Defence, 22 October 1937.
40   T. 175/94, Hopkins to Fisher and Woods, 15 December 1937; see also T. 177/42,
     Phillips to Fisher and Chancellor, June 1938, and Note by Phillips, 27 June 1938. On
     the forecasts of a slump see below p. 127.
41   T. 171/341, Memoranda by Phillips and Hopkins, 3 January 1939.
42   Clay, *Lord Norman*, pp. 432–3.
43   T. 175/94, Phillips, "Position of Exchange Equalisation Account", n.d. but internal
     evidence indicates 1 December 1936.
44   Ibid.
45   Clay, *Lord Norman*, p. 461.
46   T. 175/94, Hopkins to Chancellor, 2 December 1936.
47   Ibid.
48   T. 175/94, Phillips, "Position of Exchange Equalisation Account", 1 December 1936.
49   T. 160/1174/F 8759/3, Note by Woods, 8 December 1936.
50   T. 175/93, Phillips to Hopkins, "Economic Advisory Committee – 12th Report",
     27 July 1934.
51   Cab. 58/30, Committee on Economic Information, 18th Report, 29 July 1935,
     paras. 18, 23, 24. The members of the committee were Sir Josiah Stamp, Keynes,
     H.D. Henderson, G.D.H. Cole, Sir Arthur Salter, D.H. Robertson, Phillips (from
     October 1935) and Leith-Ross.
     Fears about the future course of housebuilding were not confined to this committee:
     see, e.g., "The Housing Boom – I", *The Economist*, 26 October 1935; the prices of
     building company shares also fell at this time (J.A. Brown, "The 1937 Recession in
     England", *Harvard Business Review*, 1940, p. 251).
52   Cab. 58/30, "The Trend of Unemployment", 4 December 1935. The subcommittee
     consisted of A.L. Bowley, H.D. Henderson, D. Caradog Jones and D.H. Robertson.
53   Cab. 58/17, 58th meeting of Committee on Economic Information, 11 December
     1935; see also Cab. 58/21, Phillips, "Housing in relation to other forms of capital
     expenditure", 19 December 1935.
     Keynes on the other hand thought the subcommittee was too optimistic (Cab. 58/17,
     58th meeting of Committee on Economic Information, 11 December 1935).
54   Cab. 58/30, Committee on Economic Information, 22nd Report, "Economic Policy
     and the Maintenance of Trade Activity", 22 February 1937; T. 177/38, Phillips to
     Hopkins, "Report of the Economic Advisory Committee on the 1st March", 13 March
     1937, paras. 1, 2 and 6, emphasis in original; the report was circulated to the Cabinet
     on 1 March.

55 T. 175/94, Hopkins to Chancellor, 13 March 1937; marginal comments by Fisher on Hopkins' and Phillips' memoranda of the same date; T. 188/175, Leith-Ross to Hopkins, 9 and 14 April 1937; Cab. 27/640, Committee on Public Capital Expenditure, 13 August 1937, and Addendum to Report, 20 December 1937; Memorandum by Chancellor, 20 January 1938; Cab. 23/92, Cabinet 2(38)5, 26 January 1938.
    It took the Treasury officials some time to persuade the Chancellor to act. Then Phillips' Committee was delayed because the Treasury took up another suggestion of the 22nd Report of the Committee on Economic Information, an interdepartmental committee on tariff policy. Leith-Ross was made chairman of that committee, on which Phillips was the Treasury representative, and the committee had to hold its meetings between Leith-Ross's visits abroad.
    On these developments see Howson and Winch, *The Economic Advisory Council 1930–1939*, Chapter 5.
56 T. 175/94, Phillips to Hopkins, 31 December 1936.
57 Ibid.
58 Sayers, *Financial Policy 1939–45*, pp. 156–7.
59 T. 175/95, Phillips to Prime Minister, 28 July 1937; see also Cab. 58/21, "Housing in relation to other forms of capital expenditure", 17 December 1935, and T. 175/70, Phillips to Hopkins, 19 October 1932 (some of which is quoted above p. 91).
60 *The Times*, 25 February 1937.
61 T. 172/1853, Phillips, "Keynes on Defence Borrowing", 25 February 1937; emphasis in original.
62 *Lord Norman*, p. 464.
63 T. 175/94, Norman to Chairman of Committee of London Clearing Bankers, 28 December 1936; Norman sent a copy to Hopkins so that he "should know on which leg to stand in the event of questions being raised from elsewhere".
64 Clay, *Lord Norman*, p. 459.
65 L.C.E.S. *Bulletin*, 24 August 1936.
66 L.C.E.S. *Bulletin*, 23 September 1936.
67 L.C.E.S. *Bulletin*, 23 December 1936.
68 *Lord Norman*, p. 464. Unfortunately Clay does not say what the Bank's policy was after the turning-point.
69 *The Economist*, Banking Supplement, 13 October 1938.
70 Clay, *Lord Norman*, pp. 463, 465.
71 Ibid., p. 436; see also pp. 423–6.
72 *The Mechanism of Cheap Money*, p. 118.
73 Ibid., pp. 118–42.
74 Ibid., p. 154.
75 Ibid., pp. 155–6; see also Goodwin, "Studies in Money", pp. 64–5.
76 L.C.E.S. *Bulletin*, 23 March and 23 May 1936.
77 L.C.E.S. *Bulletin*, 19 June 1936.
78 L.C.E.S. *Bulletin*, 24 August 1936.
79 Commercial History and Review of 1936, 13 February 1937. On the government's view of the balance of payments situation see above p. 203.
80 On the commodity boom see Hodson, *Slump and Recovery 1929–1937*, pp. 439–67; on the American recession see K. Roose, *The Economics of Recession and Revival*.
81 *The Economist*, Commercial History and Review of 1937, 12 February 1938.
82 L.C.E.S. *Bulletin*, 23 June 1937.
83 Clay, *Lord Norman*, pp. 462–3; Hodson, *Slump and Recovery*, pp. 440–2. On the gold scare see also Clay, *Lord Norman*, pp. 429–31, and Howson and Winch, *The Economic Advisory Council 1930–1939*, Chapter 5.
84 *Lord Norman*, p. 463.
85 Hodson, *Slump and Recovery*, pp. 441–2.
86 J.A. Brown, "The 1937 Recession in England", *Harvard Business Review*, 1940, pp. 251–2. Brown's evidence is the data in the *BESS* on retail sales and interviews with businessmen in 1938.
87 Stone and Rowe, *The Measurement of Consumers' Expenditure and Behaviour in the U.K. 1920–1938*, Vol. II, pp. 14–15, 52–3, 138.
88 Phelps Brown and Shackle, "British Economic Fluctuations 1924–38", *OEP*, May 1939, pp. 121–2.
89 *The Measurement of Consumers' Expenditure*, pp. 15, 52.
90 Ibid., Tables 12 and 25.

91   J.A. Brown, "The 1937 Recession in England", p. 252.
92   *Bulletin*, 23 September 1937.
93   L.C.E.S. *Bulletin*, 23 November 1937.
94   L.C.E.S. *Bulletin*, various issues.
95   "British Economic Fluctuations 1924–38", pp. 115, 126.
96   Ibid., p. 126.
97   *Economic Recovery in Britain*, pp. 31–2.
98   Ibid., p. 36.
99   *National Income*, Table 32.
100 Table 18.
101 Richardson, *Economic Recovery in Britain*, p. 34.
102 L.C.E.S. *Bulletin*, 23 April 1938.
103 L.C.E.S. *Bulletin*, 21 December 1938.
104 Commercial History and Review of 1938, 18 February 1939.
105 Bretherton, Burchardt and Rutherford, *Public Investment and the Trade Cycle in Great Britain*, pp. 83–93.
106 The phrase is Kindleberger's, *The World in Depression*, p. 278.

Chapter 7

1   Moggridge, *British Monetary Policy 1924–1931*, pp. 98–9.
2   Ibid., pp. 99–100.
3   Ibid., pp. 3–14, 18, 21–2; W.A. Brown, Jr., *The International Gold Standard Reinterpreted*, Vol. I, pp. 168–9, 178; above pp. 12–13.
4   T. 176/5, Niemeyer to Colonial Secretary, 5 October 1921.
5   José Harris, *Unemployment and Politics: A Study in English Social Policy 1886–1914*, p. 6. Prewar unemployment policy was also "primarily concerned with problems of social administration . . . [and] only rarely . . . with the regulation or elimination of unemployment by methods of economic fiscal or monetary control" (ibid., p. 6). Countercyclical public works were a matter of rephasing existing public expenditure commitments, not of increasing government expenditure in order to increase aggregate demand (D. Winch, *Economics and Policy*, 1972 edition, pp. 58–63).
6   Sayers once, when reviewing *JMK*, Vol. XVI, which covers Keynes's activities in the First World War, speculated that this may have had something to do with Keynes's influence ("The Young Keynes", *EJ*, June 1972).
7   Moggridge, *British Monetary Policy*, pp. 1, 228–9.
8   Ibid., Chapter 4 and Appendix 1.
9   Ibid., p. 236.
10   Ibid., pp. 86–7; above pp. 82–6 and Appendix 4.
11   Committee on Finance and Industry, *Report*, para. 9.
12   Cab. 58/30, Committee on Economic Information, 5th and 6th Reports, November 1932 and February 1933; Macgregor, Pigou, Keynes, Layton, Salter and Stamp to *The Times*, 17 October 1932; above pp. 91–3, 118–19.
13   Above pp. 127–30. On the evolution of Keynes's views on the goals and role of monetary policy, see Moggridge and Howson, "Keynes on Monetary Policy, 1910–46", *OEP*, July 1974.
14   Countercyclical public works thus meant something different to the Treasury in 1937–8 from what it had meant to the prewar advocates of countercyclical public works.
15   See, e.g., above p. 91.
16   Sir Edward Bridges, *Treasury Control*, Stamp Memorial Lecture, 1950, p. 15.
17   Sayers, *Financial Policy 1939–45*, pp. 146–62, 197–210; Dow, "The Economic Effect of Monetary Policy, 1945–57", Radcliffe Committee, *Memoranda of Evidence*, Vol. 3, paras. 4–11.
18   Above p. 56.
19   The balance of payments constraint would not necessarily be severe in the case of housing investment, whose import content is low.
20   Keynes's term (Moggridge and Howson, "Keynes on Monetary Policy, 1910–46", p. 244).

Bibliography

Unpublished Papers

F.R.B.N.Y. Archives

Keynes Papers

Public Record Office Papers. The call numbers of the volumes/files I have used are:

Cab. 23. Cabinet Conclusions.
Vols: 27, 66–72, 75, 77, 82, 83, 86–88, 90, 92, 94, 96.

Cab. 24. Cabinet Memoranda (G.T. and C.P. papers).
Vols: 74, 75, 86, 97, 108, 219, 222, 223, 227, 254, 259, 265, 270, 272, 273, 274.

Cab. 27. Cabinet Committees.
Vols: 58, 71, 72, 435, 454, 456, 462, 467, 503, 583, 584, 640.

Cab. 58. Economic Advisory Council (including Committee on Economic Information).
Vols: 11, 14, 17, 21, 30, 145, 169, 183.

Prem. 1. Prime Minister's Papers.
Files 96 and 97.

T. 160. Treasury. Finance Files.
The file number is preceded by the box number.
Files:
53/F 1874
66/F 2114
194/F 7380/02
198/F 7548
226/F 8469
239/F 8970
398/F 12394
402/F 12600/03
411/F 3420/02
425/F 11282/019
429/F 11721
430/F 12317/02
449/F 13047/1–2
496/F 13228
497/F 13380/1–2
527/F 12995
533/F 13296/01–03
538/F 13748
551/F 9973/1–2
633/F 14810
688/F 14996/1–4
691/F 15060
760/F 14596
770/F 15551
849/F 14370
1174/F 8759/05/3
1378/F 18064/04

T. 163. Treasury. General Files.
68/G 3788
T. 170. Bradbury Papers.
Files 125 and 140.
T. 171. Chancellor of Exchequer's Office. Budget Papers.
Vols: 180, 196, 279, 286, 287, 288, 293, 296, 301, 304, 309, 315, 317, 341.
T. 172. Chancellor of Exchequer's Office. Miscellaneous Papers.
Files: 896, 1020, 1059, 1208, 1272, 1384, 1499B, 1662, 1684, 1690, 1746, 1768, 1775, 1814, 1821, 1828, 1832, 1853.
T. 175. Hopkins Papers.
Files: 11, 15, 17, 25, 26, 40, 46, 51, 52, 53, 56, 57, 58, 59, 64, 70, 71, 72, 84, 87, 88, 93, 94, 95, 96, 100, 104, 112.
T. 176. Niemeyer Papers.
Files: 5, 11, 13, 18, 32.
T. 177. Phillips Papers.
Files: 8, 12, 24, 25, 36, 37, 38, 42.
T. 185/1–3. Committee on Currency and Foreign Exchanges after the War. Proceedings (3 vols).
T. 188. Leith-Ross Papers.
Files: 11, 14, 20, 28, 29, 48, 72, 175, 176.
T. 200/4–6. Committee on Finance and Industry. Unpublished Minutes.
These are also in the Keynes Papers.

Serial publications

BESS
Board of Trade Journal
The Economist
Hansard
L.C.E.S. *Bulletin*
The Times

Books, Articles and Official Reports

D.H. Aldcroft, "Economic Progress in Britain in the 1920s", *SJPE*, November 1966, reprinted in Aldcroft and Richardson, *The British Economy 1870–1939*.
"Economic Growth in Britain in the Inter-War Years; A Reassessment", *EHR*, 1967. reprinted in Aldcroft and Fearon (eds.), *Economic Growth in Twentieth-Century Britain*.
"The Impact of British Monetary Policy, 1919–1939", *Revue Internationale d'Histoire de la Banque*, 1970.
"British Monetary Policy and Economic Activity in the 1920s", *Revue International d'Histoire de la Banque*, 1972.
The Inter-War Economy: Britain, 1919–39, Batsford, London, 1970.
D.H. Aldcroft and P. Fearon (eds.), *Economic Growth in Twentieth-Century Britain*, Macmillan, London, 1969.
British Economic Fluctuations 1790–1939, Macmillan, London, 1972.
D.H. Aldcroft and H.W. Richardson, *The British Economy 1870–1939*, Macmillan, London, 1969.
B.W.E. Alford, *Depression and Recovery? British Economic Growth 1919–1939*, Macmillan, London, 1972.
S. Armitage, *The Politics of Decontrol in Industry: Britain and the United States*, Weidenfeld and Nicholson, London, 1969.
H.W. Arndt, *The Economic Lessons of the Nineteen-Thirties*, Royal Institute of International Affairs, London, 1944.
K. Arrow, "The Economic Implications of Learning by Doing", *REStudies*, June 1962.
T. Balogh, *Studies in Financial Organization*, Cambridge University Press, Cambridge, 1947.
Bank of England, "The Exchange Equalisation Account: its origins and development", *BEQB*, December 1968.

"The Bank of England's holdings of gold and foreign exchange, 1924–31", *BEQB*, March 1970, Supplement.

"The Balance of Payments in the inter-war period: further details", *BEQB*, March 1974.

C.R. Barrett and A.A. Walters, "The Stability of Keynesian and Monetary Multipliers in the U.K.", *REStats*, November 1966.

R. Bassett, *Nineteen Thirty-One: Political Crisis*, Macmillan, London, 1958.

Sir Harold Bellman, "The Building Trades", in British Association, *Britain in Recovery*.

Board of Governors of the Federal Reserve System, *Banking and Monetary Statistics*, Federal Reserve System, Washington, 1943.

M. Bowley, "Fluctuations in Housebuilding and the Trade Cycle", *REStudies*, 1936–7.
Housing and the State 1919–1944, Allen and Unwin, London, 1945.

A. Boyle, *Montagu Norman*, Cassell, London, 1967.

G. Braae, "Investment in Housing in the United Kingdom, 1924–38", *The Manchester School*, 1964.

R.F. Bretherton, F.A. Burchardt, R.S.G. Rutherford, *Public Investment and the Trade Cycle in Great Britain*, Clarendon Press, Oxford, 1941.

Sir Edward Bridges, *Treasury Control*, Stamp Memorial Lecture, Athlone Press, London, 1950.

British Association for the Advancement of Science, *Britain in Recovery*, Pitman, London, 1938.

A.J. Brown, "The Liquidity-Preference Schedules of the London Clearing Banks", *OEP*, 1938.
"Interest, Prices and the Demand Schedule for Idle Money", *OEP*, 1939.

Jonathan A. Brown, "The 1937 Recession in England", *Harvard Business Review*, 1940.

W.A. Brown, Jr., *England and the New Gold Standard 1919–1926*, Yale University Press, New Haven, 1929.
The International Gold Standard Re-interpreted 1914–1934, 2 vols., N.B.E.R., New York, 1940.

K. Brunner (ed.), *Targets and Indicators of Monetary Policy*, Chandler Publishing Co., San Francisco, 1969.

D. Burn, *The Economic History of Steelmaking 1867–1939: A Study in Competition*, Cambridge University Press, Cambridge, 1961.

A.F. Burns and W.C. Mitchell, *Measuring Business Cycles*, N.B.E.R., New York, 1946.

A. Buse, "The Structure of Interest Rates and Recent British Experience: A Comment", *Economica*, August 1967.

Sir Alec Cairncross, *Control of Long-term International Capital Movements*, The Brookings Institution, Washington, 1973.

L.V. Chandler, *Benjamin Strong: Central Banker*, Brookings Institution, Washington, 1958.
American Monetary Policy 1928–1941, Harper and Row, New York, 1971.

T.C. Chang, *Cyclical Movements in the Balance of Payments*, Cambridge University Press, Cambridge, 1951.

Colin Clark, "Statistical Studies of the present economic position of Great Britain", *EJ*, September 1931.

S.V.O. Clarke, *Central Bank Cooperation 1924–31*, F.R.B.N.Y., New York, 1967.

H. Clay (Sir Henry Clay), "The Financing of Industrial Enterprise", *Transactions of the Manchester Statistical Society*, 1931–2.
Lord Norman, Macmillan, London, 1957.

G. Clayton, J.C. Gilbert, R. Sedgwick (eds.), *Monetary Theory and Monetary Policy in the 1970s*, Oxford University Press, London, 1971.

Committee on Currency and Foreign Exchanges after the War (Cunliffe Committee), *First Interim Report*, Cd. 9182, H.M.S.O., London, 1918 (B.P.P. 1918 (9182), VII, 853).
Final Report, Cmd. 464, H.M.S.O., London, 1919 (B.P.P. 1919 (464), XIII, 593).

Committee on National Debt and Taxation (Colwyn Committee), *Report*, Cmd. 2800, H.M.S.O., London, 1927 (B.P.P. 1927 (2800), XI, 371).
Minutes of Evidence, H.M.S.O., London, 1927.

Committee on Finance and Industry (Macmillan Committee), *Report*, Cmd. 3897, H.M.S.O., London, 1931 (B.P.P. 1930–1 (3897), XIII, 291).
Minutes of Evidence, H.M.S.O., London, 1931.

Committee on the Working of the Monetary System (Radcliffe Committee), *Report*, Cmnd. 827,

H.M.S.O., London, 1959 (B.P.P. 1958–9 (827), XVII, 389).

Principal Memoranda and Minutes of Evidence, 4 vols., H.M.S.O., London, 1960.

D.C. Corner, "Exports and the British Trade Cycle: 1929", *The Manchester School*, 1958.

W.F. Crick, "British Monetary Policy 1931–37", *Bankers Magazine*, February 1938.

A.D. Crockett, "Timing Relationships between Movements of Monetary and National Income Variables", *BEQB*, December 1970.

D.R. Croome and H.G. Johnson (eds.), *Money in Britain 1959–1969*, Oxford University Press, London, 1970.

N. Cunningham, "Business Investment and the Marginal Cost of Funds", *Metroeconomica*, 1958.

E.W. Davis and K.A. Yeomans, *Company Finance and the Capital Market; A Study of the effects of firm size*, Cambridge University Press, Cambridge, 1974.

F. de Leeuw, "The Demand for Housing: a Review of Cross-Section Evidence", *REStats*, February 1971.

F. de Leeuw and E. Gramlich, "The Federal Reserve-MIT Econometric Model", *Federal Reserve Bulletin*, January 1968.

"The Channels of Monetary Policy", *Federal Reserve Bulletin*, June 1969.

J.C. Dodds and J.L. Ford, *Expectations, Uncertainty and the Term Structure of Interest Rates*, Martin Robertson, London, 1974.

J.C.R. Dow, "The Economic Effect of Monetary Policy, 1945–57" in Committee on the Working of the Monetary System, *Memoranda of Evidence*, Vol. 3.

The Management of the British Economy 1945–1960, Cambridge University Press, Cambridge, 1964.

J.A. Dowie, "Economic Growth in the Inter-War Period: some more arithmetic" in Aldcroft and Fearon (eds.), *Economic Growth in Twentieth-Century Britain*.

I.M. Drummond, *British Economic Policy and the Empire 1919–1939*, Allen and Unwin, London, 1972.

Imperial Economic Policy 1917–1939: Studies in Expansion and Protection, Allen and Unwin, London, 1974.

R. Eisner and R.H. Strotz, "Determinants of Business Investment", in Commission on Money and Credit, *Impacts of Monetary Policy*, Prentice-Hall, Englewood Cliffs, N.J., 1963.

Federal Reserve Bank of Boston, Conference Series no. 5, *Consumer Spending and Monetary Policy: the Linkages*, Federal Reserve Bank of Boston, Boston, 1971.

K. Feiling, *The Life of Neville Chamberlain*, Macmillan, London, 1946.

C.H. Feinstein, "Production and Productivity 1920–1962", in Aldcroft and Fearon (eds.), *Economic Growth in Twentieth-Century Britain*.

Domestic Capital Formation in the U.K. 1920–1938, Cambridge University Press, 1965.

National Income, Expenditure and Output of the U.K. 1855–1965, Cambridge University Press, Cambridge, 1972.

Douglas Fisher, "Expectations, the Term Structure of Interest Rates and Recent British Experience", *Economica*, August 1966.

G.R. Fisher and D.K. Sheppard, *Effects of Monetary Policy on the United States Economy: A Survey of Econometric Evidence*, O.E.C.D., Paris, December 1972.

H. Fleisig, "The United States and the Non-European Periphery during the Early Years of the Great Depression", in H. van der Wee (ed.), *The Great Depression Revisited: Essays on the Economics of the Thirties*, Martinus Nijhoff, The Hague, 1972.

M. Friedman, *The Optimum Quantity of Money and other Essays*, Macmillan, London, 1969.

"A Theoretical Framework for Monetary Analysis", *JPE*, March/April 1970.

(ed.), *Studies in the Quantity Theory of Money*, University of Chicago Press, Chicago, 1956.

M. Friedman and D. Meiselman, "The Relative Stability of Monetary Velocity and the Investment Multiplier in the U.S., 1897–1958", in Commission on Money and Credit, *Stabilization Policies*, Prentice-Hall, Englewood Cliffs, N.J., 1963.

M. Friedman and A.J. Schwartz, *A Monetary History of the United States 1867–1960*, Princeton University Press, Princeton, 1963.

R. Frost, "The Macmillan Gap 1931–53", *OEP*, 1954.

B.B. Gilbert, *British Social Policy 1914–1939*, Batsford, London, 1970.

C.A.E. Goodhart and A.D. Crockett, "The Importance of Money", *BEQB*, June 1970.

R.M. Goodwin, "Studies in Money, England and Wales 1919–38", Unpublished Harvard Ph.D. thesis, 1941.
(There is a copy in the Library of the National Institute of Economic and Social Research, London.)
"The Supply of Bank Money in England and Wales", *OEP*, June 1941.

R.A. Gordon, *Business Fluctuations*, Harper, New York, 1952.

A.T.K. Grant, *A Study of the Capital Market in Britain from 1919–1936* (reprint of *A Study of the Capital Market in Post-War Britain* (1937)), Cass, London, 1967.

J.A.G. Grant, "Meiselman on the Structure of Interest Rates; a British Test", *Economica*, 1964.

F.H. Hahn, "On Some Problems of Proving the Existence of Equilibrium in a Monetary Economy" in Hahn and Brechling (eds.), *The Theory of Interest Rates*, Macmillan, London, 1965.

M. Hamburger and R. Latta, "The Term Structure of Interest Rates: some additional evidence", *JMCB*, 1969.

W.K. Hancock and M.M. Gowing, *British War Economy*, H.M.S.O., London, 1949.

José Harris, *Unemployment and Politics: A Study in English Social Policy 1886–1914*, Clarendon Press, Oxford, 1972.

R.A. Harris, "A Re-analysis of the 1928 New Issue Boom", *EJ*, September 1933.

R.G. Hawtrey, "Public Expenditure and the Demand for Labour", *Economica*, March 1925.
A Century of Bank Rate, Longmans, London, 1938.
Currency and Credit, 4th edition, Longmans, London, 1950.
"The Return to Gold in 1925", *Bankers Magazine*, August 1969.

H.D. Henderson, *The Inter-War Years and other Papers*, ed. H. Clay, Clarendon Press, Oxford, 1955.

R.F. Henderson, *The New Issue Market and the Finance of Industry*, Bowes and Bowes, Cambridge, 1951.

J.R. Hicks, "Mr Hawtrey on Bank Rate and the Long-term Rate of Interest", *The Manchester School*, 1939.

U.K. Hicks, *The Finance of British Government 1920–1936*, Oxford University Press, London, 1938, reprinted 1970.

H.V. Hodson, *Slump and Recovery 1929–1937*, Oxford University Press, London, 1938.

S. Howson, "'A Dear Money Man'?: Keynes on Monetary Policy, 1920", *EJ*, June 1973.
"The Origins of Dear Money, 1919–20", *EHR*, February 1974.

S. Howson and D. Winch, *The Economic Advisory Council 1930–1939*, Cambridge University Press, Cambridge, 1976.

H.G. Johnson, "Clearing Bank Holdings of Public Debt, 1930–50", L.C.E.S. *Bulletin*, November 1951.
"A Survey of Theories of Inflation", Chapter 3 of *Essays in Monetary Economics*, Allen and Unwin, London, 1967.

P.B. Johnson, *Land Fit for Heroes: The Planning of British Reconstruction 1916–1919*, University of Chicago Press, Chicago, 1968.

T. Jones, *A Diary with Letters 1931–1950*, Oxford University Press, London, 1954.

Dale W. Jorgenson, "Econometric Studies of Investment Behaviour: A Survey", *Journal of Economic Literature*, 1971.

E.E. Jucker-Fleetwood, "Montagu Norman in the Per Jacobbson Diaries", *National Westminster Bank Quarterly Review*, November 1968.

H.B. Junz and R.R. Rhomberg, "Price Competitiveness in Export Trade among Industrial Countries", *AER*, May 1973.

A.E. Kahn, *Great Britain in the World Economy*, Columbia University Press, New York, 1946.

N. Kaldor, "Hawtrey on Short- and Long-term Investment", *Economica*, November 1938, reprinted in *Essays on Economic Stability and Growth*, Duckworth, London, 1960.

N.J. Kavanagh and A.A. Walters, "The Demand for Money in the U.K. 1877–1961; Some Preliminary Findings", *BOIS*, 1966.

C. Kennedy and J.P. Thirlwall, "Technical Progress", in *Surveys of Applied Economics*, Vol. I, Macmillan, London, 1973.

R.A. Kessel, *The Cyclical Behaviour of the Term Structure of Interest Rates*, N.B.E.R., New York, 1965.

J.M. Keynes, *A Tract on Monetary Reform* (1924) (*JMK*, Vol. IV), Macmillan, London, 1971.
   A Treatise on Money (1930) (*JMK*, Vols. V and VI), Macmillan, London, 1971.
   Essays in Persuasion (1931) (*JMK*, Vol. IX), Macmillan, London, 1972.
   The General Theory of Employment, Interest and Money (1936) (*JMK*, Vol. VII),
   Macmillan, London, 1973.
   Activities 1914–1919: the Treasury and Versailles (*JMK*, Vol. XVI), ed. E. Johnson,
   Macmillan, London, 1971.
   The General Theory and After: Part I Preparation (*JMK*, Vol. XIII), ed. D.E. Moggridge,
   Macmillan, London, 1973.
   The General Theory and After: Part II Defence and Development (*JMK*, Vol. XIV),
   ed. D.E. Moggridge, Macmillan, London, 1973.
C.P. Kindleberger, *Economic Growth in France and Britain, 1860–1960*, Harvard University
   Press, Cambridge, Mass., 1964.
   The World in Depression 1929–1939, Allen Lane, London, 1973.
D. Laidler, "The Influence of Money on Economic Activity: some current problems", in
   Clayton, Gilbert and Sedgwick (eds.), *Monetary Theory and Monetary Policy in the 1970s*.
D. Laidler and M. Parkin, "Inflation: A Survey", *EJ*, December 1975.
D.S. Landes, *The Unbound Prometheus: Technological Change and Industrial Development in
   Western Europe from 1750 to the present*, Cambridge University Press, Cambridge, 1969.
L.C.E.S., *The British Economy: Key Statistics 1900–1970*, Times Newspapers, London, 1971.
D.S. Lees, "Public Departments and Cheap Money, 1932–38", *Economica*, February 1955.
   "The Technique of Monetary Insulation, December 1932 to December 1937", *Economica*,
   November 1953.
Sir Frederick Leith-Ross, *Money Talks: Fifty Years of International Finance*, Hutchinson,
   London, 1968.
W.A. Lewis, *Economic Survey 1919–1939*, Allen and Unwin, London, 1949.
K.S. Lomax, "Production and Productivity Movements in the U.K. since 1900", *JRSS*, 1959.
   "Growth and Productivity in the U.K.", *Productivity Measurement Review*, 1964, reprinted
   in Aldcroft and Fearon (eds.), *Economic Growth in Twentieth-Century Britain*.
P.J. Lund and K. Holden, "An Econometric Study of Private Sector Gross Fixed Capital
   Formation in the U.K. 1923–1938", *OEP*, March 1968.
R.A. MacIntosh, "A Note on Cheap Money and the British Housing Boom", *EJ*, March 1951.
S. Magee, "Currency Contracts, Pass-through and Devaluation", *Brookings Papers on Economic
   Activity*, 1: 1973.
H. Makower, J. Marshak and H.W. Robinson, "Studies in Mobility of Labour: Analysis for
   Great Britain, Part I", *OEP*, May 1939.
B.G. Malkiel, *The Term Structure of Interest Rates*, Princeton University Press, Princeton, 1966.
B. Mallett and C.O. George, *British Budgets, Third Series, 1921–33*, Macmillan, London, 1933.
R.C.O. Matthews, "Some Aspects of Post-War Growth in the British Economy in relation to
   Historical Experience", *Transactions of Manchester Statistical Society*, 1964, reprinted in
   Aldcroft and Fearon (eds.), *Economic Growth in Twentieth-Century Britain*.
   "Why has Britain had Full Employment since the War?", *EJ*, September 1968.
G. Maxcy and A. Silbertson, *The Motor Industry*, Allen and Unwin, London, 1959.
J. Meade and P.W.S. Andrews, "Summary of Replies to Questions on the Effects of Interest
   Rates", in Wilson and Andrews (eds.), *Oxford Studies in the Price Mechanism*.
D. Meiselman, *The Term Structure of Interest Rates*, Prentice-Hall, Englewood Cliffs, N.J., 1962.
Memoranda by Ministers on Certain Proposals relating to Unemployment, Cmd. 3331, H.M.S.O.,
   London, 1929 (B.P.P. 1928–9 (3331), XVI, 813).
J.R. Meyer and E. Kuh, *The Investment Decision: An Empirical Study*, Harvard University Press,
   Cambridge, Mass., 1957.
B.R. Mitchell and P.M. Deane, *Abstract of British Historical Statistics*, Cambridge University
   Press, Cambridge, 1962.
F. Modigliani, "The Channels of Monetary Policy in the Federal Reserve-MIT-University of
   Pennsylvania Econometric Model of the United States", in G. Renton (ed.), *Modelling the
   Economy*, Heinemann, London, 1975.
F. Modigliani and R. Sutch, "Innovations in Interest Rate Policy", *AER*, 1966.

211

"Debt Management and the Term Structure of Interest Rates", *JPE*, 1967.

D.E. Moggridge, "The 1931 Financial Crisis – a New View", *The Banker*, August 1970.
British Monetary Policy 1924–1931: The Norman Conquest of $4.86, Cambridge University Press, Cambridge, 1972.

D.E. Moggridge and S. Howson, "Keynes on Monetary Policy, 1910–46", *OEP*, July 1974.

E.V. Morgan, *Studies in British Financial Policy 1914–1925*, Macmillan, London, 1952.

W.A. Morton, *British Finance 1930–1940*, University of Wisconsin Press, Madison, 1943.

E.T. Nevin, "Estimating Departmental Intervention", *REStudies*, 1952.
"The Origins of Cheap Money, 1931–2", *Economica*, February 1953, reprinted in Pollard (ed.), *The Gold Standard and Employment Policies between the Wars*.
The Mechanism of Cheap Money: A Study of British Monetary Policy 1931–1939, University of Wales Press, Cardiff, 1955.

N.I.E.S.R., "The Effects of Devaluation on the Balance of Payments", *NIER*, November 1967.

O.E.C.D., Monetary Studies Series, *Monetary Policy in the United States*, O.E.C.D., Paris, 1974.

A.T. Peacock and J. Wiseman, *The Growth of Public Expenditure in the United Kingdom*, revised 2nd edition, Allen and Unwin, London, 1967.

Pember and Boyle, *British Government Securities in the Twentieth Century*, 2nd edition, privately printed, London, 1950.

E.H. Phelps Brown and G.L.S. Shackle, "British Economic Fluctuations, 1924–38", *OEP*, May 1939.

A.C. Pigou, *Aspects of British Economic History 1918–1925*, Macmillan, London, 1947, and Cass, London, 1971.

S. Pollard (ed.), *The Gold Standard and Employment Policies between the Wars*, Methuen, London, 1970.

L.L.D. Price, "The Demand for Money in the U.K.: a further investigation", *BEQB*, March 1972.

H.W. Richardson, "The New Industries between the Wars", *OEP*, 1961, reprinted in Aldcroft and Richardson, *The British Economy 1870–1939*.
"The Basis of Economic Recovery in the 1930s: a review and a new interpretation", *EHR*, 1962, and in Aldcroft and Richardson, *The British Economy 1870–1939*.
"Over-Commitment in Britain before 1930", *OEP*, 1965, and in Aldcroft and Richardson, *The British Economy 1870–1939*.
Economic Recovery in Britain, 1932–9, Weidenfeld and Nicholson, London, 1967.

H.W. Richardson and D.H. Aldcroft, *Building in the British Economy between the Wars*, Allen and Unwin, London, 1968.

J.V. Robinson, "The Production Function and the Theory of Capital", *REStudies*, 1954.

A.R. Roe, "The Case for Flow of Funds and National Balance Sheet Accounts", *EJ*, June 1973.

K.D. Roose, *The Economics of Recession and Revival: an Interpretation of 1937–38*, Yale University Press, New Haven, 1954, and Archon, Hamden, Conn., 1969.

N. Rosenberg, "Science, Invention and Economic Growth", *EJ*, March 1974.

S. Roskill, *Hankey: Man of Secrets, Vol. II, 1919–1931*, Collins, London, 1972.

D.C. Rowan, "The Rate Structure and Capital Movements: a Note on Operation Twist", *Banca Nazionale del Lavoro Quarterly Review*, December 1974.

D.C. Rowan and R.J. O'Brien, "Expectations, the Interest Rate Structure and Debt Policy", in Hilton and Heathfield (eds.), *The Econometric Study of the United Kingdom*, Macmillan, London, 1970.

B.E.V. Sabine, *British Budgets in Peace and War, 1932–1945*, Allen and Unwin, London, 1970.

W.E.G. Salter, *Productivity and Technical Change*, 2nd edition, Cambridge University Press, Cambridge, 1966.

P.A. Samuelson, "The Paradoxes of Capital Theory: A Summing-up", *QJE*, November 1966.

R.S. Sayers, *Modern Banking*, 1st edition, Oxford University Press, London, 1938.
"The Springs of Technical Progress in Britain 1919–39", *EJ*, 1950.
"The Rate of Interest as a Weapon of Economic Policy", in Wilson and Andrews (eds.), *Oxford Studies in the Price Mechanism*.
Financial Policy 1939–45, H.M.S.O. and Longmans, London, 1956.
Central Banking after Bagehot, Clarendon Press, Oxford, 1957.
"The Return to Gold, 1925" (1960) in Pollard (ed.), *The Gold Standard and Employment*

Policies between the Wars.

A History of Economic Change in England 1880–1939, Oxford University Press, London, 1967.

J. Schmookler, *Invention and Economic Growth*, Harvard University Press, Cambridge, Mass., 1966.

J.A. Schumpeter, *Business Cycles*, 2 vols., McGraw Hill, New York and London, 1939.

D.K. Sheppard, *The Growth and Role of U.K. Financial Institutions 1880–1962*, Methuen, London, 1971.

L.B. Smith, *The Postwar Canadian Housing and Residential Mortgage Markets and the Role of Government*, University of Toronto Press, Toronto, 1974.

P. Snowden, *An Autobiography*, 2 vols., Ivor Nicholson and Watson, London, 1934.

R.B. Stewart, "Great Britain's Foreign Loan Policy", *Economica*, 1938.

W.F. Stolper, "British Monetary Policy and the Housing Boom", *QJE*, November 1941.

R.N. Stone and D.A. Rowe, *The Measurement of Consumers' Expenditure and Behaviour in the U.K. 1920–1938*, Vol. II, Cambridge University Press, Cambridge, 1966.

R.H. Tawney, "The Abolition of Economic Controls 1918–21", *EHR*, 1943.

J. Tobin, "The Monetary Interpretation of History", *AER*, June 1965.

"Monetary Semantics", in Brunner (ed.), *Targets and Indicators of Monetary Policy*.

A.A. Walters, "Monetary Multipliers in the U.K.", *OEP*, November 1966.

"The Radcliffe Report – Ten Years After, A Survey of Empirical Evidence", in Croome and Johnson (eds.), *Money in Britain 1959–1969*.

Money in Boom and Slump, Institute of Economic Affairs, London, 1969.

Christine M.E. Whitehead, *The U.K. Housing Market: An Econometric Model*, Saxon House, Farnborough, 1974.

K. Wicksell, *Interest and Prices*, trans. R.F. Kahn, Macmillan, London, 1936.

Lectures on Political Economy, ed. Robbins, Routledge, London, 1935.

D. Williams, "Montagu Norman and Banking Policy in the Nineteen Twenties", *Yorkshire Bulletin of Economic and Social Research*, July 1959.

"London and the 1931 Financial Crisis", *EHR*, April 1963.

"The 1931 Financial Crisis", *Yorkshire Bulletin of Economic and Social Research*, November 1963.

T. Wilson and P.W.S. Andrews (eds.), *Oxford Studies in the Price Mechanism*, Clarendon Press, Oxford, 1951.

D. Winch, *Economics and Policy, A Historical Study*, Hodder and Stoughton, London, 1969, Fontana, London, 1972.

J.H. Wood, "Expectations, Errors and the Term Structure of Interest Rates", *JPE*, April 1963.

"The expectations hypothesis, the yield curve and monetary policy", *QJE*, 1964.

A.J. Youngson, *Britain's Economic Growth 1920–1966*, Allen and Unwin, London, 1968.